Technology, Methodology, and Business Education

National Business Education Association Yearbook, No. 40

2002

Editor
Ann M. Remp
Eastern Michigan University
Ypsilanti, Michigan

Published by

National Business Education Association
1914 Association Drive
Reston, VA 20191-1596
(703) 860-8300 • Fax: (703) 620-4483
www.nbea.org

TABLE OF CONTENTS

Part I: Technology, Learners, and Learning Environments

Learners and Technology: Experience, Attitudes, and Expectations

Jim Rucker
Fort Hays State University
Hays, Kansas

Sharon Reynolds
Minot State University
Minot, North Dakota

Technology and Learning: Integrating Home, Classroom, and Community

Nancy Zeliff
Northwest Missouri State University
Maryville, Missouri

Technology, Business Education, and Young Learners

Ruth K. Shafer
Hazelwood School District
Florissant, Missouri

Customized Services for Diverse Student Needs

Martha H. Rader
Arizona State University
Tempe, Arizona

Part II: Building Relationships in a Technology- Mediated World

Part III: Business Functions and Technology

Part IV: Technology Skills for Consumer and Career-Related Uses

PREFACE

The questions that this *Yearbook,* entitled *Technology, Methodology, and Business Education,* addresses are also the challenges that business educators face in integrating technology into the learning environment. They include the following:

- How do students experience technology, and what technology needs can business teachers meet? The students that business educators work with are increasingly diverse. They are in different stages of life and have a variety of attitudes toward and expectations for technology in learning. Their diverse socioeconomic backgrounds and learning abilities also challenge teachers. Knowing and appreciating this changing audience is the first task that teachers face.
- How does technology affect how successful business and educational relationships are built? These relationships are increasingly mediated by technology. Business teachers and business students alike must employ technology-appropriate skills that are based on sensitivity to the language, culture, and other factors that result in successful local and global relationships. This is a second challenge to business teachers.
- What are the technology trends in selected business subjects that business educators can or should integrate into their classrooms? Learning may sometimes involve direct work with a particular technology. Often learning means analyzing how new technology systems manage information in the subject matter area and applying a methodology that students themselves can use to anticipate further technology changes. This process needs to be accomplished without sacrificing business principles and content. The third challenge to business teachers is to integrate sufficient content and methodology to address technology systems in the subject area and accomplish these learning goals.
- How does technology change the personal business skills that students will use on a daily basis throughout their lives? Business teachers contribute to the communication, keyboarding, personal finance, legal, and career education of students. Technology affects each of these areas. The fourth challenge that business teachers face is ensuring that meeting these needs remains an important part of the total instructional mix.

The authors of this *Yearbook* have created discussions about how and where technology fits into the work of business teachers. Some authors have suggested learning activities that can be integrated into classes as a means of gradually changing instruction. Other authors have provided maps for more comprehensive approaches to instruction. All have provided rich and comprehensive resources, most of which are readily accessible via the World Wide Web. Every effort has been made to verify the active status of the suggested Web sites. Yet the Web is dynamic, and readers may find addresses (hopefully very few) that have changed.

The *Yearbook* reviewers have worked behind the scenes to ensure that each chapter meets readers' needs. These business educators used a blind review process to make recommendations to the authors. The reviewers will learn the identities of the authors only as they read this *Yearbook*. Each manuscript received at least three reviews. The following individuals deserve special acknowledgment and sincere thanks for serving as chapter reviewers:

Norma Dell Broadway
Hinds Community College
Jackson, Mississippi

Alice Citano
Kent State University- Ashtabula
Campus
Ashtabula, Ohio

Kenneth L. Gorman
Winona State University
Winona, Minnesota

Virginia Hemby
Indiana University of Pennsylvania
Indiana, Pennsylvania

Billy R. Hix
Motlow State Community College
Lynchburg, Tennessee

Glenda Kunar
Youngstown State University
Youngstown, Ohio

Konnie G. Kustron
Eastern Michigan University
Ypsilanti, Michigan

David W. Leapard
Eastern Michigan University
Ypsilanti, Michigan

Kenneth E. Martin
University of Cincinnati
Cincinnati, Ohio

Donna McKoon
Motlow State Community College
Lynchburg, Tennessee

Bill McPherson
Indiana University of Pennsylvania
Indiana, Pennsylvania

Mary Etta Naftel
Hinds Community College
Raymond, Mississippi

Larry G. Pagel
Northern Michigan University
Marquette, Michigan

Kathleen Richards
Utah Valley State College
Orem, Utah

James Calvert Scott
Utah State University
Logan, Utah

Jean Anna Sellers
Fort Hays State University
Hays, Kansas

Beverly A. Soriano
Framingham State College
Framingham, Massachusetts

Dawn Woodland
Indiana University of Pennsylvania
Indiana, Pennsylvania

Mazie E. Will
Sul Ross State University
Alpine, Texas

I would also like to express my sincere appreciation to the many other talented and dedicated individuals who contributed to this *Yearbook*. **Ronald F. Fulkert**, of Eastern Michigan University, spent many hours discussing best teaching practices related to technology. **Nyla Hughes**, who is a graduate assistant studying technology at Eastern Michigan University and holds a bachelor's degree in writing from Michigan State University, reviewed each manuscript for writing style and clarity. The NBEA Publications Committee and the NBEA publications staff also worked diligently on behalf of NBEA members. There are many others who have made contributions. Although they are not named, they will perhaps recognize their contributions. These are the business educators who nominated authors, recommended reviewers, and gave other advice. Thanks are extended to each of these important contributors to this *Yearbook*.

Ann M. Remp, Editor
Eastern Michigan University
Ypsilanti, Michigan

Teaching in a Dynamic Technology Environment: An Overview and Introduction

Ann M. Remp
Eastern Michigan University
Ypsilanti, Michigan

Business, government, and other types of organizations, such as education organizations, face demands for improved customer, citizen, and client services. These organizations, in collaboration with educators, need to determine the role of technology in educating citizens, consumers, employees, and other clients. Business raises questions about the ability of technology to deliver training (Brown, 2001) and to generate knowledge in collaborative environments (Briton, 2001). These questions parallel educators' concerns about how technology should be used to improve learning. All of these constituents search for best practices that have improved performance and provide models that can be emulated.

Business educators have a wealth of research to validate the effectiveness of instructional approaches in many areas, including those that are related to technology. Educational standards are dictating the migration of some information technology learning outcomes to earlier grade levels. Students are also learning technology skills outside of school. Even more fundamentally, as a language for learning as well as the content of learning (Moursund, 2000a), information technology is continually "changing what it means to know and work in the various academic disciplines" (p. 1). Work has become knowledge intensive, whether the "worker" is student, teacher, employee, employer, consultant, or other. The technology environment will continue to be dynamic. Never has technology been more important to business success; never before has understanding of business principles and processes been so critical to the successful implementation of technology systems.

This introduction focuses on best instructional practices for the dynamic technology environment. The thesis of this introduction is that as technology is integrated more completely in earlier grades and learned in the home and community environment, business educators can chart new territory through knowledge-focused instructional approaches. The authors of this *Yearbook* have elaborated on ways business teachers can create and apply best practices. Following brief comments on technology and goals for learning, this introduction discusses the concept of best practices, the status of best practices in business education, and directions for business teachers as they use technology to improve learning. Definitions and suggested student activities are included throughout all the chapters to support the discussion.

TECHNOLOGY AND GOALS FOR LEARNING

Students have many goals related to school that reflect inputs from parents, teachers, peers, and society as communicated through the media. Research demonstrates the relationship between setting positive learning goals and self-direction in performance achievement (Zimmerman & Kitsantas, 1997). Besides meeting academic goals, students have other school goals that include "learning social sensitivity, . . . compliance [with rules], making friends, becoming a better person, and finding a job . . . " (Bigelow & Zhou, 2001, p. 2). Teachers need to know how students view technology in relation to these other goals in order to motivate students to learn new and sometimes challenging technologies, to apply that knowledge flexibly, and to create new knowledge (Hargreaves, 1999).

Effective learning requires the teacher to address motivation. Perspectives on the role of information technology in education differ and affect motivational approaches. Some argue that real learning results only from student-directed inquiry, while others express concern that the computer is used as the motivation to learn (Kasch, 1997). Some believe that learning technology should produce a means of collaboration and communication, not simply the skill to use a particular technology (Briton, 2001). Motivation based on some schools of thought is a predominantly mental or rational process, while, when viewed from other perspectives, is exclusively emotional in nature (Kasch, 1997).

Moursund (2000/2001), an executive officer of the International Society for Technology in Education, has described information technology proficiency as a combination of computer and Internet skills and knowledge that form a "general-purpose brain tool" (p. 1). The National Educational Technology Standards for Students, according to Moursund, "provide guidelines for levels of students' expertise with IT. Many adults [including teachers] look at these standards and dismiss them as completely unreasonable; after all, relatively few adults can meet them" (p. 2). Moursund (2000c) has argued that motivation must be based on "a compelling application that empowers its user to do things" and that "compelling is in the eyes of the beholder. Intrinsic motivation makes an application compelling" (p. 2).

Observations and case reports verify that using technology motivates students in many ways. For example, according to Zeliff (chapter 2 of this *Yearbook*), some students are technology teachers in their communities, prepared formally for that role by youth organizations. Students may be motivated to take on this role by the desire to be part of a group, share knowledge, learn about technology, help others, show off, gain status, avoid failure or embarrassment, or other purposes. What makes technology learning compelling for students is probably multidimensional.

Asking students to reflect on the relationship of technology to their broad-based school goals can provide insights into how technology can be used effectively in instruction. In addition, the process of reflecting on their goals helps students to articulate their thinking, a necessary step if they are to prepare to do knowledge work. Ramey, in chapter 12, and Everett, in chapter 15 of this *Yearbook*, extensively discuss knowledge management concepts and students' need to become knowledge managers.

DEFINITIONS

- **Knowledge** is a "personal capability . . . to do or to judge something, now or in the future . . . acquired as a result of reading, seeing, listening to, or feeling . . . something" (Gundry & Metes, 2001). This definition is used throughout this introduction, but it differs from many other definitions of knowledge.
- **Knowledge management** "examines information and human understanding, using concepts from education, information technology, cognitive psychology and library science . . . [to turn] an organization's intellectual assets . . . into greater productivity, new value, and increased competitiveness" (Open Directory Project, n.d.).
- **Knowledge creation or generation** is the "transformation of information into capabilities for effective action" (Open Directory Project, n.d.). Hargreaves (1999) has described creating best teaching practices as knowledge generation tasks and the primary responsibility of teachers and schools.

BEST PRACTICES

Best practices are successful practices and programs that communities and organizations recognize as effective and identify as models that others can emulate with the expectation of achieving similar results. The purpose of providing models is to move effective practices from isolated use to widespread implementation. Articulating and disseminating best practices is an example of knowledge management at work. Business best practices processes and projects focusing on uses of technology provide useful input for business teachers who seek to integrate technology into instruction more effectively.

Identification of Organizational Best Practices

Candidates for the designation of best practice may be found in any area that is important to a community, organization, or profession. The number of projects dedicated to identifying best practices is growing, which is a testimony to the intense desire to improve performance in all sectors—government, business, nonprofit, and education.

STUDENT ACTIVITY

Technology and Student Goals

Note to teachers: This survey can be done anonymously unless you want to use the information for individual interventions. If the activity is used for individual interventions, you should meet any school requirements for collecting the information.

Student and teacher activity: Ask students to think about all the goals they have and how technology affects them. Then ask them to complete the survey below. Tell students that there are no right or wrong answers; their opinions are what is important. Complete the survey twice yourself: once to predict how students will respond and once to reflect your own goals. After collecting the information from students, compare your predictions and your goals with the students' responses. The results should be used to identify the compelling needs for technology instruction. The survey can be modified as needed. A scale of 1 (definitely agree) to 5 (definitely disagree) should be used to answer the survey.

1. I am proud of my knowledge of computers and my ability to work with them.
2. Other students seem to know a lot more about computers and technology than I do.
3. I think I know some areas of technology well enough to help other students learn.
4. My parents really want me to be good at using technology.
5. My knowledge of computers and technology has already helped me to do better in school.
6. I like that other students think I'm a geek because I spend so much time with computers.
7. I would like to make more friends that want to share information about computers.
8. I know that if I learn more about computers and technology I will be able to help other people.
9. There's a lot about computers that I can learn on my own, so I really want to learn skills in school that are harder for me to learn on my own.
10. I need to learn as much about working with computers as I can because this knowledge will affect my career.

Identification process. The goal of the best practices process is to identify several models of successful practices for emulation. Identifying multiple models, rather than just one, allows practitioners to match models to their own environments. At the same time, the goal is to be selective. Not every effective practice is designated a best practice; to be deemed "best" a model must be likely to produce improvements when adapted by others. Although best practices projects differ in the type of best practice that they seek, all begin with criteria by which to compare the "apples and oranges" of actual practices against a standard of achievement. Best practices projects base their criteria on organization mission statements and/or standards for performance.

The first step in identifying best practices is to develop and disseminate criteria that characterize best practices. The second step is to evaluate specific candidate programs and practices against these criteria. Finally, dissemination of information about "best" programs and practices provides the basis for others to use as a model for the practices in their environments.

Example of the process. The Association of College and Research Libraries (ACRL) Best Practices Initiative provides a useful example of the process. After defining information literacy and the standards and performance indicators required to demonstrate literacy, ACRL (2000) developed a statement of characteristics that "best" programs should exhibit. These characteristics address program mission, goals and objectives, articulation with curriculum, pedagogy, assessment, and several other items. ACRL then solicited nominations for best practice status. Eight to ten programs have been selected for a 2002 best practices conference.

Aside from defining what the information-literate person must be able to do at all levels of education, this example shows the relationship of standards to criteria, and in turn, to the selection of best practices that serve as models for others. Shafer, in chapter 3 of this *Yearbook*, provides a model, based on integrated business education and information literacy standards, for building a program for young learners that business teachers can emulate. Clodfelter, in chapter 13 of this *Yearbook*, provides a model for integrating technology into entrepreneurship education. Both of these models exhibit characteristics that best practices must embody.

Selected Best Practices Projects

The business, nonprofit, education, government, and other sectors are aggressively conducting best practices evaluations. The desire to improve performance is universal. Several projects focus on the effectiveness of technology implementations that have education of clients as a goal.

Congress online project. The Pew Charitable Trusts sponsored a project to identify congressional Web sites that furthered "constituent participation in the legislative process; . . . a stronger sense of congressional accountability; . . . and . . . e-democracy" (Congress Online Project, 2001). The evaluation criteria for best Web sites first stress audience and content and then the site's interactivity. These form the first three layers of a pyramid, emphasizing that "the most fundamental component of an effective Web site is a clear understanding and acknowledgement of who its audience is . . . . [I]f the Web site fails to provide the information and services its visitors seek, visitors will leave to find the information elsewhere." Interactivity is the means for democratic conversation between citizens and their representatives. Finally, best congressional Web sites incorporate elements of design and architecture and innovative approaches to maximize the likelihood of accomplishing their goals.

National Workforce Center for Emerging Technologies (NWCET). NWCET (2002) "plays a pivotal role in informing students, business, educators, and government about IT [information technology] workforce education and development and emerging trends in the field of IT." Rather than establish criteria for evaluating other best practices, NWCET evaluated how successfully it achieved its goals in four areas and disseminated its results for other organizations to use. Evaluation activities involving focus groups, on-site visits, and conferences with consultants and "internal champions" provided feedback about what worked and what needed modification. By sharing its experience, NWCET allows other organizations with similar missions to determine what to expect should they implement similar approaches to technology learning.

World Best Website Awards. The WorldBest Network honors outstanding Web sites with its World Best Website Awards. Businesses and other organizations receive "stars" reflecting the performance of their Web sites (WorldBest Network, 2001). Web sites receive one star for functionality, the minimum performance that must be exhibited. The second star represents design, and the third reflects content—the mission and Web site goals, interactivity, information quality, and related factors. Four-star sites display originality. The fifth star indicates professionalism and effectiveness, including customer service, honesty, ethical practices, and overall site effectiveness. The evaluation instrument consists of 100 evaluation statements: Each star correlates with one of the five categories, each category encompasses five evaluation areas, and each evaluation area is defined by four statements.

In each case, best practices flow from a clear statement of mission and goals, just as instruction flows from curriculum, and curriculum from mission and outcomes. Effective interaction with clients generally is an expected component of best practices. The effectiveness of content to meet needs and of innovation to hold attention are also considered. Business education students must learn to work with best practices. Learning the concepts is part of their route to acquiring knowledge skills.

STUDENT ACTIVITY

On the Cutting Edge

Because the process of identifying best practices is a knowledge task, students who emulate the process also emulate the knowledge creation and application activities that are involved in the knowledge task. Young (2001) has developed and made available to other teachers a WebQuest entitled "On the Cutting Edge: Searching for the Perfect Website" (http://carbon.cudenver.edu/~dlyoung/webquest/wq_training/wq_t_cuttingedge/).

It includes background information; a description of the task, the product, and the individual roles that students will assume for the project; guidelines for teamwork; a design grid for evaluation; and a reflection component. Business teachers looking for a Web-oriented project and/or an example of how to raise instruction to a high knowledge level are encouraged to review the project. They will find a strong motivational element in the project. Additional WebQuests are available to teachers at http://edweb.sdsu.edu/WebQuest/matrix/. Activities are classified by grades. Some business teachers may have an interest in Plunkett's (1999) "Basic Network Design" WebQuest.

Business Education Best Practices

As an outcome of research and as business teachers communicate the results of instructional initiatives, candidates for best practices are created. Meggison in chapter 19 of this *Yearbook* summarizes the results of recent technology-related business education research. An excellent example of a best practices project disseminated to business teachers is found in Delta Pi Epsilon's (DPE's) *Best Practices in Business Education* (2001): "Each [practice] is organized in an action research format describing the area needing improvement, the suggested idea, the procedures used, the results, and the suggestions for implementation. This is followed by the resources consulted or used."

A taxonomy, or classification, of technology-related instructional needs helps to direct the collection and exchange of knowledge. Business teachers have a taxonomic project in the *Business Education Index* (Delta Pi Epsilon, 2000 and earlier). Delta Pi Epsilon indexes publication (captured) knowledge of the profession by relevant business education topic areas, including technology topics. Business teachers are thus able to access the body of business education knowledge. The National Business Education Association disseminates instructional approaches through its publications including *Business Education Forum*, *Keying In*, and the *NBEA Yearbook*. Technology is a theme throughout these publications. Delta Pi Epsilon disseminates the results of research through the *Delta Pi Epsilon Journal* and *Instructional Strategies*.

Sharing dialogue (uncaptured) knowledge is more difficult. The experience of teachers who present sessions at state, regional, and national business education meetings is available to those who hear the presentations, and efforts can be made to convert this knowledge into a form the community can share. However, the experiments of other business teachers who are improving education in their classrooms may be locked in their memories and experiences. This knowledge needs to be moved to the "publication" category, regardless of the particular form of publication that is used.

Speaking to business educators, Briggs (Delta Pi Epsilon, 2001) said, "What teachers may not realize is that they are conducting research in their own classroom when they attempt something new in response to a problem or concern they have encountered .... A decision has been made as to how to implement the new idea, and it is carried through. Either the new idea works to some degree, or it does not. Either way, the teacher has conducted a simplistic form of research" (p. 1). Briggs alludes to the losses or benefits the business education profession experiences when business teachers keep knowledge to themselves or disseminate it in some way.

CHARACTERISTICS OF BEST INSTRUCTIONAL PRACTICES

A synthesis of business, education, and business education goals and achievement standards related to instruction and technology points to a set of characteristics that describe best instructional practices for technology-related instruction. Some characteristics apply to many areas in which technology is either the content and resource delivery system or both.

DEFINITIONS
- **Knowledge management tools:** Technologies that "help capture, organize, store, and transmit source material from which an individual may acquire knowledge" (Gundry & Metes, 1996, p. 2).
- **Location of knowledge:** Knowledge is embedded in documents, that is, in recorded forms ("publication knowledge") and in the memories and experiences of individuals ("dialogue knowledge"). "Today's challenge is to capture knowledge from what people say and do as part of their day to day [*sic*] work and make it accessible to others" (Gundry & Metes, 1996, pp. 2–3).

STUDENT ACTIVITY

Examining Knowledge Tools
Note to teachers: Both Ramey in chapter 12 and Everett in chapter 15 of this *Yearbook* discuss knowledge management. Teachers should read these chapters, and students should be introduced to e-mail, audio conferencing, online conferencing, and collaborative tools and gain experience with word processing, e-mail, or a presentation application. Gundry and Metes' 1996 white paper on knowledge management is recommended reading.

Activity: Ask students to visit Knowledge Ability Web site at http://www.knowab.co. uk/wbw2a.html and read about "Tools Best Practices." Ask them to explain what the phrase "tools best practices" means. Ask them to explain why it will be important for them to figure out and share ways to work "smarter, not harder" with information tools. Ask students to explain whether working smarter, not harder requires information or knowledge, and ask them to explain what they think knowledge is. Have students communicate their thoughts via e-mail, or in a group-created word processing document or group presentation. Then ask students to discuss how they might have done this activity differently if they had used electronic conferencing or other electronic collaboration tools.

The Effective Business Education Teacher

The standards for what students should achieve in business and information technology are contained in the *National Standards for Business Education* (National Business Education Association, 2001). Additionally, the National Association for Business Teacher Education (NABTE) (1997) has stated the instructional standards that business educators should strive to achieve:

The business teacher embraces multiple approaches to learning and
- uses self-directed learning to help students gain access to knowledge, direct their own learning, and learn how to learn.
- employs teacher-directed learning where the teacher maintains primary control of the learning process through such methods as lectures, question and answer sessions, and teacher-led discussions.
- facilitates collaborative learning by having students work together in groups that may include students, teachers, business and community people, and others. (p. 13)

As part of the process of identifying instructional best practices, Hargreaves (1999) has urged teachers to collaborate at the school level to audit effective practices. Such audits provide the basis for mapping what is known about effective instructional practices and what is not known. Knowledge management requires a taxonomy, or classification system, that focuses on needs.

The NABTE performance standards provide a classification scheme for auditing successful approaches to technology-related instruction. Business teachers can audit what they have learned while working with technology using teacher-directed, student-directed, and collaborative instructional approaches. Based on the audit, teachers can map what works and broaden the base for implementation. They can also identify what does not work, as well as what is missing, and develop and test approaches to correct or fill these gaps. As part of the process of filling gaps, business teachers can ask students to identify technology approaches used in other classes that they learned from and enjoyed.

Schools that support teachers in these processes are "knowledge-creating schools" (Hargreaves, 1999, p. 124). Business teachers who engage in this process are practicing knowledge management, especially if they report their efforts to the profession. Business teachers are making knowledge that has hitherto been inaccessible and locked within their minds public and usable for others. They are also developing skills in the processes their students must learn.

Effective Business and Organizational Web Sites

The Web site best practices projects examined earlier address educational processes: exchange of information and interaction between clientele and organizations for some mutual goal. The criteria for effective Web sites generally address audience, content, interaction, innovation, design, and originality.

As business teachers increasingly use the World Wide Web as the content, resource, and delivery system for instruction, criteria for evaluation and design/architectural elements should be helpful. From a knowledge management perspective, organizational criteria for best practice sites become a second classification scheme to use with teacher-directed, self-directed, and facilitated instructional approaches.

Effective Technology-Related Educational Practices

The Software & Information Industry Association (2000) analyzed 311 research reviews and studies from a pool of more than 3,500 reports and confirmed the incomplete status of best instructional practices with and about technology. While the report suggested a number of positive impacts of technology, these impacts depended on a complex interaction of "the specific student population, the software design, the educator's role, how the students are grouped, the preparedness of the educator and the level of student access to the technology . . ." (p. 4). The similarity of business teacher standards and Web site effectiveness criteria is evident. Among the promising results are the following generalizations (Software & Information Industry Association, 2000):

- The teacher's role in facilitating effective use of technology in instruction is of "primary importance" in creating "an environment characterized by careful planning and frequent interaction among students and the teacher."
- "Instructional scaffolding—gradually decreasing the level of help available and/or gradually increasing the complexity of the task—can be effective in improving student achievement."
- "Technology has been used successfully to support constructivist, inquiry-based and project-based instruction."
- "Small group collaboration on the computer is especially effective when students have received training in the collaborative process."

What examples illustrate approaches that address these findings? Several examples of collaborative approaches appear in DPE's *Best Practices for Business Education* (2001) and are listed in DPE's *Business Education Index*. Readers are encouraged to review them. The need to plan for technology experiences that are integrated into instruction is also familiar to business teachers. What follows are examples of Web-based approaches to learning that have developed over the short life of the World Wide Web. They represent varying levels of support for learning knowledge skills.

Support for Learning

One of the most difficult tasks in instruction is determining the level of support that students need to acquire knowledge tools. Meggison (chapter 19) discusses the issue of level of support in presenting results of research. Students are "waylaid" on the knowledge route if they assume that information exists when it does not or if they fail to find information that does exist because the information has not been catalogued. Students are also "waylaid" if they repeat what they already know and do not reach higher levels of learning that involve analysis, synthesis, and evaluation. A number of Web-based approaches that are in use may provide models for business teachers.

Scaffolded Web-based approaches. When the Web made its appearance, educators in many disciplines began to use it in innovative ways. In 1995 Dodge (1997b) initiated a project with teachers to determine effective means of using the Web for instruction. The product was the WebQuest (Dodge, 1997a), a learner-oriented activity at the higher levels of Bloom's learning taxonomy. WebQuests are based on "doable," but challenging, tasks that require students to employ processes, resources, and role-play to accomplish the tasks, as well as evaluation, reflection, and transfer of learning. Support for learning is provided by teachers, students, and others who participate in the WebQuests.

March (1999, 2000), Dodge's colleague, has suggested five additional "Web-and-Flow" activity formats that would build from lower to higher knowledge skill levels to support the progressive development of knowledge skills: the Topic Hotlist, Knowledge Hunt, Subject Sampler, Insight Reflector, and Concept Builder. Seamon (2001a and 2001b) has described the progression: Students move from collecting information through "hotlists" of Web sites developed by teachers to becoming developers of "hotlist" Web pages. Students then move from the role of hotlist developers to the roles of participants and developers of other intermediate-level activities. From developing knowledge-based activities, they move to assessing their work in terms of "best practice" criteria.

Web-based approaches that move from lower to higher levels of acquiring knowledge and involve interaction among and between students and teachers are reaching critical mass, such that more and more examples are available on the Web. This makes these instructional activities reusable, which is the goal of knowledge management. This also justifies the investment of teacher time to create and share/post activities.

Teacher-directed to collaborative, student-developed approaches. Becoming capable of generating and applying knowledge requires students to learn how to cope with what it means to "know" today when the "what" will not remain static. Initially the teacher may develop a task for lower-level skill development. Then, to move students from a lower to higher level of knowledge skill, teachers may ask students to create a similar task based on their experience with the first. At the highest level, students must operate with competence in many knowledge skills in a project format producing a significant product. Although there are many types of activities, the contrast between the lowest and highest level activities will illustrate the need for progressive knowledge skill development.

The topic "hotlist" introduces a search for information on the Web. The hotlist is a teacher-prepared list of Web sites on a specific topic that students should visit. A goal of this lower-level knowledge activity is to have students focus on the information available on the World Wide Web and locate additional information to enhance their knowledge of an essential concept that has already been developed in instruction. The hotlist replaces open-ended, unstructured searches that may be unproductive (March, 1999). The teacher may begin with a question or simply a topic that has been covered in class and list the teacher-selected sites. Preferably the hotlist is a Web page. Once acquainted with the hotlist, students may then create the next hotlist based on a new course topic.

As teachers add to the hotlist targeted questions to be answered, rather than simply the topic, the knowledge level will escalate. Students must screen information to distinguish relevant from irrelevant information.

WebQuests require high-level knowledge skills as well as project and team skills. Young's (2001) WebQuest, which was cited earlier, reflects the components that Dodge (1997a, 1997b) designed into the learning experience: an introduction that provides background for role-playing, a task of sufficient complexity to challenge students to apply their knowledge from previous learning in new ways, the process the students should follow and suggested strategies, resources, an evaluation instrument, and a conclusion to facilitate reflection on learning. Dodge has indicated that WebQuests can range in duration from a few days to several weeks or more.

STUDENT ACTIVITY

Building a Personal Finance Hotlist

Read Piening and Deinert's chapter 18 in this *Yearbook* and select a lesson that can be supported by the Web resources in the chapter. For the following activity, the topic will be "How do you decide whether a Web-based business is probably reputable or might be fraudulent?" First, discuss the concept of fraud and examples from business. Discuss the risks students face when buying online. Provide students with a hotlist of Web sites (preferably on a Web page) for credit card companies, the Better Business Bureau Online, and a few others that provide basic information. Form groups of 3–4 students, depending on the number of Internet connections that are available. The task involves two steps:

First, ask students to use the hotlist and identify some information to look for on a business Web site that would help them decide whether the business is probably reputable or should be checked out further before anything is purchased from it. Have them discuss their findings.

Second, ask the students to develop their own hotlist of business sites that show some of the characteristics of reputable sites. Get them started by asking if the hotlist can include a credit card site or the Better Business Bureau Online site. Ask them to answer the question based on the criteria the site must meet to "make the list." Ask students for a few names of other businesses they might visit and have students confirm what they will be looking for. Have them copy/paste their site addresses into a word processing program to create their hotlist to minimize errors (Seamon, 2001).

Note to teachers: As you introduce another essential concept, have students create the hotlist initially. You may instruct students about effective terms to use with a search tool. Although any two searches with the same search tool using the same terms can produce different results, you should test the search terms to determine the appropriateness of the sites that are likely to result. Every chapter of this *Yearbook* provides pertinent Web sites so that readers can spend time reading and using the information from the sites rather than doing open-ended searches for information.

Young's (2001) "Searching for the Perfect Website" is relevant to business education, focuses on best practices, and hence is an exemplary model. Its dynamic and descriptive style of writing, beginning with the students' invitation to the "war room" of an Internet design firm, illustrates how motivation and interest can become compelling for students. The resource component includes a hotlist. The high-level aspect of the project is that creating the evaluation instrument is the product of the WebQuest. A partially completed sample evaluation instrument illustrates the gradual withdrawal of instructional support. Students review the evaluation instrument for a different, but related project. They must then use the model, adapt the evaluation criteria to their own project, and produce an evaluation instrument based on their research.

As a best practice, the WebQuest is a model that can be replicated. McNally (2000/2001) has emphasized the importance of using a template when designing a WebQuest. Brooks and Byles (2000) have provided a set of WebQuest resources in hotlist form interspersed with narrative explanation. One link directs teachers to a suggested template entitled "Put the Title of the Lesson Here" at http://www.memphis-schools.k12.tn.us/admin/tlapages/lesson-template.htm. Examples of WebQuests that are categorized by grade level and subject can be found at or through the EdWeb site at San Diego State University (http://edweb.sdsu.edu/WebQuest/matrix/).

Other resources for business teachers. The Open Directory Project (ODP) (http://www.dmoz.org) is an example of a knowledge management project. Because the resources available through the World Wide Web and other Internet services are vast, individuals can be overwhelmed by thousands of responses to search requests. Sites may also be missed in the cataloging processes employed by search tools. To address these problems, more than 20,000 volunteers serve as ODP editors for information categories. These editors search for sites that relate to their categories and review sites submitted by Web site owners. The ODP site at http://dmoz.org/Reference/Knowledge_Management/desc.html is an excellent starting place for business teachers who are searching for descriptions of and information about knowledge management tools. Because the resources must be classified, each business teacher must obtain a concept map of knowledge management with links to resources on each element of the map.

Coping with information overload and information obsolescence is a knowledge skill for teachers. Teachers are well served by the ODP for other educational and information technology needs, as well. Business education students and all other students must also develop this skill. Business teachers can lead in developing these needed career skills.

Effective Business Education Practices: This *Yearbook*

The chapters in this *Yearbook* address specific characteristics that best instructional practices must exhibit: knowledge of the audience so that technology-related instruction is appropriate; interaction that prepares students to build effective, technology-mediated relationships; quality content that prepares students for the business environment; and client services that respond to the need to develop career and personal skills in a dynamic technology environment.

The audience. *Part I: Technology, Learners, and Learning Environments* is dedicated to students and other educational stakeholders. This is the audience that business education addresses. Rucker and Reynolds (chapter 1) focus on what students bring to the classroom: their technology experiences, their attitudes toward technology, and their expectations about technology in learning. Zeliff (chapter 2) discusses learning opportunities in the wider technology environment of the student—the home and the community. Shafer (chapter 3) addresses the technology needs of young learners and their teachers and the contributions that business educators can make to the effective use of technology in learning in the earlier grades. Rader (chapter 4) provides methods and approaches for students facing challenges occasioned by physical disabilities, learning disabilities, and use of multiple languages.

Interaction. *Part II: Building Relationships in a Technology-Mediated World* focuses on the connected world, where relationships are supported by technology and sometimes are totally dependent on how effectively individuals handle technology tools. Blaszczynski (chapter 5) discusses citizenship and ethics in a technology-mediated world and the rights and responsibilities of those who use the global technology infrastructure. Crews, North, and McCannon (chapter 6) examine how employer-employee, customer-business, and employee-employee relationships are impacted by technology. Stout (chapter 7) focuses on technology-mediated relationships in distance learning environments. Timm (chapter 8) discusses the interrelationships of people, countries, businesses, international banking, governments, and law that facilitate global commerce. Scott (chapter 9) focuses on language, culture, and technology in the global business environment.

Quality content. *Part III: Business Functions and Technology* addresses selected business content areas affected by technology implementations. O'Connor (chapter 10) provides perspectives on instruction in marketing, management, and administration. Lehman (chapter 11) discusses enterprise resource planning concepts and how their implementation affects business procedures. Ramey (chapter 12) examines knowledge management in the business environment. Clodfelter (chapter 13) provides a plan by which business teachers can address online business and entrepreneurship concepts. Each of these chapters provides content and approaches for instruction that integrate technology and increase interaction among students. The content standards for business education (National Business Education Association, 2001) provide a comprehensive overview of what students need to know and be able to do.

The topics in this section of the *Yearbook* only begin to touch on critical areas for business education. The changes in technology systems that are currently under way require instructional practices that seamlessly integrate business principles, business procedures and processes, and technology systems. The door is open to the development of new best instructional practices by business educators.

Client services. *Part IV: Technology Skills for Consumer and Career-Related Uses* addresses individual needs as technology becomes more prevalent in daily life. Berry (chapter 14) discusses technology's impact on career paths, as it modifies existing careers and creates new opportunities. Everett (chapter 15) explores effective communication in a networked environment as well as the need for knowledge management skills. Maxam (chapter 16) advises teachers on the continuing need for and methods of teaching keyboarding and word processing, and addresses newer input skills that students will need. Clark (chapter 17) updates business teachers on legal issues in technology that affect both teachers and students. His goal is to help students apply legal concepts to decisions they make about using technology. Piening (chapter 18) provides business teachers with a comprehensive treatment of consumer aspects of online investing and shopping. Meggison (chapter 19) concludes this *Yearbook*'s search for best practices by discussing the findings of recent technology-related research.

Instruction that reflects knowledge and sensitivity to business education's audiences, interaction that strengthens the ability to build relationships, quality content that allows students to anticipate the ways that technology will be implemented in different fields, and personal and career skills development should motivate students.

CONCLUSIONS

The challenges that business teachers face in delivering instruction in a dynamic technology environment are the same challenges that students will face as they move into their careers. Work is knowledge intensive and requires knowledge skills. Best instructional practices that target knowledge skills will address this need.

Where best instructional practices in business education have stood the test of time, they should continue to be used and passed along to other teachers in earlier grades who are involved in developing information literacy. Identifying and disseminating new practices that business teachers have developed and classroom tested should be goals for the entire business education professional community. Using "best practice" candidates shared by business teachers in workshops, conferences, and publications helps to build a base for judging the "portability" of practices. Adapting practices from business and education also aids teachers.

As stated at the outset, the thesis of this introduction is that as technology is integrated more completely in earlier grades and in the home and community environments, business educators can chart new territory using knowledge-focused instructional approaches. Through best instructional practices, business teachers can accomplish this goal.

Business teachers will never master every technology, and students will arrive in business education classes with technology skills developed outside of school and at earlier levels. The knowledge of technology held by teachers and students is trading places. Methods of instruction must take more advantage of students' ability and willingness to teach technical aspects of technology. Teachers must add to students' skill base, starting at more advanced levels to address the downward migration of some skills. Business teachers must build a compelling need in students to create and manage knowledge. What students need to learn are the proficiencies that make their business teachers effective—their ability to practice knowledge skills and develop best practices.

REFERENCES

Association of College and Research Libraries. (2000, July). *Information literacy competency standards for higher education.* Retrieved December 8, 2001, from the World Wide Web: http://www.ala.org/acrl/ilintro.html

Bigelow, B. J. & Zhou, R. M. (2001, March). Relational scaffolding of school motivation: developmental continuities in students' and parents' ratings of the importance of school goals. *The Journal of Genetic Psychology, 162*(1), 75–92. Retrieved April 7, 2002, from the World Wide Web: http://firstsearch.oclc.org

Briton, D. (2001). Online worker's education: How do we tame the technology. *International Journal of Instructional Media, 28*(2), 117–35. Retrieved December 8, 2001, from the World Wide Web: http://firstsearch.oclc.org

Brooks, S. & Byles, B. (2000, November 29). *Using a WebQuest in your classroom.* Retrieved January 18, 2002, from the World Wide Web: http://www.memphis-schools.k12.tn.us/admin/tlapages/wqtetc99.htm

Brown, K. G. (2001, Summer). Using computers to deliver training: Which employees learn and why? *Personnel Psychology, 54*(2), 271–296. Retrieved December 8, 2001, from the World Wide Web: http://firstsearch.oclc.org

Congress Online Project. (2001). *Best practices criteria 2001.* Retrieved December 8, 2001, from the World Wide Web: http://www.congressonlineproject.org/criteria.html

Delta Pi Epsilon. (2000 and earlier). *Business education index.* Little Rock, AR: Delta Pi Epsilon.

Delta Pi Epsilon. (2001). *Best practices in business education.* Little Rock, AR: Delta Pi Epsilon.

Dodge, B. (1997a). *Building blocks of a WebQuest.* Retrieved January 10, 2002, from the World Wide Web: http://edweb.sdsu.edu/people/bdodge/WebQuest/buildingblocks.html

Dodge, B. (1997b). *Some thoughts about WebQuests.* Retrieved January 10, 2002, from the World Wide Web: http://edweb.sdsu.edu/courses/edtec596/about_webquests.html

Gundry, J. & Metes, G. (1996, December). *Team knowledge management: A computer-mediated approach.* Retrieved December 28, 2001, from the World Wide Web: http://www.knowab.co.uk/wbwteam.html

Hargreaves, D. H. (1999, June). The knowledge-creating school. *British Journal of Educational Studies, 47*(2), 122–144. Retrieved from the World Wide Web: http://firstsearch.oclc.org

Kasch, C. R. (1997, Spring). Engines for education [book review]. *Journal of Research on Computing in Education, 29,* 315–23. Retrieved December 27, 2001, from the World Wide Web: http://firstsearch.oclc.org

March, T. (1999). *The six Web-and-flow activity formats.* Retrieved January 10, 2002, from the World Wide Web: http://www.web-and-flow.com/help/formats.html

March, T. (2000, October). Webquests 101. *Multimedia Schools, 7*(5), 55–58. Retrieved January 11, 2002, from the World Wide Web: http://firstsearch.oclc.org

McNally, L. (2000, December/2001, January). Strategies of successful technology integrators: Part 3 - network tools. *Learning and Leading with Technology, 28*(4), 6–9. Retrieved January 10, 2001, from the World Wide Web: http://firstsearch.oclc.org

Moursund, D. (1999, October). Powerful lesson plans. *Learning and Leading with Technology, 27*(2), 4–5. Retrieved December 8, 2001, from the World Wide Web: http://firstsearch.oclc.org

Moursund, D. (2000a, February). IT as language and content. *Learning and Leading with Technology, 27*(5), 4–5. Retrieved December 30, 2001, from the World Wide Web: http://firstsearch.oclc.org

Moursund, D. (2000b, September). Roles of IT in improving our educational system. *Learning and Leading with Technology, 28*(1), 4–5. Retrieved December 30, 2001, from the World Wide Web: http://firstsearch.oclc.org

Moursund, D. (2000c, October). Roles of IT in improving our educational system—part 2: Compelling applications. *Learning and Leading with Technology, 28*(2), 4–5, 21. Retrieved December 30, 2001, from the World Wide Web: http://firstsearch.oclc.org

Moursund, D. (2000/2001, December/January). Roles of IT in improving our educational system—part 4: Brain and body tools. *Learning and Leading with Technology, 28*(4), 4–5, 62. Retrieved December 30, 2001, from the World Wide Web: http://firstsearch.oclc.org

National Association for Business Teacher Education. (1997). *Business teacher education curriculum guide & program standards.* Reston, VA: National Business Education Association.

National Business Education Association. (2001). *National standards for business education.* Reston, VA: Author.

National Workforce Center for Emerging Technologies. (2002). *NWCET best practices.* Retrieved April 7, 2002, from the World Wide Web: http://www.nwcet.org

Open Directory Project. (n.d.). *Reference: Knowledge management.* Retrieved December 28, 2001, from the World Wide Web: http://dmoz.org/Reference/Knowledge_Management/desc.html

Plunkett, D. (1999, June 30). *Basic network design: A WebQuest for 9–12 technology classes.* Retrieved January 10, 2002, from the World Wide Web: http://www.yorkville.k12.il.us/webquests/webqplunkett/webqsplunkett.html

Seamon, M. (2001a, January/February). Changing instructional practices through technology training. *Book Report, 19*(4), 44–8. Retrieved April 7, 2002, from the World Wide Web: http://firstsearch.oclc.org

Seamon, M. (2001b, March/April). Changing instructional practices through technology training, part 2. *Book Report, 19*(5), 40–42. Retrieved April 7, 2002, from the World Wide Web: http://firstsearch.oclc.org

Software & Information Industry Association. (2000, July 26). *2000 research report on the effectiveness of technology in schools: Executive summary.* Retrieved January 19, 2002 from the World Wide Web: http://www.siia.net/sharedcontent/store/e-edtech-sum00.pdf

WorldBest Network. (2001). *Quality criteria for Website excellence.* Retrieved December 8, 2001, from the World Wide Web: http://www.worldbestwebsites.com/criteria.htm

Young, D. L. (2001, August 4). *On the cutting edge: Searching for the perfect Website* [a WebQuest, rev. ed.]. Retrieved January 10, 2002, from the World Wide Web: http://carbon.cudenver.edu/~dlyoung/webquest/wq_training/wq_t_cuttingedge/

Zimmerman, B. & Kitsantas, A. (1997). Developmental phases in self-regulation: Shifting from process goals to outcome goals. *Journal of Educational Psychology, 89*(1), 29–36.

Learners and Technology: Experience, Attitudes, and Expectations

Jim Rucker
Fort Hays State University
Hays, Kansas

Sharon Reynolds
Minot State University
Minot, North Dakota

In the 21st century the notion of a self-contained classroom located in an identifiable physical space is evolving into that of a virtual classroom, one that offers the potential for interacting with students and teachers all over the world. Some experts have gone as far as to predict that the "residential-based model"—with students attending classes at prearranged times and locations—will eventually disappear, having been replaced by distance and online learning delivery systems (Blustain, Goldstein, & Lozier, 1999; Drucker, 1997).

In distance and online learning delivery systems teachers and students are operating "blind." Each participant in the teaching and learning process is "invisible" to the others, and therefore is challenged to find new or adaptive ways of relating to and functioning in this environment. The success or failure of new educational delivery methods will depend to a large extent, then, on the participants' experiences, attitudes, and expectations.

Just as customers are best served by the businesspeople who know the most about their needs and lifestyles, students are best served by instructors who are knowledge-able about students' needs and about what they bring to the learning environment. Consequently, this chapter focuses on the diversity of the current and future student population, students' attitudes and expectations with regard to the use of technology for learning, stakeholder expectations in the emerging workplace, and the implications of these expectations for teaching about business and careers. This chapter also presents some examples of best practices for using technology as an educational delivery method.

TODAY'S AND TOMORROW'S LEARNERS: POPULATIONS CHARACTERIZED BY DIVERSITY

Less than a decade ago, one predictor of computer know-how was affluence: more affluent households were more likely than less affluent ones to own a computer for home use. In 2001 more than 50 percent of the U.S. population was online; this number is expected to exceed 75 percent by 2005 ("Race for First Impressions," 2001). Today there is an overall downward trend in affluence among those who use the Internet, although Net users have higher household earnings than the general public (62.6 percent of the online population earns an annual household income above $50,000) (Thompson, May 22, 2000).

Yet it is important to remember two things: (1) many households are still not "wired," thus students may be unfamiliar with even the basics of computer technology; and (2) online users differ widely in age, experience, level of technological literacy, and in what they value about being online.

Elementary and Secondary School Students

Washington Post writer Laura Sessions Stepp has characterized today's students as more savvy about money, technology, and business than any previous generation (Glenn, 2000). Most of today's students used and experimented with technology long before they began their formal education and often are more technologically advanced than many educators. For example, many students are wed to cell phones, palm and wireless devices, and pagers. To these students, technology has always been ubiquitous, a staple of the music, entertainment, television, and cable industries. Computers, CD-ROMs, video games, VCRs, and videos are, if not "old hat," at least as comfortable as an old pair of shoes. And DVD players are just now being "broken in."

Many of today's students live in a world that extends far beyond their desks: they are using the Internet and chat rooms to communicate with people all over the world, and they are carrying handheld or laptop computers that allow them to access wireless communications or to download homework assignments from the Web. If they have not used these technologies at home, they have most likely used some combination of them in their communities, for example, in libraries or schools. But the Digital Divide is real. For instance, a child in a low-income white family is three times more likely to have Internet access than a low-income Hispanic child (Thompson, May 28, 2000).

The prevalence of technology and the fact that many users take it for granted can cause students to harbor some misconceptions about their expertise in the medium. For instance, many students approach learning technology applications on a need-to-know basis, which can cost them dearly. A classic example occurred at Central Washington University in Professor Kimberly Bartel's software applications class. When she tried to teach the concepts behind software functions such as "save" and "save as," her students weren't listening. So she deliberately walked them through a procedure and intentionally had them make a mistake.

Bartel's students created a word-processed file. "Save it," she told them, "and give the disk to your neighbor." The students passed each other their disks. "Now open the file," Bartel said. The students tried, but couldn't find the file because they had saved it only to their hard drives not to the disks. The resulting disbelief made them sit up and pay attention to what she could teach them (Glenn, 2000, p. 12).

Computer labs, hubs of activity in many schools, are excellent places to offer one-on-one instruction in basic software functions like those taught by Bartel. (Interestingly, however, according to Mitra [2000], isolating computers in laboratories makes them seem abnormal and disconnected from practical daily uses.) If students are supervised and coached individually, their "teach me on a need-to-know basis" approach to learning is often appropriate and effective in such an environment. However, the literature raises issues of access and available software with respect to gender equity, especially if student use of computer labs is unregulated. In 1996, for example, an article in *Educational Leadership* credited girls' apparent disinterest in technology to the lack of gender-sensitive computer games and to "boys hogging the computers" (Dooling, 2000).

Yet girls are beginning to outpace boys in their use of the Internet (for example, accessing sites like chickclick.com); this surge is expected to continue into 2003 (Thompson, June 19, 2000). In fact, girls prefer communicating by e-mail and in chat rooms to using the phone. Girls also use the Internet for sports-related purposes: for example, to buy tickets, to watch game highlights, and to play online sports trivia games. Whereas girls shop the Internet for clothes and shoes, boys shop it for electronics and video games (Runne, 2001).

Seventy-four percent of 754 teens (ages 12 to 17) who were surveyed (eStatNews, 2001) use the Internet for instant messaging, 92 percent for e-mail, and 84 percent for fun, for example, to visit an entertainment site. Computer game use remains widespread, and games tend to be biased toward males (Butler, 2000); boys still use computers more at home than girls do, a situation reinforced (wittingly or unwittingly) by parents (Sadker & Sadker, n.d.). Internet access among those who have it seems to be fairly freewheeling. That is, although 61 percent of parents say they set rules for Internet use at home, only 37 percent of teens reported time restrictions for Internet usage (eStatNews, 2001).

Adult Learners

In addition to traditional students—the ones in elementary and secondary school who matriculate directly to community colleges or universities—the undergraduate student population now includes more students who are older, married, employed, and of nonresidential status.

Women comprise 49 percent of all online users. As of this writing, this figure is expected to reach parity with men, and by 2002, women online will outnumber men online by 2.1 million (Thompson, June 7, 2000). However, fewer women than men enroll in computer programming courses and fewer women than men are computer educators (Butler, 2000).

With regard to gender differences in computer usage, the only difference lies in initial expectations for performance—these differences do not affect actual use (Gefen & Straub, 1997). As a group, middle-aged to older adults have vastly different abilities with respect to computer technology. Their comfort level may be affected by whether or not they have had to use computers on the job (and their success or failure in this context), whether or not they have children who grew up in the Digital Age, and their own interest in keeping up with new technology.

ATTITUDES AND EXPECTATIONS

Two decades ago, the "average" user viewed computers as fragile scientific instruments; today, computers are perceived to be trouble-free information appliances, much like telephones or refrigerators. Consequently, the average user assumes the computer can do whatever he or she needs—e.g., run any number of application programs simultaneously, regardless of minimum operating requirements—with sometimes disappointing results. This naive confidence in computers, and especially in hard drives, has made users complacent about doing systematic data backups and stunned when their attempts to recover lost files fail (Van Horn, 1998).

Researchers have studied a variety of factors related to the successful use of computer and other technologies. These include specific characteristics such as gender (Ayersman & Reed, 1995), computer self-efficacy (Delcout & Kinzie, 1993), computer anxiety (McInerney, McInerney, & Sinclair, 1998; Koohang, 1997), and general attitudes about computers (Bandalos & Benson, 1999). The ability to respond to a request (in the classroom and/or the workplace), access information on the Web, use videoconferencing, or deliver a multimedia presentation may be affected by one or more of these factors.

Bame, Dugger, deVries, and McBee (1993; in Boser, 1998) have argued that experience with technology is the basis for attitudes. Those who have had positive experiences with technology develop positive attitudes towards it; those who have had negative experiences with technology will likely develop negative attitudes toward it.

Bame has suggested that an informed user (i.e., one who uses the Internet in creative ways such as for e-commerce, online shopping, and distance learning) will have more positive attitudes towards networked computers. Positive past experiences with communication technology generally orient users to expect positive gains from the Internet, reinforcing positive motivation to study and learn about technology itself. The reverse is also likely to be the case. Continuing research is needed to investigate how a variety of experiences over longer periods of time might influence students who do not already hold positive attitudes about technology and who experience higher levels of computer apprehension.

The Elementary and Secondary School Classroom

Computer use is an expected and "natural" development in pedagogy (Mitra, 2000). Because of their constant exposure to technology, today's students have grown to expect many of their courses to center around technology or to have a significant technology base. They also expect their teachers to use technology more sophisticated than chalkboards, overheads, or simple slide shows and to access information from the Internet while teaching a class. Students believe computers can positively affect the way they interact with teachers and that such interactions can be quite gratifying (Mitra, 2000).

Using a less-interactive teaching method, such as lecture, "goes against everything researchers have discovered about the way children learn" (Lerner, 1997, p. 1). The student should be active rather than passive. Likewise the teacher's role has shifted from being the expert to being a collaborator or guide (Lerner, 1997).

Though teachers and students can benefit from capitalizing on technology's educational advantages, there is room for caution. More sophisticated presentation methods may encourage attention but not necessarily retention. The best learning occurs when students are actively engaged in activities that are meaningful to them; students should, as far as possible, manipulate educational technology tools themselves as they solve problems, manipulate information, and demonstrate other skills required in the emerging workplace. The more experienced users become, the less apprehension they are likely to have about using technology as a tool for learning.

A reader of scientific literature and the popular press may observe some apparent contradictions in whether boys and girls differ in their attitudes about and expectations for technology use. For example, whereas the popular press reports that girls are outpacing boys in their use of the Internet, the scientific literature reports that girls are more ambivalent about technology than boys (a shift that appears at about the seventh-grade level), perhaps due to cultural biases, few female role models, and boys' virtual monopoly of computer usage (Butler, 2000). These differences may be explained by time lags: it takes much longer to conduct studies, report results, peer-review the studies, and publish the articles than it does to conduct simple, one-pointed surveys. It is entirely possible that information reported in sources such as *e-Marketer* and the *New York Times neXt* column may appear as peer-reviewed and validated studies in future issues of *The Clearing House* and the *Journal of Research in Computing in Education*. In any case, both boys and girls believe that computers are essential to their future success in the workplace (Dooling, 2000).

Adult Learners

Adult students start classes expecting to see technology used based upon the subject matter of the class (for example, spreadsheet applications in accounting, project planning software in management) and believe that technology-assisted instruction may increase the organization and clarity of instructor presentations. However, these students do not necessarily believe technology-assisted instruction increases their own skills in synthesis and reasoning (George & Sleeth, 1996). Three representative studies, below, discuss the reaction university students had to technology-assisted learning.

Self-efficacy with regard to computer use. The Ohio Higher Education Study (McCain, Morris, Green, & Al-Najran, 1999) focused on the relationship between one's experiences with and attitudes toward technology and their effect on one's sense of confidence about using technology tools.

Eighty percent of students who used technology while participating in the Ohio higher education system believed technology aided learning. These students used computers to access news and weather reports, turn in assignments electronically, download computer programs and files for research papers, join listservs related to research interests, gather information from stock reports, e-mail friends, access electronic magazines, join discussion groups for learning and for fun, and meet people electronically.

The other twenty percent, who held negative attitudes toward technology, stated that computer networks threaten workers' privacy and shorten people's attention spans. They also stated that the Web and network computing weaken the social relationships that should be developed in the classroom, that government should regulate the Internet more carefully, and that computers and technology on the whole are boring and too time-consuming.

College students enrolled in a course that was designed to help them learn technology skills and processes and address issues of a technology-infused environment reported the following:

- More experience with technology increases one's sense of power and self-confidence and reduces the intensity of strongly held negative attitudes towards the role of computing in society.
- Positive experiences with using technology for gaining information and for maintaining social relationships increase one's sense of power and control over networked computing.

Perceived effectiveness of distance learning technologies. Distance education, although not new in the United States, is becoming increasingly popular as an educational delivery method in institutions of higher education and sometimes in elementary and secondary schools. The education is interactive, but students and instructors are in different geographic locations. The instruction can be synchronous (occurring at the same time for all participants) or asynchronous (accessed at will by students to accommodate variations in their schedules). The delivery system can use many technologies, including but not limited to the Internet, video- and audioconferencing, closed-circuit television, and computer-based training. Students' perceptions of distance education are mixed, as the studies discussed below illustrate.

The perceived effectiveness of distance technologies is assumed to reflect, to some extent, attitudes toward technology itself. Henchy's (1998) descriptors illustrate a range of existing attitudes:

- "Enthusiasts" see technology as a problem solver capable of enhancing learning.
- "Revolutionaries" see technology as transforming education.
- "Indifferents" or "cautious ones" have little or nothing to contribute to what can be considered important learning.
- "Skeptics" believe that technologies have yet to prove their potential.
- The "concerned" believe technology may lead to serious inequities in access and services.
- "Hostiles" believe technologies are being driven by elitist and corporate interests for their own benefit. (p. 1)

Two surveys offer insights into student's reactions to this method of learning.

A survey of students in an online course at William Paterson University (Presby, 2001) was conducted toward the middle of the semester to determine students' perceptions of this delivery method for education. The survey asked seven questions:

1. What is the best thing about taking an online course?
2. What is the worst thing about taking an online course?
3. Compared to a traditional course, do you put more work into an online course?
4. Does this online course meet your expectations?
5. Using a rating of 1 to represent the lowest and 10 the highest, what were your thoughts about the course before the semester began, and what are your thoughts now?
6. Do you feel class contact time is important in an online class?
7. Do you have additional suggestions?

Students' shared some interesting insights (see Table 1).

Table 1. Selected Quotes and Comments From William Paterson University Study

- "There is no real contact with other students or the teacher and some students need that contact."
- Fear that not all e-mails, assignments sent through the assignment drop box, etc., had been properly received.
- "A lot of reading and research is required in order to use the course technology."
- "Too time consuming if you don't know the technology."
- "I feel I am always on the computer and that doesn't keep me motivated."
- "A lot of work for an online class when technology is involved, but [I] guess that's why one takes the course" (Presby, 2001).

A second study, completed by Everett Rogers (1995) at Minot State University, attempted to further illustrate how Internet technologies impact student perceptions of learning. The study was based on Roger's model of the diffusion of innovation (1995). Rogers has identified several important conditions that influence the decision to use an innovative approach rather than a traditional approach for a given task: prior educational conditions, characteristics of students, and perceived characteristics of distance and online learning. Rogers' instrument addressed the following items:

- Students' prior educational/technology practices
- Students' perceived needs
- Sociological changes
- Student characteristics, personality variables, and communication behaviors

Rogers collected his data by having students respond to five statements related to the effectiveness of online learning (Rogers, 1995):

1. Most people believe that online learning is more effective than traditional methodologies.
2. In a course with both traditional and online learning methodologies, I learn better through the online learning portion.
3. I prefer online learning courses to traditional courses.
4. I believe I can learn the same amount in an online learning course as in a traditional course.
5. I believe I can make the same grade in an online learning course as in a traditional course.

Rogers reported that students believed they could make the same grade in an online learning course as in a traditional course. When asked if they believed that online learning was more effective than traditional course formats, most respondents disagreed, even though they tended to agree that they could learn the same amount in an online course.

Most of the relative advantages of online learning involved saving time, scheduling classes, and being able to take more courses. The students agreed that the difficulty of contributing to class discussions and the inability to see other students were disadvantages to online learning courses.

The same survey asked students to rate the value of contact time in the course. Table 2 reports some responses.

Table 2. Reported Value of Course Contact Time

- "Chat room interaction is very important because at least everyone can express feelings and problems at the same time."
- "It is good to discuss through e-mail or chat rooms to see how things are going."
- "When you don't have contact, it is easy to lose focus."
- "It is good getting other opinions and 'hearing' the other answers."
- "The class should be divided equally, meaning half time in class and doing work online the second half" (Rogers, 1995).

THE EMERGING WORKPLACE: STAKEHOLDER EXPECTATIONS ABOUT TECHNOLOGY

The relentless advance of technology continues to challenge business educators to provide students with quality educational experiences. The National Center for Education Statistics (U.S. Department of Education, 2000) reported that teachers who have nine or fewer years of teaching experience were more likely than teachers who have twenty or more years of experience to teach using computers or the Internet. If more recently matriculated teachers are more likely than less recently matriculated teachers to use technology in the classroom, one obvious challenge is for all business educators to use technology as a delivery system for various teaching objectives. Another challenge, however, is to determine whether even technology-literate students can demonstrate the technology competencies needed in the emerging workplace.

Various educational, governmental, and employer-issued reports communicate perceptions of what educators should be doing with respect to developing and using technology as a tool for learning. For example, professional organizations like the National Business Education Association (NBEA) and the International Society of Technology Education (ISTE) have addressed the use of technology as an educational delivery system, the interrelationship of technology to various business disciplines, and the application of technology to achieve literacy and career success. ISTE's standards for digital learning spell out the minimum requirements for technology literacy (see Table 3). Government and private sector commissions have addressed the uses of technology for career advancement and are particularly applicable at the adolescent and adult learning levels.

Reports compiled by the U.S. Department of Labor reflect the economic shift from the Industrial to the Digital Age: of 54 jobs expected to grow most significantly by 2005, only eight do not require technological fluency ("The Power of Digital Learning," 2000). According to the U.S. Secretary of Labor's Commission on Achieving Necessary Skills the following five workplace competencies are necessary for solid job performance:

- Ability to productively use resources
- Interpersonal skills

- Skill in locating and manipulating information
- Comfort with systems thinking
- Ability to operate technology

All five competencies, directly or indirectly, involve applying technology as a resource, as a tool, or as a system (SCANS 2000 Center, 2000).

Table 3. Standards for Digital Learning

Competence in "digital learning" involves the ability to
- Be proficient in the use of technology
- Communicate information and ideas using a variety of media and formats
- Access, exchange, compile, organize, analyze, and synthesize information
- Draw conclusions and make generalizations based on information gathered
- Know content and be able to locate additional information, as needed
- Evaluate information and sources
- Construct, produce, and publish models, content, and other creative works
- Become self-directed learners
- Collaborate and cooperate in team efforts
- Solve problems and make informed decisions
- Interact with others in ethical and appropriate ways

Note. From "The Power of Digital Learning: Integrating Digital Content," by The CEO Forum on Education and Technology, 2000, June, *The CEO Forum: School Technology and Readiness Report,* p. 10. Copyright 2000 by the CEO Forum on Education and Technology. Adapted with permission.

The advancement of technology continues to drive what students need to learn in order to be successful in the business environment. And technology skills are becoming more complex, raising the bar for what students need to know and be able to do. Whereas in the Industrial Age, students may have needed to know how to operate basic word processing or spreadsheet software, in today's and tomorrow's Digital Age, students may also need to know, at a minimum, how to build Web pages or conduct a dialogue via two-way videoconferencing. And in a technology-obsessed society, in which students will be barraged by digital images, students will need to develop multimedia literacy in order to understand the nuances of technology and form their own decisions about its significance or meaning ("The Power of Digital Learning," 2000).

This complexity has made it more important than ever for employers and business teachers to work together to ensure that students are equipped with the skills to be successful. "Technology advances have changed the way information is gathered and utilized," write Szul and Moore, "therefore, it is important to develop a plan for constant revision of curriculum [that reflects these changes]" (Szul & Moore, 1999, p. 42).

IMPLICATIONS FOR USING TECHNOLOGY TO TEACH ABOUT BUSINESS AND CAREERS

Today's and tomorrow's employees will be managing their own careers, acquiring new skill sets as needed, and demonstrating flexibility with regard to career "ladders" (Beller & Or, 1998). Educational institutions recognize this need for lifelong learning, and competition for students is stiff. Students have a wider range of degree programs at their disposal and more flexibility in course offerings. They are no longer limited to obtaining their education within the geographic territory in which they live. Moreover, technology-assisted learning is viewed as a natural evolution in pedagogy.

Teachers who wish to prepare students for the emerging workplace will find it useful to examine the following considerations related to incorporating technology-assisted learning into their classrooms: access, inclusion, climate, empowerment, teaching strategies, and flexibility issues.

Access

Elementary and high school teachers can create a more technology-accessible environment (with respect to gender) by providing optional supervised computer lab time (if computers are not already integrated into the regular classroom), or by considering the potential advantages of single-sex computer technology classes. A wide variety of computer activities, especially general reading and writing activities, and attention to software that allows collaboration and communication, will appeal to female students (Butler, 2000).

Teachers in elementary and high schools may need to educate parents about unconscious biases against socializing girls to take risks—e.g., by studying mathematics or technology. Socialization based on unconscious stereotypes and expectations begins early and influences a girl's decision about taking certain courses in high school. Additionally, parents are often willing to invest more money in their sons' education. Attitudes like these help perpetuate assumptions that girls cannot excel in mathematics or technology (Hanson, n.d.).

Teachers at the community college and university levels, as well as those involved in adult education, are using computers to enhance classroom discussion, and many instructors are using Web-enhanced lecture courses, in which students can view the course Web site from their homes.

Yet there are specific limitations to this technology application. Even though individual computers are now relatively inexpensive and the computer hardware and software markets are very competitive, technology is still too costly for many individuals. Student budgets may not be able to keep pace with the latest technical advances. Limited access means limited computer literacy, presenting problems for the student who wants to use online learning technologies. Many students lack access to computer networks or even to individual computers. Students must be highly motivated and proficient in computer operations before they can perform successfully in an online learning environment.

However, administrators should not rule out offering distance and online learning opportunities as part of nonresidential education services. Educational delivery via the Internet takes advantage of drastic price reductions for personal computers and increased telecommunications capabilities. Reductions in state funding for colleges and universities force administrators to seek new ways of limiting expenditures. Initial costs for distance and online learning may be high, but administrators have found that costs per credit hour decrease as more students use these delivery systems.

Inclusion

Females often focus on the social function of machines whereas males often focus on the machine itself as the "subject" to be mastered. Curriculum that presents the machine as an end in itself is less likely to appeal to young women than to young men: girls value richly textured video and audio, collaborating rather than competing, and interactions and simulations (Houtz & Gupta, 2001). Curriculum that incorporates gender-neutral software creates a more inclusive environment. Teachers and curriculum directors should be selective when purchasing software applications, be aware of possible negative gender messages in the software, and discard any such exclusionary software already in use (Butler, 2000). Once girls are excluded, even through very subtle verbal patterns, it is hard for them to reconnect even with gender-sensitive instruction.

Teachers who have classes of mixed gender or cultures may want to consider how cultural differences manifest themselves: through acceptance of unequal power distribution, avoidance of unfamiliar cultural roles, degree of acceptance of individualism, and disposition towards masculine attitudes and behavior (Gefen & Straub, 1997). It is important to note, however, that gender/cultural differences do not affect actual use of computers; they affect only initial expectations for performance. Therefore, teachers can concentrate on creating a classroom in which these perceptions are acknowledged yet not given undue importance. Instead, teachers should focus on small successes designed to allay computer anxiety and to develop feelings of confidence and self-efficacy in their students.

Climate

Teachers' expertise and enthusiasm directly impact student success. Yet teachers vary in their technological proficiency, and therefore, in their enthusiasm for technology-assisted learning. It is thus important to free oneself enough to change roles with the students: let them teach, and let the teacher become the facilitator of learning (Dooling, 2000). This role reversal is also a strategy for empowerment.

Empowerment

It is important to train female teachers (Butler, 2000) so that elementary and high school girls will be presented with successful role models, especially since it has been reported that female high school seniors are half as likely as male seniors to see themselves working in a technical field at age 30 ("Indicators," 1996). Recognize the power of technology to motivate students and enhance satisfaction in the learning process, particularly with regard to increasing retention, creating enjoyment of learning, and generating interest in course materials.

With respect to online learning, it is fine for a student to take a course exclusively on the computer. He or she can correspond with class members and the professor by using e-mail, chat rooms, or bulletin boards; however, most students still prefer some tradi-tional (face-to-face) contact with their professors. The benefits include reducing unneces-sary computer anxiety, enabling the student to share any concerns about the course before beginning the class and the professor to show students how to speed delivery of assignments, and allowing students to discuss any problem they are experiencing while using the course technologies (J. Angell, personal communication, October 12, 2000).

Teaching Strategies

The most important strategy to remember with respect to technology-assisted instruction is that it is one more strategy for learning and not an end in itself. There-fore, technology should be used where appropriate, and when it can authenticate learning. Instruction should be scaled to each type of user group, taking into consider-ation students' experiences, expectations, and attitudes. Especially in the case of younger students, teachers need to take into account the expectations and attitudes of parents with respect to their own level of technological proficiency and their expecta-tions for their children's education.

In addition, the following approaches to technology-assisted learning are worthy of consideration (Dooling, 2000; Mitra, 2000; George & Sleeth, 1996):

- Integrate the curriculum to use computer technology as a tool for teaching and learning.
- Redefine the teacher as a facilitator of learning.
- Allow students to take on the role of teacher, not only within their grade level but also across different grade levels.
- Create learning communities that include peers, teachers, and other experts. Collaborative, learner-centered approaches offer opportunities for all students, regardless of their individual learning styles, to succeed.
- Use authentic and relevant learning experiences that include real-world data, simulations, and students' reported experiences.
- Let students accommodate technology to their preferred learning styles. For example, Dooling's article in *Educational Leadership* (2000) reported that 30 percent of students surveyed in grades four to seven preferred to figure things out themselves or with the support of a book or manual.
- Teach on a "need-to-know" basis. But counter the naiveté of some learners by remembering to teach essential technology basics like file maintenance and systematic backup.
- Remember that learning by doing increases retention and improves performance. Students must become active participants in the process of finding, organizing, analyzing, and applying information in order to solve problems.

- Find new ways to teach and to reinforce critical-thinking skills. Employers are looking for people who can solve problems, manipulate and make meaning of information, and evaluate different business solutions.
- Instead of measuring learning from traditional perspectives of grades and test scores, measure how students perceive the changes brought forth in the learning environment because of the introduction of computers.
- Use parent volunteers as one-to-one coaches in computer labs.
- Take advantage of professional development technology courses that are linked to authentic instructional work.
- When offering online and/or distance learning options, preview the technology and how it will be used.
- Remember that online learning must offer opportunities for genuine interaction.

Flexibility Issues

The authors' experiences in online teaching argue for flexibility in working with students who are not proficient with technology, including all of its variations: e-mail, chat rooms, computer conferencing, electronic bulletin boards, computer-based multimedia, Internet browser features and search engines, and video- and audioconferencing. To reach as many students as possible, incorporate as many tools as is practical, and let students choose the ones that work for them.

Using e-mail for informal one-to-one correspondence allows students to read messages at their convenience and store them for later reference. An electronic bulletin board to which everyone is free to respond can encourage student-to-student interaction in a classwide conference or through individually posted comments or questions to the class, even though students may at first have to overcome the challenge of learning basic and more advanced computer, software, and online communication skills.

Yet such challenges offer opportunities for collaborative learning. In one class, for example, an electronic drop box was selected as the tool used to submit assignments. Many students, however, had no prior experience using it. In the chat room, other students provided the help that was needed. This alleviated the frustration that might have otherwise occurred while learning new skills.

While students can learn from one another, it is beneficial to provide access to the teacher comparable to that provided in a traditional classroom setting. In addition, resources for context-sensitive help or tutorials that students can access at will should be provided.

EXAMPLES OF BEST PRACTICES IN TECHNOLOGY-ASSISTED INSTRUCTION

Technology is always evolving; it can serve as a tool for learning but one that undergoes constant change. One useful approach is to consider its major roles and how they can be integrated with content mastery, for example,

- As a delivery method (such as in distance learning)
- As a method for inquiry and exploration (such as in research, I-search, and connecting to the rest of the world)
- As a tool for shaping and making meaning of information (such as with spread-sheets)
- As a way to organize and manage one's own business processes (such as with project management software and contact databases)

Teachers are making extraordinary uses of technology-assisted instruction throughout the country:

- In Middlebury (Connecticut) Elementary School second graders use art software to produce scientific drawings of penguins as they study Antarctica. Fourth graders chart and graph the growth of bulbs using spreadsheets (Dooling, 2000).
- At Woodbury Middle School, also in Connecticut, teacher Jeff Turner has already implemented an eighth-grade memory book project. He dreams of a future in which his students create interdisciplinary portfolios that include animation, sound effects, and video. He intends to connect students more closely to the community by developing touch-screen menus for local restaurants and is considering creating a town Web site that would feature oral histories by local senior citizens (Dooling, 2000).
- At Petaluma (California) High School senior Kris Ivarson designed and built the Petaluma Community Network (http://www.petalumanet.org), a Web site for community residents and for individuals thinking about relocating there. The site features a guest book, bulletin board, and interactive calendar, and it offers links to education, community, government, business, tourism, and health resources (Glenn, 2000, pp. 12–13).

The Virtual High School

One of the most innovative inclusions of technology in education, the Virtual High School (VHS) is a collaborative of participating high schools that offer content-rich, accredited high school courses over the Internet (Virtual High School, 2001).

When a participating school offers a VHS NetCourse, that school can enroll up to 20 students in other existing VHS courses. A limited number of student-only schools are allowed to enroll 10 students per semester on a trial basis, for a single year, after which they must train a teacher and join VHS as a fully participating school.

Currently more than 150 schools and 3,000 students participate, up from the initial consortium of 28 schools. Schools are scattered throughout the country (visitors to VHS's Web site can access an interactive map that hyperlinks to participating schools). So that teachers remain current and able to meet student needs for new and innovative courses, VHS developed two graduate-level online professional development courses.

Though the school exists only in cyberspace (it has a mailing address in Concord, Maine, however), it abides by formalized policies, procedures, and guidelines and operates as a nonprofit organization. Funding comes primarily from a U.S. Department of Education-sponsored five-year Technology Innovation Challenge Grant awarded to Hudson Public Schools in October 1996. The school charges tuition for professional development and an annual membership fee to all participating schools.

Comments from VHS students praise the opportunity to take charge of their own learning and the access VHS offers to disabled learners such as the hearing-impaired. A third-year evaluation report prepared for Hudson Public Schools cited that courses met the high-quality standards set by panels of experts, but that teachers expressed significantly less satisfaction about the amount of interaction they experienced in VHS courses compared to that experienced in face-to-face courses.

Based on case study analyses focusing on courses in advanced placement statistics, modern classics, photographic vision, and preengineering,

- VHS students were reported to be better prepared academically than students in corresponding face-to-face courses.
- Student dropout rates were low for both sets of courses but lower for the face-to-face courses than for the VHS courses.
- VHS students were more likely than face-to-face students to use the World Wide Web, but there were no significant differences between groups in their use of computers, e-mail, or the Internet.
- There were no significant differences in scores teachers gave to assignments from face-to-face students and VHS students, and no significant differences in external graders' scores of face-to-face students and VHS students in two of three courses.
- In every course more VHS students than face-to-face students passed the technology-use portion of the Internet assessment. In only one course (modern classics), for only one skill area (reasoning and information), did face-to-face students significantly outperform VHS students.
- In general, technology enables VHS students to take high-quality courses that would not be available to them otherwise. There are significant technology-based problems that limit student-student and student-teacher interaction in ways that negatively affect teacher feedback, student input, and the sense of community. However, according to the report, the VHS project is addressing these issues and expectations are high that the quality of interaction in VHS courses will match the quality of interaction students get in face-to-face courses (Kozma et al., 2000).

Mindquest Learning Network

Operated by the Bloomington, Minnesota, Public Schools, Mindquest is an alternative education program designed for adults and older teens who have dropped out of school. Currently, 40 students are enrolled in this Internet-based curriculum. Contemporary topics are the basis for the science, math, and technology courses offered through this program. The courses explore connections and patterns, using inquiry and problem-solving strategies, and provide a framework for exploring careers and work and for completing a self-directed learning project. The cost is free to in-state students. Out-of-state students pay tuition (Mindquest, n.d.).

SUMMARY

In the next few years, most jobs will require employees to use technology. Employees will need to become lifelong learners, increasing the importance of nontraditional educational delivery methods such as distance and online learning.

The attitudes and expectations of today's and tomorrow's learners may be as diverse as the student populations themselves, and perhaps as positive as teachers' own experiences learning various technology applications. Teachers will need to understand the unique backgrounds of their students with respect to technology use, and consider that, especially at the elementary and high school levels, teachers are working not only with student expectations and experiences but also with parental expectations and attitudes.

Because technology removes the confines of the traditional classroom through global access to information, interaction with peers and experts, and opportunities for simulated and real experiences, technology also adds elements of adventure and fun to learning. Students will expect teachers to incorporate sophisticated technology into their lessons, presentations, and education delivered at a distance. Teachers will work with classes in which they never meet their students face to face. Studies indicate that students perceive online learning to offer significant relative advantages over traditional approaches, including saving students time, easing course scheduling, and enabling students to take more courses. Many students do not believe, however, that they learn more in online course, and they have concerns related to being able to contribute to class discussions.

The younger the student, the more natural it is for that student to consider technology as a primary learning tool and to expect his or her teacher to use it as a teaching tool. However, technology in and of itself is not a substitute for good pedagogy. Teachers must capitalize on their younger students' predisposition towards active learning and use technology as one tool in the teaching-learning continuum, being mindful of student learning styles and the need to teach thinking and reasoning skills as well as technology applications.

Older learners will also expect instructors to demonstrate similar or more sophisticated competence in using technology as a tool to enhance learning. The degree of technological competence among young adult and adult learners may be more diverse than among younger students because adults will have developed attitudes and expectations based on their experiences with technology in their own workplaces, in their children's education, and with respect to their own inclinations to stay "ahead of the curve."

Because technology advances relentlessly, the American work force must continuously retrain. So, too, must teachers retrain so they can make their students not only computer literate but also technology proficient.

Teachers can benefit themselves and their students by approaching technology as a tool for learning, but one that will continue to evolve and advance. It may be useful to consider technology's major roles and how they relate to subject matter mastery, for example, as a delivery method, as a method for inquiry and exploration, as a tool for shaping and making meaning of information, and as a way to organize and manage one's own business processes.

Teachers across the country and around the world are finding innovative ways to incorporate technology into the classroom and to make it a primary vehicle for distance education. Some examples include the Virtual High School and the Mindquest Learning Network. Professional groups, government agencies, and private-sector companies are useful sources of information about projected needs in the emerging workplace and ideas for continually transforming the technology curriculum to keep pace with advances in how business is conducted.

REFERENCES

Ayersman, D. J., & Reed, W. M. (1995). Effects of learning styles, programming, and gender on computer anxiety. *Journal of Research on Computing in Education, 28*(2), 148–161.

Bame, E., Dugger, W., Jr., deVries, M., & McBee, J. (1993). Pupils' attitudes toward technology–PATT–USA. *Journal of Technology Studies, 19*(1), 40–48.

Bandalos, D., & Benson, J. (1999). Testing the factor structure invariance of a computer attitude scale over two grouping conditions. *Educational and Psychological Measurement, 30*(1), 49–60.

Beller, M. & Or, E. (1998, December). The crossroads between lifelong learning and information technology: A challenge facing leading universities. *Journal of Computer–Mediated Communication, 4*. Retrieved July 30, 2001, from the World Wide Web: http://www.ascusc.org/jcmc/vol4/issue2/beller.html

Blustain, H., Goldstein, P., & Lozier, G. (1999). Assessing the new competitive landscape. In R. N. Katz & Associates (Eds.), *Dancing with the devil*. San Francisco: Jossey-Bass Publishers.

Boser, R., Palmer, J., & Daugherty, M. (1998). Students' attitudes toward technology in selected technology education programs. *Journal of Technology Education, 10*(1).

Butler, D. A. (2000, March/April). Gender, girls, and computer technology: What's the status now? *The Clearing House 73*(4), 225–9.

Delcout, M. A. B., & Kinzie, M. B. (1993). Computer technologies in teacher education: The measurement of attitudes and self-efficacy. *Journal of Research and Development in Education, 27*(1), 35–41.

Dooling, J. (2000, October). What students want to learn about computers. *Educational Leadership 58*(2), 20–4.

Drucker, P. (1997, March 10). An interview with Peter Drucker. *Forbes Magazine*, pp. 126–127.

eStatNews. (2001, June 25). US teens in trouble, or in takeover, online? *eMarketer.* Retrieved August 2, 2001, from the World Wide Web: http://www.emarketer.com/analysis/edemograhics/20010625_pew_teens.html

Gefen, D., & Straub, D. W. (1997, December). Gender differences in the perception and use of e-mail: An extension to the technology acceptance model. *MIS Quarterly 21*, 389–400.

George, G., & Sleeth, R. G. (1996). Technology-assisted instruction in business schools: Measured effects on student attitudes, expectations, and performance. *International Journal of Instructional Media 23*(3), 239–44.

Glenn, J. M. (2000, February). Teaching the net generation. *Business Education Forum, 54*(3), 6–14.

Hanson, K. (n.d.). *Gender, discourse, and technology, center for equity and diversity* (Working Paper 5). M.A.D. Solutions for Gender Equity Issues Fact Sheet. Retrieved January 1, 2002, from the World Wide Web: http://www.alphaci.com/equity/need.htm

Henchy, N. (1998, October 30). *Attitudes toward technology in education.* Retrieved July 30, 2001, from the World Wide Web: http://ceris.schoolnet.ca/e/tech4.html

Houtz, J. E., & Gupta, U. G. (2001, Spring). Nebraska high school students' computer skills and attitudes. *Journal of Research on Computing in Education 33* (3), 316–27.

Indicators. (1996). M.A.D. Solutions for Gender Equity Issues Fact Sheet. Retrieved January 1, 2002, from the World Wide Web: http://www.alphaci.com/equity/need.htm

Koohang, A. A. (1997). A study of the attitudes of pre-service teachers toward the use of computers. *Educational Communications and Technology Journal, 35*(3), 145–149.

Kozma, R., Zucker, A., Espinoza, C., McGhee, R., Yarnall, L., Zalles, D., & Lewis, A. (2000, November). *The online course experience: Evaluation of the virtual high school's third year of implementation, 1999–2000.* Hudson, MA. SRI Project 7289.

Lerner, M. (1997). *The current state of technology and education: How computers are used in K–12 and Brown University classrooms.* Retrieved from the World Wide Web: http://www.netspace.org/~mrl/handbook/int_ed.htm

McCain, T., Morris, S., Green, C., & Al-Najran, T. (1999). *To do is to empower: Relationships between experience with networked computing, efficacy, and attitudes toward life online.* Retrieved July 30, 2001 from the World Wide Web: http://jac.sbs.ohio-state.edu/cable/papers/nca/ToDo.htm

McInerney, V., McInerney, D. M., & Sinclair, K. E. (1998). Student teachers, computer anxiety, and computer experience. *Journal of Educational Computing Research, 11*(1), 27–50.

Mindquest Learning Network. (n.d.). *Case studies: Virtual high schools outside California.* Retrieved January 1, 2002, from the World Wide Web: http://www/vhs.ucsc.edu/vhs/casestudies.htm

Mitra, A. (2000, Spring). Changes in student attitudes and student computer use in a computer-enriched environment. *Journal of Research on Computing in Education 32*(3), 417–33.

The power of digital learning: Integrating digital content. (2000, June). *The CEO Forum: School Technology and Readiness Report.* Washington, DC: CEO Forum on Education & Technology.

Presby, W. (2001, February). Increasing productivity in course delivery. *T.H.E. Journal, 28*(7), 52–8. Retrieved July 30, 2001, from the World Wide Web: http://www.thejournal.com/magazine/vault/A3298.cfm

Race for First Impressions. (2001, June 12). *eBusiness Trends.* IDC Research Corporation. Retrieved January 1, 2002, from the World Wide Web: http://www.idcresearch.co.nz/Newsletters/eBusiness_news/ebt20010617.htm

Rogers, E. M. (1995). *Diffusion of innovations* (4th ed.). New York: The Free Press.

Runne, J. (2001, April 9). The difference between boys and girls online. *e-Marketer.* Retrieved August 2, 2001, from the World Wide Web: http://www.emarketer.com/analysis/edemograhics/20010409_edemo.html

Sadker, M., & Sadker, D. (n.d.). *Failing at Fairness.* M.A.D. Solutions for Gender Equity Issues Fact Sheet. Retrieved January 1, 2002, from the World Wide Web: http://www.alphaci.com/equity/need.htm

SCANS 2000 Center. (2000). *Workplace know-how.* Retrieved July 20, 2001, from the World Wide Web: http://www.scans.jhu.edu/General/workplace.html

Szul, L. F., & Moore, W. A. (1999, October). Preparing career-ready students: A process for curriculum revision. *Business Education Forum, 54*(1), 42–44.

Thompson, C. (2000, May 22). America Online, Part 1: Income. *e-Marketer.* Retrieved August 2, 2001, from the World Wide Web: http://www.emarketer.com/analysis/edemograhics/052200_income.html

Thompson, C. (2000, May 28). America Online, Part 2: Race. *e-Marketer.* Retrieved August 2, 2001, from the World Wide Web: http://www.emarketer.com/analysis/edemograhics/052900_race.html

Thompson, C. (2000, June 7). America Online, Part 3: Gender. *e-Marketer.* Retrieved August 2, 2001, from the World Wide Web: http://www.emarketer.com/analysis/edemograhics/20000606_gender.html

Thompson, C. (2000, June 19). America Online, Part 4: Teens. *e-Marketer.* Retrieved August 2, 2001, from the World Wide Web: http://www.emarketer.com/analysis/edemograhics/20000619_teens.html

U.S. Department of Education, National Center for Education Statistics. (2000, April). *Teacher use of computers and the Internet in public schools* (NCES 2000-090). Washington, DC: Author.

Van Horn, R. W. (1998, June). The changing user. *Phi Delta Kappan 79*(10), 794–795.

Virtual High School. (2001). *Virtual high school: Bringing innovative education to the world.* Retrieved May 18, 2001, from the World Wide Web: http://vhs.concord.org/Content/About+Us-What+is+VHS

Technology and Learning: Integrating Home, Classroom, and Community

Nancy Zeliff

Northwest Missouri State University

Maryville, Missouri

Technology permeates our homes, schools, and communities. The Baby Boom Generation has literally given birth to the Net Generation—those individuals born between 1977 and 1997 (Tapscott, 1998). "N-Geners" were born into the Digital Era, while Baby Boomers have been assimilated into it. Yet, not all Americans across all generations have access to computers and the Internet in the same way, creating a divided society of information "have's" and "have-not's,"—a Digital Divide.

This Digital Divide widens and narrows for different groups as the telecommunication and technology infrastructure improves and progresses. Those who have access to technology develop computer knowledge and skills as technology advances. Those without technology at home must access computers and Internet services in the community and schools or remain without the knowledge and skills necessary for careers and economic success, a factor that attaches important responsibilities to the schools.

This chapter includes examples of best practices to help business teachers find ways to integrate school, home, and community opportunities to benefit students and address the technology gaps that may exist within classrooms and curricula. Business teachers will also find a basis for anticipating how classrooms can and should evolve to deal with the technology experiences of future students. This chapter begins with technology in the home, how information "have's" use technology, and the Digital Divide. The chapter then outlines community efforts that increase access to technology and finally presents selected school applications, such as networked classrooms and virtual high school opportunities, that are increasing access to educational opportunities for larger segments of the population. Selected activities illustrate how this material can be integrated into the classroom.

TECHNOLOGY ACCESS IN THE HOME

Falling Through the Net is the main title of four reports that examine access to computers and the Internet. "Defining the Digital Divide" (U.S. Department of Commerce, 1999) reported the status of technology households in December 1998, just as federal government efforts authorized by the 1996 Telecommunications Act to improve the telecommunications infrastructure were beginning. "Toward Digital Inclusion" (U.S. Department of Commerce, 2000) reported dramatic changes just 20 months later, in August 2000.

Home applications affect all members of households regardless of age. Yet a Digital Divide still exists, and business teachers must teach students whose backgrounds are not only increasingly economically and ethnically diverse, but also diverse in technology experiences.

Falling Through the Net

To appreciate the rate at which the technology environment is changing, here is a short quiz. The answers are discussed later in the section and are based on 1998 and 2000 data reported in the *Falling Through the Net* reports; in some cases there are different answers reflecting changes over the 20-month period that the reports span. The reader should predict the answers before reading them:

1. The percentage of U.S. homes that have access to the Internet is about (circle one):

   85 percent   70 percent   55 percent   40 percent

   25 percent   10 percent

2. Of those who access the Internet outside the home, the most prevalent point of access is (circle one):

   Community centers   Schools   Work   Public libraries

3. What percentage of home Internet users complete online courses? About (circle one):

   5 percent   20 percent   35 percent

   50 percent   More than 50 percent

4. The single most reliable predictor of Internet use is (circle one):

   Level of education   Age   Income   Family structure

5. True or False: Less than one quarter of unemployed Americans who have home Internet access use it to search for employment?

6. Use of computers and access to the Internet is lowest in which community?

   Urban   Suburban   Rural

7. True or False: Gender is a significant predictor of access to the Internet, with men more than twice as likely as women to go online?

8. True or False: Individuals with disabilities are only slightly less likely to access the Internet than those without disabilities?

Home Applications

The Net Generation accesses technology everywhere, but access in the home is particularly important. Home access can be both wired and wireless. Internet users are quickly moving from the initial view of the Web as a novel, discovery-oriented medium, where surfing was a prevalent activity, to a more focused, resource-oriented use (Harmon, 2001). The following home life scenarios illustrate what access to computers and the Internet makes possible.

A four-year-old girl holds a mouse in her right hand clicking away, her legs dangling from an adult-sized chair. She abruptly stops, takes a CD from the computer, pops another CD in the drive, clicks, and begins interacting with the second CD she has used in 30 minutes.

What were business teachers playing with or watching when they were four years old? Some had no televisions. Some were watching Captain Kangaroo. Some were singing with Big Bird and counting with "the Count."

A young teenager tells his parent "just ten more minutes" before coming to the dinner table. Another MSN Messenger alert pops on the screen, and he cannot postpone chatting with the friend with whom he has just shared the last six hours at school.

Two parents are seated at the kitchen table early Monday morning planning the family's busy week. They activate their personal data assistants (PDAs) to check work, social, and children's schedules. A press of a button synchronizes the wireless exchange of data, and the family sets off to school and work, confident that each knows where everyone will be!

Ordering flowers for Aunt Emma's 80th birthday takes just a few clicks of a mouse. A book for one's graduate class can be ordered online to save money on the campus bookstore price. Is a favorite Beatle's album not available anywhere locally? One is sure to find it through an online auction. Is there no time to shop for holiday gifts? Millions of Americans make purchases online through e-commerce sites. And before taking a vacation, anyone can access the World Wide Web to make hotel reservations, check the forecast for weather and road conditions, as well as print discount coupons, maps, driving directions, and information about tourist attractions.

Access to knowledge affects virtually every endeavor. With global positioning satellite (GPS) technology, a farmer can measure the acreage of each field. The farmer can adjust planting rates to coincide with the fertility levels of the soil and can apply chemicals and fertilizer precisely based on previous year's data. During harvest, yields can be calculated per acre.

It is important for teachers to understanding the home technology experience. The portraits just painted apply to the homes of some students, but not to others. How will experiences like the ones described above impact education? What kind of school environment will be needed? The following activity can be done by students, preservice teachers, or teachers.

STUDENT ACTIVITY

Planning School Learning Environments

Ask teams of three to four to design a school learning environment for a family such as the one described above and present their reports with visuals.

- Assign one or two teams to address the four-year-old: What kind of elementary school environment will facilitate a seamless transition to and from the home learning environment?
- Assign another one or two teams to the parents: When the parents seek adult learning opportunities, what will enable them to move seamlessly from their home to the learning environment?
- Assign another team to address the teenager: What does the teenager think of his school's learning environment? What can be changed to provide challenging learning opportunities?

The Net Generation uses digital media for entertainment, learning, communication, and shopping. N-Geners typically prefer collaboration to isolation, have a sense of immediacy over patience, are creative rather than accepting, and choose to seek out information on the Internet rather than use other information sources.

Building on Marshall McLuhan's characterization of mass media, Tapscott (1998) has said that N-Geners perceive the computer as a "cool" medium—a device they can personalize with their own screen savers and digitized voice output. A "cool" medium is interactive, personal, and original. A "hot" medium, on the other hand, is mechanical, uniform and repetitive. Parents of N-Geners tend to perceive the computer as a "hot" medium—one that symbolizes productivity.

The Digital Divide

Even with the growing number of Americans accessing the Internet, according to U.S. Department of Commerce data (1999 & 2000), there is a distinct divide between the "have's" and the "have-not's." However, the focal points of this divide are changing rapidly. Gender is disappearing as a factor in Internet access, but disability is an increasingly significant factor. Households in central city areas still have lower access rates than the general populace. But in rural areas the changes in the telecommunication infrastructure are reversing earlier access problems (quiz question 6: rural in 1998, but urban/city center in 2000). Income and education directly correlate with access and interact with ethnic background.

Overall home access. Access to technology at home is a major factor in the Digital Divide. In 2000 slightly more than half of U.S. households (51 percent) had computers, up from 42.1 percent in 1998. In 1998 26.2 percent of Americans had Internet access at home. Another 17 percent accessed the Internet outside the home at community centers, libraries, work, or schools. In 2000 41.5 percent of all U.S. households had Internet access. Of those whose Internet use is increasing, most report school or work reasons for the increase (Harmon, 2001). The overall rise in access to the Internet from December 1998 to August 2000 is dramatic (quiz question 1: about 25 percent in 1998, and about 40 percent in 2000).

In 1998 the majority (56.3 percent) of those who accessed the Internet outside the home used work sites (quiz question 2). Schools were the second most prevalent places of access at 21.8 percent. Public libraries provided access for 8.2 percent of the respondents. E-mail was the most prevalent home application, with 77.9 percent of home users communicating primarily with family and friends, increasing to 79.9 percent in 2000. The Internet was used to search for jobs by 53.9 percent of unemployed people who had home access (quiz question 5: false), and in 2000 the unemployed continued to use the Internet to search for employment. In 1998 online courses were completed by 38.8 percent of home users (quiz question 3).

Income level. Income level is a useful and reliable predictor of overall Internet use because of the costs of access and basic computer technology, but education level is also a reliable predictor (quiz question 4). In 1998 individuals making over $75,000 used the Internet predominantly at home, and those with incomes less than $35,000 more commonly used the Internet outside of the home. This disparity in home Internet use between those at the highest and lowest income levels actually widened by 29 percent from 1997 to 1998. By 2000, households in all income ranges had made dramatic strides in access, but the correlation between income and access was still clear. In 1998 19.1 percent of people whose income levels were $25,000–34,999 had household Internet access; in 2000 34 percent did. In 1998 29 percent of individuals whose incomes were $35,000–49,999 had household Internet access; in 2000 46.1 percent did.

Geography. In 1998 Americans living in rural areas lagged behind the national average for Internet access. Schools provided Internet access to 30 percent of rural persons, compared to the national average of 21.8 percent. This rural divide was due to a more antiquated telephone infrastructure in rural areas. Small, independent phone companies are prevalent in rural areas and often cannot provide high-speed lines and Internet connectivity. In addition, most phone calls in rural areas, except to immediate neighbors, are long distance calls. The telephone companies, however, have made attempts to eliminate the Digital Divide in rural areas by charging flat fees for accessing Internet providers rather than long distance charges based on connection time. Federal assistance is also reducing the divide. In 2000 Internet access in rural areas rose dramatically to 38.9 percent, still below the national average of 41.5 percent, but up from the 1998 figure of 22.2 percent. In 2000 households in central city areas had lower access to the Internet than households in rural areas did.

Education. The education level of heads of household directly relates to their likelihood of owning a computer or accessing the Internet. From 1997 to 1998 the divide between those at the highest and the lowest levels of education widened by 25 percent. Those with a college degree were over 8 times more likely to use a computer at home than the least educated and about 16 times more likely to access the Internet at home. In 2000 the greatest increase occurred in households of individuals with some college education but not bachelor's degrees. This group rose to 49 percent from 30.2 percent in just 20 months.

Family structure. Single-parent households had lower computer and Internet usage rates than two-parent households, and about half the level of access that two-parent households had in 2000. Single-parent households headed by men were more likely to have Internet access than those headed by women. For African Americans, Asians, and Native Americans at all income levels, two-parent families were twice as likely to have Internet access in 1998 than single-parent families.

Ethnic background. African American and Hispanic households were twice as likely to own computers in 1998 as in 1994, and ownership increased by almost 10 percent in 2000. In spite of almost doubling access, African American (23.6 percent) and Hispanic (23.5 percent) households had only slightly higher than half the national access average of 41.5 percent. African American and Hispanic households had lower levels of access than households of Whites and people of Asian/Pacific Island descent. Asian/Pacific Island households had the highest level of Internet access of all ethnic groups, followed by White households. Income and education levels account for fully half of the disparity; raising the education and income levels of African Americans and Hispanics would reduce the divide significantly.

Age. About 12 percent of senior citizens in rural areas and central city areas use computers and have access to the Internet (Morley, 2000). However, while the rate of Internet access by individuals aged 50 or older was 29.6 percent in 2000 and is lower than that of the population as a whole, the number of people over the age of 50 who accessed the Internet increased by 53 percent between 1998 and 2000, compared to an increase of 35 percent for all users.

Gender. The effect of gender on the Digital Divide is changing. "[W]hen females and males have had the same amounts and types of experiences on computers, studies show that females' achievement scores and attitudes are similar to those of males" (Kirkpatrick & Cuban, 2000, p. 156). But males use computers more often and for more purposes than females, and the disparity increases with age. Currently, the computer-related labor force is estimated at 25 to 33 percent female. This is due to the fact that fewer females than males apply for computer-related programs or enroll in computer classes (Kirkpatrick & Cuban, 2000).

Males take more classes, use computers more in their free time, and stay on computers for a longer duration than females. Equally revealing is where the computer skills are used. Fifty-six percent of females, but only 35 percent of males, learned about computers at school. However, previous differences in access to the Internet have virtually disappeared. In 2000, women (44.2 percent) were almost as likely to access the Internet as men (44.6 percent) (quiz question 7: false).

Disability. The 2000 data show a distinct divide between those with and without disabilities. In 2000 those with a disability (21.6 percent) were half as likely to access the Internet as those without a disability (42.1 percent) (quiz question 8: false). "[T]hose who have impaired vision and problems with manual dexterity have even lower rates of Internet access and are less likely to use a computer regularly than people with hearing difficulties. This difference holds in the aggregate, as well as across age groups" (U.S. Department of Commerce, 2000, p. xvi).

Initiatives to equalize access. The surge of computer use and Internet access in the United States can be attributed to several initiatives: (1) Pro-competition policies, which have reduced computer prices; (2) the FCC's Universal Service program, which strives to provide telecommunication service to rural and low-income areas at a level equaling that of other areas; (3) universal service to schools, libraries, and rural health care providers through the E-rate program; (4) the U.S. Department of Agriculture's efforts to help establish a telecommunication infrastructure in rural areas; and (5) public and private sector efforts to provide Internet access at community access centers. It is also relevant to ask how wireless technology will change the access picture.

The E-rate program was created by the 1996 Telecommunications Act "to provide discounts on the cost of telecommunication services and equipment to all public and private schools and libraries" (U.S. Department of Education, 2000, p. vii). Funding has been made available through an application process, with special efforts made to increase technology access in the poorest communities.

TECHNOLOGY ACCESS IN THE COMMUNITY

The following scenarios from various communities illustrate how pervasive the demand for technology is:

Children in the slums of New Delhi, India, use a computer that is permanently connected to the Internet and mounted on a boundary wall. Having no instruction or previous knowledge, children are now accessing Internet sites, playing games, and using applications to assist their parents with their jobs (Ghosh, 2000).

Members of a 4-H club assist younger members with their PowerPoint projects, teach senior citizens about computers and the Internet, and help the disabled access technology (4-H, 2001).

A senior citizen, born long before any N-Gener, connects to the Internet at a housing center. She checks e-mail from her children, grandchildren, and great grandchildren and then logs onto a genealogy site to continue researching her family's lineage from Europe (U.S. Department of Housing and Urban Development, n.d.).

Community Computing Centers

Community computing centers are needed to provide Internet access to minority groups, lower-income groups, and less-educated individuals who do not have access at home, school, or work. Access points to nonprofit Internet service providers (ISPs) have been placed in public libraries, laundromats, supermarkets, and other heavily trafficked public places where individuals can access the Internet free of charge. Additionally, FreeNets offer kiosks with Internet access in public places (Tapscott, 2000).

According to the Community Technology Centers' Network (CTCNet) (2001), there are more than 450 nonprofit community computing centers in the United States. These centers provide free or low-cost access to computers and the Internet. Computers are ranked ahead of video games and swimming pools in their effectiveness at helping youth centers provide positive alternatives to juvenile crime (Tapscott, 2000). Recognizing that socially or economically disadvantaged populations can become further disadvantaged if they lack access to computers and the Internet, CTCNet fosters partnerships with other nonprofit agencies, philanthropies, businesses, and industries.

PowerUP strives to help underserved youth acquire skills, experiences, and resources needed in the Digital Age. PowerUP's mission (2001) is to provide

- Caring adults who serve as mentors
- Safe places in which to explore computers and the Internet
- A healthy start through snacks and online programming
- Marketable skills via technology
- Opportunities to serve

PowerUP has partnered with AmeriCorps*VISTA to work where youths are most susceptible to the Digital Divide. Some VISTA mentors work full-time for one year to promote digital literacy and community involvement. Other volunteers assist in the operation of the PowerUP site.

Youth Organizations

Intel has supported 100 Intel computer clubhouses in underserved communities worldwide. The computer clubhouses provide learning environments where youths can explore their interests after school and gain experience and confidence with technology. There are sites throughout the United States as well as in Columbia, Germany, Israel, and the Netherlands. These clubhouses are housed primarily in Boys and Girls Clubs, but the first Clubhouse was in Boston's Museum of Science (Computer Clubhouse, 2000).

Not all community computing centers have up-to-date computers and technologically savvy volunteers or staff members. Many community computing centers are in the back rooms of community centers or YMCAs. These centers may use cast-off computers from industries or schools, some capable of Internet access and others not (Tapscott, 2000). From an infrastructure perspective, centers have several concerns: outdated computers, lack of volunteers, and lack of funding (Tapscott, 2000).

Other youth groups, such as 4-H, have launched their own efforts to bridge the Digital Divide by forming statewide technology teams. These teams reach out in communities to bring technology and Internet skills to all populations. The Teens Teaching Internet Skills (TTIS) project was launched with 4-H members teaching seniors how to access the Internet for information on Medicare. An Iowa TTIS success story reported that both generations benefited from the experience (4-H, 2001). The newly formed Missouri 4-H technology team has plans for launching similar technology-oriented activities and centers.

Not only are youth-oriented service groups, such as 4-H, targeting seniors and crossing generations in efforts to diminish the Digital Divide, so is the U.S. Department of Housing and Urban Development (HUD) (1999). In 1995 HUD launched a community-based initiative called Neighborhood Networks to encourage the development of community technology centers. In December 2000 more than 644 centers were in operation with another 700 or more in the planning stage. A Michigan center hosts an Internet café, where seniors can send e-mail messages worldwide while enjoying the company of their neighbors.

STUDENT ACTIVITIES

Focus on Community Technology Resources

Activity 1. As an entrepreneurship assignment, allow students to write a business plan for a neighborhood network center following the HUD guidelines. The HUD Resource Guide (1999) can be found at http://www.hud.gov/nnw/resourcesforcenters/nnwresourcegude_99fall.intro.html.

Activity 2. In a class that includes interviewing skills, ask students to interview a volunteer or a participant of a community center that provides Internet access. Have the students report on the center's services and uses, as well as participant satisfaction levels with center access. The report can be in written or in multimedia format accompanied by an oral report or discussion. To locate a center, students can visit CTCNet at http://www.ctcnet.org.

Activity 3 (for preservice teachers). Arrange to have a guest speaker or a virtual field trip (or an actual one, if feasible) to a 4-H training session, a computer clubhouse (see http://www.computerclubhouse.org/usa.htm for locations), or other local computer center for children and teens. Explore the role of volunteers and the possible relationship business students may want to establish with centers. Discuss the implications of computer and Internet literacy experiences for children on the future of business education.

TECHNOLOGY ACCESS IN THE CLASSROOM

The classroom scenarios included in this section illustrate differences in various stages of education ranging from the elementary to graduate levels. Specific initiatives illustrate the need for teacher development within a supportive school system, whether the initiative is to network classrooms or integrate education from virtual sites with that available in the local school.

Classroom Applications

Two fourth-grade students share a computer and develop a multimedia presentation on animals of the rain forest for their science class. They open a shared file prepared by their teacher with hyperlinks to the Web and use the links, their creativity, and their inquiry skills to research their chosen animal, an orangutan. Their next class is social studies, and they word process their report on Thurgood Marshall. Their teacher has a classroom workstation, takes a laptop computer home, and interacts with the students in class with an electronic whiteboard rather than a chalkboard or wipe board.

Classrooms in Missouri, like the one described above, are called eMINTS (Missouri's Instructional Networked Teaching Strategies) classrooms (MOREnet, 2001). What will the 10-year-olds enrolled in these classrooms expect from their high school or college classes?

High school students, all with headsets on, are seated at computers, and the room is abuzz with speaking. Is this a "free day" to play CDs and converse with friends? No, it is speech recognition software—an alternative to keyboarding—at work. The students speak, and the computers recognize the words and display them on the monitors.

Business teachers across the nation are being trained in speech recognition software and ways to implement the software into the business curriculum. Such software is especially useful for students with disabilities and for those who are experiencing signs of repetitive stress injury (Barksdale, n.d.).

It is 11:30 p.m., and a college student returns to his apartment after working the second shift at a manufacturing plant. He grabs a soda, turns on the computer, and accesses his online class. Actually, he is enrolled in two courses online and takes two "on-ground" classes, enabling him to be a full-time student as well as work full-time to make ends meet. He looks at the daily announcements where he gets directions from his instructor, checks the discussion board for postings from his peers, and begins to download the PowerPoint lectures that have video and audio attached. He takes a shower while the downloads occur. He'll hear and view the lecture before turning in for the night.

An Army soldier plugs in her laptop in a barrack across the globe and, like the college student, clicks a few times to be online with her instructor and classmates, a hemisphere away. As an enlisted soldier, she seeks college credit as a means to become a better soldier as well as to guarantee a spot in the competitive workforce upon her discharge from the service. Online classes from nearly 30 colleges and universities across the United States are available to her, both in technical and core academic areas through Army University Access Online (Web-based Education Commission, 2000).

These are scenes from schools, colleges, and military locations around the world. Today learning environments exist where technology supplements traditional teaching strategies and learning styles. Are these scenes ubiquitous? No. While wealthy districts and some universities can invest in technology and teacher training, poorer districts and schools with less state support have more-pressing needs, such as building maintenance and teacher salaries, to address first.

In 1996 65 percent of U.S. public schools had access to the Internet, but school districts with richer student populations were 25 percent more likely to be connected than school districts with poorer students. Only 58 percent of schools where more than one third of students were eligible for free or reduced-price lunch were connected to the Internet. Yet, 78 percent of schools where only 10 percent of students were eligible for free or reduced-price lunch were connected. Getting connected is expensive, with an average cost of $50,000 per school. For the 65 percent of U.S. schools that were connected in 1996, equal access within the district and its buildings was not assured (Tapscott, 1998). The picture is less severe today for some groups, but the divide still exists (U.S. Department of Commerce, 2000; U.S. Department of Education, 2000).

The U.S. Congress established the Web-based Education Commission (2000) to develop policies and make decisions to ensure that universal access is realized and that the power of the Internet reaches schools, college campuses, and even corporate training centers.

Networked Classrooms

Two programs that have realized the power of the Internet are Missouri's eMINTS classrooms and West Virginia's Wetzel County laptop program within the NetSchools program.

The eMINTS (Missouri's Instructional Networked Teaching Strategies at http://emints.more.net) project was piloted in the 1997–98 and 1998–99 school years in six St. Louis County elementary schools with funding from Southwestern Bell and MOREnet, the state's research and education telecommunications network. The project provided one computer for every two students. In the pilot program, test scores, attitudes, teaching styles, and learning rates improved. Fifty eMINTs classrooms were added in 1999–2000, and another 40 were added in the 2000–2001 school year.

Critical elements of the eMINTS project include professional development and support for teachers. Schools selected through a proposal process and by location are grouped into clusters. Teachers in each cluster meet regularly either in person or virtually to discuss teaching strategies and activities and to receive training in the technology used. Teacher support is another element leading to success. Teachers receive workstations, SmartBoards, related peripherals (scanners and digital cameras, for example), software, laptops for home use, and cluster training. Both the school district and state education agency provide funding for the classrooms (MOREnet, 2001).

At the elementary level there can be as many as 100 or more students per grade level, and a digital divide can exist within a school building. Classroom projects have included Hyperstudio projects in science and Missouri history and social studies. Internet work is done continuously as reinforcement of basic skills using sites such as the following:

- Fun Brain at http://www.funbrain.com/
- PBS Kids at http://pbskids.org/
- Quia.com at http://www.quia.com
- Sci 4 Kids at http://www.ars.usda.gov/is/kids/
- Wacky Web Tales at http://www.eduplace.com/tales/
- Yahooligans at http://www.yahooligans.com/

Keyboarding skills are taught starting at the kindergarten level, so students have the skills to adeptly work on computers. Students meet with their peers in other eMINTS classrooms via videoconferencing and Web cameras and evaluate peer projects from other schools over the Internet (MORENet, 2001).

NetSchools, like Missouri's eMINTS classrooms, are striving to bridge the Digital Divide and train teachers in technology. The mission of the NetSchools (2001a) program is to facilitate the following:

- Equitable one-to-one access to technology (no Digital Divide)
- Increased student engagement and motivation
- Improved student achievement
- Extended learning opportunities after school and on weekends
- Increased parental involvement
- Improved home-school connections
- Increased opportunities for higher-order thinking
- Timely and standards-based curriculum integration
- Efficient classroom management
- Improved opportunities for cooperative learning
- Innovative changes in teacher methodology and collaboration

For example, a wireless network for laptop computers was established at the Hundred High School in Wetzel County, West Virginia. With infrared network ports in the library, lunchroom, and all classrooms, students essentially have computer labs throughout the campus. Students enjoy lunch with food in one hand and a keyboard in the other! Six months after the project began, test scores soared. Funds were received through the E-rate program, but E-rate funding is available only for school programs, not home-based programs. Additional funding sources are being sought so the students can continue with dial-up service from their rural homes (NetSchools, 2001b).

Other laptop-based school initiatives have been instituted on college campuses and in K–12 school districts using the following five models (Belanger, 2000):

1. Each student has his or her own laptop for use at home and school.
2. A set of laptops purchased by the school is shared by teachers and classrooms.
3. In any given classroom there are students with and without laptops.
4. Each classroom is assigned a few laptops on a permanent basis.
5. A combination of the above models.

Portable alternatives to laptops (e.g., Alpha Smart and DreamWriter) are available for lower-end use of keyboarding and word processing software. For example, Geometer's Sketchpad and Computer Extender work with graphing and geometry software. Research, although rather limited in nature, shows an increase in cooperative learning and project-based instruction among students using laptops. A middle school program in South Carolina that uses laptops showed a continued level of academic achievement during a period of the learners' lives when academic achievement usually drops. This was even more apparent among at-risk learners (Belanger, 2000).

Virtual Learning Environments

The number of students enrolled in distance education courses nearly doubled between 1994–95 and 1997–98. In 2000 the Web-based Education Commission predicted that by 2002, 15 percent of postsecondary students would be enrolled in distance education courses. According to the National Business Education Association (2001), nearly 2 million individuals enroll in online courses, which allow them a 24/7 time frame in which to complete course requirements. Over 26,000 Web-based courses were available in 2001, and an estimated 100 new college courses go online each month.

Virtual high school classes are also available. Virtual high schools are flourishing in Minnesota, Maryland, Kentucky, and Nebraska (Class.com, 2000). An entire high school diploma program is now available to homebound students or students who do not attend traditional high schools. The Virtual High School (http://vhs.concord.org/home.htm) supplements the local school's curriculum, providing options for students who seek courses not offered at their local school, are not able to attend school for reasons such as illness or injury, need a course in a time frame that is different from that of other students, or other reasons. Schools become members of the Virtual High School and can secure fee-free enrollments for students by offering virtual courses. Several evaluation reports on results should be helpful to others who are interested in starting distance education initiatives (http://vhs.concord.org/About+Us-Project+Evaluation).

Use of the Internet by Teachers

How do teachers—the facilitators of learning in a technology-rich learning environment—use the Internet? According to Becker, in 2000 39 percent of U.S. teachers had Internet access in their classrooms and another 25 percent could find an Internet connection in their school. Slightly lower than this combined 64 percent, 59 percent of all teachers had Internet access at home. Of the teachers with Internet access, 68 percent used the Internet directly for classroom instruction, seeking information that supplemented their teaching. Professional communications with teachers at other schools and publishing on the World Wide Web constituted only 16 percent of all teacher use. Only 18 percent of the teachers posted lesson plans, suggestions, or student work on the Internet. Teachers with home computers were three times as likely as those without home computers to communicate with their peers online (Becker, 2000).

Teachers using technology in the classroom asked their students to use the following types of software, which are listed in order from the most to the least commonly used: word processing, CD-ROMs, Internet resources, games and drills, simulations, graphics, spreadsheets and databases, multimedia authoring, and e-mail (Becker, 2000, p. 84). The richer the application delivered by network, the greater the need for bandwidth, or capacity to handle high volumes of information. Insufficient bandwidth can cause poor performance of technology.

According to the Web-based Education Commission (2000), "greater access to broadband connectivity" is needed. In response to this need, a consortium of 180 U.S. universities, as well as industry and government agencies, was formed and named Internet2. Internet2 develops and tests new technologies needed to "ensure the transfer of new network technology and applications to the broader education and networking community" (Internet2, 2001).

This author is one of two faculty members selected by Northwest Missouri State University to represent the University on a statewide Internet2 K–12 Initiative committee. This committee's purpose is to explore at all levels of education the range of opportunities in Missouri to partner with industry and government and develop and deploy advanced network applications and technologies.

SUMMARY

To prepare today's youth for success as consumers, citizens, and workers, it is critical to integrate computers and access to the Internet into all phases of life. Access to computers and the Internet is restricted to some of the U.S. population. Minority populations, populations living in rural areas, and those with lower incomes and less education do not have the same levels of access as the rest of the populace. This divide will grow if efforts to build universal access slacken.

Many factors contribute to an individual's success. Knowledge and access to information may be as important as motivation. One cannot become more educated and better trained for today's digital workplace without access to information and

STUDENT ACTIVITIES*

Exploring Educational Initiatives

Activity 1a. Ask preservice teachers to locate a local school or a school in the state that is a member of a virtual high school consortium or delivers online instruction. Have them interview a teacher about the backgrounds of students, as well as the challenges, results, and successes of teaching online.

Activity 1b. As an alternative to conducting interviews, have preservice teachers evaluate online virtual high school programs, selecting from those identified in the chapter already (Class.com or Virtual High School) or from sites like the New Technology High School (http://www.nths.nvusd.k12.ca.us/about_nths/default.htm), the Digital Divide Project (http://www.washington.edu/wto/digital), or other sites discovered through searches.

Note to teachers: Prepare or have preservice teachers prepare a set of questions that they will address during their evaluations. It may be helpful to review the evaluations of the Virtual High School program in order to frame questions. Preservice teachers may report results in a class or online discussion or in a written or multimedia report at the teacher's discretion.

Activity 2. Ask preservice teachers to compare the uses of technology identified by Becker (2000) with those observed in computer or technology classrooms. Ask preservice teachers to observe the effects of bandwidth on student "wait time" during Internet access. In discussion, have preservice teachers recommend alternative ways to use technology to better match the bandwidth available to the class. A variation on this activity is to ask members of a computer literacy class to examine the concepts of bandwidth and the effects of bandwidth on their Internet activities.

*For presrevice teachers

---

computer skills. Education affects income, and both are factors that would halve the disparity in access that currently exists for various ethnic groups. Integrating technology and learning in the home, the classroom, and the community will foster students' pride in themselves and in their communities and will ensure the strength and safety of the nation's citizens and communities and increase the quality of life for all Americans.

REFERENCES

4-H. (2001). *Access the future coalition: Success stories.* Retrieved March 17, 2001, from the World Wide Web: http://www.4h.org/access/success_stories.html

Barksdale, K. (n.d.). *Speaking solutions.* Retrieved March 18, 2001, from the World Wide Web: http://www.speakingsolutions.com/

Becker, H. J. (2000). Internet use by teachers. In R. D. Pea (Ed.), *The Jossey-Bass reader on technology and learning* (pp. 80–111). San Francisco: Jossey-Bass.

Belanger, Y. (2000, May). Laptop computers in the K–12 classroom. *ERIC Digest.* Retrieved August 28, 2001, from the World Wide Web: http://www.ed.gov/databases/ERIC_Digests/ed440644.html

Class.com (2000). *Expand your universe*. Retrieved August 28, 2001, from the World Wide Web: http://www.class.com

Computer Clubhouse. (2000). *Intel presents computer clubhouse*. Retrieved August 27, 2001, from the World Wide Web: http://www.computerclubhouse.org

CTCNet. (2001, March 19). *Computer Center Technology's Network*. Retrieved August 27, 2001, from the World Wide Web: http://www.ctcnet.org/

Ghosh, N. (2000, September). India's slum kids latch onto IT. *ED Education at a Distance, 14*. Retrieved from the World Wide Web: http://www.Usdla.org/ED_magazine/illuminactive/SEOP00_Issue/story05.htm

Harmon, A. (2001, August 26). Exploration of World Wide Web tilts from eclectic to mundane. *The New Your Times*. Retrieved August 26, 2001, from the World Wide Web: http://www.nytimes.com/2001/08/26/technology/26ONLI.html?/todaysheadlines

Internet2. (2001). *Frequently asked questions about Internet2*. Retrieved August 28, 2001, from the World Wide Web: http://www.internet2.edu/html/faqs.html#

Kirkpatrick, H. & Cuban, L. (2000). Should we be worried? What the research says about gender differences in access, use, attitudes, and achievements with computers. In R. D. Pea (Ed.), *The Jossey-Bass reader on technology and learning* (pp. 155–167). San Francisco: Jossey-Bass.

MOREnet. (2001). *About eMINTS*. Retrieved August 28, 2001, from the World Wide Web: http://emints.more.net/about/

Morley, J. (2000, January). Falling through the Web: Inequality in access to distance education. *ED Education at a Distance*. Retrieved from the World Wide Web: http://www.usdla.org/Ed_magazine/illuminactive/Jan00_Issue/Falling.htm

National Business Education Association. (2001, March). Assessing online learning. *Keying In, 11*. Reston, VA: Author.

NetSchools. (2001a). *FAQs*. Retrieved August 28, 2001, from the World Wide Web: http://www.netschools.com/whynetschools/FAQs.htm

NetSchools. (2001b). *Hundred high school, Hundred, West Virginia*. Retrieved August 28, 2001, from the World Wide Web: http://www.netschools.net/whynetschools/cs_hundred.htm

PowerUP (2001). *PowerUP: Bridging the Digital Divide*. Retrieved August 28, 2001, from the World Wide Web: http://www.powerup.org

Tapscott, D. (1998). *Growing up digital: The rise of the Net Generation*. New York: McGraw-Hill.

Tapscott, D. (2000). Digital Divide. In R. D. Pea (Ed.), *The Jossey-Bass reader on technology and learning* (pp. 127–154). San Francisco: Jossey-Bass.

U.S. Department of Commerce. (1999, November). *Falling through the net: Defining the Digital Divide*. Washington, DC: National Telecommunications and Information Administration and Economic and Statistics Administration. Retrieved August 27, 2001, from the World Wide Web: http://www.ntia.doc.gov/ntiahome/fttn99/contents.html

U.S. Department of Commerce. (2000, October). *Falling through the Net: Toward digital inclusion*. Washington, DC: National Telecommunications and Information Administration and Economic and Statistics Administration. Retrieved August 27, 2001, from the World Wide Web: http://www.ntia.doc.gov/ntiahome/digitaldivide/

U.S. Department of Education. (2000, September). *E-Rate and the Digital Divide: A preliminary analysis from the integrated studies of educational technology* (Doc #00-17). Washington, DC: The Urban Institute. Retrieved May 2000 from the World Wide Web: http://www.ed.gov/offfices/OUS/eval/elem.html#technology

U.S. Department of Housing and Urban Development. (1999). *HUD.* Retrieved March 17, 2001, from the World Wide Web: http://www.hud.gov/nnw/resroucesforcenters/nnwfactsheet003.html

Web-based Education Commission. (2000, December). *The power of the Internet for learning.* Retrieved August 28, 2001, from the World Wide Web: http://interact.hpcnet.org/webcommission/index.htm

Technology, Business Education, and Young Learners

Ruth K. Shafer

Hazelwood School District

Florissant, Missouri

Business educators can bring their expert computer skills, teaching strategies, and software knowledge to all aspects of the elementary setting. There is a pronounced void of computer literacy curricula directed to the needs of young learners. The main goal of computer learning at the lower levels should be the use of the computer as a tool. To achieve learning goals in core learning areas, young learners create e-mail, write stories, and perform other writing tasks. Students also search the Internet for information and may use spreadsheets and databases. They should develop basic keyboarding skills to use all fingers effectively, format word processing documents, and use database and spreadsheet applications for reports required in core subjects. They should also have a working knowledge of hardware use and software applications.

There are many issues involving technology. Technology is often talked about in relation to science and mathematics achievement standards and to the designs and inventions that characterize human progress. Technology is also spoken of in terms of computer knowledge and the comprehensive application of computer and research techniques to academic learning objectives. Related issues include the selection of appropriate technology for solving problems and making decisions. Further, "all literacies—even those involving technology—are powerfully interconnected. Vast and ever-increasing quantities of information, images, graphics, video, and audio are available with new software, hardware, and Internet connections" (Raffery, 1999).

How can business educators contribute to developing literacy among young learners? One premise of this chapter is that children cannot achieve other learning objectives effectively and efficiently without acquiring keyboarding as an enabling skill.

Technology literacy, however, goes beyond keyboarding. Another premise of this chapter is that business teachers can make significant impacts on the technology literacy of young learners by partnering with elementary educators to develop curriculum and train the personnel who work with young learners.

This chapter discusses facets of elementary education that impact technology literacy and the contributions that business educators can make. The chapter then describes a program that is based on a leadership and collaborative role for business educators with elementary school personnel. Business teachers in districts without an elementary technology curriculum can (and are invited to) adapt this program for their local school districts. Several student activities for preservice business teachers and graduate business education students focus on technology for young learners.

TECHNOLOGY IN THE EARLY GRADES

Technology holds great promise for young learners. There are also significant impediments to the development of technology learning skills, such as the lack of grade level-appropriate curricula. Impediments also originate from the time constraints of elementary teachers, doubts that technology enhances learning, and the lack of professional development available to elementary educators. Business educators can help address some of these issues.

Teacher Time Constraints

While economics employs a "trickle down" analogy to explain certain developments, business educators know that they face a "push down" phenomenon in technology literacy. Some objectives recently targeted for the secondary level are now identified for the primary grades. As these change takes place, elementary educators are challenged because little of their responsibility is moved up to other levels of education, and there are high expectations that integration of technology will enhance learning and transform education.

"Trying to Beat the Clock," a study prepared for the U.S. Department of Education (Adelman, 1998), presented a clear picture of what it is like to face a classroom of students hour after hour, day after day, with little time to prepare and few opportunities to interact with colleagues. Instruction and the host of chores required for the smooth running of their classrooms leave elementary educators with few opportunities to plan for other aspects of education reform.

U.S. teachers bear a heavy responsibility to use time for instruction, but the school time is structured in blocks that are often too short for meaningful professional development, planning, or collaboration. Teachers have few opportunities to exchange lesson plans or teaching techniques with peers or more experienced colleagues. They must often rely on hallway conversations to make decisions. "Education officials must consider ways of reallocating the ways teachers spend their time so that they and their students can find school a more rewarding and productive place" (Stevenson, 1998).

Among the many reasons for leaving the teaching profession, Hong (2001) cited the increasing pressure to do more in less time. "One such 'minor' addition to our curriculum was keyboarding practice. . . . The explanation was that this would not be an 'add-on' to our curriculum but could be incorporated as part of our existing writing period" (p. 2). Hong explained other incursions on time for instruction, and the frustration she felt at having to say, "We don't have time" to finish, to discuss, or to learn. Keyboarding was only one of several examples, but a meaningful one for examining how teachers may feel about the impact that teaching technology in the early grades has on their time to teach.

Conflicts in Learning Priorities

Teachers who are asked to integrate technology into learning may or may not be convinced that technology will contribute positively to learning or that technology literacy should take precedence over core learning outcomes. Barlow (1999) quoted a National Center for Education Statistics report on teacher preparedness: "At a time when 78 percent of public schools have access to the Internet, . . . only 20 percent of teachers reported feeling well prepared to integrate educational technology into classroom education." He described his nonteaching work that involves his use of computer technology, but then observed, "Most of what teachers need to do as teachers has no essential connection to modern technology. . . . My students need to read, discuss ideas, and then write about them. We can do all of those things without a lot of modern technology" (p. 3).

Barlow illustrated a basic fact: elementary educators are not trained to be specialists. Often they do not see the computer as a tool and do not know teaching strategies for keyboarding and software instruction that are enablers for other learning outcomes. Although many educators use a computer daily for personal and professional use, they do not transfer this knowledge to their daily teaching. Barlow's challenge also reflects the lack of tested practice for introducing technology into instruction. Schmid, Fesmire, and Lisner (2001) have stated that "[i]ntegrating technology into an elementary school's daily instructional routine . . . can be 'a school of hard knocks' where good intentions are soundly thumped and sound practices are often discovered through trial and error" (p.36).

Technology literacy instruction becomes a low priority when the evidence of its effectiveness in learning is not communicated and when effective curricula and methods do not accompany the directives to integrate technology into instruction.

High Expectations and School Curriculum

Hong and Barlow's commentaries are not antitechnology, but they do reflect the perception that the use of technology in their classrooms is not related to the learning that should take place. According to Bickart and Pierrel (1999, p. 3), the results of the heavy investment made by schools in computer technology "fall short of expectations," because meeting technology standards in the primary grades is an "extra" that is not integrated into core learning.

According to Angulo (2001), "Technology platforms and the Internet have created tremendous opportunities for new education paradigms. . . . Those who are effectively educated and trained will survive economically and thrive in our global, knowledge-based economy" (p. 1). Few would dispute this, but Angulo goes on to explain that this opportunity will not be realized without significant change: "Helping teachers effectively use technology in instruction goes way beyond simply teaching them how to use Microsoft Office. Fundamental changes in classroom strategy and management are required" (p. 2). Even more fundamental than these needs are the need for curricula, methods, and professional development that address new responsibilities.

Current Technology Literacy Efforts

Many efforts are related to using age-appropriate educational software, which is widely available. The *Children's Software & New Media Revue,* which *is* both a conventional publication and a Web site (http://www.childrenssoftware.com/default.htm) with over 5,000 reviews of children's interactive media, is evidence of the interest and pressure to produce technology literacy early. The Open Directory Project site (http://www.dmoz.org) has a category for kids and teens with subcategories for technology and learning.

Much of the software currently used in elementary classrooms and computer labs is subject oriented and menu driven. Instructional software for the early grades is often developed for reading and quick response and generally requires only limited use of keyboarding techniques. At most there might be some form of software program to teach the keyboard in a shortened period of time by a teacher's aid. So when students are required to create documents, their keyboarding skills are greatly challenged.

These products are often reviewed in library publications (see Troutner, 2000; Elders, 2000; Watson, 2000) because librarians often share responsibility for technology literacy in the early grades and equipment is often located in the media center. Reviewers frequently mention the need for adult supervision and assistance to maximize the learning of proper fingering, a point emphasized by business educators. Bartholome (1998) has stressed that the type of supervision needed requires knowledge of psychological and pedagogical principles of skill learning. Erthal (1998) has stated that "[k]eyboarding software packages should be carefully scrutinized to ascertain if they follow sound pedagogical, psychomotor principles" (p. 4). Whether educators in the early grades have the interest and ability to make these evaluations has not been demonstrated.

Even reports on the emerging use of handheld computers in the elementary classroom (Soloway, Norris, & Curtis, 2001) reinforce this continuing theme: for the technology to be effective, time for the learning processes (doing, reflecting, collaborating, and sharing) must be incorporated into the curriculum.

CONTRIBUTIONS OF BUSINESS EDUCATORS

Business educators have not only expressed interest in and concern about the technology literacy of young learners, they have acted in a number of ways. This is

STUDENT ACTIVITY*

Technology Standards for the Elementary Level

Ask preservice business teachers or graduate business education students to investigate the learning standards for elementary keyboarding, computer literacy, and/or technology literacy in their state. Then ask them to examine how different school districts in the state actually implement curriculum and instruction at the elementary level to achieve these standards. Finally, have students discuss how business education can play a role in the delivery of technology literacy instruction.

Note to teachers: This activity can be done as an outside assignment, in an online class, or started in a class session with access to the Internet. The activity can be done by groups in the class.

*For preservice business teachers or graduate business education students

particularly evident in the area of keyboarding. Business educators also have other expertise that is needed to make technology literacy instruction work in the early grades. Business educators have technical expertise with hardware and software, effective teaching methods, and knowledge of how to apply technology to learning. They also have the pedagogical preparation to evaluate and recommend software and hardware. Additionally, they are skilled at developing curricula, especially in conjunction with the diverse community representatives and businesspeople who serve on their advisory committees.

Business Education Initiatives

Integration of technology frequently relates technology to the improvement of writing. Activities include composing e-mail, creating newsletters, and other activities (Bickart & Pierrel, 1999). The keyboard is an enabler for achieving learning outcomes. This is not a new concept for business educators.

Research and policy on keyboarding. According to Bartholome (1998), research evidence

> . . . is very positive that elementary school youngsters can learn how to keyboard (type). Keyboarding (typewriting) skills also enhance their language art abilities. A half hour a day for three days a week for one semester can provide students with the necessary keyboarding skills to automate their responses so that they can keyboard faster than they can write. Keyboarding should be taught when students start to input words and sentences on the keyboard. (p. 14)

Bartolome (1998) has reported a long history of typewriting and keyboarding initiatives at the elementary level from the 1930s on. The absence of a universal elementary keyboarding curriculum and a teacher education component through the 1980s can be explained, he said, by the lack of a "compelling reason" for the elementary student to keyboard. By the 1980s, however, "computers ha[d] been introduced to the elementary schools," creating that "compelling reason to teach students to keyboard" (Bartolome, 1998, p. 3).

The Policies Commission for Business and Economic Education and the *National Standards for Business Education* (NBEA, 1995; NBEA, 2001) have addressed keyboarding and information technology objectives and standards for the elementary level in very specific ways. The National Business Education Association (NBEA) (1997) developed and disseminated the *Elementary/Middle School Keyboarding Strategies Guide* demonstrating the commitment of the profession to the young learner. NBEA's (2001) information technology achievement standards emphasize the impact of technology on society, computer system knowledge, application and business functions, in addition to the critical input and information retrieval literacy skills needed by young learners.

Teaching methods for young learners. Business educators have articulated instructional methods for the primary grades. The main goal of computer training at the lower levels should be the use of the computer as a tool. Students should develop basic keyboarding skills to use all fingers effectively, to format word processing documents, and to use database and spreadsheet applications for reports required in core subjects. Students should also have a working knowledge of hardware use and software applications.

Bartholome (1998) has emphasized many principles for developing keyboarding skills at the elementary level (http://www.usoe.k12.ut.us/ate/keyboarding/Articles/Bartholome.htm). Several are paraphrased here, but the reader is encouraged to study the full document:

- Evaluate students' keyboarding technique. Students value elements that are graded.
- Have students rely on the sense of touch. Have them learn to value touch as an alternative to sight when they lose their place.
- Ask students to help each other learn to sit up straight and use proper fingering. Make each student a peer tutor for others in the class.
- Try to anticipate errors that students will make and watch for signs of fatigue that lead to errors.
- Make students feel successful when they make progress in order to motivate further progress.
- Spread practice over time, using several shorter practice periods rather than one longer one.
- Strengthen fingers with "finger gymnastics" and build practice stamina by progressing from shorter to longer practice periods.

Nieman (1996) has also provided an extended discussion of curriculum and methodology at the elementary level well worth reviewing in original form. She has emphasized teacher involvement and attention to technique whether the instructional approach involves teacher-called drills, practice, or tutorials.

Related instructional needs. Many schools fail to design computer workstations ergonomically and to attend to questions of posture and position of children using computers. Bartholome, Nieman, and others have identified methods and related competencies that only a prepared professional would be able to deliver: proper position of body and feet, as well as "hand span check for distance of body from the keyboard" (Neiman, 1966). Business teachers must ensure that this does not go unnoticed by school district administrators and educational personnel.

Roles for Business Teachers

Business educators can bring their expert computer skills, teaching strategies, and software knowledge to all aspects of the elementary setting. There are several roles for business teachers in this process.

Teaching. Teaching at the elementary level is one option for business educators to consider. In states where business education certification provides a role for the business teacher at the elementary level, some business educators teach technology literacy skills. However, business educators have generally endorsed a broader approach regarding who should or can teach these skills in the early grades. McLain's position (Erthal, 1998) is that "instruction can be supplied by elementary teachers who have taken a keyboarding methods class, a business education teacher with elementary learning methods, or a combination of business education and elementary education teachers" (p. 37).

Nieman (1996) has encouraged business educators to realize that, for elementary children,

> . . . learning an abstract concept, such as touch keyboarding, is difficult . . . and children do not have the attention span for traditional drill . . . In addition, younger children are more emotional than older students and they respond to and need constant teacher smiles, praise, and a winning atmosphere. (p. 28)

According to Hoggatt (1998), "Working with elementary students presents new and different challenges and opportunities than . . . working with middle school and high school students. Additional training may be required by the keyboarding instructor in order to meet successfully the opportunity of working with elementary students." Business educators who decide to teach at the elementary levels generally have a substantial interest in and preparation for teaching at these grade levels and must also work within the certification or licensure requirements of their states.

Collaborative leadership. Another way for business educators to get involved is through a collaborative, leader-oriented approach to curriculum development. Business educators can become proactive with district administrators and curriculum coordinators by offering model curricula with proven instructional strategies and by assisting with teacher training and student instruction. By taking the initiative to

STUDENT ACTIVITY*

Certification or Licensure for Elementary Business Education

Ask preservice business teachers or graduate business education students to think about teaching business education at the elementary, middle, or secondary levels. Ask them to consider whom they would teach, what they would teach, and how they would teach. As a group, have the students identify critical factors that would differ based on the level of teaching.

If the state in which the preservice teachers or graduate students reside has a K–12 business education certificate or license, have them complete their research by interviewing (face-to-face or by e-mail or telephone) a teacher at the level least familiar to them. If the state in which the students reside does not have a K–12 business education certificate or license, ask the students to discuss whether one should be created and why.

*For preservice business teachers or graduate business education students

ensure that effective keyboarding and computer applications are taught to young learners, business education can remedy some of the dilemmas faced by elementary educators. Curriculum and instructional leadership ensures that students reach secondary school ready for a business education curriculum that will focus on the use of technology in careers.

Besides making effective use of business teachers' technical and instructional expertise, this approach utilizes the business teacher's extensive experience with advisory committees and other stakeholder groups in developing technology curricula. This approach is likely to be endorsed by the school district. Bickart and Pierrel (1999) have encouraged principals to form grade-level or multigrade-level task forces that involve teachers "in thinking about how and when to integrate technology learning into the curriculum" (p. 3). Community involvement should be present as well. These are collaborative processes that business educators know well.

A Missouri survey. A Missouri business education survey suggests that teachers are willing to participate using a collaborative approach. Missouri business educators sought information to develop statewide competencies for curriculum development. Business educators completed a survey that was distributed and evaluated by the Missouri Business Education Association (2001) and the results were reported to the state department for reference and future use. Table 1 presents the questions and the responses that Missouri business educators provided.

In view of the general absence of preparation, business teachers ranked preparation in the preservice program as their first preference. Once elementary teachers are employed, however, business teachers preferred to provide the training themselves rather than return the elementary educators to universities for training. This may reflect the interest of teachers in working in partnerships within their school systems.

Table 1. Missouri Elementary Keyboarding Survey

1. How are the elementary teachers in your school district prepared to teach keyboarding?

Number (n=130)	Response
5	By the district through special workshops
5	By the district business teachers
1	Through summer workshops
106	No training is provided
13	Other—please describe

2. How should elementary teachers be trained to teach keyboarding? Rank the following from 1–3, with 1 as the first choice.

Average	Response
1.7	As a part of their undergraduate degree (a methods course in teaching keyboarding in elementary schools)
1.8	Through special training sessions taught by the business teachers in the school district
2.0	Through summer workshops at universities with teacher education programs

3. If summer workshops are provided for teaching elementary keyboarding, how do you feel the fees should be covered?

Number (n=121)	Response
13	Paid by the teachers
69	Funded through the state department
39	Funded by the teachers' schools

A MODEL FOR CURRICULUM DEVELOPMENT

At the local level, states are addressing the need for business educators to be involved in all aspects of technology curriculum development and instruction. For instance, the Hazelwood (Missouri) School District keyboarding and technology curriculum was developed to meet the need for improved student performance using technology. The role of business education in this districtwide initiative illustrates an approach to collaboration that may work for others.

The Need for Change and the Curriculum Committee

Before the technology curriculum was developed, primary grade students in the Hazelwood School District worked on computers in all subjects but had no effective

STUDENT ACTIVITY*

The Future of Keyboarding

Ask preservice business teachers or graduate business education students to discuss the future of keyboarding as an enabler of core learning at the elementary, middle, secondary, and postsecondary levels. Ask them to consider the growth of wireless, portable information devices and handheld computers and their use in business education. Also have them consider speech recognition technologies. Then ask them to explain whether and how keyboarding will (or will not) remain a technology literacy skill as other technologies become increasingly prevalent.

*For preservice business teachers or graduate business education students

techniques for using the technology. Children were unable to complete tasks efficiently. Teachers and students were frustrated with lack of accomplishment; and thus a districtwide committee was formed to develop a technology curriculum. The committee was made up of elementary teachers, elementary principals, business educators, and media specialists. The district's business education coordinator chaired the committee.

As the committee began its work, members developed a statement of mission, philosophy, and rationale for the curriculum, describing the continuous need for teacher technology training and ongoing curriculum revision as technology evolved (Hazelwood School District, 2000). The mission of the curriculum "is to empower students through the utilization of computers to become effective communicators, lifelong learners, and citizens of a global society." The rationale is that "technology is an essential tool, and communication in this global society is limited without basic skills in word processing, information retriev[al], manipulation of data, and records management."

Now the curriculum delivered by elementary teachers on a daily basis incorporates significant keyboarding and computer literacy content. The district also has a second technology literacy curriculum. This second curriculum, developed by librarians and instructional media professionals, focuses on databases and access to resources. Teachers may also have their students take advantage of these extended services.

The Elementary Technology Curriculum

In Hazlewood School District, the "building block" approach to curriculum design ensures that young learners achieve computer proficiency. Starting in first grade, the curriculum introduces computer knowledge. In subsequent grades, the learning skills are organized into a manageable step-by-step procedure with a set of teacher instructions, time frame, and hands-on practice activities. For closure, a culminating project provides enrichment.

The curriculum follows the elementary portion of the technology section of the *National Standards for Business Education* (NBEA, 1995; NBEA, 2001). The curriculum preceded the release of the International Technology Education Association's *International Standards for Technology in Education*, but alignment with these standards is appropriate where learning outcomes apply. Table 2 lists the skills to be taught at each grade level:

Table 2. Elementary Level Technology Skills for Hazelwood School District

GRADE 1
1. Turn computer on and off
2. Manipulate the mouse
3. Open the word processing software option
4. Open, close, resize, and move a window
5. Quit the word processing software option
6. Change text font, size, style, color
7. Print
8. Choose a graphic
9. Create a heading on a document
10. Save a document to a disk and to a teacher folder
11. Eject a disk

GRADE 2
1. Learn alphabetic keys using the Herzog method
2. Insert and delete using the mouse and the arrow keys
3. Left-align, right-align, center, and justify text
4. Cut, copy, and paste
5. Change line spacing
6. Set left tab stop

GRADE 3
1. Learn number row using the Herzog method
2. Open and close ClarisWorks
3. Use spell check
4. Change line spacing
5. Insert a graphic
6. Set tab using left tab marker
7. Change left/right paragraph indentations and first-line indentation

GRADE 4
1. Learn numeric keypad (using the numeric keypad guide)
2. Format document using left, right, center, and decimal tab markers
3. Change page to horizontal orientation and display formatting characters
4. Use thesaurus
5. Apply zoom controls
6. Create columns using icons and insert header/footer
7. Use find/change option

GRADE 5
1. Copy a picture to the clipboard and into a document
2. Apply the shortcuts palette to enhance a word processing document
3. Use the format menu to effectively arrange a document
4. Create an outline
5. Create a spreadsheet in a word processing document to organize numerical/text data, produce charts, and calculate numerical data

GRADE 6
1. Create a master page by using the "save as" function
2. Create a spreadsheet to organize numerical/text data, produce charts, calculate numerical data, and sort text
3. Create a database to merge the fields of a record into a word processing document and create data records
4. Create a draw document

The curriculum was developed so that as students learn the technology skills at each grade level, they complete activities on the computer that are a part of the core curriculum requirements. Hence, teachers do not feel that required curriculum is being eliminated to make time for technology instruction. Teachers can integrate daily instruction in all subject areas by demonstrating the computer application and use as a tool—not an additional area of instruction for the teacher.

Training Elementary Teachers

Technology curricula have not been included in teacher preparation programs. In Hazlewood School District it was necessary, therefore, to develop a training program for instructors that was effective and easy to deliver. Doing so required motivation and in-class teacher support. The program needed to provide instructional strategies, creative ideas, and techniques for teaching keyboarding.

Business educators had the expertise to meet this challenge. Elementary teachers welcomed the use of technology in their curriculum and sought help in delivering these necessary skills. Elementary teachers were open and receptive to expertise in areas where they were deficient. As business educators integrated and trained teachers to deliver technology at the elementary level, they heeded several factors that could have hampered program success. Time and availability for teacher training required effective planning. A routine follow-up with staff was a vital element of program success. Additionally, an ongoing training program was essential to deal with teacher transfers and new hires.

This teacher training is now conducted by means of a three-day program in the elementary computer lab. Because the elementary teachers and their students are assigned to use the computer lab on a daily basis, the elementary teachers instruct the keyboarding curricula during this assigned lab time. The teachers learn the Herzog method of keyboarding instruction (Herzog Keyboarding, 1999). Several reasons dictated this choice: (1) the Herzog method uses a known alphabetic system of instruction and is easily transferred into new learning by elementary students; (2) no new software had to be purchased to implement the program effectively, which is a very important point for existing elementary computer labs that have already installed word processing software; (3) the system is well organized for developmental keyboard learning in a logical, sequential manner, and there is appropriate practice material that is motivational for elementary learners; (4) the program provides tactile keys for proper finger placement on the keyboard for better techniques and speed development.

Technology Literacy and the Instructional Media Center

The Hazlewood School District has also implemented a complementary technology literacy curriculum delivered by librarians through the instructional media center in each school. This curriculum is taught and implemented in the library setting by the librarians and interested classroom teachers. The term "interested teachers" refers to elementary teachers who want to use the service for their students.

STUDENT ACTIVITY*

The Herzog Approach

Have students research the approaches to introducing the keys to elementary students using the "home row" and Herzog approaches (see http://www.herzogkeyboarding.com/). This may be an individual assignment resulting in a position paper or it may be a group assignment with one group responsible for studying each approach followed by a formal or informal discussion in class or via electronic means.

*For preservice business teachers or graduate business education students

The scope and sequence of learning activities, shown in Tables 3 to 7 (see pp. 50–54), are designed to develop skills for using electronic information systems, doing searches, and transferring written data to visual formats.

Table 3. Technology Literacy Skill 1: Understand and Use Electronic Information Systems and Computer Platforms

Awareness (grades K-4)

Librarians/Teachers

- Introduce shared terminology and technology
- Introduce district online catalog
- Introduce an online catalog such as that of the St. Louis County library system
- Collaborate with interested teachers on resource-based teaching to facilitate student use of electronic information systems and computer platforms

Students

- Use electronic information systems and computer platforms independently or with assistance

Implementation (grades 5-8)

Librarians/Teachers

- Facilitate use of automated information systems with focused information gathering
- Facilitate access to the county library and other systems' online catalogs for additional sources for science fair and research projects
- Collaborate with interested teachers on resource-based teaching to facilitate student use of electronic information systems and computer platforms

Students

- Use electronic information systems and computer platforms independently or with assistance

Reinforcement (grades 9-12)

Librarians/Teachers

- Collaborate with interested teachers on resource-based teaching to facilitate student use of electronic information systems and computer platforms

Students

- Independently use computers in subject-specific areas
- Access county library and other systems (such as academic and special libraries) online catalogs

Table 4. Technology Literacy Skill 2: Identify Appropriate Databases for Specific Purposes

Awareness (grades K-4)

Librarians/Teachers

- Teach terminology needed for utilization of programs
- Introduce databases; books, and materials (online public access catalog); periodicals (magazine index for children and/or reader's guide); encyclopedias (Grolier's Electronic, World Book Info Finder, etc.)
- Collaborate with interested teachers on resource-based teaching that will enable students to identify appropriate databases for specific purposes

Students

- Identify appropriate databases for specific purposes independently or with assistance

Implementation (grades 5-8)

Librarians/Teachers

- Introduce additional databases available in IMC specifics, i.e. Newsbank indexes

- Assist students in selecting appropriate databases for assignments
- Collaborate with interested teachers on resource-based teaching that will enable students to identify appropriate databases for specific purposes

Students

- Identify appropriate databases for specific purposes independently or with assistance

Reinforcement (grades 9-12)

Librarians/Teachers

- Introduce additional databases (both CD-ROM and online) available in the instructional media center
- Assist students in selecting appropriate databases for assignments
- Collaborate with interested teachers on resource-based teaching that will enable students to identify appropriate databases for specific purposes

Students

- Select and use available databases independently

CONCLUSION

Students will benefit from curricula like those used by Hazlewood School District as they advance to middle school programs and then to high school business education programs. Students should come to high school programs with the following:

- Basic knowledge of keyboarding and software applications
- Enhanced formatting techniques and technical skills
- A preparation for new learning in advanced software, Web design, desktop publishing, and network administration in high school
- Research skills to retrieve and interpret electronic information

As evidenced by research, instruction in keyboarding and technology is strongly needed at the elementary level. More and more children are entering school having experience with computers, the Internet, and other forms of technology at a younger

---

Table 5. Technology Literacy Skill 3: Develop Viable Search Strategies

Awareness (grades K-6)

Librarians/Teachers
- Introduce search strategy methods
- Brainstorm topics
- Do background reading
- Brainstorm terminology/synonyms
- Collaborate with interested teachers on resource-based teaching of viable search strategies

Students
- Brainstorm descriptors (keywords for searches)
- Develop search strategies independently or with assistance

Implementation (grades 7-8)

Librarians/Teachers
- Introduce more complex search strategies such as Boolean logic searches with "and/or operators," etc., using DIALOG/Classmate

Educator's Program, the NEWSBANK PLUS database, and UMI PROQUEST Magazine Express
- Collaborate with interested teachers on resource-based teaching of viable search strategies

Students
- Develop and use viable search strategies in available databases

Reinforcement (grades 9-12)

Librarians/Teachers
Collaborate with interested teachers on resource-based teaching of viable search strategies

Students
- Independently use search strategy techniques, e.g., plot a Boolean search using dialog databases

---

age. Business educators must lead and collaborate in developing school curricula at the elementary level. Addressing technology literacy at the elementary level can and should be a joint effort of elementary educators, other elementary professionals, and business educators who are involved in developing a technical, research-based curriculum. The scope of this effort should include

- Hardware and software use with proper keyboarding skills
- Research use and strategies
- Software application to related core subjects
- Use of telecommunication technologies to access documents
- Transfer of written data to and from audio and visual formats

How can business educators become involved? First, they can contact the technology director or the person who develops the technology plan for their school district. Many district personnel may be unaware of the business educator's expertise and knowledge of how to deliver technology curricula to K–12 students. District personnel may not know that they should and can seek help from business educators. Business educators should inform district personnel of their expertise and willingness to become involved at all levels.

Table 6. Technology Literacy Skill 4: Understand and Use Telecommunication Technology to Access Documents, Ideas, and New Technologies

Awareness (grades K-3)
Librarians/Teachers
- Introduce electronic mailboxes, bulletin boards, teleconferences, etc., (e.g., Fredmail, Introlink, and MOREnet)
- Collaborate with interested teachers on resource-based teaching to enable students to use telecommunication technologies to access documents, ideas, and new technologies

Students
- Practice keyboarding skills
- Use telecommunication technologies with assistance

Implementation (grades 4-8)
Librarians/Teachers
- Introduce advanced telecommunication technologies (e.g., AT&T learning networks, global networks, and bulletin boards)
- Introduce access skills

- Collaborate with interested teachers on resource-based teaching to enable students to use telecommunication technologies to access documents, ideas, and new technologies

Students
- "Log on and off" on their own
- Practice keyboarding skills
- Use features of various systems proficiently

Reinforcement (grades 9-12)
Librarians/Teachers
- Collaborate with interested teachers on resource-based teaching to enable students to use telecommunication technologies to access documents, ideas, and new technologies

Students
- Use telecommunication technologies in assignments and projects

Business educators can also contact the media specialists in targeted buildings to discuss joint curriculum development efforts at the district level. Additionally, business educators can volunteer to train elementary teachers in keyboarding instruction and/or develop keyboarding workshops to prepare the elementary teachers. As they have in the past, business educators must continue to take the steps to ensure that current and future students will excel in using and applying technology in a global society.

REFERENCES

Adelman, N. E. (1998). *Trying to beat the clock: Uses of teacher professional time in three countries.* (Contract No. EA94053001). Washington, DC: U.S. Department of Education, Planning and Evaluation Service. Retrieved September 23, 2001, from the World Wide Web: http://www.enc.org/topics/timss/kit/documents/0,1946,ACQ-137042-7042.shtm

Angulo, M. (2001, March). Leveraging learning for generation i. *School Administrator, 58*(3), 28–31. Retrieved September 23, 2001, from the World Wide Web: Wilson Select Plus, pp. 1–4.

Table 7. Technology Literacy Skill 5: Transfer Written Data to and From Audio and Visual Formats

Awareness (grades K-5)

Librarians/Teachers
- Collaborate with interested teachers on resource-based teaching about the transfer of written data to and from audio and visual formats
- Demonstrate the transfer of data from one format to another, e.g., use of a computer to present text in graph format, use of HyperCard, laser disks, etc.

Students
- View a visual or listen to an audio presentation and write about it
- Create a visual for a story independently or with assistance

Implementation (grades 6-10)

Librarians/Teachers
- Collaborate with interested teachers on resource-based teaching about the transfer of written data to and from audio and visual formats
- Demonstrate the transfer of data from one format to another, e.g., use of a computer to present text in graph format, use of HyperCard, laser disks, etc.

Students
- View a visual presentation and create an interpretation in another format

Reinforcement (grades 10-12)

Librarians/Teachers
- Collaborate with interested teachers on resource-based teaching about the transfer of written data to and from audio and visual formats
- Demonstrate the transfer of data from one format to another (e.g., use a computer to present text in graph format, use a HyperCard, or use laser disks)

Students
- Research a topic and independently produce a video, slide show, or laser disk with interactive video, etc. (new technologies to be incorporated as they are developed and become available)

Barlow, D. (1999, April). Are our teachers well prepared? *The Education Digest,* 64(8), 44–47. Retrieved July 30, 2001, from the World Wide Web: Wilson Select Plus, pp. 1–4.

Bartholome, L. W. (1998). Typewriting/keyboarding instruction in elementary schools, pp. 1–15. Retrieved September 23, 2001, from the World Wide Web: http://www.usoe.k12.ut.us/ate/keyboarding/Articles/Bartholome.htm

Bickart, T. S., & Pierrel, E. (1999, May). Technology learning in the K–3 classroom. *Principal,* 78(4), 19–20. Retrieved September 23, 2001, from the World Wide Web: Wilson Select Plus, pp. 1–4.

Elders, A. (2000, November). KidKeys 2.0 (teacher edition). *School Library Journal,* 46(11), 82. Retrieved September 23, 2001, from the World Wide Web: Wilson Select Plus, p. 1.

Erthal, M. (1998, October). Who should teach keyboarding and when should it be taught? *Business Education Forum,* 53(1), 36–37. Retrieved September 23, 2001, from the World Wide Web: http://www.usoe.k12.ut.us/ate/keyboarding/info.htm

Hazelwood School District. (2000). *District Technology Plan.* Hazelwood, MO: Hazelwood School District Board of Education.

Hazelwood School District. (1995, May 6). *Elementary keyboarding and technology curriculum, grades 1–6.* Hazelwood, MO: Hazelwood School District Board of Education.

Herzog Keyboarding. (1999). The Herzog system of computer keyboarding. Retrieved November 9, 2001, from the World Wide Web: http://www.herzogkeyboarding.com/html/system_summary.html

Hoggatt, J. (1998). A master plan for evaluating and updating your keyboarding program. *Business Education Forum, 52*(4), 34–36.

Hong, L. K. (2001, May). Too many intrusions on instructional time. *Phi Delta Kappan, 82*(9), 712–714. Retrieved September 23, 2001, from the World Wide Web: Wilson Select Plus, pp. 1–5.

Missouri Business Education Association. (2001, March). *2001 Strategic Plan Survey.* Unpublished.

National Business Education Association. (1997). *Elementary/middle school keyboarding strategies guide* (2nd ed.). Reston, VA: Author.

National Business Education Association. (1995). *National standards for business education: What America's students should know and be able to do in business.* Reston, VA: Author.

National Business Education Association. (2001). *National standards for business education: What America's students should know and be able to do in business* (2nd ed.). Reston, VA: Author.

Nieman, P. (1996, October). Introducing early keyboarding skills. *Business Education Forum, 51*(1), 27–30.

Raffery, C. D. (1999, October). Literary in the information age. *Educational Leadership,* pp. 22–25.

Schmid, R. E., Fesmire, M., & Lisner, M. C. P. (2001, April). Riding up the learning curve: Elementary technology lessons. *Learning and Leading with Technology, 28*(7), 36–39. Retrieved September 23, 2001, from the World Wide Web: Wilson Select Plus, pp. 1–5.

Soloway, E., Norris, C., & Curtis, M. (2001, April). Making palm-sized computers the PC of choice for K–12. *Learning and Leading with Technology, 28*(7), 32–34, 56–57. Retrieved August 16, 2001, from the World Wide Web: Wilson Select Plus, pp. 1–6.

Stevenson, H. W. (1998, September). Guarding teacher's time. *Education Week.* Retrieved from the World Wide Web: http://www.edweek.org/ew/1998/02steven.118

Troutner, J. (2000, April). Type to learn, Jr. *Teacher Librarian, 27*(4), 53–54. Retrieved September 23, 2001, from the World Wide Web: Wilson Select Plus, p. 1.

Watson, B. C. (2000, June). Kid keys 2.0. *T.H.E. Journal, 27*(11), 88. Retrieved September 23, 2001, from the World Wide Web: Wilson Select Plus, pp. 1–2.

Customized Services for Diverse Student Needs

Martha H. Rader

Arizona State University

Tempe, Arizona

Not long ago public schools routinely excluded students simply because they differed from school standards for "normal" students. As recently as the 1960s and 1970s millions of children were denied access to public school programs throughout the United States because of race, learning and physical disabilities, pregnancy, and medical conditions such as epilepsy (Henley, Ramsey, & Algozzine, 1999).

These exclusionary practices along with restrictive national immigration policies created a more homogeneous school population than is present in today's public schools. The continual increase in the diversity of students, including those with special needs, is the effect of the shift toward inclusion practices and the liberalization of immigration policies. Many business educators are inadequately prepared to deal with the new student demographics that have been brought about by the integration and mainstreaming of students with physical and learning disabilities and enrollments of multicultural students with limited English proficiency.

The "one-size-fits-all" approach to education that characterized many classrooms in the past does not fit today. Instead of requiring students to conform to an inflexible curriculum, learning services must be customized for diverse students. This chapter is intended to help teachers maximize the learning potential of their students. Because diversity is expected to continue to increase throughout the 21st century, business educators at all levels must learn to implement new teaching strategies.

The chapter begins by focusing on legislative and other governmental actions affecting diverse student populations, including students with physical and learning disabilities and those with limited English proficiency. Throughout the chapter teachers will find strategies and resources to help address students' various needs. The final discussion identifies how to obtain resources for the classroom.

LEGISLATION AFFECTING SPECIAL POPULATIONS

The *Brown v. Topeka Board of Education* Supreme Court decision in 1954 prohibited public schools from segregating students by race. In 1964 the Civil Rights Act forbade discrimination based on race or ethnicity. These two legal milestones provided the basis for today's multicultural education, with its emphasis on equal opportunity and diversity in race, ethnicity, gender, and language (Ford, 1992).

In the 1970s two major laws affected how schools treat students with disabilities. Section 504 of the Rehabilitation Act of 1973 prohibited discrimination against handicapped persons in any program or activity receiving federal funds. In 1975 Public Law 94-142, now called the Individuals With Disabilities Education Act (IDEA), required schools to provide special-needs students with individualized education programs (IEPs), which are individualized plans for modifications and supplementary services, as needed for success in the classroom (Bakken & Kortering, 1999).

In 1990 IDEA was amended, mandating the inclusion of a statement of "transition services" in each student's IEP. The intent of this provision was to reduce the dropout rate for special-needs students and to help them make successful transitions to adulthood through gainful employment or by continuing their education in appropriate postsecondary programs (Storms, O'Leary, & Williams, 2000).

The 1997 amendments to IDEA strengthened the requirement for transition services. They also emphasized that students with disabilities should be educated in regular classes to the maximum extent appropriate. These students should learn alongside their nondisabled peers but should have appropriate supplementary aids, services, modifications, accommodations, and support. Under the 1997 amendments transition service needs must be identified in the IEPs of all students with disabilites who are 14 years of age or older, and the transition service needs must be reviewed annually.

Transition services must now prepare students with disabilities for postsecondary education, employment, and independent living. These new requirements effectively mandate tracking special-needs students into vocational education programs. In some high schools the number of special-needs students in a typical business class has increased from one or two students to nearly half the enrollment. In the mid 1980s the Carl Perkins Act shifted vocational education funding emphasis to special-needs and at-risk students. The 1990 Perkins amendments and the 1997 IDEA amendments have continued this trend. The result will undoubtedly be further increases in the number of mainstreamed special-needs students enrolled in business education classes at both the middle school and secondary school levels.

Concurrent with these changes the federal Assistive Technology Related Assistance for Individuals with Disabilities Act was passed in 1988 (James & Meske, 1998). This legislation, known as the Tech Act, established an office in each state to provide centers and funding for assistive technology training projects focusing on computer access, communication, and activities of daily living. These centers provide trainers to assist schools. The goal is to help schools set up their own teams to provide assistive technology to students with disabilities. The assistive technology services and vocational rehabilitation agencies can provide funding and other aid to students with disabilities under IDEA transition services.

In the past vocational rehabilitation agencies did not provide services to students with disabilities at the secondary level on a widespread basis. Now, however, vocational rehabilitation assessments and assistance may be provided under transition services if schools request them from the agencies. Services from vocational rehabilitation include information and referral, demonstrations or presentations, training, device selection assistance, technical support, short-term equipment loans, and purchases of assistive devices (Southwest Human Development, 2000). Upon request from the special education department, an inclusion specialist can visit a school to provide assessments and assist with various types of accommodations including assistive technology.

MEETING THE NEEDS OF STUDENTS WITH PHYSICAL DISABILITIES
Physical disabilities are temporary or permanent biological conditions including visual impairments or blindness; hearing impairments or deafness; orthopedic and neurological impairments affecting mobility, language, or communication; and other serious health problems that limit students' activities and affect educational performance (Gordon & Keiser, 1998). Physically challenged students often require physical modifications to the classroom or assistive technology to accommodate their disabilities.

Assistive Technology, Accommodations, and Modifications
Assistive technology includes any piece of equipment or device that can be used by a person with a disability to perform specific tasks and improve functional capabilities (Lewis, 1998). Assistive technology can help students overcome many obstacles to learning. The cost of assistive technology and other devices ranges from free to expensive, and the types of devices vary from low tech to high tech.

In many cases a student with a physical disability can be effectively assisted using only accommodations to assignments and the environment, modifications to the workstation or task, and low-cost devices. Accommodations are minor changes, such as allowing more time, giving shorter assignments, moving a desk, or adjusting a chair. Modifications are major changes requiring documentation in the IEP (Davey, 1999). Modifications may include various types of assistive technology that are used to address visual, speech/hearing, motor, and cognitive impairments.

Many assistive technologies are available to help individuals with disabilities use computers. Information about assistive technologies is readily available on the Internet.

Closing the Gap (http://www.closingthegap.com), Integrated Network of Disability Information and Education (INDIE) (http://www.indie.ca), and Alliance for Technology Access (http://www.ataccess.org) are three resource sites. The *Closing the Gap 2000 Resource Directory* (2000), a comprehensive resource, includes hardware, software, and other computer-related products. An online directory search tool is available at http://www.closingthegap.com.

Classroom/furniture adaptations. The aisle in a classroom or computer lab should be a width sufficient to maneuver a wheelchair. The recommended width is five feet. Students in wheelchairs should work at ergonomic desks that are 30 inches high with adjustable keyboard trays (Davey, 1999). Some orthopedically impaired students can benefit from minor adaptations such as placing the keyboard on the lap on top of a beanbag. The special education department may be able to recommend appropriate workstation adaptations for students with disabilities.

Computer software and keyboard adaptations. Current Microsoft software provides a variety of accessibility utilities, including the Accessibility Wizard and a screen magnifier, that can be added during installation. FilterKeys helps individuals with limited motor control avoid typing errors caused by involuntary hand movements or by pressing a key too long. The StickyKeys feature allows individuals to type combination keys, such as dollar signs and capital letters, without using both hands. Microsoft's Web site at http://www.microsoft.com/enable/products provides links to accessibility features and Accessibility Wizard for the specific version of Windows being used.

Macintosh computers feature the Easy Access program under the control panel, which includes Sticky Keys and Slow Keys, the Macintosh equivalent of FilterKeys. Apple Computer's Web site at http://www.apple.com/disability/easyaccess.html contains detailed instructions for downloading, installing, and using the features.

Plastic key guards are available from various vendors to reduce keyboarding errors for users with hand tremors. Miniature keyboards are available for users with a limited range of motion. The online *Closing the Gap 2000 Resource Directory* at http://www.closingthegap.com includes hundreds of keyboard products. Wrist splints equipped with pointers help users with a limited range of motion type by pointing (Davey, 1999). For students unable to type with both hands, South-Western Publishing Company's classic text, *Type With One Hand*, by Richardson (1999), contains keyboarding lessons and drills in left-handed and right-handed versions.

A variety of keyboard products may also meet needs. A special alternative keyboard with only seven keys is available from Infogrip, Inc., for one-handed computer users who have good coordination but lack the range of motion to use a regular keyboard (http://www.infogrip.com). This type of keyboard, which is called a "chord" keyboard, works somewhat like a court reporting keyboard; the user types certain letters by holding combinations of other letters (Davey, 1999). IntelliKeys by IntelliTools is an alternative keyboard resembling an Etch-a-Sketch. This device has various overlays to change or customize the keyboard for the user (http://www.intellitools.com). Don Johnston Incorporated makes a special keyboard called Discover:Kenx for users who can type only by sip and puff (*Closing the Gap 2000 Resource Directory*, 2000). Individuals with the most severe disabilities can use an LC Technologies device to keyboard with their eyes. The keyboard is shown on the screen, and an infrared device allows the user to type a letter by focusing his or her eyes on the letter for two or three seconds (Davey, 1999).

Word prediction software can be very effective for dyslexic individuals and users with mobility impairments because users can operate a computer without having to type an entire word. As the user types the first letters of a word, the word prediction program compares it to a dictionary of words beginning with those letters. A window appears on screen with a list of words, and the user finds the intended word and inserts the word in the document by typing only one keystroke.

Dragon NaturallySpeaking by Dragon Systems (http://www.dragonsys.com) is a popular voice recognition software product that allows disabled users to operate computers using voice commands (*Closing the Gap 2000 Resource Directory*, 2000). However, individuals with inconsistent speech patterns or diction may have trouble using voice recognition software.

Mouse adaptations. Controlling the mouse can be a problem for students with physical disabilities or poor hand-eye coordination. A student can speed up or slow down the mouse by changing control panel settings in Windows or activating the MouseKeys feature in Macintosh's Easy Access utility. MouseKeys converts the number pad to a mouse controller so that numbers move the mouse in different directions. The zero key locks the mouse key down for click and drag, and the decimal point key releases it.

A trackball is simply a mouse with the ball on top. Trackballs available from various vendors range in size from as large as a tennis ball to as small as a pea (Davey, 1999). Many of these devices are illustrated in the National Assistive Technology Research Institute's Viewer Index. Individuals with limited hand mobility can place a trackball so that it can be operated by the elbow, upper arm, or foot. Joysticks and touchscreens are alternatives that can be adapted to work like a mouse.

HeadMaster, by Prentke Romich, and HeadMouse, by Origin Instruments, are infrared devices that allow users to operate computers with only head movements (http://natri.uky.edu). HeadMouse is so precise that it allows users to operate Autocad without using their hands (DiGangi, Wijesariya, & Jones, 2000).

Monitor adaptations. For the hearing impaired, the standard computer monitor requires modification to convert audible error messages or "beeps" to text that can be read on the screen. The computer monitor is inaccessible to blind users or those with limited vision. Screen magnifications or conversions of text to speech or text to Braille may help some of these users.

CloseView is a Macintosh Easy Access utility that enlarges the image on the screen. Keying "command option k" allows the user to enlarge the screen view, and the magnifying glass icon allows the user to zoom in on small items (Davey, 1999). Microsoft has expanded its screen utilities with new versions of Windows. ZoomText is a stand-alone screen magnifier that works with various versions of Windows (*Closing the Gap 2000 Resource Directory,* 2000).

A wide variety of high-tech hardware and software allows blind users to read the screen (*Software Focus,* 2000). Refreshable Braille is a strip containing plastic pins that move up and down to allow the user to feel screen output in Braille. Documents can be printed in Braille by using special Braille software translators and embossers.

Screen-reading software supports speech synthesizers that read onscreen information aloud. Headphones prevent others in the classroom from hearing output from the speech synthesizers. The most advanced screen reader today is called JAWS. JAWS reads text on the screen and tells the user where the cursor is located. JAWS can also read PowerPoint presentations and Web pages. Freedom Scientific, Inc., the developer of JAWS also has Braille note takers, embossers, and displays (http://www.freedomscientific. com).

Internet accessibility. Web pages should be designed so that they are accessible to users with disabilities (Crockett, 2000). Faculty offering online courses and online materials for student access need to be aware that federal regulations require all institutions receiving funds under the Tech Act to make their Web pages accessible to people with disabilities. Poorly designed sites are difficult to navigate. Some color schemes may frustrate color-blind individuals. Some formats like Word documents and HTML formats are readable by screen readers such as JAWS, but others are not. For example, Adobe PDF formats and JavaScripts are presently inaccessible via JAWS (DiGangi, Wijesariya, & Jones, 2000).

Web pages should be designed with links to textual descriptions of all graphics and multimedia objects. These links, called ALT tags, are created by linking an object on the screen to a text box. An ALT tag appears on the screen as text contained in a "bubble" that pops up when an object is selected. All images on a Web page should be identified with descriptive ALT tags that can be read by the screen reader; for example, "man opening car door."

The World Wide Web Consortium (W3C) provides Web page accessibility guidelines at http://www.w3.org/WAI/. "Bobby" is a free service that evaluates a Web site's accessibility (http://www.cast.org/bobby). "Prompt Toolkit" is a more sophisticated Web accessibility evaluation service (http://aprompt.snow.utoronto.ca).

Today business educators can access a variety of solutions that were not available a short time ago. Although it may seem that these solutions are for some but not all students, it is likely that a solution introduced in the business education classroom will benefit someone outside of the classroom, as well. As future business professionals, all students will need to know what is available and how to access technology for individuals with disabilities. They may be responsible at some future time for making the workplace accessible for employees and customers or for developing Web sites that meet accessibility criteria.

MEETING THE NEEDS OF LEARNING-IMPAIRED STUDENTS

Mainstreamed students who have difficulty learning are often classified as having learning disabilities, mild mental retardation, or behavior disorders. The categories are not mutually exclusive, so students with different disorders may exhibit similar problems.

Students with learning disabilities often have trouble understanding or using written or spoken language due to perceptual handicaps, brain injury, minimal brain dysfunction, dyslexia, or other conditions (Henley et al., 1999). High school students with learning disabilities are often identified by severe discrepancies between academic achievement and intellectual ability. Their achievement scores in reading, language, and math may correspond with those expected of someone several years younger (Mercer, 1987).

Mild mental retardation is characterized by impaired intellectual and social functioning. Behavior disorders are characterized by constant behavior problems that interfere with adapting to classroom routines and that inhibit learning. The disorders result from emotional or neurological disturbances and may be associated with hyperactivity, impulsiveness, distractibility, or depression (Henley et al., 1999).

Students in all three groups tend to have low academic achievement levels and lack intrinsic motivation and interest in school. These students generally have poor memories and few study skills; lack strategies for test taking, note taking, listening, and reading comprehension; and have difficulty paying attention and proofreading (Carlson & Alley, 1981; Moran, 1980; as cited in Mercer, 1987). They also tend to have trouble solving problems and following instructions (Schumaker, Hazel, Sherman, & Sheldon, 1982; as cited in Mercer, 1987).

Curriculum Modifications for Students With Learning Disabilities

In classrooms that rely on the lecture method, students must excel at listening and taking notes. In these instances students are frequently dependent on their own devices to acquire information from textbooks, worksheets, or computer tutorials. Oral feedback and reinforcement might be given only at the end of a lesson and directed to the entire class rather than to individual students.

Students with learning disabilities may be unsuccessful in such an environment and may require significant modifications or adaptations to the curriculum, different instructional strategies, and changes in classroom management techniques. Before the teacher can act, however, he or she must know what the student's special needs are. In order to understand each component of the student's IEP, ideally, the business teacher should participate in IEP meetings along with the student, his or her parents, and the special education teacher.

According to Platt and Olson (1997), the IEP should include the following components:

- Present performance levels
- Annual or long-range goals
- Short-term instructional objectives
- Extent of participation in regular classroom activities
- A statement of special education services to be provided and who will provide them
- The dates and duration of special services to be provided
- Criteria and procedures for assessing progress
- A statement of transition services that are needed

A typical IEP may recommend simple accommodations such as shortening assignments, not penalizing the student for spelling errors, permitting the student to use a tape recorder, or providing the student with the teacher's notes. The curriculum may be modified for the student in various ways such as by (a) providing special textbooks that are written at a lower reading level; (b) adapting textbooks used in regular classes, for example, by providing supplementary vocabulary sheets or skipping difficult sections; (c) allowing more time to complete assignments; and (d) providing alternative assignments or assessments. Additionally, the business educator or an aide provided by the special education department can use a special textbook to provide individualized instruction for a student.

Some consumer math, business math, or basic business textbooks have been developed at a fifth- or sixth-grade reading level specifically for students with learning disabilities. The content of these special textbooks generally focuses on real-life application of the subject matter to develop transition skills such as paying bills, making change, and budgeting. Many regular textbooks contain supplementary materials and activities for students with learning disabilities. Either commercially prepared or teacher-made study guides can be used to assist students with their lessons.

Curricular materials should reinforce effective study skills. Testing should cover the content specified in the long-range or short-term goals for the student, rather than all the information presented to the entire class. Ideally the special education department should provide alternative testing for students who are unable to take a regular written test. Shorter tests, special tests with a lower readability level, oral tests, checklists, and process or product assessments are frequently used for students with learning disabilities. Additionally, these students are often allowed to retest after a teacher or aide reteaches the material to them (Gordon & Keiser, 1998).

Instructional Strategies for Students With Learning Disabilities

IEPs do not provide the details required for day-to-day decisions about instructional strategies. To meet the needs of students with learning disabilities, teachers should develop a positive attitude and classroom climate; facilitate a high degree of student-engaged time; and provide frequent question periods, review, and reteaching. Lessons should include previewing, modeling, guided practice, independent practice, and immediate feedback (Sabornie & deBettencourt, 1997). These are strategies that will work for all students.

Developing a positive attitude. A proactive approach is crucial for successful teaching and learning. Taking the time to help special-needs students succeed can be very rewarding. In order to increase their expertise and confidence in working with these students, business educators can read articles, attend workshops, and network with colleagues. Business teacher education programs can assist by offering new courses, adding units on special needs to existing methods courses, and encouraging research in the area of special needs.

Establishing a positive classroom climate. A positive climate in the classroom is not created when special-needs students are ignored or given busy work to occupy their time. Teachers should interact with special-needs students by maintaining good eye contact, asking questions that the student can answer correctly, providing positive feedback, and displaying willingness to provide extra help. Teachers should avoid discriminatory practices such as displaying the work of only the best students, calling on good students more often than slower students, and providing less response time when questioning slower students. Showing an interest in all students and providing opportunities for all students to be successful will convey the care and concern that builds student self-esteem and motivates students to learn.

Providing a high degree of student-engaged time. Students with learning disabilities may be unable to benefit from independent work. They need direct teacher-led instruction (Sabornie & deBettencourt, 1997). To provide maximum levels of student-engaged time, the teacher should be well organized, keep lessons on schedule, and discourage students from digressing from the task at hand. Students should begin to work as soon as they enter the classroom instead of waiting while the teacher prepares materials, passes out papers, and takes the roll. Lessons should be individualized ahead of time to allow for different rates of learning. When an assignment is completed, students should immediately proceed to the next task or lesson, rather than waiting for the teacher to assign the next task.

Organizing content into short lessons. Lessons for students with learning disabilities can proceed more quickly if the teacher divides appropriate content into short lessons with small increments of change, lets each student participate in each activity and have the opportunity to answer questions correctly, and provides smooth transitions between activities.

Previewing each lesson. Students with learning disabilities may be unable to organize perceptual information or differentiate important concepts from illustrative material. The teacher should structure each lesson with an "advance organizer" to preview learning (Platt & Olson, 1997). The preview should state reasons that the lesson is important, objectives for student learning, and the relationship of the lesson to previous lessons. This will help prepare students for the activities that follow and focus their attention on the most important concepts.

Modeling behaviors. The constructivist or problem-solving approach that encourages students to figure out how to do a task is usually ineffective for students with learning disabilities. For these students, the teacher should model (demonstrate) each behavior rather than simply discussing how to do it. Students with learning disabilities may have difficulty following oral instructions (Sabornie & deBettencourt, 1997). To show exactly how to complete a task, the teacher may work a problem on the board or use a computer or conventional projector to provide additional examples. Additionally, discussing "nonexamples," or ways *not* to do an assignment, can prevent students from making common errors.

Providing guided and independent practice. In guided practice the teacher supervises a group that practices tasks together, such as spelling aloud, repeating information in unison, or typing short passages to build speed. The use of strategies such as rhyme, mnemonics, and subvocal speech can increase students' retention of information (Henley et al., 1999).

Independent practice involves giving students a task to perform without help from the teacher. However, the teacher should move around the room to observe the independent practice closely and provide immediate positive and negative feedback to students. When a student is observed making errors, the teacher should provide feedback without telling the student the correct answer. The best strategy for both guided and independent practice is to prompt the student with reminders and cues that allow the student to correct his or her own behavior.

Asking students questions frequently. The teacher should provide frequent review and summarization. Pausing every six to eight minutes in a lesson for questions elicits feedback on the content that has just been presented (McNamara, 1998). The teacher should ask questions to check student understanding, directing most task-related questions to the individual student to assess the student's ability to answer the question correctly. If answers reveal a lack of understanding, prompt reteaching is necessary. Calling on students to summarize important concepts again at the end of the lesson is an effective strategy for closure.

Preteaching vocabulary and providing study guides. Preteaching new vocabulary before each lesson can enhance students' comprehension of the content. Students can learn new vocabulary by making flash cards and drilling each other on the words in pairs. The use of teacher-made study guides allows students to record information about a lesson or chapter on a partial outline. Study guides help students organize information and encourage them to recall what they have read or heard.

Facilitating cooperative learning. Cooperative learning is a very effective strategy for having students work together in heterogeneous small groups (Vallecorsa, deBettencourt, & Zigmond, 2000). The teacher selects the members of each learning group to prevent disparities between groups. The groups generally consist of three to six students ranging in achievement level from high to low. The groups should contain equal numbers of males and females, with no more than one student with a learning disability in each group.

Cooperative learning differs from other small-group activities that do not emphasize the method of working together. In cooperative learning the teacher not only assigns group activities but also instructs the students in how to work cooperatively. To avoid having a few students do all of the work, tasks are divided equally among group members. For example, in the "jigsaw" approach the teacher divides a task into subtasks and specifically assigns tasks to each student based on his or her ability to complete them. Another approach is to assign each member a specific role to facilitate completion of a task. For example, one student may be responsible for writing down suggestions, while another student keeps track of the time.

Utilizing peer tutoring. Peer tutoring illustrates the adage that the best way to learn something is to teach it to someone else. Research has shown that the test scores of both special education students and their student tutors improve when they work together (Henley et al., 1999). In peer tutoring students give and receive immediate feedback while practicing, discussing, and evaluating learning. Peer tutoring works particularly well in the computer lab. Advanced students who may be bored with concepts they already know can be identified as tutors for students who are having difficulty grasping concepts. Peer tutoring works best when student tutors are carefully selected and trained by the teacher. Tutors must understand that their job is to help rather than to actually do other students' work.

Although special instructional approaches may appear to benefit only students with learning disabilities, other students who observe their teachers adapting and adjusting to all students may carry that behavior over into the workplace and other areas of their lives. The teacher thus becomes a role model for all students when he or she demonstrates instructional approaches appropriate for the learning disabled.

MEETING THE NEEDS OF STUDENTS WITH LIMITED ENGLISH PROFICIENCY (LEP)

Linguistically diverse students are those who speak languages other than English at home. Data from the 1990 census showed that one out of six youth in the United States between the ages of 14 and 19 either spoke a language other than English at home, was born outside the United States, or both (Waggoner, 1999). Linguistically diverse students are especially concentrated in the states of California, Texas, New York,

Florida, Illinois, Arizona, and New Mexico (Solorzano & Solorzano, 1999). Liberal immigration policies in Canada have led to even greater diversity there (Ward, 1998).

Spanish is the language spoken most commonly by students with limited English proficiency. Census Bureau projections show that Latinos will become the dominant ethnic minority in U.S. schools. By mid-21st century, they will make up 30 percent of the K–12 population (Waggoner, 1999). In California Latinos already make up more than 30 percent of the state population and by the year 2020 are expected to surpass Whites as the largest ethnic group in the state (Solorzano & Solorzano, 1998).

Curriculum Modifications for LEP Students

LEP students are taught in various kinds of programs: transitional bilingual education programs, sheltered English programs (also referred to as "sheltered content teaching" or "specially designed academic instruction in English"), structured immersion programs, and submersion programs. In transitional bilingual education programs students receive all or part of their academic content instruction in their native language along with English language instruction. In sheltered English programs LEP students receive their content instruction in specially structured classes taught in English. At the elementary school level sheltered English programs are often referred to as structured immersion programs. In submersion programs students are mainstreamed into regular classes with little or no special assistance (Faltis, 1997).

Although few regular teachers are able to communicate with LEP students in their native language, they must provide appropriate instruction to these students. In many schools bilingual teaching assistants with little or no content knowledge instruct LEP students. Another ineffective practice is grouping LEP students together for busy work. Assignments that focus on rote memorization or drill and practice must be replaced with those that require problem-solving and critical-thinking skills. Curricular content should not be simplified for LEP students unless they have other special learning needs (Bernhardt, Hirsch, Teemant, & Rodriguez-Munoz, 1996).

Instructional Strategies for LEP Students

Business educators all too often are left to devise strategies on their own to help LEP students. These teachers may have little information about the students and little support from the school. Teachers need information about achievement test scores, if available, and students' proficiency levels in speaking and writing English. To be culturally responsive, teachers should also seek information about students' backgrounds and experiences from the students, other teachers, and the counseling department.

LEP students have a tendency to avoid interaction with their teachers and others in the classroom. Teachers should encourage LEP students to interact because social interaction is crucial to language development (Verplaetse, 1998). The most effective instructional strategies simultaneously promote language development and academic learning. The strategies for mainstreamed LEP students discussed in this chapter were developed for students in sheltered English programs (Short, 1999). Some strategies suggested for students with learning disabilities can also be used effectively to teach LEP students.

Including multicultural content in teaching. Business educators should include multicultural content in business courses, such as marketing, basic business, and entrepreneurship. A focus on international business can develop students' appreciation of and respect for other cultures. Keyboarding and computer applications courses can include exercises in keying short passages in other languages, such as Spanish, and learning how to key Spanish-language punctuation marks. Students learning to use e-mail can exchange messages with pen pals or companies located in other countries. Accounting, business math, and marketing students can learn about metric and foreign currency conversions by solving problems related to international business transactions and business travel to foreign countries. LEP students can share their knowledge of business practices and customs in their native countries with the class. The business educator may need to encourage this participation.

Modifying speech to aid comprehension. When lecturing, teachers need to break difficult concepts into shorter, more understandable parts, speak slowly, and pause frequently to give LEP students opportunities to catch up (Bernhardt et al., 1996). LEP students have increased comprehension when teachers elaborate rather than using simplified language. Providing more information and several examples gives students more than one path to comprehend a lesson. Likewise, providing synonyms and explanations for difficult vocabulary is beneficial to LEP students. Key words can be written on the board or given to students on handouts to help them follow discussions.

Providing nonverbal cues. A teacher's nonverbal cues—smiling, shaking or nodding the head, and hand gestures—should support verbal communication (Faltis, 1997). Facial expressions convey emotions such as happiness, displeasure, or surprise. These nonverbal cues can contribute to student comprehension, prevent students from "tuning out" a lesson, and let students know that their teacher is enthusiastic and concerned about them.

Offering alternative pathways for student comprehension. Explaining or reinforcing vocabulary visually by using pictures, diagrams, flowcharts, graphs, maps, PowerPoint presentations, videos, and computer simulations increases comprehension. The use of manipulatives can also be very effective. The teacher can, for example, use play money and actual products to demonstrate sales techniques in a marketing class or pass around actual parts of a computer such as RAM chips or a motherboard to illustrate concepts in a computer class. Teachers can increase comprehension of the textbook and other written materials by providing vocabulary previews, study guides, dictionary practice, and demonstrations, as well as by facilitating class discussions (Short, 1999).

Using questioning techniques. The teacher should make an effort to ask questions frequently and give LEP students more than the average three-second pause to answer.

If a student fails to answer, the teacher can provide hints or follow up with an easier question rather than going on to the next student. Many LEP students are reluctant to speak because they are afraid of being corrected by the teacher.

Two nonthreatening strategies for determining student understanding are confirmation checks and clarification checks (Long, 1987; Schacter, 1984; as cited in Faltis, 1997). Confirmation checks are repetitions of all or part of what a student said in the form of a question, as shown in the following example:

Student: The spell chickler doesn't work.
Teacher: The spell checker?
Student: Yes.

Clarification checks ask a student to clarify his or her unintelligible speech, as shown in the following example:

Student: The spillshaker doesn't work.
Teacher: The what? (clarification request)
Student: The spillshaker.
Teacher: What does that mean? (clarification request)
Student: The thing that shows what words you typed wrong.
Teacher: Oh, I see. The spell checker. It doesn't work on timed writings.

These checking questions are excellent ways to "scaffold" an LEP student's understanding of the lesson content simultaneously with his or her ability to articulate it in English (Faltis, 1997). Scaffolding, or assisting an LEP student in developing language skills, should be provided by the content teacher so that the student understands and can participate in learning (Peregoy & Boyle, 1999). Checking questions force the student to articulate his or her thought processes. The following example is an illustration of the use of checking questions:

Teacher: What's the answer to problem number three?
Student: $105
Teacher: How did you get that answer?
Student: $300 minus $195
Teacher: Why did you subtract?
Student: The gross profit is the selling price minus the cost of goods sold. That is $300 minus $195, which equals $105.

Encouraging interaction among students. Peer tutoring and cooperative learning are excellent strategies to use with LEP students. Bilingual students who are fully fluent in English can serve as peer tutors and translators for LEP students. Cooperative learning enhances social interaction, allowing students to develop social skills as well as content knowledge and English language skills. Teachers should encourage peer tutors to converse with LEP students in their native language as well as in English. Peer interaction reinforces the learning of subject content and facilitates language development at the same time (Short, 1999). Cooperative learning groups should be structured heterogeneously, with equal numbers of LEP students in each group. The teacher should carefully assign the tasks in each group to students so that the LEP students are given tasks that they can accomplish successfully.

OBTAINING RESOURCES FOR DIVERSE STUDENT NEEDS

Business educators can obtain resources for diverse student needs from a variety of sources. To assist students with physical or learning disabilities, teachers can request funding from the school's special education department for specialized equipment, software, curricular materials, and aides. IDEA funding from various sources (federal, state, and local) is available through the special education department. The special assistance mandated in the IDEA legislation requires schools to provide resources such as supplementary aids and services, modifications, accommodations, and supports to help special-needs students succeed in the regular classroom.

In the past special education departments and business educators have not generally worked together in teams. In accordance with current legislation, special educators will undoubtedly collaborate more closely with business educators to meet IDEA transition requirements. Business educators are likely to be asked to participate in IEP meetings, which will enable them to acquire necessary information to develop strategies for helping their special-needs students and take advantage of additional resources that should be provided.

Parents and teachers can write requests for special equipment or other resources through IDEA. Some schools have an IDEA transition specialist who can make recommendations for resources from the Assistive Technology Resource Centers and Technology Access Programs in that state. In many states vocational rehabilitation departments already provide services in schools, and these services should increase as more schools comply with the IDEA transition service provisions. For students with mild disabilities that do not fall under IDEA criteria, teachers may request assistance by making Section 504 requests for regular school funds. Requests should be made in writing, as schools typically have ten days to respond to each written request from a teacher or parent.

Carl Perkins funds may also be available for business education students with mild disabilities who do not meet IDEA criteria for special-needs students. A portion of a school's Carl Perkins funding should be set aside for special-needs students, and the definition of a special-needs student under Carl Perkins legislation is much broader than under IDEA. Teachers seeking Carl Perkins funding should contact their school's career and technical education director. The federal projects coordinator in the school district may be able to provide project funding such as Title I funds for at-risk students, dropout prevention funds, or Title IX funds to pay for adaptive equipment, an aide, or a work-study student.

Bilingual and English as a second language (ESL) funding for LEP students is provided to school districts through federal Title VII grants. If a teacher requests assistance through Title VII, the bilingual education/ESL director or federal projects coordinator in the school district may be able to provide a bilingual aide or other special resources to assist the LEP students in business classes.

SUMMARY

Business educators and special educators need to improve the articulation of services for students with diverse needs who are being mainstreamed into business education classes in increasing numbers. Business educators need to demonstrate positive attitudes and build positive classroom environments for special-needs and LEP learners to prosper. Students with physical disabilities, learning impairments, and limited English proficiency, are part of the business classroom and need accommodations of various sorts. Business educators must be open to modifying the environment, equipment, and curriculum in order to meet their students' special needs.

Business educators cannot, however, customize the learning environment without a toolkit of instructional approaches that work with various students and work within a classroom of both regular and special-needs students. Best practices for one type of need may or may not work for all students, so teachers need to gather information about students and begin to make interventions to determine what works best for each class.

Teachers also need resources. Current legislation increases the likelihood that resources will be available to help teach special-needs and LEP students, if teachers are able to take the time to obtain assistance. The legislation also increases the likelihood of cooperation from various professionals in school and educational agencies.

REFERENCES

Bakken, T., & Kortering, L. (1999). The constitutional and statutory obligations of schools to prevent students with disabilities from dropping out. *Remedial and Special Education, 20*(6), 360–366.

Bernhardt, E., Hirsch, G., Teemant, A., & Rodriguez-Munoz, M. (1996). Language diversity and science: Science for limited English proficiency students. *Science Teacher, 63*(2), 24–27.

Closing the Gap 2000 Resource Directory. (2000, February/March). *18*(6).

Crockett, R. (2000, April 3). Helping the disabled navigate the net. *Business Week, 22.*

Davey, B. (1999, October). *Accessible computers for everyone.* Paper presented at Abilities Expo, Santa Clara, CA.

DiGangi, S., Wijesariya, R., & Jones, R. (2000, September). *Expanding accessibility to on-line instruction.* Seminar presentation at Arizona State University, Tempe, AZ.

Faltis, C. J. (1997). *Joinfostering: Adapting teaching for the multilingual classroom* (2nd ed.). Upper Saddle River, NJ: Merrill.

Ford, B. A. (1992). Multicultural education training for special educators working with African-American youth. *Exceptional Children, 59*(2), 107–114.

Gordon, M., & Keiser, S. (1998). *Accommodations in higher education under the Americans with Disabilities Act (ADA)*. DeWitt, NY: GSI Publications.

Henley, M., Ramsey, R. S., & Algozzine, R. F. (1999). *Characteristics of and strategies for teaching students with mild disabilities* (3rd ed.). Boston: Allyn and Bacon.

James, M. L., & Meske, M. W. (1998). Using technology to assist disabled students in their quest for success. *Business Education Forum, 52*(4), 45–46, 49.

Lewis, R. B. (1998). Assistive technology and learning disabilities: Today's realities and tomorrow's promises. *Journal of Learning Disabilities, 31*(1), 16–26, 54.

McNamara, B. A. (1998). *Learning disabilities: Appropriate practices for a diverse population*. Albany, NY: State University of New York Press.

Mercer, C. D. (1987). *Students with learning disabilities* (3rd ed.). Columbus, OH: Merrill.

Peregoy, S. F., & Boyle, O. F. (1999). Multiple embedded scaffolds: Support for English speakers in a two-way Spanish immersion kindergarten. *Bilingual Research Journal, 23*(2 & 3), 113–124.

Platt, J. M., & Olson, J. L. (1997). *Teaching adolescents with mild disabilities*. Pacific Grove, CA: Brooks/Cole.

Richardson, N. K. (1999). *Type with one hand* (3rd ed.). Cincinnati, OH: South-Western Educational & Professional Publisher.

Sabornie, E. J., & deBettencourt, L. U. (1997). *Teaching students with mild disabilities at the secondary level*. Upper Saddle River, NJ: Merrill.

Short, D. J. (1999). Integrating language and content for effective sheltered instruction programs. In C. J. Faltis & P. M. Wolfe (Eds.), *So much to say: Adolescents, bilingualism, and ESL in the secondary school* (pp. 105–137). New York: Teachers College Press.

Solorzano, R. W., & Solorzano, D. G. (1999). Beginning teacher standards: Impact on second-language learners and implications for teacher preparation. *Teacher Education Quarterly, 26*(3), 37–70.

Software focus on special needs. (2000, February). *T.H.E. Journal, 27*(7), 78–83.

Southwest Human Development. (2000). *Assistive technology services* [Brochure]. Phoenix, AZ: Author.

Storms, J., O'Leary, E., & Williams, J. (2000). *The Individuals with Disabilities Education Act of 1997 transition requirements: A guide for states, districts, schools, universities and families*. Minneapolis, MN: National Transition Network Institute on Community Integration.

Vallecorsa, A. L., deBettencourt, L. U., & Zigmond, N. (2000). *Students with mild disabilities in general education settings: A guide for special educators*. Upper Saddle River, NJ: Merrill.

Verplaetse, L. S. (1998). How content teachers interact with English language learners. *TESOL Journal, 7*(5), 24–28.

Waggoner, D. (1999). Who are secondary newcomer and linguistically different youth? In C. J. Faltis & P. M. Wolfe (Eds.), *So much to say: Adolescents, bilingualism, and ESL in the secondary school* (pp. 13–41). New York: Teachers College Press.

Ward, B. (1998). California learning. *American Language Review, 2*(5), 14–17. Retrieved July 22, 2001, from the World Wide Web: http://www.alr.org/alo/so98/fcl14.html

Citizenship, Business Ethics, and Technology

Carol Blaszczynski
California State University
Los Angeles, California

Promoting good citizenship is a vital aspect of business education instruction. Not only do business educators strive to educate for business, they also seek to educate about business so that students become savvy investors, entrepreneurs, and citizens. Business education has expanded its boundaries to include all types of information technology and the Internet. The discipline now encompasses educating for global citizenship and Internet citizenship with a focus on how technology is used. Citizenship bestows certain privileges, often viewed as rights, and entails responsibilities.

This chapter focuses on the relationships of three facets of the business education curriculum: citizenship, technology, and business ethics. With the exponential rise in the usage of the Internet and other technologies, ethical concerns have also increased. This chapter discusses the ethical use of technology and the rights and responsibilities of technology users. Instructional activities for business educators who teach traditional and online classes are also included. The activities should hone the ethical decision-making skills of students to prepare them to deal with dilemmas involving current and future technologies.

RIGHTS AND RESPONSIBILITIES OF TECHNOLOGY USERS
Technology users are, in effect, citizens of a global, technologically connected society who have rights and responsibilities.

Rights of Technology Users
Technology users claim two fundamental rights: the right to privacy and the right to ethical treatment. Privacy may be defined as "the right of individuals to control the

collection and use of personal information about themselves" ("What is privacy?," n.d.). The Policies Commission for Business and Economic Education (PCBEE) (1992), described the components of ethical behavior, stating, "Personal integrity, honesty and fairness, and respect for the rights of others are measures of ethical behavior. Evolving technology and the expanding global economy intensify the need for ethical business practices" (p. 17). Although citizens expect to be treated ethically, behaving ethically is also a responsibility of citizens of the global environment.

Privacy plays a pivotal role in global business (Melymuka, 2001). Concern about privacy has created a demand for privacy-enhancing goods and services. According to Lester (2001), "People are coming to accept the notion that the protection of privacy is a pervasive and lasting concern in the computer age—and that, indeed, it may turn out to be *the* true enabler of the information economy" (p. 28). Remp (1999) has asserted that, "Privacy is essential for a workplace culture that fosters creative thinking" (p. 126).

Businesses have recognized the privacy concerns of consumers, as the posting of privacy policies on Web sites attests. In fact, privacy career paths were recently identified by *U.S. News & World Report* ("Hot Job Tracks," 2001), with the creation of chief privacy officer (CPO) positions in organizations, as well as related certifications being offered through several firms. By the year 2005, most firms of medium to large size are likely to have a CPO on board.

Responsibilities of Technology Users
Technology users have three responsibilities: acting ethically, maintaining vigilance, and staying knowledgeable. Individuals should have some basis for determining whether or not an action is ethical and then know the general and specific business and technology standards that apply.

Guffey (2000) has recommended that individuals consider five factors when faced with an ethical conundrum:

1. The legality of the action being contemplated
2. How individuals with opposing viewpoints will perceive the action
3. The viable options, if any
4. The opinion of a trustworthy colleague
5. The reactions friends, family, coworkers, and employers are likely to have to action or inaction

According to Brooks (2000), "North American society now endorses the position that an individual's personal rights are more important than those of an employer's, unless it can be shown that, in a particular circumstance, the employer's interest is reasonable, legitimate, and morally acceptable" (p. 237).

There are also guidelines for ethical action in specific areas. Two policy statements by PCBEE address ethical concerns. "This We Believe About Business Ethics" (Policies

STUDENT ACTIVITY

Privacy Tolerance Levels

In 1999 Sun Microsystems CEO Scott McNealy (Lester, 2001, p. 27), was asked about the existence of privacy safeguards in a just released Sun computer-networking system. McNealy answered that "Consumer privacy issues were nothing but a 'red herring' . . . You have zero privacy anyway. Get over it."

Ask student teams to debate the statement and/or write a response indicating their level of agreement or disagreement with the statement. Ask students to mark an X on the continuum shown in Figure 1 that indicating their standards for privacy.

Figure 1. Privacy Standards Continuum

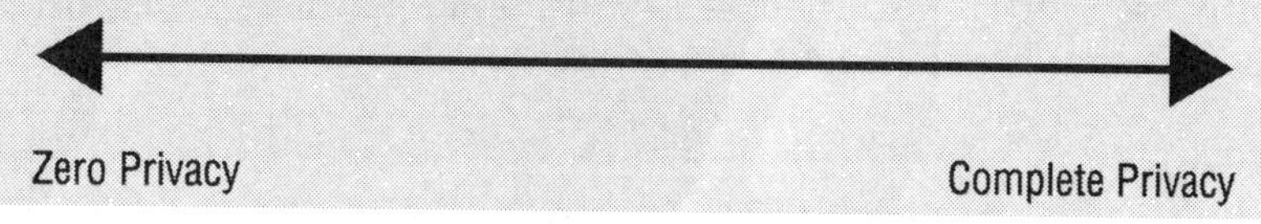

Zero Privacy   Complete Privacy

A variety of discussions can be based on the impacts that different standards for privacy have on the Internet environment. The next two scenarios can provide a basis for discussion:

Scenario I: *You walked into your divisional meeting a few minutes late. During the course of a heated discussion about the organization's privacy policy, you expressed some strong sentiments. Later you learned that the meeting had been recorded. You were appalled; you had had no idea that your comments were being recorded.*

Have students discuss the scenario from an ethical standpoint. What questions would they want answered? What will happen to the tapes after the meeting notes are distributed? What would students recommend for the future in terms of policies and practices? Do the positions of students reflect their standards of privacy?

Scenario II: *When you began your employment with Sterling Communications, a publicity photograph was taken of you. The photo was not flattering, and you requested that it not be used. All executives are required to have a home page, and you carefully crafted the contents of your Web page. When you learned that it had been uploaded, you accessed the page. Much to your annoyance, you found that your unflattering photograph was staring back at you. You were disturbed because photographic images can be modified by others and distributed in creative ways.*

Have students discuss what action they would likely take in this situation and whether photographs of employees be placed on Web pages.

Commission for Business and Economic Education, 1992) underscores the importance of teaching ethics for business: "Students must be aware of their ethical responsibilities as consumers, workers, and citizens" (Policies Commission for Business and Economic Education, 1992, p. 17). "This We Believe About Electronic Business in Business Education" highlights ethics and security as critical electronic business issues (Policies Commission for Business and Economic Education, 2000).

Ethics play a central role in the business education standards developed by the National Business Education Association. The information systems achievement standards require students to "describe, analyze, develop, and follow policies for managing privacy and ethical issues in organizations and in a technology-based society" (2001, p. 90). The business education performance expectations for management (2001, p. 114) state that students should be able to "identify ethical considerations resulting from various situations" including technological advances.

MAINTAINING VIGILANCE AND REMAINING KNOWLEDGEABLE

Individuals apply ethical standards in many settings. To do this, they must maintain vigilance and remain knowledgeable about many issues that affect their roles as employees, consumers, and citizens. The treatment of individuals and individual information is central to discussions of surveillance, identity theft, fraud, cyber crime, personally identifiable information, and intellectual property.

Surveillance

Jesdanun (2001) reported that Civil Libertarians and advocates for privacy believe that "technology is getting so good and cheap that we could be entering an era of surveillance everywhere, privacy nowhere" (p. B4). Surveillance can be done on e-mail, computer files, and telephone conversations, and by using video cameras and tracking Web sties visited (American Management Association, 2001). According to Parsons (2001), a recent career services firm survey revealed that 80 percent of organizations have implemented monitoring systems and policies to reduce employee Internet use. Additionally, in the field of biometrics, facial characteristic recognition technology is being developed not just to record as video security cameras do in convenience stories, grocery stores, and banks, but also to identify (Jesdanun, 2001).

Identity Theft

According to Davis (2001), identity theft is the fastest-growing white-collar crime in the United States. Over 700,000 Americans experienced illegal use of their personal information in 2000 (Identity Theft Resource Center, 2001). In 2000 over 27,000 phone calls were made about stolen or lost identification to the identity theft hotline operated by the Federal Trade Commission (Clark, 2001). To reduce the likelihood that identity theft will occur, experts, such as Richard Cinnamon (Davis, 2001), recommend taking precautionary steps. These steps include lowering credit card limits to reduce the potential damage an identity theft could do and requesting that issuers of credit cards stop mailing unsolicited convenience checks.

Fraud

Approximately 35.6 million citizens have participated in online auctions. Most of the participants have been content with their experiences. On the other hand, the National Consumers League reported, through Internet Fraud Watch at http://www.fraud.org/internet/intset.htm, that the number one consumer Internet fraud complaint involves online auctions, which constitute 78 percent of reported complaints.

On average, the typical fraud victim lost $326 in 2000 (National Consumers League, 2001). Online auction sales continue to be popular. According to an eBay spokesperson ("Fraud Complaints," 2000), the auction site experiences one instance of fraud for every 25,000 auctions completed or about 168 on an average day.

STUDENT ACTIVITY

Great Deal for You or E-Rip-off?

Ask students to read the online auction scenario below, which presents the possibility of fraud. The scenario, based upon an actual experience, can be used in business classes for a variety of purposes.

Scenario: *You are a book-lover and have set a goal of collecting every book ever written by your favorite author, Victoria Keyes. Unfortunately, ten of the titles you wish to buy are out of print. A friend told you that you might consider auction sites as a source for the books needed to complete your collection. Following your friend's advice, you check out the newest online bidding site, GreatDealForYou.com.*

On GreatDealForYou.com you discover that Simple City, one of the books by Victoria Keyes that you are missing, is on auction for $8.50—a bargain! You decide to bid on the book. Following the directions for setting up an account, you place your bid and sit back. Two days remain before the auction closes, and you check back occasionally to see if you are still the highest bidder. You are uncontested and win the bid.

The seller of the book, David Kramer, e-mails you that the shipping will cost $2.90 (bringing the total cost of your purchase to $11.40) and includes his mailing address for payment. Once he has received your payment, he will mail the book to you. In response, you send David an e-mail message informing him that you'll mail the check to him tomorrow morning. The next morning, as promised, you drop the check in the mail.

Two weeks later you are pleased to receive the book. Upon closer inspection, you discover that it looks like pages are missing from the book. The seller had declared the book in fair condition but "with all pages intact." Worriedly, you then check your records to determine that the edition you purchased should have 200 pages, while the book in your hands has only 138. Since this is your first experience with online auctions, you are suspicious that this could be a scam.

Have students discuss the situation: What are the ethics involved in this case? Could the seller perhaps have been unaware of the missing pages? What regulations exist for this type of a situation? What recourse, if any, do buyers of online merchandise have in cases where the item received differs from the item advertised? Have students write an e-mail message to David Kramer explaining the situation and requesting a mutually acceptable solution.

This scenario serves as the basis for a group research project framed around the questions above. If students review the major auction sites, they will become familiar with the rules that each site has in place for such sensitive situations. Students who are unfamiliar with online auctions will learn that the buyer can always leave negative feedback about the transaction on the auction site to warn future buyers. Since sellers depend on a stellar reputation, negative feedback can be harmful.

To minimize the likelihood of online auction fraud, consumers should be familiar with how auctions are conducted, research the seller before bidding by examining buyer feedback, and obtain content information about the seller (National Consumers League, 2001).

Cyber Crime

Over 20 percent of Fortune 1000 organizations reported computer network attacks during 2000; viruses accounted for 65 percent of these attacks. Moreover, about 65 percent of corporate cyber crimes are never reported because firms fear negative publicity. As a result, software sales of security products are predicted to reach $50 billion in 2002 up from $7.4 billion in 1999 (Weinstein, 2001). According to Weinstein, "since the Internet has ascended to an incomprehensible commercial force, cyber-security has ascended to a vital information-technology field" (p. F1). Concomitantly, 60 percent of Fortune 500 organizations are hiring cyber sleuths to combat cyber thieves.

STUDENT ACTIVITY

Web Browser Security

Have students explore and report on the security update pages for their respective Web browsers: Internet Explorer, Netscape Navigator, or other software. Students should determine how to set security preferences, check passwords and certificates, and determine whether encryption is in use. Students should also check the developer site for software patches that can be downloaded at home, if needed, to increase the security of their online activities. This activity reinforces the need to be vigilant and to remain knowledgeable about changes.

Elements of an effective risk management program for e-business include monitoring vendor sites for software program updates, staying knowledgeable about computer security, and promoting a workplace environment where security is the responsibility of all (Glover, Liddle, & Prawitt, 2001).

Personal Profiles

Personally identifiable information (PII) is information gathered about an individual from online transactions and Web surfing that can be used to profile an individual's buying behavior and interests. Marketers can use this information to target advertisements and e-mail messages to individuals.

"PII refers to anything in an electronic network that can be linked in some way to a flesh-and-blood human being; to someone with a name, an address, and a life: to you, for example" (Jennings & Fena, 2000, p. xviii). PII has become so important that some analysts on Wall Street are "valuing some companies based on the quantity and quality of their customer PII profiles . . . [S]oftware developers are reengineering their products to become 'PII-compliant'" (Jennings & Fena, 2000, p. xviii).

The bright side of collecting PII is that it can help users personalize settings and obtain interesting information. On the other hand, it can be used in identity theft, racial redlining (electronic profiling that includes zip code, age, and gender and allows companies to exclude demographic groups that may be considered risky), online fraud, identity spoofing (when an individual is impersonated online), online revenge, stalking, and harassment (Jennings & Fena, 2000, p. xx).

To counter the concerns about what happens to data that are collected, increasing numbers of e-commerce operations are including privacy policies or statements on their Web sites. "Disclosure by a Web site of how it treats private information not only leads to accountability but also builds user trust and confidence" (Jennings & Fena, 2000, p. xx). Consumers view the inclusion of privacy policies positively and are more inclined to trust those organizations that post them.

In late 2000 and early 2001 banking and financial institutions mailed written privacy policy information to customers detailing how information is collected and disclosed. Moreover, procedures for how to opt out of information disclosure were also communicated to customers. Along with exercising opt-outs, consumers can request that their names be removed from direct-mailing lists.

STUDENT ACTIVITY

Personal Information Search

Ask students to estimate how many hits they will get in an Internet search for information about themselves. Then have students go to a major search engine, such as Yahoo! or Google, and run a search on their full names to determine what information can be accessed about them online. Then ask students to compile a list of personal information that has been collected about them and assess the accuracy of the information.

Much of this information is used in designing a PII profile. Students should be able to brainstorm the types of information that might go into such a profile, such as full name, date of birth, mother's maiden name, bank account numbers, credit card numbers, address, phone numbers (home and work), cell phone number, pager information, PIN numbers, voice mail access codes, e-mail user names and passwords, computer system or account user names and passwords, access codes to buildings and rooms, medical records, dental records, driving records, travel records, work/employment history, library records, and school records. If individuals travel online, then there may also be a record of purchases, Web sites visited, auctions bid on, and the like.

Intellectual Property

In its Code of Ethics for Information Systems, the National Business Education Association's Computer Education Task Force in 1999 identified the need for users to develop a respect for intellectual property. This respect includes "not copying copyrighted materials belonging to a business, education institution, or another individual."

In addition, an individual should not copy the work of another and distribute it as his or her own (National Business Education Association, 1999).

Ethical individuals make careful attributions of their sources. Web managers can trace the unauthorized use of copyrighted images through digital watermarks (Harnack & Kleppinger, 2000). According to Schick (2001), individuals can copy code from Web pages as long as graphics, links, and text are changed. He advocates that individuals give credit to the authors of the code in the comments section of the script.

Disclaimers on some organizations' sites state that the organizations will not be held responsible for any errors in the information presented on the sites. Thus, the credibility of site information may be questionable.

Net citizens, or netizens, should follow guidelines for ethical use of e-mail and other technologies. For example, it is generally considered illegal to forward an e-mail chain letter (Schwartau, 2000). Good netizens avoid negative behaviors such as spamming, flaming (using all caps to convey yelling in an e-mail message), and forwarding e-mail without the consent of others. Employees should avoid using company computers to send personal e-mail messages (Guffey, 2000). Organizations should develop, implement, and enforce policies for e-mail use.

PRIVACY ENHANCING TECHNOLOGIES AND PRACTICES

The growth of privacy-enhancing technologies and programs corresponds with the growth of existing online technologies. Among these are privacy seal programs, history file maintenance, encryption, cookie deletion and blocking practices, filtering software, and technology to prevent e-mail from being forwarded and to make Web site visits undetectable.

Privacy Seal Programs

Third-party privacy seals signify that a Web site submits to a third-party compliance review and oversight. An outside agency verifies practices to ensure that the Web site complies with the privacy statement published on the site (Jennings & Fena, 2000). The purpose of privacy certification programs is to provide online consumers some assurance of information privacy. The leading privacy seal programs include TrustE (http://www.truste.org/); BBBOnline (http://www.bbbonline.org/); and WebTrust (http://www.cpawebtrust.org/), which is sponsored by the American Institute for Certified Accountants (Sanders, 2000).

BBBOnline, a program of the Better Business Bureau, developed a Code of Online Business Practices for business to consumer (B2C) activities (http://www.bbbonline.org/code/code.asp). The five Principles for Ethical Business to Customer Conduct (http://www.bbbonline.org/code/principle.asp) include (1) communicating truthfully and accurately; (2) disclosing business, product, and transaction information for online purchases; (3) practicing sensitivity to customers' and potential customers' information (including posting and following a privacy policy); (4) satisfying customers by engaging in fair business practices; and (5) protecting children (Better Business Bureau, 2001).

Rendering Web Site Visits Undetectable

A visitor may enter a Web site undetected by pressing the CTRL and O keys simultaneously—the open page command—while using a Web browser (Jennings & Fena, 2000). The dialog box that appears allows the URL to be keyed. Such a practice avoids leaving a trail of personal information for marketers to follow. In addition, technology users can take several other actions.

Erasing History Files

A good practice is to erase history files so that they do not entice prying eyes that would seek to trace a user's steps online. Browsers will vary in the exact location of this option, but consulting the Help Index for the history topic should lead the user to instructions and information.

Encrypting Bookmarks

To protect the Favorites list or the bookmarks on a browser, a bookmark encryption program can be used to warrant the list undecipherable to others. SiegeSoft's Private Bookmark (http://www.siegesoft.com/) is an example of this type of encrypting utility.

Deleting Cookies

Much has been written about the importance of information stored in cookies. Web browser settings can be modified to prompt users to accept cookies or to reject them. More information about eliminating cookies can be found on the EPIC Cookies Page (http://www.epic.org/privacy/internet/cookies).

Using Filtering Software

Organizations use filtering programs to prohibit employees from accessing Web sites that are not work related or are unsavory ("Internet Content Filtering," 2001). Parents and certain family-oriented sites also employ password-protected filtering software to protect children from undesirable Web sites. Furthermore, filtering software is used to prevent spam from entering e-mail boxes on Web-based mail accounts.

Other Technologies and Practices

Subscribers to America Online and CompuServe can take advantage of a feature that allows e-mail to be unsent. For this feature to work, both the sender and receiver must be subscribers to the same Internet service provider. Other e-mail tools allow for the self-destruction of e-mail after a set period of time. A message can be unsent after it has been read and may be designated as "read only." This designation means that the message receiver is unable to save, forward, or print the message ("How to 'Unsend' E-Mail," 2001).

INSTRUCTIONAL STRATEGIES

Scenarios, such as those provided in this chapter, can be used for traditional class discussions or for threaded discussion on online course management systems, such as

STUDENT ACTIVITIES

Examining Privacy Issues

The WebQuest model was developed by Bernie Dodge at San Diego State University (SDSU), along with Tom March, in 1995. In essence, WebQuests are inquiry-based activities in which a majority of the information is captured from the Web (www.edweb/sdsu/edu). "WebQuests are designed to use learners' time well to focus on using information rather than looking for it and to support learners' thinking at the levels of analysis, synthesis, and evaluation" (WebQuest Site Overview, 2001). The SDSU WebQuest homepage (http://www.edweb.sdsu.edu/webquest) contains a thorough guide to WebQuests, materials for reading and training, and templates for creating WebQuest activities.

Activity 1. Privacy Policy WebQuest

Direct students to complete a WebQuest designed to have them use the Web to analyze privacy statements or policies appearing on the Web sites of various organizations. The quest can begin with sites of the privacy seal organizations such as TrustE (http://www.truste.org), BBBOnline (http://www.bbbonline.org), and Web Trust (http://www.cpawebtrust.org). Then students can be directed to sites of other organizations. Criteria for evaluating the policies can be brainstormed in teams. Teams of students can then develop privacy policies for the class or for fictitious e-businesses. Additionally, if Web page construction knowledge is required for the course, students can design Web pages using the previously written privacy policy as content.

Activity 2. Advice to a Friend

After students have researched various privacy-enhancing technologies, have students write an e-mail message to a friend describing preventive measures that can be taken to increase one's privacy when using technology.

WebCT, or Blackboard. Over 1,500 universities use the WebCT site (http://www.webct.com) as the framework for their online learning communities. WebCT serves as a repository for resource libraries, materials, and online course discussion groups (De Meyer, 2001). The quiz and survey feature of WebCT provides a vital tool that educators can use to conduct pre- and posttests of student learning.

Many instructors prefer the simplicity of Blackboard (http://www.blackboard.com) to WebCT as an online learning community. Blackboard accounts are easy to set up; course materials, such as PowerPoint slides, can be posted; and instructor-monitored discussion groups can be formed. Although Blackboard is user-friendly, the trade-off is the customizability that WebCT allows for designing an online course or elements of an online course.

For electronic classrooms and distance learners, electronic surveys can be designed. These surveys can be used as pre- and posttests of knowledge. The quiz area of WebCT can be used to generate and distribute the surveys. The mean responses can then serve as a starting point for class discussion about various ethical e-commerce technology issues.

Bubblegrams

Bubblegrams or crossword puzzles can be used by business educators to teach vocabulary (Schrag & Poland, 1987) particularly, but not exclusively, at the secondary level. A privacy bubblegram is illustrated in Figure 2. In addition to being used as a handout in traditional classes, the puzzle can be included on a course Web page for distance learners.

Figure 2. Privacy Bubblegram

Vocabulary Word	Definition
P _ _	Information gathered about Internet users
_ _ R _ _ _ _	Send e-mail you receive to another person
_ _ _ I _ _	Statement posted on a Web site about privacy
_ _ _ V _ _ _ _ _ _ _	Electronic monitoring of employees
_ _ A _	Unsolicited e-mail messages from advertisers (junk mail)
C _ _ _ _ _	Web site data stored on your system
_ _ _ _ Y _ _ _ _	Technology that does not reveal sender of e-mail messages

(Key: PII, Forward, Policy, Surveillance, Spam, Cookies, Anonymize)

SUMMARY

Technological advances have produced many benefits for citizens and organizations. However, these advances have also resulted in a plethora of ethical concerns in the areas of security and privacy. Knowledge, vigilance, and appropriate actions will aid both individuals and organizations in protecting two fundamental rights—the right to privacy and the right to have personal, consumer, and business information used ethically. Inherent to the concept of privacy is the right to protect one's good name by fulfilling the responsibilities of citizens.

Good citizenship entails exercising vigilance against surveillance, identity theft, fraud, and cyber crime; staying knowledgeable about privacy issues and privacy-enhancing technologies; and acting ethically in situations created by current and emerging technologies.

Business educators need to respect the privacy of students and strive to create a culture of respect and trust, where ethical technological behavior is encouraged and valued. In their roles as citizens, consumers, and employees, students will need to cultivate the savvy to resolve the ethical dilemmas resulting from both existing and emerging technologies.

REFERENCES

American Management Association. (2001). *2001 electronic monitoring and surveillance.* Retrieved August 7, 2001, from the World Wide Web: http://www.amanet.org/research/emssurvey.htm

Better Business Bureau. (2001). *BBBOnLine code of online business practices.* Retrieved August 7, 2001, from the World Wide Web: http://www.bbbonline.org/code/code.asp

Brooks, L. J. (2000). *Business and professional ethics for accountants* (2nd ed.). Cincinnati: South-Western College Publishing/Thompson Learning.

Clark, B. J. (2001). The day they stole my name. *Kiplinger's Personal Finance, 55*(3), 81–85.

Davis, K. (2001). Anatomy of a fraud. *Kiplinger's Personal Finance, 55*(3), 89–96.

De Meyer, D. (2001, February). Get smart. The best technology investment you'll make this year (really). *SmartBusiness, 14*(2), 92–99.

Fraud complaints spur eBay to suspend seller, call police. (2000, March 29). *The Los Angeles Times,* p. C3.

Glover, S. M., Liddle, S. W., & Prawitt, D. F. (2001). *Ebusiness: Principles & strategies for accountants.* Upper Saddle River, NJ: Prentice Hall.

Guffey, M. E. (2000). *Business communication: Process and product* (3rd ed.). Cincinnati: South-Western Publishing Company/Thompson Learning.

Harnack, A., & Kleppinger, E. (2000). *Online! A reference guide to using Internet sources.* Boston: Bedford/St. Martin's.

Hot job tracks 2001: Privacy. (2001). *U.S. News & World Report.* Retrieved August 7, 2001, from the World Wide Web: http://www.usnews.com/usnews/edu/careers/cc2001pr.htm

How to "unsend" e-mail sent in error. Stay out of the e-mail hall of shame. (2001, March). *Smart Computing, 12*(3), 88–91.

Identity Theft Resource Center. (2001). *Facts and statistics.* Retrieved August 7, 2001, from the World Wide Web: http://www.idtheftcenter.org/html/facts_and_statistics.htm

Internet content filtering. (2001, March). *Smart Computing, 12*(3), 104.

Jennings, C., & Fena, L. (2000). *The hundredth window: Protecting your privacy and security in the age of the Internet.* New York: The Free Press.

Jesdanun, A. (2001, March 11). Looking over our shoulders. Technology has ways to chip away privacy. *San Gabriel Valley Tribune,* p. B4.

Lester, T. (2001). The reinvention of privacy. *The Atlantic Monthly 287*(3), 27–39.

Melymuka, K. (2001, May 28). Data privacy key to global business, panel says. *Computerworld.* Retrieved August 7, 2001, from the World Wide Web: http://www.computerworld.com/cwi/story/0,1199,NAV47_STO60876,00.html

National Business Education Association. (1999). *NBEA computer education task force code of ethics for information systems.* Retrieved August 7, 2001, from the World Wide Web: http://www.nwmissouri.edu/~oisbe/telecom/ethicscode.html

National Business Education Association (2001). National standards for business education: What America's students should know and be able to do in business. Reston, VA: Author.

National Consumers League. (2001, January 31). *Online auction survey summary.* Retrieved August 7, 2001, from the World Wide Web: http://www.nclnet.org/onlineauctions/auctionsurvey2001.htm

Parsons, J. (2001, March 18). Internet triggers work issues. Companies worry about loss of productivity, private use of Web in the office. *San Gabriel Valley Tribune*, p. B4.

Policies Commission for Business and Economic Education. (1992). Policy statement no. 51: This we believe about teaching ethics for business. *Business Education Forum, 47*(1), 17–18.

Policies Commission for Business and Economic Education. (2000). *Policy statement no. 66: This we believe about electronic business in business education.* Reston, VA: National Business Education Association. Retrieved August 7, 2001, from the World Wide Web: http://www.nbea.org/curfpolicy.html

Remp, A. M. (1999). Workplace privacy, confidentiality, and surveillance. In P. A. Gallo Ville & M. G. Curran (Eds.), *The 21ˢᵗ century: Meeting the challenges to business education* (Yearbook No. 37, pp. 115–127). Reston, VA: National Business Education Association.

Sanders, E. (2000, December 11). Leading privacy programs are scrutinized. Government may intervene as self-regulation falters. *Los Angeles Times*, p. C1, C5.

Schick, G. (2001). Stealing code from other Web pages. *Smart Computing, 12*(2) 92–94.

Schrag, A. F., & Poland, R. F. (1987). *A system for teaching business education* (2ⁿᵈ ed.). New York: McGraw-Hill, Inc.

Schwartau, W. (2000). *CyberShock: Surviving hackers, phreakers, identity thieves, Internet terrorists and weapon of mass destruction.* New York: Thunder's Mouth Press.

WebQuest site overview. (2001). Retrieved August 13, 2001, from the World Wide Web: http://edweb.sdsu.edu/webquest/overview.htm

Weinstein, B. (2001, May 27). Tech watch: Wanted, cyber sleuths. *San Gabriel Valley Tribune*, p. F1.

What is privacy? (n.d.). *Privacy Journal.* Retrieved August 7, 2001, from the World Wide Web: www.townonline.com/specials/privacy/

Soft Skills for Building Customer and Employee Relationships

Tena B. Crews

State University of

West Georgia

Carrollton, Georgia

Alexa B. North

State University of

West Georgia

Carrollton, Georgia

Melinda McCannon

Gordon College

Barnesville, Georgia

The relationship between employers and employees is changing. Today, and certainly in the future, employers will treat employees more like customers—internal customers (Srikonda & Connell, 2000). The field of internal marketing, which emphasizes employees as internal customers, identifies internal support activities and operations as a key link to external customer satisfaction. Research indicates that the existence of service-oriented human resource management practices and procedures correlates strongly with customer perceptions of high-quality service (Sergeant & Frenkel, 2000). In other words, how internal customers are treated within the organization affects how they will treat customers outside the organization.

Business teachers must address these new customer concepts and focus instruction on skills in building and maintaining positive relationships. The purpose of this chapter is to help teachers integrate these concepts and skills into instruction by addressing several questions: Why are the soft skills emphasized so strongly as a factor for success in technology environments? How has technology influenced customer recruiting and service? What changes in the way work is done demand attention to soft skills? How technology use policies and practices affect employee-employer relationships, particularly in relation to privacy and remote work environments? This chapter also suggests what teachers can do to prepare students to practice appropriate customer service skills. Student activities are included to illustrate how to bring the concepts into the instructional environment. A list of additional resources supplements those used in the chapter to provide teachers with more complete information as they engage their students in learning activities.

TECHNOLOGY AND SOFT SKILLS

Business education instruction focuses on the skills necessary to use technology to generate new information and to access and modify existing information. However, as the Policies Commission for Business and Economic Education (2000) has noted,

> ... [s]tudents entering today's dynamic workplace must possess business-related, nontechnical (soft) skills as well as technical competence. Success in the twenty-first century business environment is dependent on a refocus on skills that were emphasized in the twentieth century.

Technology, as it is implemented and used, affects employees' relationships with customers, with each other, and with supervisors and employers. Soft skills have become critical in the technology environment. Teachers can reinforce this point through activities focusing on customer service.

STUDENT ACTIVITY

Customer Service

Have students discuss their experiences with customer contact personnel in technology areas. Start by asking the following questions and building on students' answers:

- Have you ever dealt with customer service personnel at a store? Describe your experience.
- Have you ever returned something for an exchange or refund? Describe your experience.
- How many of you own a computer?
- Have you ever had a problem with your computer and had to take it in for service? Describe your experience.
- Have you ever had a problem with your computer and had to call a help desk? Describe your experience.
- Have you ever had a problem with you computer and had to solve it yourself by contacting an online help desk through the Internet or e-mail? Describe your experience.

In the last 15 years information technology (IT) has evolved from mainframe-based applications to network systems with many different types of technology (LANs, WANs, telecommunications equipment, and UNIX or PC file servers) providing around-the-clock services (McBride, 2000). Employees need access to the information that technology can provide at all times to support themselves. Additionally, relationships with external customers have changed as a result of changes in technology.

Changes in Customer Recruiting and Service

Sir Colin Marshall, British Airways chairman, has illustrated the importance of this customer orientation in the business sector: "If those of us who head companies don't keep our customers in sight and earshot all the time, we deserve to be passed over." The world's largest and most consistently profitable international airline owes much to what Sir Colin calls his "evangelistic determination to strive for customer-service excellence" (PricewaterhouseCoopers, 1998, p.1). This view is being echoed throughout the economy.

Forms of customer service delivery are evolving rapidly with changes in technology. Simultaneously, IT is undergoing a process of migration, from a support function to a customer-contact function (Sergeant & Frenkel, 2000). Effective use of customer service technologies adds value to organizations by enhancing service quality and contributing to competitive advantages in service delivery.

As technology becomes more closely integrated with the achievement of marketing and strategic objectives, greater attention is being paid to ensure that technology operates effectively to meet or exceed appropriate service levels (Sergeant & Frenkel, 2000). Marketing practices to recruit new customers are viewed as the start of a business relationship that is then maintained by delivery of high-quality customer service.

Changes in customer recruiting. Marketers expect to spend $73 billion on e-mail marketing by 2005 (James, 2000). E-mail marketing can generate a 10- to 20-percent response rate compared with banner ads, which generate a rate of less than one percent (Merrick, 2000). E-mail marketing is an effective and legitimate marketing technique. However, to collect e-mail addresses, marketers must ensure that customers are willing to provide contact information and grant permission to receive electronic messages. Otherwise, the companies that the marketers represent may be accused of "spamming" (James, 2000).

Spamming is sending unsolicited e-mail messages, usually advertising, in bulk to thousands of people (Foster, 2000). Spamming can cause customers to view a company unfavorably and will cause some Internet service providers to block a company's Internet access. To avoid being labeled a spammer, a company must not only get permission to send electronic advertising but must also give customers an easy way to remove their names from the mailing list (Merrick, 2000).

Companies that take care of their customer relations can look forward to productive use of their marketing dollars. If they do not follow these rules, companies may not only face a loss of marketing dollars but also irreparable damage to their reputation.

Changes in customer service. The customer service environment has changed dramatically in the past ten years, mainly as a result of technology. The appearance of electronic commerce on the Web, for example, is one of several factors that has changed the demand for customer service delivery. Electronic commerce and business activities include buying and selling goods or services via the World Wide Web and the Internet, transferring electronic funds, and exchanging data (McBride, 2000).

Due to the volume of these common transactions, help desks and support centers have been renamed "contact centers" to emphasize the fact that they are more directly involved in company business. Information is frequently received at these contact centers via the Internet or e-mail. Excellent customer service requires a comprehensive approach based on good communication skills as well as appropriate technology systems.

A customer service system should be an "invisible" system. The system should be designed so that the external customer is not inconvenienced by or even aware of the steps being taken to fulfill his or her service requests (Huggins, Long, & Sundberg, 1997). Many companies now use a form of computer/telephone integration. This technology unites a computer system with a telephone system so that the two technologies function seamlessly as one system. The multifunctional structure is designed to assist customers in an efficient, effective manner. Examples include automated attendants, automatic call distributors, and interactive voice response systems to meet customers' needs.

Changes in Work Relationships

Competition in business today has created a desire and need for teams. The delegation of duties is being changed through a redesign of the work process. This delegation process is, in turn, creating team environments in organizations. Teams are essential for tasks that are too complex for one person to complete or that require the expertise of several individuals (Stiger, 1998). Cleland (1996) has stated, "The traditional model of organizational design is an endangered species" (p. vii). Many businesses have modified their organizational design because they view teams as an effective way to involve employees and solve problems. Consequently, Cleland (1996) has described teams as the "common denominator of organizational change" (p. 9).

With the obvious influx of teams and the changing technology in today's businesses, employees must go beyond a traditional team environment and use today's technology effectively. Schwartz (1991) has stated that simple distinctions between information and data are not enough. Teams can interact and discuss possibilities, implications, and meaning. Humans learn about possibilities and implications from stories rather than from facts, checklists, and process descriptions. Rather than answering the traditional business question, "Are the data correct?", teams allow members to discuss the more innovative business question, "What is the meaning of the information we have?"

As companies have begun to cooperate globally, they have discovered the value of collaborative work (Kimball, 1997). As teams shift to more virtual environments, they are not bound by physical locations and may never meet in person; consequently, they must work harder during the team-forming stage. During this stage, the members get to know each other and learn about each member's strengths and weaknesses. This may be difficult or take longer in a totally virtual environment. Learning activities can help students to experience and evaluate this process.

STUDENT ACTIVITY

Virtual Teams

Group students in teams and have each team complete an entire project virtually. For example, task each team with researching and recommending the purchase of new computers for the computer lab. Include requirements, such as that each team compare prices on hardware, software, peripherals, etc., and that the teams never meet in person, but conduct all interactions electronically. Impose other restrictions to enhance the "virtual" nature of the experience. After students complete the project via totally virtual teams, have them word process a two-page report documenting the pros and cons of working in virtual teams. Also have students discuss the "getting-acquainted" aspects of their experience.

The mission of the organization must provide a common goal for all team members. This mission will be carried out by team members and enforced by managers in the organization. Managers must change their mindset to one of managing processes and not necessarily managing individuals. Telleen (1997b) has noted that "[s]ome managers are beginning to realize that successful management has been accomplished by managing knowledge and facilitating the flow of information. As the trend continues, we can expect knowledge management to become the business of managers" (p.1). Likewise, successful management will bond with effective teams that create new knowledge.

ISSUES IN EMPLOYER-EMPLOYEE RELATIONSHIPS

With the increased use of the Internet for communication and work, employers and employees are faced with questions about acceptable practices in the workplace. What rights do employees have? What should employers expect? What can employers do to protect their employees and themselves from problems stemming from the use of the Internet? These issues can be discussed using two categories: privacy and remote work.

Employee Privacy

Employees want to feel that they have a certain amount of privacy at work. The manner in which the employer handles supervision affects the employee's feelings of privacy. Employer monitoring of electronic mail is a case in point. Many employees may believe that e-mail is protected from being opened and read by others in the same way that postal mail is. However, there is no federal law that prohibits an employer from reading any e-mail or computer file, including bookmarks or lists of Web pages that an employee has visited.

Monitoring practices by employers have led to employee reports of physical and mental stress and increases in sick leave due to stress. Continued stress ultimately leads to low employee morale and high employment turnover rates (Jitendra & Crampton, 1998).

Legislation has been introduced to address the issue of employee privacy. Though the Notification of Employee Monitoring Act (H.R. 4980) died in subcommittee hearings in 2000, some expect it to be resurrected in the near future. This bill is supported by the American Civil Liberties Union, which is lobbying hard for stricter privacy laws to protect employees (Borck, 2000).

Some individuals ask why companies resort to monitoring their employees' e-mail and other Internet activities if this monitoring is associated with claims of employee stress and possible government intervention. There are a number of reasons. First, monitoring gives employers an idea of which employees are being productive and which employees are wasting company time. For example, employers want to know whether Web and e-mail resources provided by the company are being used for personal or job-related purposes. Second, employers want to protect themselves from employees who might engage in corporate espionage. Knowing that employers have access to the e-mail system may discourage employees from revealing corporate information.

The main reason for monitoring, however, is the employer's responsibility for the actions of their employees. Companies may be held liable if their employees send electronic messages that are threatening, harassing, or sexually explicit, or if employees download pornographic or copyrighted material from the Internet to company computers (Jitendra & Crampton, 1998). Until companies can find other ways to keep their employees from straying from the proper use of the Internet, employers will continue to scrutinize employee activities.

Employees should be made fully aware of what is acceptable use of the Internet at work. First, companies should have a formal, written electronic communication policy that is distributed to all employees (Anonymous, 2000; Morgan, 2000). The policy should state clearly that any means of electronic communication is the exclusive property of the employer and that the employer reserves the right to monitor all communications. The electronic communication policy should also refer to the company's guidelines against sexual harassment and discrimination. In addition, the employer should state that the company reserves the right to block access to chat rooms and inappropriate Web sites. With such a detailed policy, employees should not be able to claim that the employer has violated their privacy. Nor should employees be able to claim ignorance of the rules (Morgan, 2000).

Some companies take the policy issue one step further by appointing a chief privacy officer (CPO). This person not only educates employees about the privacy they can and cannot expect at work but also educates the employer about customer privacy issues. Companies must be extremely careful with their customer databases when doing business. A CPO can help a company maintain confidentiality and avoid losing customers (Nash, 2000).

Remote Work and the Virtual Office

With the use of technology, employees can work anywhere at anytime with little or no direct supervision. This ability brings new challenges to both employers and employees. More companies are giving their employees an opportunity to work from a remote location, generally called telecommuting. In fact, an estimated 19.6 million

STUDENT ACTIVITY

Company Internet and E-Mail Policies

Have students contact local companies to ask for examples of or details about their Internet and/or e-mail policies. Also, have students search the Internet for companies to see if their Internet and/or e-mail policies are posted online. Using these examples, have students create an Internet and e-mail policy for the school.

Note to teachers: You may want to have this activity precede discussion of the school policy. Students can compare the policy they have written with the school's policy.

Americans now telecommute on either a full- or part-time basis (Greenwald, 2000). Companies have found that telecommuters consistently (1) prove themselves to be more productive, (2) are less apt to call in sick, and (3) accomplish more in the same number of hours than employees who come into the office every day (Wilde, 2000).

When a telecommuting program is successfully implemented, companies can give up costly office space and attract and retain talented employees who cannot or will not relocate to a fixed office site (Schilling, 1999). Yet, not everyone should telecommute. Successful telecommuters are people whose job requires them to spend most of their work-related time on the computer or telephone. Telecommuters should be people who (1) can organize and manage their time because there will not be someone to physically supervise them, (2) are good performers and are self-motivated to meet deadlines, and (3) are comfortable with a relative degree of isolation from other employees (Schilling, 1999). Once telecommuters have been chosen, there are other issues that must be addressed before the work relationships can be successful.

STUDENT ACTIVITY

Telecommuter Self-Assessment

As a critical-thinking activity, provide a case study about a hypothetical candidate for a telecommuting position. In groups or in full-class discussion, ask students to analyze this candidate's strengths and limitations. As a follow-up activity, ask students to list the attributes that would make them successful as telecommuters and attributes that would make them less likely to succeed. This may be done in a journal or personal log. Ask students to decide what comments they want to contribute to a general class discussion so that they are not required to reveal facts that they consider private or personal. Conduct a brief follow-up discussion during the next class period.

Issues Affecting Telecommuters

A concern for individuals who work at a distance and their employers should be the ergonomics of whatever location is used as the virtual office, such as the home office. Employers must also be concerned about security, supervision, and benefits when employees work at a distance.

Ergonomics. An employee cannot set up a computer on the kitchen table and call it an office. Having a well designed, ergonomically correct, and safe office, may reduce the risk of injury and resulting claims against the employer. Although telecommuters tend to file fewer worker's compensation claims per employee than do those who work at the employer's location, employers still must take ultimate responsibility for the safety of the home office (Atkinson, 2000).

A home office that does not have an ergonomically correct workstation can cause a telecommuter to experience musculoskeletal disorders. According to the Occupational Safety and Health Administration (OSHA), these disorders account for 34 percent of all work-related injuries and illnesses. Although OSHA established and then rescinded rules specifically about the home office, telecommuters should be concerned with their own health (Hoffman, 2000; Loiacono, 2000). To minimize the possibility of experiencing injury or illness, the workstation must have adjustable chairs, desks with adjustable keyboard platforms, and adequate lighting (Tyler, 1998).

In addition to ergonomically correct workstations, a home office should, at a minimum, conform to the following safety checklist:

- Does the space seem adequately ventilated?
- Is the space reasonably quiet and free of distractions?
- Are all the stairs with four or more steps equipped with handrails?
- Are all circuit breakers and/or fuses in the electrical panel labeled as to intended service?
- Do circuit breakers clearly indicate if they are in open or closed position?
- Is all electrical equipment free of recognized hazards that would cause physical harm (e.g., frayed wires, bare conductors, loose wires, flexible wires running through walls, exposed wires fixed to the ceiling)?
- Are electrical outlets three pronged (grounded)?
- Is the computer equipment connected to a surge protector?
- Are aisles, doorways, and corners free of obstructions to permit visibility and movement?
- Are file cabinets and storage closets arranged so drawers and doors do not open into walkways?

STUDENT ACTIVITY

Ergonomics

Have students conduct research using the Internet, the media center, and other resources to find information about ergonomically correct office design such as furniture, layout, color, lighting, etc. Using the information from this research and if available, a painting/drawing software package, have students create an ergonomically correct home office for a telecommuter. Have them include with the design a word-processed one-page document to defend their choices or be prepared to give a five-minute oral presentation to the class.

- Is the space crowded with furniture?
- Are the phone lines, electrical cords, and extension wires secured under a desk or along a baseboard?
- Are floor surfaces clean, dry, level, and free of work or frayed seams?
- Are carpets well secured to the floor, and free of frayed or worn seams? (Laws, 2000, p. 32)

Security of remote sites. Employers should establish policies that cover home security topics such as who has access to the company computer, how to store or destroy sensitive data, how often to back up information, and what types of virus-protection or firewall software to install (Greenwald, 2000; Reidy, 2000). Involving the IT department in decisions about security and computer applications at the beginning of the telecommuting process is important because the IT department will probably have to diagnose and solve any problems that arise (Wilde, 2000).

Other telecommuting issues. Another issue that employers must address is the employee's job functions. Each telecommuter should have a written job description just as office-bound employees do. In addition, employers should cover such topics as how often a telecommuter comes to the office, how new assignments are received, how a telecommuter's job performance will be measured, and how a telecommuter will interact with supervisors. Having such policies in writing will help to decrease problems and misunderstandings when it is time for performance reviews (Greenwald, 2000).

Insurance issues that are unique to telecommuters are sometimes overlooked. Employers need first-party property insurance to cover damages to company property taken or removed from the telecommuter's control and loss of or damage to personal property of a third party that was in the telecommuter's care, custody, or control. Also, error and omissions insurance coverage can protect against the inadvertent loss of company information or property due to a telecommuter's negligence (Reidy, 2000).

TRAINING FOR CUSTOMER SERVICE

Support environments, which are made up of personnel who assist a variety of internal and external customers, vary to support the roles or the goals of business. For example, support environments for a government agency or educational institution are different than for a for-profit organization. However, because support environments have common requirements, they use many of the same processes (McBride, 2000).

A support model with at least two to three levels is the norm. A level is defined by the amount of interaction a support person or group has with customers. Level one, or frontline, support is involved in the point of first contact; level two consists of members with more experience in or knowledge of a particular subject. These levels deliver services that range from answering simple questions to solving in-depth technology problems. These levels deliver service via technologies such as personal computers, telephones, fax machines, and e-mail.

Processes common to support environments include logging calls and managing and resolving problems (McBride, 2000). The process of logging calls creates records to detail problems, requests, and questions. Managing and resolving problems require discovering the causes of problems and removing or correcting them. Communication is vital to this process.

The Front Line: First-Level Skills

Quite often, a caller's first contact is with an automated attendant that answers calls with a recorded message, identifying the company and giving instructions for reaching specific extensions or departments. However, if a caller does not know this information, the call is typically directed to a first-level customer contact employee who can properly forward the call.

First-level customer contact employees perform a clearinghouse function. Consequently instead of solving the customers' problems themselves, they determine the nature of the customer's problem or request. Customer contact employees must be active listeners, able to relay information correctly to and from the external customer, and able to route information to a professional staff member who has the training and authority to answer questions or take the necessary action.

Organizing data meaningfully is an essential function, and the success of the customer contact employee depends on this process. The employee must be prepared to turn raw facts or data into information. The customer contact employee must be an active listener and able to relay information to the customer on an appropriate language level.

Many phone systems currently have automated attendants, and customers simply press numbers on the phone that guide them through the phone system electronically. Because of this, many people believe that phone skills are not as important today as in previous years. This is not so, however. Customers often prefer human interaction and may need an explanation or the calming effect of a human, not a machine.

Referrals: Second-Level Skills

Once an external customer is referred, customer service representatives perform a problem-solving function. As problem solvers, these individuals should complete training to handle customer questions or to take the necessary action. In addition, customer service representatives have electronic access to customer information files and can add information to a customer database.

A call management strategy is a collection of tools, techniques, and approaches that successfully move a call from the initial customer contact employee through the end of the call. Call management has four goals: (1) to provide the user with the needed information, (2) to manage stress levels for both the caller and the support specialist, (3) to ensure that the call progresses in an effective and efficient manner, and (4) to make the user more self-reliant (Beisse, 1999). A call management strategy should be based on comprehensive company policy, philosophy, and expectations.

Whether the student prepares specifically for a support position or some other position, their responsibilities are likely to bring them into direct contact with customers. Developing listening, telephone, problem-solving, and other customer service skills will contribute to their success and that of the organization.

STUDENT ACTIVITY

Clearing Up Muddy Points

This exercise will facilitate peer teaching, problem solving, and the development of critical thinking—skills that are needed in customer service roles. This exercise may be used with any new topic that is introduced to a class, including a discussion of the multilevel support model and its levels.

As students enter class, give each an index card with "muddiest point" written at the top. During the class discussion on the chosen topic, have students use the reverse side to note points on which they are not clear (muddy). For closure, have students write the one point they found most confusing or unclear (muddiest).

When the presentation is complete, divide the students into groups. Have them compare their "muddiest points" and have them work together to clear up the confusion. At the end of the group discussion, if any questions still remain "muddy" to all members of the group, a member of each group should write the questions on the card and be prepared to discuss it with the class and teacher.

Note to teachers: Encourage students to answer the "W-H" questions in relation to the topic: Who did/does what? When? Where? How? and Why? Emphasize that individuals sometimes provide the wrong support to customers when the customer's problem is "muddy." They may need to interact with the customer to clarify the customer's request using the "W-H" questions.

ATTITUDE CHANGE AS A SOFT SKILL

The need to pair technology skills and soft skills in business education is dramatically illustrated when employment facts are considered. Between 1998 and 2008 U.S. employment is expected to rise from 140.5 million to 160.8 million (Kelinson & Tate, 2000). In addition to supporting an increasing number of telecommuters, technology will play an even more important role in shaping the future world of work. Three predictions by futurists (Challenger, 2000) deal specifically with technology:

1. Most workers' primary activities will involve IT. Computer networks will be interconnected with information systems that will affect all industries, and workers who can step into the new job categories created by these networks and their implementation will be in strong demand.
2. With the increased use of portable technology tools, companies will want individuals who can work extremely flexible schedules. Workers who can be available to employers and clients at a moment's notice will be highly sought after. The traditional weekend will no longer exist.
3. Employees will become increasingly isolated. The portable technology tools that allow for flexibility in scheduling will also contribute to the decrease in face-to-face

exchanges. The result may be a decline in social skills and a hindrance to team problem solving.

A few examples of technology trends include increased use of wireless data transmission, the "ever-shrinking PCs, the replacement of CD-ROM drives with DVD, speech and handwriting recognition, 'smart' appliances, virtual reality interfaces, and the first non-military applications for ultra-wideband wireless communication" (PricewaterhouseCooper, 2001a, p.1). Technological changes are complex and continually influence the knowledge base required by all individuals. "People will become the key element, not as versatile machines but as repositories of unique knowledge to be shared and blended" (Telleen, 1997a, p.3).

From these trends, one can see that success for employees, employers, and educators will depend on embracing technology and on flexibility and adaptability. Positive attitudes toward increasingly rapid changes in technology are also part of the soft skill set. This encompasses attitudes of students toward technology careers and attitudes of teachers toward teaching the soft skills.

Changing Attitudes Toward Technology Careers

According to the U.S. Bureau of Labor Statistics and industry observers, the country faces a critical shortage of high-tech workers. Approximately 800,000 IT jobs are expected to be vacant by 2002 and one million by 2003. The technology field will create more than five million new jobs between now and 2008. However, women, who comprise half the U.S. population, currently fill only a small fraction of the IT jobs. Further, the Commission for Advancement of Women and Minorities in Science, Engineering, and Technology Development reports that today only seven percent of science, engineering, and technology jobs are filled by minorities (Gaudin, 2000).

Business teachers must address basic attitudes toward technology careers so that underrepresented groups will seek and prepare for those opportunities. Teachers may want to engage students in discussions of how they feel about handling the hardware and software components of systems, designing technology environments for people, and careers involving help desks and other information management areas.

Teaching Soft Skills

Just as employees are internal customers of businesses, students are internal customers of educational institutions. Most students come into schools empowered by technology. It is a challenge for educators to stay abreast of ever-changing technology and the limitless amounts of information that the Internet brings.

No teacher can have total mastery of technology knowledge or every subject. However, there are certain soft skills that all students should know. In every class, teachers can prepare students to interact with and appreciate others, to solve problems, to think and function independently, and to think and functions in teams. Teachers can also help students transfer their knowledge base from one situation to another.

Just as business managers do, educators need to understand the people they are working with and themselves. Teachers need to know when to redefine themselves, others, and goals. The business world has shifted away from traditional assets towards intellectual assets, and companies are increasingly judged by their knowledge assets and their use of those assets to create value (PricewaterhouseCoopers, 2001b). Similarly, educators are held accountable for their students' learning. Businesses increasingly depend on educators to provide them with intellectual assets—students with knowledge, technical skills, and soft skills.

Evaluating Attitudes Toward Pace of Change

As the list of topics about which business educators should heighten their awareness grows, business educators will have to decide how to address their own attitudes toward the increasingly rapid changes in technology and help students adjust to the pace they will face throughout their careers. The following are a few examples of emerging technology education topics:

- Development of Internet2—test bed for advanced technologies like digital video, multicasting, and distributed storage
- Advancement of wireless technologies to alleviate the boundaries of wires
- Advancement of networking technologies moving toward Gigabit Ethernet and Terabit Ethernet
- Convergence of voice and data that will give new meaning to "voice-mail"
- Placement of pace-based satellite networks to serve remote locations
- Production of digital-signal processor (DSP) power to squeeze more data onto smaller lines
- Advancement of computer security and demand for security specialists
- Creation of new chief knowledge officer positions to help manage users and help them put data to competitive use
- Utilization of Extensible Markup Language (XML) to pick up where HTML leaves off
- Building of Linux platforms offering more immediate response than Microsoft platforms
- Advancement of DSL technologies to include high-bit-rate DSL, very-high-density DSL, symmetric DSL, and ISDN DSL
- Introduction of micropayments as companies may charge small amounts for products and services (i.e., charge a nickel to view an article)
- Advancement of collaborative tools to combine historical data, predictive analysis, and real-time discussion to create a faster decision-making process (International Association of Administrative Professionals, 2000)

Change is evidenced by developments in materials, equipment, and processes to improve goods and services. Individuals must change their attitudes, skills, and knowledge bases, as well. Eckhard Pfeiffer, CEO of Compaq Computers Corporation, has summed it up by stating, "Compaq employees know that individual and collective success can only continue if they embrace change as an opportunity rather than reacting to it in a crisis mode" (PricewaterhouseCoopers, 1998, p.1).

CONCLUSION

This chapter's message is that soft skills must be partnered with technology skills for students to be successful. Technology directly and indirectly changes relationships. Changes in the importance of the external customer have brought about changes in the ways employers view employees. Both are customers with needs, and building and maintaining positive relationships depend on understanding common concerns about privacy, as well as clarifying policies and maintaining consistent and respectful practices.

Because technology is influencing and will continue to influence work, this chapter discussed customer service skills and the organization of these support services. Telephone, listening, and problem-solving skills are valuable for every student, and vital for those who will pursue careers working in help desks and other customer service areas. Attitudes toward technology and toward the pace at which technology changes must also be addressed by teachers and students. The business education classroom must be one that addresses both soft skills and technical skills, and the activities included in this chapter illustrate some ways that teachers can develop soft skills.

RESOURCES

Teachers frequently ask for additional resources. The following list includes ergonomics, workplace privacy, and telecommuting resources:

Ergonomics

Cherniak, M. (Ed.). (1999). *Office ergonomics*. Philadelphia: Hanley & Belfus.

International Ergonomics Association—Federation of ergonomics and human factors societies around the world. Retrieved from the World Wide Web: http://www.iea.cc/index.cfm

Meister, D. (1999). *The history of human factors and ergonomics*. Mahwah, NJ: Lawrence Erlbaum Associates.

Occupational Safety & Health Administration. (n.d.). *Comprehensive rules and regulations about ergonomics* [Video]. Retrieved February 14, 2000, from the World Wide Web: http://www.osha.gov/

Oborne, D. (Ed.). (1995). *Ergonomics and human factors*. Aldershot, UK: Elgar.

Privacy in the Workplace

American Civil Liberties Union. *Statement on privacy*. Retrieved from the World Wide Web: http://www.aclu.org/privacy/

Center for Social & Legal Research. *Privacy & American business*. Retrieved from the World Wide Web: http://www.pandab.org/

Lessig, L. (1999). *Code and other laws of cyberspace*. New York: Basic Books.

Privacy Rights Clearinghouse. Retrieved from the World Wide Web: http://www.privacyrights.org/

Whitaker, R. (1999). *The end of privacy: How total surveillance is becoming a reality*. New York: New Press.

Telecommuting

Dinnocenzo, D. A. (1999). *101 tips for telecommuters: Successfully manage your work, team, technology, and family*. San Francisco: Berrett-Koehler.

Igbaria, M. & Tan, M. (Eds.). (1998). *The virtual workplace*. Hershey, PA: Idea Group Pub.

International Telework Association and Council. Retrieved from the World Wide Web: http://www.telecommute.org/

Nilles, J. M. (1998). *Managing telework: Strategies for managing the virtual workforce*. New York: Wiley.

Smart Valley telecommuting guide—Step-by-step guide to implementing a telecommuting program. Retrieved from the World Wide Web: http://smart2.svi.org/PROJECTS/TCOMMUTE/TCGUIDE/

REFERENCES

Anonymous. (2000, November). The need to be "fair" with employees. *Agency Sales, 30*(11), 18–21.

Atkinson, W. (2000, July). Is worker's comp changing? *HRMagazine, 45*(7), 50–61.

Beisse, F. (1999). *A guide to computer user support*. Cambridge, MA: Course Technology/Thomson Learning.

Borck, J. R. (2000, November). Full, open disclosure of e-resource policies yields better feelings from your employees. *InfoWorld, 22*(47), 80.

Challenger, J. A. (2000, September/October). 24 trends reshaping the workplace. *The Futurist, 34*(5), 35–41.

Cleland, D. I. (1996). *Strategic management of teams*. New York: John Wiley & Sons, Inc.

Foster, E. (2000, November). What's it worth to you to get off the 'legitimate' spammers' mailing lists? *InfoWorld, 22*(45), 101.

Gaudin, S. (2000, July 17). Women, minorities could fill more high-tech jobs. *Network World, 17*(29), 9, 16.

Greenwald, J. (2000, January 24). Are workers safe at home? *Business Insurance, 34*(4), 1,28.

Hoffman, M. A. (2000, January 31). OSHA allays concerns over telecommuting. *Business Insurance, 34*(5), 2, 4.

Huggins, K., Long, D. L., & Sundberg, C. W. (1997). *Customer service in insurance: Principles and practices* (2nd ed.). Atlanta, GA: Life Office Management Association (LOMA) Associate Customer Service Program.

International Association of Administrative Professionals. (2000). *Future technology trends—coming your way*. Retrieved July 3, 2001, from the World Wide Web: http://www.iaap-hq.org/ResearchTrends/futuretrends.htm

James, D. (2000, October). Addresses are the issue. *Marketing News, 34*(21), 19–20.

Jitendra, M. M., & Crampton, S. M. (1998, Summer). Employee monitoring: Privacy in the workplace. *S.A.M. Advanced Management Journal, 63*(3), 4–14.

Kelinson, J. W. & Tate, P. (2000, Spring). The 1998–2008 job outlook in brief. *Occupational Outlook Quarterly, 44*(1), 2–39.

Kimball, L. (1997). *Teams strategies conference*. Toronto, Canada: Federated Press.

Laws, J. (2000, March). Online telecommuting resources. *Occupational Health & Safety, 69*(3), 32.

Loiacono, K. L. (2000, April). Ergonomics causes quite a stir. *Trial, 36*(4), 11.

McBride, D. (2000). *A guide to help desk technology, tools & techniques*. Cambridge, MA: Course Technology/Thomson Learning.

Merrick, B. (2000, October). Beware of e-mail marketing pitfalls. *Credit Union Magazine, 66*(10), 20.

Morgan, C. (2000, May). The write stuff. *Rough Notes, 143*(5), 28–30.

Nash, (2000, November). Chief privacy officers: Forces? or figureheads? *Computerworld, 34*(46), 62.

Policies Commission for Business and Economic Education. (2000). Policy statement no. 67: This we believe about teaching the soft skills: human relation, self-management, and workplace enhancement. Reston, VA: National Business Education Association. Retrieved July 3, 2001, from the World Wide Web: http://www.nbea.org/curfpolicy.html

PricewaterhouseCoopers (2001a). *PricewaterhouseCoopers assesses the future of technology*. Retrieved December 11, 2000, from the World Wide Web: http://www.pwcglobal.com

PricewaterhouseCoopers (2001b). *Six forces shape the future of business*. Retrieved July 3, 2001, from the World Wide Web: http://www.pwcglobal.com/sixforces/PwC_html/index.html

PricewaterhouseCoopers. (1998). *Words of wisdom*. Retrieved July 3, 2001, from the World Wide Web: http://www.pwcglobal.com/gx/eng/ins-sol/spec-int/ceo/wisdomLeadership.html

Reidy, A. M. (2000, January). Home work problems. *ABA Journal, 86,* 70.

Schilling, S. L. (1999). Implementing a successful telework program. *Compensation & Benefits Management, 15*(4), 58–60.

Schwartz, P. (1991). *The art of the long view*. New York: Doubleday Publishing.

Sergeant, A. & Frenkel, S. (2000). When do customer contact employees satisfy customers? *Journal of Service Research, 3*(1), 18–34.

Srikonda, S. L. P. & Connell, L. D. (2000, August). *Industrial Distribution, 89*(8), 52–53.

Stiger, R. R. (1998). *The team*. Presentation in EM 510 Engineering Management Principles Course, University of Idaho at Idaho Falls. Retrieved July 3, 2001, from the World Wide Web: http://www.if.uidaho.edu/~bobs/EM510/Class2stuff/Class2Part%202/sld001.htm

Telleen, S. L. (1997a). *Intranet organization: Chapter 7—Work changes*. Retrieved July 3, 2001, from the World Wide Web: http://www.iorg.com/intranetorg/chpt7.html

Telleen, S. L. (1997b). *Intranets: The new knowledgebase*. Retrieved July 3, 2001, from the World Wide Web: http://www.oracle.com/oramag/oracle/98-Sep/58ind.html

Tyler, K. (1998, September). Sit up straight. *HRMagazine, 43*(10), 122–128.

Wilde, C. (2000, April 10). Telework programs are on the rise. *InformationWeek, 781,* 189–194.

Building Relationships With Learners at a Distance

Vickie Johnson Stout
University of Tennessee
Knoxville, Tennessee

A variety of emerging technologies make teaching and learning possible at any time and from any place. Computer-mediated instruction and satellite-televised instruction top a growing list of avenues for professional and personal development. Piskurich (1998) has identified eight learning technologies as future forces in distance education: (1) Web-based training, (2) desktop conferencing, (3) interactive distance learning through satellite or landline linkages, (4) high-definition television, (5) portable computers, (6) voice recognition technology, (7) wireless personal communication devices, and (8) virtual reality processes. Although these technologies enhance learning opportunities, they do not guarantee that learning will occur. Distance instruction may or may not translate into distance learning.

Building learner relationships is critical in all forms of instruction but requires special attention in virtual learning environments. Distance learning involves more than posting instructional content in cyberspace. Because of the lack of opportunity for face-to-face communications, educators must proactively build relationships with learners. Paradoxically, as access to instruction at a distance grows easier and more plentiful, building relationships with learners at a distance grows more complex.

The purpose of this chapter is to equip educators with insights into specific challenges of and strategies for building relationships with learners at a distance. The challenges facing teachers emerge from using technology for content delivery, interaction, and applications. Challenges also emerge in the form of barriers to learning at a distance. Principles of instructional design suggest strategies for teachers, and a process of continuous quality improvement should help teachers build positive learning relationships. The experience teachers have with conventional learning provides a good starting point for discussion.

COMPLEXITY OF BUILDING RELATIONSHIPS AT A DISTANCE

Two factors contribute to the complexity of relationships in distance learning: teachers' experiences with face-to-face learning and elements of interpersonal relationship building.

Face-to-Face Instruction

The persistent comparison of distance instruction with traditional face-to-face instruction is one source of the complexity in building relationships with distance learners. Face-to-face instruction is a real-time, multisensory experience. Teachers perceive face-to-face instruction as an instructional modality that can adjust rapidly when learning difficulties occur. However, the validity of this perception hinges on two premises. The first is that the instructor and learner have a positive relationship. The second is that the teacher can discern when learning difficulties cause the learner to disconnect from instruction.

If the instructor and learner do not have a relationship or have an unhealthy relationship, even real time, multisensory face-to-face instruction can fall short of fostering learning. While face-to-face instruction does not always lead to learning, it is the instructional modality with which most instructors and learners are accustomed and through which they have engaged in instructional relationship building.

Elements of Interpersonal Relationship Building

The complexity of building relationships with learners at a distance also stems from the status and mix of critical elements associated with building interpersonal relationships. According to Miller, Wackman, Nunnally, and Miller (1988), interpersonal relationships are influenced by: (1) space, (2) energy, (3) time, and (4) choice.

Space. The proximity or closeness of people in interpersonal relationships is only partly physical or geographic. Perception of interpersonal space is also mental, spiritual, and emotional. Individuals determine closeness or distance in terms of values, emotions, beliefs, interests, and comfort zones. A substantial challenge for distance educators is minimizing or alleviating the effects of perceived separation between learners and instructors. Deliberate efforts in the instructional processes should encourage closeness in a learning environment.

Energy. Energy is the drive or vitality that people project in a relationship. Whether a learner is engaged in learning and channeled along a desired learning path depends in part on the energy in the relationship. Energy may be positively or negatively charged and may vary in intensity from moment to moment. Energy can be generated or dissipated and focused or diffused, influencing the satisfaction of the learner. Participation in instruction grows or diminishes in response to satisfaction with the interaction process and/or results. Teachers must channel energy in ways that build and maintain relationships that promote learning.

Time. One person's action becomes the stimulus for another person's response, which, in turn, becomes the basis for alternating interaction. Miller et al. (1988) have emphasized that "relationships become systems which perpetuate the status quo or initiate and incorporate change" (p. 8). The element of time helps people view and value relationships as interactional systems.

Learning is a deliberate form of change, and the scope and sequence of interactions are critical to producing change. Distance learning involves systems that use both asynchronous and synchronous interaction. Crafting the scope and sequence of interactions in each system influences the learner's comprehension and retention levels.

Choice. People choose to either sustain a relationship or change it. Either person in a relationship can change the relationship by changing the interaction system, and every communication exchange becomes a potential turning point for the relationship. Interactions in distance instruction are no different. Every volleyed message has the potential of changing *whether* and *how* the participant—instructor or learner—listens to and values what the other has to convey.

THE INSTRUCTIONAL RELATIONSHIP-BUILDING PROCESS

Building instructional relationships involves cultivating three different but interdependent relationships: the instructor-learner relationship, the learner-content relationship, and the learner-learner collaborative relationship. Through these relationships, the instructor can assist learners in expanding their knowledge, skills, and attitudes. There are varying depths to which each relationship can be built, and achieving some depth in one relationship may be a prerequisite to developing depth in another relationship.

Instructor-Learner Relationship

Relationships develop as instructors and learners build a history of shared experiences. According to Miller et al. (1988), a relationship increases in significance as its history leads to anticipation of future interactions. Regardless of the instructional modality, relationship building is the vertex of teaching and learning.

Building instructional relationships requires "constructive togetherness" (Miller et al., 1988). This refers to processes by which individuals attend and attune to others within the interaction system. Through affirming, energizing, and productive interactions, instructors and learners achieve a state of "we" and "us." Creating opportunities for constructive togetherness is vital because sharing, creating, deciding, and building something together produce high-performance learning. By contrast, "negative togetherness" results in confusion, isolation, lack of cooperation, and lack of energy.

The instructor-learner relationship often serves as the lens through which the learner develops a relationship with the instructional content. Although learners commonly have varying degrees of experience with content, positive instructor-learner relationships enable learners to expand their relationship with the content.

Distance instructors can encourage constructive togetherness through use of a clear and common language about the instructional process and learning performance expectations. Through nonverbal and verbal communications, instructors and learners initiate, build, maintain, and destroy relationships—instructional or otherwise. Nonverbal and verbal communications not only serve as vehicles for interacting, they also serve as indices of whether a relationship exists and, if one exists, how healthy it is.

Distance instructors must incorporate nonverbal communication with verbal communication, using technology as an intermediary. This is no small feat, even for experienced educators. Building relationships from a distance using technology is analogous to instructors and learners turning their backs to one another and then attempting to view each other through hand-held mirrors. Skillful viewing of another person's reflected image depends upon both persons knowing what to look for and how to use the mirror effectively.

Without the benefit of speaking face-to-face and using body language, instructors at a distance must creatively use text and multimedia and capitalize on the potential of distance communication to foster necessary instructional relationships.

STUDENT ACTIVITIES

Distance Media and Communication

Activity 1. Ask students to research/discuss what types of humor or emoticons are appropriate to personalize and help enliven the tone of text messages exchanged between instructors and learners at a distance. Teachers might have novice distance learners demonstrate appropriate use of emoticons and Internet acronyms.

Note to teachers: Calgary Separate School District No. 1 (2001) posts a list of common emoticons and acronyms on its site at http://ww.cssd.ab.ca/tech/learn/email.html.

Activity 2. Have students build a collection of acronyms for frequently used phrases unique to their course.

Activity 3. Have students evaluate the effectiveness of live digital cameras in helping learners and instructors view one another while communicating. Have them examine the impact of the distortion and jerkiness that is associated with minute time delays in real-time communications via the Web.

Learner-Content Relationship

Subject matter content affords a focal point for or touchstone around which communication occurs. The learner and instructor come to know one another in the context of studying subject matter content. The learner-content relationship is the lens that learners use to focus on and progress through the three levels of comprehension: recall, inference, and application.

At the recall level, learners become acquainted with or made aware of content features and relevance. The learner's relationship with content at this level is limited or superficial—lacking context. At the inference level, the learner grows moderately in contextual learning. Based on understanding the features and relevance of content, learners become capable of determining what knowledge, skills, or attitudes they do and do not possess. At the application level, learners possess an advanced or maturing contextual relationship with the content. The learner-content relationship is a prerequisite for the learner-learner collaborative relationship.

Learner-Learner Collaborative Relationship

Learners collaborate most effectively when they have already developed a working relationship with the instructor and with subject matter or instructional content. Until the learner-content relationship is established, learners have nothing with which to collaborate. Consequently, distance instruction should incorporate collaborative problem solving and decision making only after the instructor-learner and learner-content relationships have been cultivated.

As instructors adapt to distance instruction, they should carefully reflect on the relationships in traditional face-to-face instruction that they are trying to build in the distance setting. Generally, instructors work to develop each relationship and then integrate them. In the distance setting, the three relationships—the instructor-learner relationship, the learner-content relationship, and the learner-learner collaborative relationship—in tandem, allow learners to focus on learning in a progressive, integrative manner.

STUDENT ACTIVITY

Growth in Relationships

To help learners understand the connectivity of the three relationships and their own growth over time, have them create a spreadsheet that includes each relationship as a column heading under which entries are made. Ask learners to record examples of interactions that reflect their growth in relationships with the instructor, the content, and other learners in collaborative efforts. As they record entries, encourage learners to look for examples of how their growth in each relationship area impacts the growth of relationships depicted in the other columns.

USES OF TECHNOLOGY IN DISTANCE INSTRUCTION

Distance instruction often involves technology used for an array of instructional functions. These may include using technology to enhance instructional methodologies, delivery, administration, evaluation, and/or communication. Table 1 provides examples of some of the most innovative uses of technology for: (1) content delivery, (2) interaction, and (3) applications.

Table 1. Examples of Technology Used for Distance Instruction and Learning Based on Instructional Methodology

Instructional Methodology	Example
Content Delivery	
Lecture	Streamed video, streamed audio, audio overlaid on/ embedded in presentation graphics, audio used in conjunction with digital still photographs, audio accompanying brief digital photograph-based videos
Demonstration	Synchronous Web-casting, network conferencing, real-time chats accompanied by text, asynchronous use of CD-ROM files, streamed video, streamed audio accompanied by text, presentation graphics with text, audio and digital photographs, series of links
Panel	Streamed video, streamed audio, audio accompanied by text, audio and digital photographs, audio overlaid on/ embedded in presentation graphics
Interaction	
Discussion	Synchronous chats or asynchronous discussion boards
Questioning	Asynchronous discussion boards, large- or small-group discussion pages
Applications	
Role-Play	Streamed video, streamed audio, links, digital photographs and audio, structured chats, threaded discussion
Case Study	Text, audio overlaid with/embedded in text files, audio with digital photographs, video
Simulation	Links; asynchronous text- and graphic-based discussion, exercises, or experiments; CD-ROM files

Content Delivery Methodology

Faculty must learn how to use content delivery technology. Content delivery methods, whether asynchronous or synchronous, include various forms of lecture, demonstration, and panel presentations. However, selected distance instruction experts have reported that synchronous instruction is more efficient than asynchronous, because synchronous delivery is sequential. Asynchronous delivery lends itself to nonlinearity and thus the need for branching (Jones, 2001).

Robert Jackson of the University of Tennessee (Jones, 2001) has suggested that preparation for video conferencing takes 20 to 30 percent more time than preparation for traditional classes. By comparison, Jackson has estimated that asynchronous instruction requires up to 200 to 300 percent more development time than traditional classroom instruction. Jackson has also reported that distance instructors have to design interactive moments when they do not have face-to-face classes. Instructors who teach asynchronously may invest not only two to three times as much time to develop a course, but at least twice as long to produce the course as they would using a traditional delivery system. However, one advantage of asynchronous instruction is its reusability. Jackson's (n.d.) award winning Web-based learning resources library is available online at www.outreach.utk.edu/weblearning.

Information design specialists Hackos and Stevens (1997) have emphasized that information systems design (ISD) conventions or protocol *can*, and generally *do*, condition Internet users to expect predictability in the structure and positioning of information (pp. 53–73). Hackos and Stevens (1997) have recommended that distance instructors determine whether subject matter content information is procedural, conceptual, reference, or hybrid (a combination of procedural and conceptual information). Based on the nature of information, instructors should adhere to information systems design (ISD) conventions.

Positioning information based on category aids users in accessing and consuming information efficiently. An example of such conditioning is the expectation of reference links within Web sites for repeatedly used information or rare and difficult to locate information. Hackos and Stevens have recommended that distance instructors use such categorization of information to their advantage when designing and developing instructional content.

The bottom line is that content delivery methodology should accommodate the building of instructional relationships. Costly investments in instructional development and production can, and often do, compete with methods of interaction that are critical to relationship building.

Interaction Methodology

Table 1 includes examples of technology-based interaction methodologies. Teachers should expect an increased volume of interactions with distance learners. With seemingly 24/7 access to their instructor and classmates, distance learners communicate to clarify messages, report difficulties, and seek feedback. Unlike traditional face-to-face instruction that affords message clarification only during a class session, distance learners may interact at any time. Some learners appear to be more vocal at a distance because they are veiled by the technology that connects them with others.

Teachers can take some steps to manage increased communication: Learners can learn to batch related questions and comments to the instructor. Additionally, rather than entertaining five different inquiries from one learner about an assigned reading, the instructor can encourage students to write questions as single, multipart inquiries. Also, publishing procedures for reporting difficulties can coach and condition learners to communicate succinctly from a distance. Rather than having the instructor and students volley e-mail messages about problems with downloading a lesson file, published guidelines for reporting difficulties can guide learners to report concrete diagnostic information.

By tracking and cataloging commonly asked questions across different iterations or offerings of instructional content, instructors can actually anticipate questions and provide learners with answers to frequently asked questions in the announcements section of a course. Monitoring discussion threads and scheduled chats as well as reviewing archives of discussions can help to document problems and solutions.

Major implications for instructors and learners at a distance include developing written communication skills and proficiency in using technology as a communication tool (Brewer, DeJonge, & Stout, 2001). Effective written communication skills allow instructors and learners to share complete, concise, and clear messages that minimize miscommunication.

Application Methodology

Methodologies that enable learners to apply their learning include, but are not limited to, role-play, case studies, and simulations. These methodologies range from incorporating low- to high-level technology and can provide safe opportunities for learners to practice using knowledge, skills, and attitudes. Collaborative application of learning should occur only after learners have demonstrated maturing relationships with the subject matter content.

Distance instructors frequently use application methods to evaluate learner performance. Through peer review, learners can review their classmates' deliverables. When properly applied using clearly defined rubrics or review criteria, the peer review process can reinforce recognition, comprehension, and retention of key concepts. Peer review can also assess targeted performance results associated with the subject matter content. Teachers should obtain permission and note the creator and other pertinent source information when posting entire or excerpted student work to illustrate exemplary work.

CHALLENGES TO BUILDING DISTANCE RELATIONSHIPS

Learners and instructors communicating at a distance may face a myriad of challenges. Of these, several that recur in distance education deserve special attention: the readiness of instructors and students, time, and technology.

Readiness

Instructor readiness entails: (1) determining the suitability of instructional content for delivery from a distance; (2) accessing resources for building and maintaining virtual learning environments; (3) designing, developing, producing, and delivering content (synchronously and asynchronously); and (4) using technological tools to build connections with learners. Instructor readiness also includes learning about students. Clark (2000, October) has provided a simple online survey for gauging learner preferences for visual, auditory, or kinesthetic learning. Optimally, learners complete such a survey prior to enrolling in instruction so that the teacher knows learning styles and preferences in advance of instruction. Western Governors University (2001) provides an online survey for learners to use in determining whether a distance-delivered course is appropriate for them.

Learner readiness means having the requisite resources to participate in a virtual learning environment. Resources include: (1) reading skills that accommodate consumption of a great deal of predominantly text-based subject matter content in a self-directed manner; (2) network navigation skills; (3) requisite hardware, software, and network access to participate in distance instruction; and (4) ability to adapt to expected and unexpected changes in learning conditions based on and infused with technology.

Lack of instructor *or* learner readiness can impede instructional relationship building. The challenge for instructors is to deal with readiness through aggressive, up-front assessment of self and learners for participation in distance instruction.

Time

Another challenge is whether or not distance instruction conforms to organizational or accreditation time constraints and requirements. For instructors, the challenge involves (1) having limited time to create and deliver distance instruction, and (2) interacting with learners in a timely manner. Instructors must provide timely responses to inquiries, as well as feedback on learner performance. The challenge for instructors and learners is to practice good time management skills and develop a mutually understood and observed rhythm for journeying through distance instruction.

For learners, the challenge involves fixed entry into and exit from instruction. Fixed time parameters for instruction may require learners to move through subject matter content at a pace that does not match their immediate needs and preferences. Distance learners who don't stay abreast of their studies can be quickly engulfed by cumulating work. Disconnected and/or out-of-step learners also miss out on the benefits of incrementally building the instructional relationship.

Technology

Technology poses a challenge because it is constantly evolving. Instructors and learners have to contend with controllable and uncontrollable technological issues. The same technology that makes distance instruction accessible is often unwieldy and unpredictable. The primary challenges posed by technology are anticipating probable difficulties, employing proper practices, and being flexible when uncontrollable difficulties arise.

Meeting these and other challenges depends upon early (1) consideration, (2) detection/recognition, and (3) troubleshooting of problems. By making recording and monitoring problems a standard part of instruction, instructors can more rapidly detect patterns (the *who, what, when, where, why,* and *how* aspects) as they manifest themselves. Instructors can proactively neutralize or minimize the effects of challenges involving readiness, time, technology, and other issues in the distance environment.

RELATIONSHIP BUILDING BY DESIGN

When asked what it takes to formulate effective distance instruction, Hall (2000) recommended examining quality by following principles of good instructional design. Instructional relationships can be built as a function of design and as a result of continually improving processes and practices.

Principles of Instructional Design

The instructional systems design (ISD) model enjoys widespread use by business, industry, and education. It consists of five core processes that make up instructional design and lend themselves to the design of distance instruction. *General Instructional Design Phases* (n.d.) provides an overview of and guidelines for using ISD to develop effective instruction regardless of modality—distance or traditional—and Clark (2000, November) compares and contrasts ISD with other models for planning instruction.

Following the Principles

As shown in Table 2, strategies for relationship building should permeate ISD—from analysis to evaluation. To illustrate, instructor-learner relationship building can begin in the ISD analysis process, as the instructor asks prospective learners about themselves prior to the onset of instruction. Analysis questions can help determine (1) learners' interest in the subject matter content, (2) how much learners already know and can do using the content, (3) learners' learning styles and preferences, and (4) learners' experience with distance learning.

Using these insights, the instructor can design and develop learning experiences that match or complement student learning styles and preferences. Learning experiences are likely to emerge that expand contexts for using subject matter content, thus building the learner-content relationship. If students represent a wide range of learning experiences and subject matter content mastery, instructors can separate content information into granules. These can then be developed into modules that learners can access in either a linear fashion or through nonlinear branching. Modules can be customized to contain text and media consistent with learning styles and preferences. The instructor should develop opportunities for interaction that will cultivate the learner-content relationship.

Instructors can consciously build rapport with students as individuals and as group members during ISD implementation. This is a continuation of the ongoing, design-based process. As learners demonstrate agility in applying content, they can develop their learner-learner collaborative relationships by making decisions and solving problems using subject matter content. At evaluation junctures throughout instruction, learners can confirm whether and to what magnitude they are developing relationships with the subject matter content.

Table 2. Strategies for Relationship Building Through Instructional Design

Instructional Process	Strategy
Analysis	• Use the analysis process for initiating instructional relationship building with learners • Determine learner stages of use and proficiency in receiving and sending different types of information

Design	• Incorporate instructional relationship building within the design process
	• Build learner-centered, information-type foci, and instructor-facilitated instructional designs
	• Build instructional focus that includes learner mastery and emphasizes performance outcomes
	• Relate instructional information to tasks that learners need to perform
	• Design instruction to link rather than combine profound and philosophical information
	• Organize content to support
	  a) Learner stage of use
	  b) Learning styles
	  c) Learning preferences
	  d) Opportunities to assess learner performance
	• Select information design building blocks on the bases of
	  a) Learner stage of use
	  b) Whether information provides context
	  c) Whether the learner needs to make a decision or perform an action
	  d) Whether descriptions are necessary to complete a task
	  e) How the instructional content topic supports learning representative of a particular learning domain

Development	• Incorporate instructional relationship building within the development process • Create instructional resources that accommodate integration of conversational communications within content delivery, interaction, and application methodologies • Use language tools such as analogies and metaphors within content, as appropriate • Adhere to visual principles in the creation of instructional resources such as text and media resources

Instructional Process	Strategy
Table 2. Strategies for Relationship Building Through Instructional Design (continued)	
Implementation	• Incorporate instructional relationship building within the implementation process • Limit evaluative communications during the implementation of an instructional design
Evaluation	• Incorporate instructional relationship building within the evaluation process • Capture evaluation process information at multiple junctures in the instructional cycle

The major processes affected by the introduction of distance instruction technologies are the design, development, and implementation phases (Sanders, 1998). However, instructional relationship building can be optimized in the analysis and evaluation processes. During analysis, the instructor investigates who the learners are and what learning characteristics they possess. During evaluation, the instructor helps learners gauge what has been learned. The instructor can also build connections to future content, helping to develop contextual learning.

Process and Practice Improvement

Improving the process of building instructional relationships involves improving the analysis, design, development, and implementation processes. These are the processes that lead to building instructional relationships.

Honing communication processes (input process, output, feedback, and control) is key, as well, because relationships develop as individuals communicate. Stout and Perkins (1987) have emphasized the importance of practices, such as (1) communicating honestly and respectfully, (2) extending the benefit of doubt, and (3) infusing humor into communication as appropriate and needed. These practices contribute to the development of healthy instructional relationships.

SUMMARY

As access to instruction at a distance grows easier and more widespread, building relationships with learners at a distance grows more complex. Sources of complexity include persistent comparison of distance instruction with traditional face-to-face instruction and the status and mix of the critical elements of space, energy, time, and choice associated with interpersonal relationships.

Successful instructional relationships result from developing three different, but interwoven relationships: the instructor-learner relationship, the learner-content relationship, and the learner-learner collaborative relationship. Through these relationships, the instructor helps learners expand their knowledge, skills, and attitudes. Cultivating the relationship between the instructor and the learner supports the development of the relationship between the learner and the content. This, in turn, equips the learner to collaborate meaningfully with other learners for the purposes of content-related problem solving and decision making.

As instructors adapt to distance instruction, they must reflect on the relationships that foster learning in traditional face-to-face instruction. These relationships must be developed in a distance environment involving technology used for content delivery, interaction, and applications. Instructors should monitor their investments of time in content delivery to preserve time for the interaction that is so critical to relationship building. The implications of interaction between and among instructors and learners at a distance include the growing importance of written communication skills and the need for proficiency in using technology for communication.

In building instructional relationships at a distance, readiness, time, and technology pose challenges to both learners and instructors. Instructors must address these challenges proactively through adherence to principles of good instructional design and continual improvement of processes and practices.

REFERENCES

Brewer, E., DeJonge, J., & Stout, V. (2001). *Moving to online, making the transition from traditional instruction and communication strategies.* Thousand Oaks, CA: Corwin Press.

Calgary Separate School District No. 1. (2001, September). *Enhance learning with technology, be e-mail wise!* Retrieved September 7, 2001, from the World Wide Web: http://ww.cssd.ab.ca/tech/learn/email.html

Clark, D. (2000, October). *Vision, auditory, and kinesthetic survey.* Retrieved September 7, 2001, from the World Wide Web: http://www.nwlink.com/~donclark/hrd/vak.html

Clark, D. (2000, November). *Introduction to instructional system design.* Retrieved September 7, 2001, from the World Wide Web: http://www.nwlink.com/~donclark/hrd/sat1.html

General instructional design phases. (n.d.). Retrieved September 7, 2001, from the World Wide Web: http://www.student.seas.gwu.edu/~sbraxton/ISD/general_phases.html

Hackos, J. R., & Stevens, D. M. (1997). *Standards for online communication: Publishing information for the Internet and World Wide Web, corporate intranets, and help systems.* New York: John Wiley & Sons.

Hall, B. (2000, June). Hall monitor, who's doing it best? *Inside Technology Training, 4,* 44.

Jackson, R. H. (n.d.). *Web based learning resources library.* Retrieved March 2001 from the World Wide Web: www.outreach.utk.edu/weblearning

Jones, C. (2001, January). Ain't got time to teach. *Online Learning, 5,* 62, 66, 68.

Miller, S., Wackman, D., Nunnally, E., & Miller, P. (1988). *Connecting with self and others.* Littleton, CO: Interpersonal Communication Programs, Inc.

Piskurich G. (1998). Future forces. In G. Piskurich & E. Sanders (Eds.), *ASTD models for learning technologies, roles, competencies, and outputs* (pp. 5–6). Alexandria, VA: American Society for Training & Development.

Sanders, E. (1998). Framework for thinking about learning technologies. In G. Piskurich & E. Sanders (Eds.), *ASTD models for learning technologies, roles, competencies, and outputs* (pp. 7–11). Alexandria, VA: American Society for Training & Development.

Stout, V., & Perkins, E. (1987). *Practical management communication.* Cincinnati, OH: South-Western Publishing/Thompson Learning.

Western Governors University. (2001). *Self-assessment for distance education.* Retrieved September 13, 2001, from the World Wide Web: http://www.wgu.edu/wgu/self_assessment.asp

International Business Online

Judee A. Timm
Monterey Peninsula College
Monterey, California

Most people would concur that in the 21st century all business is global business. However, global electronic commerce (e-commerce) is still in its infancy. There are many benefits associated with conducting business when the world is an expanded market for every business, and opportunities for effective and efficient collaboration are limitless. There are also challenges.

The Internet has the ability to free trading partners from the limitations of time, cost, distance, language, and logistics. "It allows suppliers an opportunity to collaborate online, address chain inefficiencies, and provide integrated forecasting of product and logistical needs" ("Suppliers Follow E-Business," 2000, p. 1). The Internet can enable a company to strategically match the right customer to the right supplier using the right channel. More refined services are available to e-commerce business customers worldwide with the Internet providing better discovery services, financial services, sourcing services, and logistics and supply chain management. According to economist Jason Meyers (1999), "Around the world, success will depend on the competitiveness of supply chains and on companies' abilities to work efficiently and effectively with their business partners" (p.1).

In this business world, (1) change is the norm, (2) business rules and paradigms built for regional or national markets may not be valid, and (3) adaptability is the key to success. The challenge for business educators lies in providing quality experiences that will prepare students for tomorrow's business world.

This chapter looks first at the influence of technology on the global marketplace, then presents skills needed for the global business world, and finally recommends some strategies for educating students for their world. Throughout the chapter, student activities illustrate ways to integrate international and technology skills. Readers will see that integrating technology into the global marketplace is a work in progress—a journey so-to-speak—that the global business world is undertaking. On this journey of trial and error, pitfalls and successes, dreams and innovations, a new way of conducting business is emerging that will have far-reaching consequences worldwide.

THE EMERGING GLOBAL INTERNET ECONOMY

The international potential of the Internet cannot be underestimated. "Electronic commerce will be an engine of economic growth in the twenty-first century, with the potential to invigorate economies by enhancing productivity, streamlining distribution, and revamping corporate structures" (Industry Group 91, 1999, p. 1). E-commerce is rapidly spreading beyond U.S. borders. "[B]y yearend [1999] almost 60% of the world's online population will reside outside the U.S., and non-U.S. Internet commerce will explode from 26% of worldwide e-commerce spending in 1998 to 46% by 2003" ("Non-U.S. Internet," 1999, p. 1).

Economic projections business-to-business e-commerce for the year 2004 and beyond show further acceleration. Many feel that business-to-business e-commerce will increasingly dwarf business-to-consumer transfers. "A study by the Boston Consulting Group forecasts that business-to-business e-commerce will quadruple from $1.2 trillion in transaction value this year to $4.8 trillion by 2004" (Miller, 2001, p.3).

The challenges for international online businesses derive from general challenges facing businesses, whether international or not. There are also unique challenges that derive from interacting with actual or potential international markets.

General Challenges for International Online Businesses

Businesses today must be productive, customer oriented, and value added. Productivity requires effective use of technology. All businesses must build customer relationships and implement practices that add value. These relationships and practices must carry over into an international marketplace.

Productivity. Using technology to increase efficiency is part of the productivity picture. Virtual sites allow "a large number of vendors . . . to help large businesses set up hosted marketplaces so their customers will be able to aggregate their purchasing power to obtain better prices from a set of common suppliers" ("Asia's Internet E-Commerce," 1999, p. 1). Covisint, an online automotive business-to-business site, is an example of a hosted marketplace. "General Motors Corp., Ford Motor Co., DaimlerChrysler AG, Renault and Nissan established Covisint . . . as an online automotive B2B aiming to improve the supply chain for auto parts and to pool buying power" (Ross, 2000, p. 2).

Broader gains will be realized when the brick-and-mortar economy incorporates the Internet to increase its productivity. As noted by IBM's Internet strategist, Wladawsky-Berger, "traditional companies will increasingly use the Internet in supply chains, customer relationship management, in ways that integrate all the channels a company has, including the physical infrastructure and the phones" (Holstein, 2001b, p. 40). Treasury Secretary Paul O'Neill projected that "[w]e've only realized about 20 percent of the productivity gains that are available just with existing knowledge and technology" (Holstein, 2001a, p. 40).

Customer relationships. Success involves finding the right niche and figuring out the best way to serve customers. Customer service expectations will shift from quality products, service, and support to relationship marketing, self-service, and value (Kalakota & Robinson, 1999, p. 63). A recent study by American Management Systems, Inc. (AMS, 1999), concurred, listing several strategies to exploit the vast opportunities available in e-commerce to enhance business success.

STUDENT ACTIVITY

Customer Loyalty

Have students determine how an online business leverages customer data to build loyalty by examining a successful online business such as Amazon.com. Ask students to visit the Amazon.com Web site to determine what types of consumer information are collected and how they are used (or can be used) to increase sales and service. What other strategies are used to encourage sales on the Web site? Compare Amazon's techniques to those of another Web-based company.

In courses that include international business or culture content, have students evaluate the online business site for how well it develops customer loyalty and meets cultural expectations for the country or culture under study. For courses that do not have an international or cultural component, ask students who come from different cultural backgrounds or have international experiences to discuss how the online business would meet or fail to meet cultural expectations.

Whether the focus is on the consumer segment or the business customer segment, building international relationships and customer loyalty is key and must be based on a backbone of trust. International customers must be able to trust that their privacy is being protected and transactions are safe. Jeff Kann, who is executive vice president of Visa U.S.A. Inc., said in his testimony to the U.S. Congress, "The future success of international electronic commerce depends on achieving a balance between the need for information and the adequate protection of consumer privacy" ("Electronic Commerce," 1999, p.5). International online businesses must know and observe the privacy laws that affect business conducted in different countries.

Self-service and customer empowerment will play an increasingly important role in the electronic business environment. Customers will not come to the Web unless given a legitimate reason to do so. Companies must identify and use strategies that will motivate each customer segment to use this technology. Integrated marketing activities, where all campaigns, promotions, and marketing initiatives integrate the Web, will help in this effort. Savings or convenience may motivate consumers. Greater control and efficiency may draw in business customers. Easy navigation and online payment options should be interactive, providing information on enhanced payment options, bill analysis, and cost allocation. These practices must be translated for international markets.

STUDENT ACTIVITY

Consumer Sales Approaches

Have students investigate how a traditional (brick-and-mortar) retail establishment (for example, JCPenney, Target, or other business) has incorporated the Internet in its consumer sales approach. Ask students to discuss these questions: What has this businesses done to encourage consumers to use the Web site? What advantages have been realized by the company and by the consumer by using the Internet? What assumptions does the site make about its customer base? Does the site market to international customers? How can you tell?

Value-added practices. Providing value may be the most critical component of success in e-commerce. Several strategies have proven useful to add value and strengthen a Web site for consumers and business customers. Mined intelligence of all customer interactions can be used to improve effectiveness and add value to subsequent interactions. Web alliances also can be formed that add value to the site as a portal to extended services. Additionally, a site that is integrated with suppliers and other partners that strengthen business processes will add value for the business customer. For example,

> Suppliers use the Internet based method to see what parts the factory needs, confirm that the factory has received the shipment, and figure out when they'll get paid. The factory can also use the system to conduct auctions for basic commodities such as masking tape. (Holstein, 2001a, p. 39)

This type of business-to-business automation can provide tremendous value in productivity savings through efficiency.

All of the strategies to increase productivity, serve customers, and add value require diligent effort and constant attention. Gomes (2001) stated that, "In order to make it, Web sites will need to be smartly conceived, well-managed, continually fine-tuned and appropriate for the business sponsoring them" (p. R4).

International Issues for Online Businesses

The Internet has made amazing impacts on the world economy and the way that business is conducted. This, however, is just the beginning of a comprehensive

STUDENT ACTIVITY

Ethics of Data Mining

In small teams, have students discuss the ethical implications of mined intelligence of consumer interactions on the Internet as it relates to consumer privacy and protection. Why is this technique useful for companies? For consumers? What can companies do to maintain consumers' trust that their rights and privacy have been protected?

This activity may be preceded by a presentation (or a student research activity) on the meaning of mining data. Where possible, integrate an international element into the discussion, for example, by having students examine privacy statements of other nations.

transformation that will affect jobs, practices, relationships, and thinking. The full potential of Internet technology will be severely challenged, however, given the constraints of culture, language, infrastructure, governments, and laws. The potential of the Internet will only be realized if people, governments, and businesses are willing and able to embrace this new, dynamic trade medium.

Trade issues. The borderless nature of the Internet makes traditional trade issues quite complex. This is especially evident when dealing with taxation and tariffs.

Current methods of taxing, regulating, and assisting businesses are based on increasingly outdated models. What happens when the unit doing business is no longer the corporation or even the multinational, but an extended enterprise of companies electronically integrated on a global basis? Local content will be impossible to determine, let alone enforce; business income will become more difficult to tax; and transactions will become more difficult to regulate. (Meyers, 1999, p. 1)

It is not clear how countries will deal with these issues, but traditional trade strategies will not apply. Internet-based transactions worldwide must be supported by global initiatives that encourage neutral, fair, and simple trade practices.

Knowing the customer and being assured that business dealings are legitimate can also be quite complex when dealing with global Internet transactions where ". . .e-commerce is conducted remotely between buyers and sellers who may have had no relationship or contact before" ("Electronic Commerce," 1999, p. 3). Authenticating the seller, buyer, and sender is an extremely important global issue. Ensuring that transactions and messages have integrity and have not been altered during transmission is critical to a fair and productive global market.

Advanced electronic authentication mechanisms—digital signatures and digital certificates—have been developed; however, the level of acceptance and the laws regarding the validity of these mechanisms vary around the world. Issues that address whether a digital signature or contract is legally binding as an original have not been universally resolved. International agreements on electronic authentication must be addressed to provide support for worldwide electronic transfers.

Cultural challenges. Although the Internet may someday create its own global culture, e-commerce today still occurs in an environment with many cultural differences. Success in global e-commerce requires strategies that incorporate multilingual, multicultural Web sites. "Companies that sell on the Web will face technical, logistical, and organizational challenges as they try to develop a global Internet strategy that incorporates multilingual e-commerce sites" ("Non-U.S. Internet," 1999, p. 1). An effective global strategy involves thinking locally in each individual market. The electronic environment requires businesses to know the cultural nuances, practices, traditions, and customs of various groups that may frequent the online businesses.

STUDENT ACTIVITY

Research on Countries and Cultures
Assign teams to develop PowerPoint presentations for research projects focusing on various countries. Students should include information on languages spoken in the country, cultural factors, imports and exports, and any other variables of the teacher's choosing based on the business education course objectives.

Note to teachers: Help student develop effective team management skills and schedule class time for teamwork. Meet periodically with the teams to solicit progress reports and answer project questions. This project can complement many of the other student activities in this chapter. Projects that include technology, research, cultural awareness, business awareness, and group interaction serve a multitude of proposes in preparing students for the challenges of the e-business environment.

Technology access and literacy. Another challenge for global e-commerce may involve less-developed countries where the potential for business growth is tremendous. Infrastructure to support technology and technological literacy are lagging in these areas. Daley ("Global Electronic Marketplace," 1998) reported that ". . .telecommunications infrastructure development is quite uneven around the world, ranging from advanced, digitalized networks and applications to very limited and often inefficient basic telephone services" (p. 4). For example, Cornelio A. Bos, director and founder of Direcciones S.A., said that Mexico's "infrastructure cannot yet support the scope that e-commerce has reached in the U.S." This was especially noted in the area of telemarketing, which exploded in the last five years. "With only 10 phone lines per 100 people, . . . The most effective direct marketing technique [in Mexico] remains the old workhorse, direct mail" ("International Round-Up," 2000, p. 8).

Swanson ("International Round-Up," 2000) reporting on conditions in Latin America, said that,

STUDENT ACTIVITY

Internet Access
Have students gather data on the level of Internet access in developing, under-developed, and industrialized countries. Ask students to discuss in small teams the consumer access challenges faced by an international online entrepreneur. What, if anything, can be done to prepare for or overcome this challenge?

> If the Internet is to become an integral part of Latin commerce and communication, it must be woven deeper into the rungs of Latin society. . . . This is going to be a long, costly process, beginning with material technology investment into education systems and less capitalized segments of the private sector. (p. 7)

Another challenge to e-commerce in many parts of the world involves technology literacy levels. In Mexico "only four out of 100 people own a computer and no more than 18 percent of the population has access to a computer at home" ("International Round-Up," 2000, p. 8). The same holds true for many other parts of the world. This issue was addressed in the U.S.-Philippines Joint Statement on Electronic Commerce (Industry Group 91, 1999):

> To avoid the creation of a digital divide on a social, cultural, or geo-graphic basis, we should promote universal technological literacy and encourage the wide availability of information technology at public institutions such as schools, libraries, and community centers. Govern-ments also have an important role to play in ensuring universal access to telecommunications services, particularly for consumers in underserved areas. (p. 2)

It is apparent from these examples that local conditions will continue to shape e-commerce for many years to come.

Many observers feel these challenges are so monumental that it is hard to envision the full potential of global e-commerce ever being realized. In testimony to the U.S. Congress, Kann noted that:

> For global electronic commerce to thrive, it is essential that there be certainty in core electronic commerce legal infrastructure areas, and some degree of uniformity or at least compatibility between countries' laws. Because these laws undergird the tools that help build the highway on which electronic commerce travels, global electronic commerce will not develop to its full potential until these issues are addressed. ("Electronic Commerce," 1999, p. 3)

STUDENT ACTIVITY

Threats to Successful International Online Businesses

Assign groups of students the task of developing a list of possible threats to the success of electronic businesses worldwide. For example, each group can be assigned one component (e.g., culture, infrastructure, education or technological literacy, government, laws, regulations) to focus on by answering the question, "How can [the component] threaten e-business success?" If the component is "culture," for instance, students may note that some cultures do not readily accept technology or that language and traditions may limit productive use of technology, or students may share other observations.

Once the lists of threats are developed, ask students to think of strategies that may help companies prepare for the threats. Each team can then present its ideas to the class. Once all the teams have presented, the class should have a comprehensive view of the challenges of doing business electronically.

As a follow-up assignment, students can research a particular country to identify possible threats to the success of an electronic business strategy.

ESSENTIAL SKILLS FOR THE GLOBAL ELECTRONIC BUSINESS ENVIRONMENT

As new ways to conduct business emerge, companies will face keen competition, globalization, and rapid changes in information technology. To stay ahead of the competition, companies will seek employees who possess skills and competencies that allow them to successfully function in an environment of uncertainty. Workers must know how to obtain information, manage change, and develop effective strategies. According to Davis (1996), a business development consultant,

Workers at all levels need technical skills, the skills to adapt to rapid change, take on increasing responsibility, cooperate more closely with one another, and even demonstrate a strategic understanding of their industries, their jobs, job functions of related departments and their corporate mission. The skill set needed to perform today is broader and deeper—broader involving technical skills and deeper involving problem solving, creative and people skills. (p. 21)

Yet at the very time when these skills seem to be so crucial, businesses encounter an increasing mismatch between available jobs and the competencies of potential employees.

International Skill Set

Table 1 presents a basic skill set that has been adapted for the international online business environment.

Skill Development

Success in an e-business environment requires employees to be computer literate and skilled in using information technology functions, beginning with word processing, spreadsheets, data entry, electronic transfers, and the Internet. More important

Table 1. Global E-Commerce Skills and Competencies

Basic	Employers need employees who can read, write, calculate, and communicate effectively. Today's global e-commerce environment also requires an appreciation and awareness of different languages and cultures.
Technical	Employees "must be computer literate and skilled in using information technology, beginning with word processing, spreadsheets, data entry, and electronic information transfers" (Dudley & Dudley, 1995). Effective use of technological tools in a global business environment will demand an increasing awareness of the issues and responsibilities related to maintaining the integrity and trust involved in sending and receiving transactions worldwide.
Communication and Interpersonal	Communication and interpersonal skills are especially critical because employees must be able to work and interact with global stakeholders including customers, suppliers, investors, and governments. To accomplish organizational goals in the global business environment, employees must be able to collaborate effectively with coworkers from a variety of educational disciplines and cultures.
Critical Thinking	Workers will be asked to use judgment and make decisions. "Critical thinking involves the elements of reasoning: purpose of the thinking, key issue or question being considered, assumption, point of view, evidence, concepts and ideas, inferences or interpretations, and implications of consequences" (Celuch & Slama, 1999, p. 35). Sound decisions will increasingly demand awareness of and sensitivity to the complexities of the global business environment.
Self-Direction and Active Learning	"The most important skill in a knowledge economy is an advanced ability to think and learn" (Davis, 1996, p. 10). Employees in a global business environment must be willing to continually retrain to deal with emerging technologies, systems, and world events.
Creativity	Employers will need creative thinkers who are able to see the possibilities of an emerging global business environment and to embrace the challenges of meeting organizational goals.
Cultural Awareness	To be effective in the global business environment, employees must have an understanding and appreciation of the diverse ethnic, cultural, and socioeconomic backgrounds of their customers, suppliers, competitors, and partners.

than basic computer literacy, however, is possessing a comfort level with technology and the willingness to learn and adapt to new technological developments as they emerge. Employees in this environment must continually train and be trained to keep their competitive edge. They will be responsible for their own learning and must have the ability to search for and access resources that will better enable them to perform their duties effectively.

In addition to technical skills, the global e-business environment will require teams of experts from different disciplines and different cultures to tackle emerging challenges. Employees must be able to work effectively in a multidisciplinary and multicultural environment. This requires good interpersonal and communication skills. As the world of business becomes increasingly complex, companies have realized that effective strategies and solutions are better achieved when individuals from diverse disciplines, viewpoints, and expertise collaborate toward a common objective.

STUDENT ACTIVITY

Creating Slogans for International Markets

Form teams of students so that each team includes at least one student who can speak or is studying a language other than English. Have each team create a short slogan in a foreign language for a product or service. The slogan should include appropriate words, symbols, and currency numbers. Students should submit the slogan in the foreign language with an English translation and explanation of currency values, numbering systems, and units of measurement. Subsequent class discussions may involve students sharing their slogans and reporting their findings. Students can also discuss the implications of conducting business in an electronic environment.

Note to teachers: Good resources for team members to meet with may include students from other countries, speakers of other languages (parents or community members), or foreign language instructors and their classes.

Creativity and critical thinking may be the most important skills for individuals working in an environment where possibilities and opportunities are limitless. As technology becomes increasingly sophisticated, those who can harness these capabilities to better understand their customers, partner with associates, or streamline their procedures will be ahead of the competition. Doing so requires a higher level of thinking and learning. Employees who can see possibilities and carry them into realistic plans and methods will be invaluable contributors in this keenly competitive environment.

In today's highly technical business world, one must never forget that business—all business—involves people. Building positive and binding relationships based on trust and respect is the key to success. This is especially true in global electronic business dealings where the businessperson may never set eyes on the customer being served.

STUDENT ACTIVITY

Respect for International Consumers

Have students develop a list of ways that a company can exhibit respect, integrity, and social responsibility in dealing with overseas customers in an e-business environment. Have students identify ways that a business can convey lack of sensitivity to other cultures and countries.

This can be an individual or group assignment. The result can be a class Web page on guidelines for international business Web sites. This task requires students to think critically about both the presence and absence of text, about the use of graphic information, and about assumptions that are revealed by choices of content for a Web site.

Those who can demonstrate respect and appreciation of cultural differences and respond to diverse demands will be able to seize the vast opportunities that the world has to offer.

Educating for Global E-Business

Preparing students for work in the global e-business environment has never been more challenging for business educators. What experiences can be offered that will allow students to embrace this environment of uncertainty, excitement, and endless opportunity? Doing so is especially difficult when no one really knows where the e-commerce revolution is going. The only thing known for sure is that conducting business in the 21st century will be unlike anything known in the past. It will require individuals who have business and technical knowledge, but more importantly have the initiative and ability to learn independently.

For this reason the best preparation for students entering global e-business occupations may be a series of experiences that allow them to learn by reading, doing, collaborating, researching, and developing. A student who "learns to learn" will be given the greatest tool for success.

Learning by reading. The basic skills of reading, comprehending, and synthesizing information are crucial in international business. Students must be made aware of the social, political, economic, and environmental issues of countries around the world in order to understand the opportunities and risks involved in conducting business. Students also must develop the habit of consistently reading, scanning, and searching for information. There are many good resources online and many excellent journals available for this purpose (e.g., *The Economist* and *The Wall Street Journal*).

Students can keep a reading journal, develop a bibliography of readings, or follow a current event in a market area of interest. Students may also find it interesting to compare and contrast how various current events are reported in different countries. Consistent reading is the foundation upon which all other learning can build. It is imperative that this exercise be incorporated throughout the business curriculum.

Learning by doing. Hands-on experiences give students opportunities to put learned theories and practices into action. Experiences working with various software packages and the Internet are essential to develop a level of comfort with technology as well as the realization that new functions are constantly emerging. Simulations provide supervised opportunities for students to experience how technologies or software programs can work together to solve a business problem or meet an organizational objective. Internships, job shadowing, and cooperative work experiences give students firsthand exposure to how technologies and disciplines can work together in a business environment. When students are actually able to experience the interconnectedness of business processes and procedures they can develop an appreciation for the challenges they will face in the future.

Learning by collaborating. Using teams to solve complex problems is the norm in the e-commerce environment. Not everyone can be an expert in all areas. However, in global e-commerce, expertise in a variety of disciplines is a must. Learning to work productively in a team by being able to communicate, collaborate, and appreciate the value of the process, will enhance a student's potential to succeed.

Teamwork should be an integral part of any business program. Students need opportunities to work with peers from different disciplines and cultures to solve problems or create projects. In order to be successful, students should receive instruction on effective team approaches prior to engaging in teamwork. Virtual teams can be established to give students exposure to working and communicating through electronic media. Using this approach, team members can be assembled from almost any part of the world. Preplanning and prior instruction are essential for learning that involves team processes and management.

Learning by researching. Information overload is the key dilemma in today's business environment. The Internet provides a limitless source of information that students can use. However, they must learn how to manage the information to use it effectively. There are many Web sites that can support research on global e-commerce. Country and market information for most countries is readily available over the Internet. Web sites offer virtual tours of countries and their cultures, virtual marketplaces, and information highlighting and describing the overseas operations of companies. Video clips can often give students added insights into the cultures and people of a country. In their search process, students may be able to acquire firsthand information about expatriates or natives in another country via e-mail.

The Internet is an invaluable research tool. Students should also become familiar with hard copy journals, indices, and papers, as well as trade associations and commercial agencies that provide research assistance and access to data banks that are not available on the Web. Whatever the source, information must be managed. It is critical that students understand and are able to carry out the research process, from problem definition to reporting. Research processes help students learn to focus in an environment of innumerable options.

Learning by developing. Students need a chance to be creative, whether the project is to develop a marketing plan, a new product or service, a PowerPoint presentation, or a new process or procedure. Students need opportunities to think and act "out of the box." These opportunities may be the first that allow students to bring their many diverse skills and interests, such as art, history, science, and language, into focus.

There are many ways that instructors can encourage creative thinking and development activities: posing a problem with many alternative solutions, bringing forward a current international event that has a variety of implications on business, or evaluating electronic tools to increase effectiveness and efficiency. These or other problems can be starting points for students to come up with creative ideas and solutions.

Teachers who encourage students to propose projects of their choosing within the parameters of the class give them the chance to pursue something that they are interested in. Once a project proposal is accepted, instructors can work with a student or students to develop expected outcomes for grading purposes. Students should be encouraged to use the Internet and multimedia in their development and presentation efforts. Whether a project involves developing a marketing plan, creating an advertisement, constructing a board game in e-commerce, or identifying a new product given future trends, students who initiate the idea often enthusiastically follow through to complete it. Being able to create, develop, and conclude a project that they can call their own from start to finish is very exciting and rewarding for students.

SUMMARY

The global e-commerce environment, with all its volatility and challenges, not only demands a new approach to working but also demands a new approach to teaching and learning. Success in this environment not only depends on providing a quality product, but also on the effective use of technology to accomplish higher levels of efficiency, productivity, and service. Global competition has become so keen that the very survival of a company will be contingent on its taking advantage of emerging technologies that will achieve these outcomes.

Businesses that are able to understand the complexities, challenges, and opportunities the Internet has to offer will be able to harness its true potential in the international arena. In preparation for a customer-driven international environment, education should be learner driven, and students should be challenged to research, analyze, and create solutions for this new frontier. Essential skills and competencies include the basic skills of reading, writing, and mathematics; computer literacy; communication and interpersonal skills; critical thinking; self-directed learning; creativity; and cultural awareness and sensitivity. Each of these competencies must be developed in the context of world issues, cultures, and affairs.

The only certainty in this emerging field is change. For this reason, students must be able to think for themselves and learn to learn. Learning activities that encourage new experiences and that challenge students to embrace change, stimulate ideas, solve problems, and collaborate to reach a desired result will best prepare students for the demands of this new world. There is no doubt that the future of international online business will present a host of challenges, pitfalls, and opportunities. The level of success that business educators achieve will depend on how well students learn to think, create, learn, and grow.

REFERENCES

AMS study finds vast opportunity for telecommunications firms to exploit e-commerce. (1999, August 25). *PRNewswire.* Retrieved January 18, 2001, from the World Wide Web: http://elibrary.com/s/edumark/
getdoc.cgi?id=185871107x…:US;EL&dtype=0~0&dinst=

Asia's Internet e-commerce applications markets to top U.S. $1.3 billion by 2003, says IDC. (1999, July 13). *PR Newswire.* Retrieved January 18, 2001, from the World Wide Web: http://elibrary.com/s/edumark/
getdoc.cgi?id=185871107x…:US;EL&dtype=0~0&dinst=

Celuch, K., & Slama, M. (1999, Jan./Feb.). Teaching critical thinking skills for the 21st century: An advertising principles case study. *Journal of Education for Business, 74,* 134–140.

Davis, E. L. (1996). The future of education. *Education and Technology.* Retrieved January 18, 2001, from the World Wide Web: http://www.wco.com/%7Emktentry/edfutur.html

Dudley, S. C., & Dudley, L. W. (1995, May/June). New directions in the business curriculum. *Journal of Education for Business, 70,* 305–311.

Electronic commerce: Jeff Kann. (1999, October 13). *Congressional Testimony.* Retrieved January 18, 2001, from the World Wide Web: http://elibrary.com/s/edumark/getdoc.cgi?id=185871107x…:US;EL&dtype=0~0&dinst=

Global electronic marketplace: William M. Dailey. (1998, July 29). *Congressional Testimony.* Retrieved January 18, 2001, from the World Wide Web: http://elibrary.com/s/edumark/getdoc.cgi?id=185871107x…:US;EL&dtype=0~0&dinst=

Gomes, L. (2001, February 12). Fix it and they will come. E-commerce isn't dead. Just broken. *The Wall Street Journal,* p. R4.

Holstein, W. J. (2001a, February 26). Old dogs, new tricks using the Internet… and, yes, getting their groove back. *U.S. News & World Report,* 38–40.

Holstein, W. J. (2001b, February 26). I love the Internet. [An interview with Irving Wladawsky-Berger, IBM vice president, Technology and Strategy Server Group]. *U.S. News & World Report,* p. 40.

Industry Group 91. (1999, August 25). U.S.-Philippines joint statement on electronic commerce. *Regulatory Intelligence Data.* Retrieved January 18, 2001, from the World Wide Web: http://elibrary.com/s/edumark/
getdoc.cgi?id=185871107x…:US;EL&dtype=0~0&dinst=

International round-up 2000: Market updates. (2000, May 1). *Circulation Management.* Retrieved January 18, 2001, from the World Wide Web: http://elibrary.com/s/edumark/getdoc.cgi?id=185871107x…:US;EL&dtype=0~0&dinst=

Kalakota, R., & Robinson, M. (1999). *E-business roadmap for success.* Boston: Addison-Wesley.

Meyers, J. (1999, June 25). Rewire your business plan. *Canadian Business, 72*, 198. Retrieved January 18, 2001, from the World Wide Web: http://elibrary.com/s/edumark/getdoc.cgi?id=185871107x...:US;EL&dtype=0~0&dinst=

Miller, P. (2001, January 1). Eye on b-to-b: Using web-customer data. *Catalog Age.* Retrieved January 18, 2001, from the World Wide Web: http://elibrary.com/s/edumark/getdoc.cgi?id=185871107x...:US;EL&dtype=0~0&dinst=

Non-U.S. Internet commerce to account for almost half of worldwide spending by 2003, IDC Reports. (1999, August 25). *PR Newswire.* Retrieved January 18, 2001, from the World Wide Web: http://elibrary.com/s/edumark/getdoc.cgi?id=185871107x...:US;EL&dtype=0~0&dinst=

Ross, R. Online b2b trade poised to soar, study predicts. (2000, November 1). *The Toronto Star.* Retrieved January 18, 2001, from the World Wide Web: http://elibrary.com/s/edumark/getdoc.cgi?id=185871107x...:US;EL&dtype=0~0&dinst=

Suppliers follow e-business trend. (2000, June 1). *Flame Retardancy News.* Retrieved January 18, 2001, from the World Wide Web: http://elibrary.com/s/edumark/getdoc.cgi?id=185871107x...:US;EL&dtype=0~0&dinst=

Global Technology, Communication, Language, and Culture

James Calvert Scott
Utah State University
Logan, Utah

Contrary to widespread perceptions around the world, today's information-technology revolution is not a new phenomenon. The first major information revolution was the invention of writing; the second involved the creation of written books. During the third information revolution, both movable-type printing and engraving were invented. The fourth and current information revolution involves the meaning of information and its purpose. Each of these four profound revolutions has brought about (1) major cultural upheavals affecting societies' ways of life; (2) significant increases in the quantity, quality, and value of information that could be communicated to others; and (3) substantial decreases in the costs of communicating that information to larger and more widespread audiences (Drucker, 1998).

Throughout recorded time, human beings have struggled with the consequences of technological advances. People have tried to maximize the advantages and to minimize the disadvantages of all innovations, altering and ultimately enhancing their ways of life in the process. Bringing about acceptance of change is a complicated process that is not only technological but also behavioral (Scott, 1985). To control ongoing technological change involving information, human beings must learn how to understand and manage themselves.

To bring about this understanding and self-management in their students, business educators must prepare students with knowledge of basic concepts; critical interrelationships involving culture, language, communication, and technology; and the reasons for their importance. Teachers need to formulate instructional goals, identify resources, and select instructional approaches. This chapter addresses these needs and suggests learning activities that can be used in instruction.

BASIC CONCEPTS AND INSTRUCTIONAL APPROACHES

Understanding the complex interrelationships between culture, language, communication, and technology requires definitions of some basic concepts and instructional approaches that apply those concepts.

Basic Concepts

Culture reflects the way of life of a group of people. A culture is composed of the learned, shared, interrelated, and unifying beliefs, values, and assumptions that guide its members' behaviors and the values they attach to tangible artifacts. As Jackson observed, "Cultures are maps of meaning through which the world is made intelligible" (Swerdlow, 1999, pp. 4–5). Lifelong acculturation by family, friends, and societal institutions is a powerful indoctrinating force that allows members of a society to function in generally similar and predictable ways as a cohesive and ordered society.

Language is a collection of words, sounds, signs, symbols, and the related systems for their use that allow people to communicate meaning. Speakers of a particular language might be in the same locality, political subdivision, or geographic region or be geographically dispersed.

Communication is the complex process of trying to convey information from the sender to the receiver without altering meaning. The initiator encodes the message in symbolic form and transmits it via some channel to the receiver. During decoding, the receiver ascribes meaning to the symbols and ultimately to the message. When the symbols used by the sender match those within the message-meaning repository of the receiver, the receiver understands the message with little or no distortion. Without this shared meaning, message failure results. The receiver transmits feedback to the sender to seek common meaning and to respond to the sender's message, thus completing the communication flow.

Technology is the collection of methodologies, processes, and inventions or tools of a culture that allows that society to function. Technology is the sum of the ways that groups and individuals provide themselves with whatever their civilization values. Information technology comprises the set of tools for acquiring, manipulating, and distributing information in various forms.

The term "online" refers to resources accessible through connections to the Internet and other networks. The devices attached to networks are used to receive, transform, and send data. "Business environment" refers to the operating locale in which decisions are made. "Global business" is transacted with little or no regard for national boundaries. An organization that functions in the global business environment will operate in a number of countries but not necessarily in every country in a trading region or in every part of the world.

Instructional Approaches

Applying concepts is critical to learning. Research will almost invariably be needed about cultures and international business. Table 1 lists several useful Web sites for students.

Table 1. Web Sites for Cultural and International Research

Sources	URLs
Executive Planet	http://www.executiveplanet.com/community
Library of Congress Country Studies	http://1cweb2.loc.gov/frd/cs/cshome.html
Michigan State University CIBER	http://globaledge.msu.edu/index.asp
Web of Culture	http://www.webofculture.com/
World Fact Book	http://www.odci.gov/cia/publications/factbook/index.html
Yahoo Countries	http://dir.yahoo.com/Regional/Countries

STUDENT ACTIVITY

Understanding Key Concepts

After reviewing key terminology, have students define such terms as "culture," "language," "communication," "technology," "online," "domestic business environment," and "global business environment" in their own words. Next, divide the class into small groups to analyze Web sites that sell goods and/or services. The Yahoo Countries Directory (see Table 1) provides access to many overseas sites. Finally, students can summarize the content of the sites in written or oral form by addressing the following questions:

1. What is the URL of the Web site, and what organization created the Web site?
2. What are the visible and hidden cultural assumptions that underlie the Web site, and how did you discover those cultural assumptions?
3. What language is used on the site, and why was it selected? Does the site use more than one language? Why were the languages chosen?
4. Does the Web site effectively use technology to market goods and/or services in both the domestic and global business environments? Why or why not?
5. Would you consider buying goods and/or services from this Web site if you were a native of the following countries: the United States? Brazil? Switzerland? Egypt? Indonesia? Why or why not?

Mini-case studies can emphasize cultural, communication, language, and technology elements and engage students in other types of analysis and problem solving.

STUDENT ACTIVITY

Developing Cultural Sensitivity

The company you work for, Worldwide Webs, employs a wide variety of highly skilled technical staff from 37 countries, including Vidhya Nagarajan, who is from India. A devout Hindu, she dresses in colorful saris and has a red dot painted on her forehead between her eyebrows. While relaxing in the employee lounge, you overhear several of your coworkers ridiculing Vidhya's appearance. You know that Vidhya is the most talented Web site designer at Worldwide Webs and that such unflattering comments would seriously alienate her if she were aware of them, perhaps causing her to seek employment at a competing business.

1. What action, if any, would you take to try to stop coworkers from making unkind public comments about Vidhya's appearance? Why?
2. Why do you think your coworkers ridiculed Vidhya's appearance?
3. Since Worldwide Webs employs a multicultural workforce, do you think it should provide cultural sensitivity training for all of its employees? Why or why not?
4. What do you think should be the goals of company-sponsored cultural sensitivity training?
5. What cultural sensitivity training topics would you suggest for all Worldwide Webs employees? Why?
6. In addition to company-sponsored training, do individuals who work in multicultural environments bear personal responsibility for independently learning about other cultures and for being tolerant of cultural differences? Why or why not?

Note to teachers: While the analysis may initially focus on the concepts of technology, language, culture, and communication, a later return to the case can promote analysis of key relationships.

UNDERSTANDING CULTURE, LANGUAGE, COMMUNICATION, AND TECHNOLOGY RELATIONSHIPS

The complex relationships of information technology to culture, language, and communication should be the focus of instruction for and about the global business environment.

Importance of Understanding Relevant Relationships

Justifying the effort to learn about technology relationships involves five assumptions: (1) culture shapes people and their ways of life, (2) language reflects how a culture perceives reality, (3) language facilitates communication with others, (4) technology allows a culture to achieve what it values, and (5) technological change is ongoing and pervasive.

First, culture is widely regarded as a powerful force that shapes the behaviors and ways of life of members of a group. Nevertheless, culture is an enigma whose inner workings are not well understood. Prominent researchers and theorists (Hall, 1959, 1976; Hofstede, 1980, 1991) have conceptualized culture in business settings in significantly different ways. Hall (1959), for example, has equated culture and communication, while Goodenough has postulated that culture governs communicative behavior (Baxter, 1983).

Second, language reflects how a culture perceives reality. The letter "e" (as in "e-mail" and "e-commerce") and the prefix "cyber" have taken on meanings in the United States, and their pervasive use reflects a changed view of how communication is conducted. Language also helps to differentiate cultural groups around the world. Some countries have profound internal cultural differences, which are reflected in their use of two or more mainstream languages, English and French in Canada, for example, and German, French, Italian, and Romansch in Switzerland (Victor, 1992).

Third, the language of a culture facilitates communication inside and outside of the cultural group. Because similar cultural factors and life experiences shape native speakers, their message-meaning repositories are apt to be similar. For nonnative speakers, the likelihood that individuals can extract the full message meaning increases with linguistic skill and cultural knowledge (Scott, 1999). For those not fluent in the language, some form of intervention, such as technology-enhanced translation or interpretation, must bridge language and cultural gaps.

Fourth, technology consists of the tools that a culture uses to achieve whatever it values. In that sense, technology is a means to an end. Technology extends human inputs in order to attain those things desired or valued by members of a society (Rybczynski, 1983; Scott, 1985).

Fifth, technological change is ongoing and pervasive and reflects the continuing efforts of a culture to extend its resources to attain something of value. Concurrently, technological change can generate potentially dangerous results if not carefully managed. Judiciously balancing the positive and negative aspects of technological innovation presents difficult choices for all cultures (Rybczynski, 1983; Scott, 1985).

When business educators introduce these complex relationships to students, the goal is to have students understand that culture is a powerful force that shapes people and their societies and that language reflects a culture's perception of reality. Business students develop deep and useful insights about international communication if they understand that the implementation of technology allows cultures to achieve what they value while at the same time producing ongoing and pervasive societal change.

Identifying Relevant Relationship Insights
The implementation of new technologies always brings about change. Society determines whether change has positive or negative cultural consequences. Several significant relationships—technology to culture, technology to language, and technology to communication—are of particular importance to business educators. Technology (1)

facilitates international business communication, (2) enhances intercultural communication competencies, (3) interacts with factors that determine the success of online international business communication, (4) requires a choice of language—English and/ or other—to conduct online business, (5) facilitates translation and interpretation services, and (6) relates to other aspects of culture and language.

Culture and technology acceptance. Cultures differ in their acceptance of technology and, hence, in their use of technology to facilitate international business communication. These differences can be described on a continuum of control over technology. Some cultures, such as that of the United States, view technology positively and readily embrace change in order to achieve whatever they value. Such "control cultures" use technology liberally to master their environments (Victor, 1992).

At the other end of the continuum are cultures, such as that of fundamentalist Iran, that view technology at best as neutral and often as negative. These "subjugation cultures" are reluctant to embrace change because they believe it is either undesirable or impossible to control in their environments. People from these cultures believe that they should be subject to their environments. Technological change threatens—and may possibly destroy—their ways of life (Victor, 1992).

Between these extremes are cultures, such as that of Japan, that view technology as a means to achieve a balance with nature that has been disrupted by the actions of people. Such "harmonization cultures" view themselves as part of their environments and try to implement change judiciously in order to achieve balance (Victor, 1992).

Control cultures are quick to embrace new technologies and place faith in the latest technological devices to improve communication. They believe that large investments in these technologies will yield domestic and global competitive advantages. Most members of control cultures and many members of harmonization cultures respond favorably to the use of technology to facilitate international business communication. But some members of harmonization cultures and most members of subjugation cultures respond much less favorably to this use of technology.

International businesspeople from technology-oriented control cultures frequently and mistakenly assume that, because a particular technology exists in another country, it is appropriate to use it for communication. Even a relatively easy-to-use, quick, efficient, and inexpensive means of international business communication may be inappropriate in certain circumstances. In "high-context" cultures, such as those in most Latin American, Middle Eastern, and Far Eastern countries, personal relationships must be built up over time before people can engage in business together. Businesspeople from those countries use Internet communication for selected purposes after working relationships are well established. Even so, for substantive and sensitive business matters, these businesspeople often continue to prefer more verbally and nonverbally rich means of communication, such as face-to-face meetings, that provide quick feedback (H. M. Al-Lawatia, personal communication, November 6,

2000; Z. Huang, personal communication, November 1, 2000; and M. L. Lamb, personal communication, November 6, 2000).

STUDENT ACTIVITY

Control, Subjugation, and Harmonization Cultures

After discussing control, subjugation, and harmonization cultures, have students individually or in small groups list five examples of countries for each of the three cultural types along with brief explanations that justify each of the categorizations.

Intercultural communication competencies. Any one country can contain many cultures within it. That is evident in the United States, and the term "intercultural" can be applied to communication between members of different cultural groups within the same larger society. As Cummings has observed, technology can make communication possible with people around the world, but it cannot overcome the cultural differences that separate them ("Cultural Differences," 1994).

The code of ethics of the Association for Computing Machinery (ACM) says, "In a fair society, all individuals would have equal opportunity to participate in, or benefit from, the use of computer resources regardless of race, sex, religion, age, disability, national origin, or other similar factors" (Shneiderman, 2000, p. 85). Earlier technologies, such as the telephone and television, have attained a state of universal usability where almost everyone can make effective use of them. Such is not yet true for computer-related technologies.

How might a lofty goal for information and communication technologies, such as the one stated in ACM's code of ethics, become a reality? According to Shneiderman (2000), human-computer interaction research focusing on technology variety, user diversity, and gaps in user knowledge can lay the groundwork for the empowerment of all people and can facilitate intercultural communication both domestically and internationally.

STUDENT ACTIVITY

ACM Code of Ethics

Following a presentation about the ACM code of ethics (http://www.acm.org/constitution/code.html), ask students to suggest realistic ways for people around the world to gain "equal opportunities to participate in, or benefit from, the use of computer resources regardless of race, sex, religion, age, disability, national origin, or other similar factors" (Shneiderman, 2000, p. 85). Encourage follow-up discussion by asking students how long they think it will take to reach this goal—if they believe that the goal is attainable. Students who think this goal is unattainable should debate whether efforts to create equal access to computer resources worldwide should be abandoned, and justify their positions. Business educators can then change the wording of the topic from "people around the world" to "cultures within your community."

Factors contributing to successful online international communication. Perhaps the most critical factor for success in online international business communication is whom the communication can reach. According to one recent survey, 35 percent of the "rich world" population but only 6 percent of the entire world population is online ("The New Economy," 2000). Unless a business wants to restrict its customer base to computer-savvy people from developed countries, online communication will not effectively reach a large worldwide audience in the foreseeable future. Less technologically advanced means of international business communication remain critical for organizations that aspire to engage in business with most of the world's population.

Another important factor for success is the choice of language(s) used online. According to Forrester Research data, 46 percent of all Web site orders received by U.S. businesses are from customers outside the United States (Sawhney & Mandal, 2000b), many of whom are not native speakers of English. As the number of online nonnative speakers of English grows, the ethnocentric use of English will exclude an increasingly significant portion of the worldwide potential customer base. Put another way, American businesses must realize that the "e" in e-commerce does not refer to "English" (Shannon, 2000).

Successful businesses in the global environment must use the languages of targeted customers in culturally sensitive ways, including domain names written in targeted languages and appropriate ideographic or letter characters and diacritical or other punctuation marks. Yahoo, for example, operates in 22 countries in 13 different languages using both Western and Eastern character sets. Businesses should also customize their Web sites to reflect local characteristics such as market structures, customer preferences and tastes, business practices, goods and services suppliers, logistics, infrastructures, and legal systems (Sawhney & Mandal, 2000a).

Using culturally acceptable communication media with international target groups contributes to successful online communication. For example, the Japanese generally respond well to Internet communication because it is based on a community of communicators. Internet communication methods allow time to reflect and to reach consensus before responding and to encourage active involvement with others. These factors are valued by the Japanese culture. On the other hand, Thais, who are members of a relatively "high-context" culture, tend to prefer more personalized means of international business communication, such as face-to-face meetings, rather than technologically mediated means, such as teleconferences (Ulijn, O'Hair, Weggeman, Ledlow, & Hall, 2000).

It is a mistake to assume that all individuals will respond to the same type of information in the same way. Three types of information exist: (1) free information that is widely shared with others, (2) commercial information that is created and sold for a price, and (3) strategic information that is shared only with those few who need to have access to it (Keohane & Nye, 1998). While online communication is a good method of distributing free information to large audiences in technology-rich countries, it may be less well-suited to distributing tightly controlled commercial and strategic information. The communicator must assess cultural expectations about how such information is shared.

Online international business communication can be successful when the barriers to its implementation are minimized so that, overall, it is the most effective way of communicating with customers worldwide. The following factors can limit the success of online international business communications:

- The high costs of online access, particularly in developing and underdeveloped countries
- Lack of convenient access to online technologies, especially in developing and underdeveloped countries
- The unreliability of some online systems, especially during periods of peak use
- The high costs of customizing online systems to accommodate cultural differences within specific market segments
- Inadequate technology to cost-effectively convert online sites into target languages
- The purchase of unproven online technologies that waste resources, alienate customers, and require users to struggle to make the new technologies work
- The perception that online technologies will be panaceas and the failure to focus on the customer
- Limited and insecure methods of accepting payments, especially in business environments where credit cards are not widely used or where credit card theft is common
- Suspicion of invasive customer tracking on sites
- Failure to consider the characteristics of online communication, including its distinctive elements, communication models, and usage guidelines (Bingi, Mir, & Khamalah, 2000; Brock, 1998; Stuller, 2000; "Writing for the Screen," 1998)

Once a business decides that online international business communication is the best alternative for customer interaction, that business must addresses complex challenges such as those presented in Table 2 (Bingi, Mir, & Khamalah, 2000).

Table 2. Challenges to Operating an International Business Online

Types of Challenges	Examples of Challenges
Economic	Cost justification, Internet access, telecommunication infrastructure, and skill shortages
Technical	Security, reliability, protocols, bandwidth, and integration
Social	Privacy and security, cultural diversity, trust, and absence of "touch and feel" (media richness)
Legal	Intellectual property rights, validity of transactions, taxation issues, and policing and regulation

International businesspeople must carefully choose communication media that are sanctioned by the cultures of their overseas business partners for particular communication purposes and stages in business relationships.

STUDENT ACTIVITY

Online Technologies in More or Less Wealthy Countries

Follow a presentation about the status of online technologies in countries of varying wealth with a student research project. Have students research the roles of governments of countries around the world in facilitating widespread implementation of technology. Useful insights should emerge after students compare and contrast strategies used by governments in adjacent developed and developing countries, such as the United States and Mexico, or Japan and South Korea.

Note to teachers: The results of the research can be shared with others in written and/or oral form. Additionally, students can use their research results to debate the following proposition: All national governments should facilitate access to online technologies for all of their citizens.

English and other languages for online business sites. The English language dominates worldwide communication for business, technology, science, and academia. More than 80 percent of all information stored worldwide in electronic retrieval systems is written in English (Crystal, 1995). English is dominant not because of its superior innate linguistic features but for historical, political, economic, practical, intellectual, and entertainment reasons (Crystal, 1995). English is the language of power and influence in spite of the fact that it is the native language of a mere 5 percent of the world's population (Crystal, 1995).

What will the future hold for English? While the number of native and nonnative speakers of English around the world rivals—and probably exceeds—the number of native and nonnative speakers of its closest competitor, Mandarin Chinese (Crystal, 1995; Fox, 2000), the importance of English may diminish in the technologically mediated global marketplace. Forty-three percent of Internet users do not read English (Shannon, 2000). In 1999 about 54 percent of Web users worldwide used English as their primary language, but by 2005 this number will decline to about 42 percent (Reed, 1999). The onus for bridging the growing language gap is primarily on the English-speaking international business community.

In some regional marketplaces, such as Western Europe, the fluency rate for English is about 47 percent, far surpassing that of any other language (Fox, 2000). This ensures a future role for English in communicating with some prospective and existing international customers. In Western Europe, 77 percent of college students, 69 percent of managers, and 65 percent of young adults speak English. In European Union countries where English is not the primary language, 91 percent of secondary school students study English (Fox, 2000). Such statistics suggest that English will continue to be an important, but certainly not exclusive, online language of global business in Western Europe, especially among better educated, more influential, and younger customers for the foreseeable future.

In a recent Forrester Research survey, 46 percent of respondents acknowledged that their organizations turned away international orders because they did not have appropriate processes to cope with them (Shannon, 2000). This shocking statistic does not bode well for the primarily monolingual American business community in the global marketplace.

What major languages other than English predominate online? According to a Business Wire news release, 19.7 million native speakers of Japanese, 15.4 million native speakers of Spanish, 14 million native speakers of German, 9.9 million native speakers of Chinese, and 9.9 million native speakers of French use the Internet ("InterLingua.com," 1999). Companies that aspire to be successful in the global business environment should seriously consider using these languages if they want to communicate effectively with the largest number of possible online customers in the foreseeable future.

STUDENT ACTIVITY

Future of Languages
Given the likelihood of a diminishing role for the English language in Web sites in the years ahead, have students speculate about which languages they think will increasingly be used in Web sites and the reasons for this increase. Also, ask students to develop a rationale for why the English language should remain a major language for Web sites around the world and to devise strategies to ensure that the English language continues to be a major Web site language. Or have students debate both sides of the issue.

Translation and interpretation services. The results of technology efforts to translate from one language to another are still far from perfect. Wagstaff (2000) has called the misunderstandings created by computers engaged in machine translation "the last significant barrier to global Internet communication" (p. 26).

While English is the dominant language of global business (Victor, 1992) and of the Internet (Wagstaff, 2000), the number of non-English speaking people who would like to communicate in their own native languages continues to grow. In the United States only two percent of the existing Internet sites are designed to accommodate the 32 million non-English-speaking residents of the country (Wagstaff, 2000). This effectively excludes many people from the online world. While some companies, such as Yahoo and Amazon, have included some information in other languages to meet the needs of non-English-speaking audiences, such customized sites represent a distinct minority of Web sites.

Less than one third of online companies that aspire to communicate with international audiences have Web sites tailored to the varying language needs of potential and current customers (Kushner, 2000). In an effort to address the language mismatch, companies are developing and improving machine translation software.

Babelfish, a popular machine translation program for the World Wide Web, is available through the AltaVista search portal. It translates between 13 pairs of languages. The user keyboards or cuts and pastes text into a window, selects the desired language pair, and clicks on a button for a rapid translation (Kushner, 2000). The translation is accomplished by three programs that assess the meaning of the sentences, translate the results, and synthesize the results into a whole (Wagstaff, 2000).

While machine translation programs have been devised by a variety of companies for both Western and Eastern languages, they typically provide only the gist of the message—sometimes with major, even comical, distortions (Kushner, 2000). Machine translation does not provide the same quality of translation that is available from a human translator. Some organizations combine machine and human translation to reduce time delays and costs of human translations, while significantly increasing the accuracy and the value of machine translations.

Technology also assists professional interpreters by allowing them to broadcast via headsets the equivalent version of the spoken message in other languages with only a few seconds' delay, as is done during sessions of the United Nations. Technology has also been used to amplify the interpretation of spoken messages for audiences when one or more sentences are spoken in one language and then converted by an interpreter into the equivalent oral form in another language.

Global Voice Limited has released its FirstVoice software. FirstVoice provides interpretations of spoken messages, translations of written information, and interlingual dictation. FirstVoice can also aid vocabulary development and improve pronunciation in a foreign language. A speaker first acquaints the software with his or her voice, and then speaks English into the PC's microphone. In turn, the software delivers a fluent masculine or feminine French-, German-, or Spanish-speaking voice. The product, designed for business and travel situations, has a vocabulary of about 200,000 words and 4,000 phrases. The British software developer plans to introduce other languages, including Arabic, Russian, Mandarin Chinese, Portuguese, and Italian, and to develop technical dictionaries for specialized business applications (M. Huckerby, personal communication, June 9, 2000). Like similar programs for machine translation, FirstVoice may have shortcomings in spite of its multiple capabilities.

Other Relationships to Culture and Language

Teachers should also discuss with students the relationships between technology and (1) cultural preservation and destruction and (2) native and nonnative language skills.

Cultural preservation and destruction. A minority of cultures, those usually found in economically developed countries in the West, tends to enthusiastically embrace technologies so that they can dominate nature. The majority of cultures—those usually found in underdeveloped countries—in order to remain one with nature, tend to be much less inclined to apply technologies. Technology is a powerful force that can alter and even destroy cultures. Such cultural devastation was illustrated by the displacement of Native Americans by technologically more sophisticated settlers. Technology can also safeguard fragile cultures and languages by recording them for posterity (Mims, 2000).

Native and nonnative language skills. Technology can be used to help native and nonnative speakers and writers acquire language skills. Some Web sites, such as the Online Writing Laboratory (http://owl.english.purdue.edu/), provide writing tools to assist with message composition, grammar, and the like. Other sites, such as Presenters Online (http://www.presentersonline.com), provide speaking-related tips, advice, and clip art (C. L. Bovee & J. V. Thill, personal communication, November 1, 2000). Teachers of English as a second or foreign language have long used available technologies to develop skills in new languages.

Business educators must work with students to develop understanding of the importance of relevant relationships between culture, language, communication, and technology. Related insights should be developed about culture and technology acceptance, intercultural communication competencies, factors contributing to successful online international business communication, English and other languages for online business sites, and translation and interpretation services. Other relationships, including cultural preservation and destruction and native and nonnative language skills, also deserve attention.

TEACHING ABOUT CULTURE, LANGUAGE, COMMUNICATION, AND TECHNOLOGY RELATIONSHIPS

With an understanding of the complex relationships between culture, language, communication, and technology, business teachers can begin to infuse this information into their instruction for and about business. To develop related knowledge, skills, and attitudes, business educators need to focus attention on instructional goals, methodologies, and resources.

Instructional Goals

Programs that provide education for and about business should enable students to achieve the following general instructional goals:

- Understanding the complex relationships between culture, language, communication, and technology in the United States and in other countries
- Understanding how culture-related factors profoundly influence human behaviors
- Minimizing ethnocentrism—the belief that one's native culture is superior to all other cultures—and maximizing respect for other cultures as credible and legitimate ways of life

143

- Understanding how language-related factors influence success in technologically mediated domestic and international business environments
- Understanding how communication-related factors influence success in both domestic and international business environments
- Understanding how to implement technology to function effectively in domestic and international business environments
- Developing the knowledge, skills, and attitudes necessary to function effectively as workers and as consumers in local, national, and international business environments

These instructional goals should be adapted for specific educational settings on the basis of the backgrounds and characteristics of the learners; the nature of the units, courses, and programs in which the instruction is provided; the environment in which the related instruction is delivered; and the preferences of important constituent groups such as parents, the public, the business community, and instructional administrators.

Instructional Methodologies

Teacher-directed, collaborative, and self-directed instructional methodologies are useful for developing knowledge, skills, and attitudes about relationships between culture, language, communication, and technology. When using teacher-directed learning activities, a business educator might ask learners to fill in the missing parts in an outline or study guide as he or she delivers a presentation about the use of English and other languages on the Internet. The business educator might reinforce key ideas in the presentation by asking learners to respond to questions about the use of various languages on the Internet.

Collaborative learning occurs through interaction with others in group settings. When teaching about culture, language, communication, and technology, a business educator might divide students into small groups, asking the groups to list ways in which a business might reduce resistance to the implementation of new technology in its overseas offices. Groups might then compare the advantages and disadvantages of the approaches and select the five best ways of making the new technology more acceptable to company workers worldwide.

Self-directed learning occurs when the student assumes primary responsibility for learning. The learner may function relatively independently of both the teacher and other students. The business educator might have learners (1) identify the cultural beliefs, personal values, and assumptions that influence their technology-related behaviors and (2) explain in writing how these beliefs, values, and assumptions were acquired. Learners might then individually create collages that pictorially depict important aspects of their technology-related cultural beliefs.

Instructional Resources

A wide variety of relevant instructional resources exist that business educators can use when teaching about culture, language, communication, and technology. Business educators should choose varied resources that meet the needs of diverse learners. Instructional resources that are suitable for elementary students may not be suitable for secondary students because their reading skills, interests, and knowledge levels differ. However, some instructional resources suitable for the upper end of the secondary school level may also be suitable for use at the collegiate level and/or in private sector education and training of adults outside of educational institutions.

Printed instructional resources are plentiful. While books address major topics in comprehensive ways, they may be updated infrequently. Periodicals usually address much narrower topics and are published regularly on a weekly, monthly, or quarterly basis. Printed resources may be most valuable for studying concepts and analyzing cultural and technological topics. But the content of printed resources will not be as current as that of online resources, which constitutes a weakness for technology-related topics.

Roakes (1999) has called the Internet a gold mine of foreign language resources and has identified a wide variety of sites that teachers can use to enrich their instruction. Electronic instructional resources include Web sites, online versions of printed resources that may or may not be available locally, and discussion groups, to name but a few. Electronic resources tend to provide more current information than printed resources, but online content is not often subjected to the same level of quality control as printed resources are. For example, because anyone can post information to a Web site, the consumer of that information must evaluate that site and its information critically prior to deciding on its suitability for instructional purposes. Generally speaking, electronic resources from colleges and universities, government agencies, nationally and internationally known businesses, and major research and publication companies have acceptable quality-control standards.

People from various walks of life can be very useful resources to those who instruct about culture, language, communication, and technology relationships. For example, individuals can provide needed information, suggest instructional strategies, make referrals to other sources of information, serve as guest speakers, or provide free or inexpensive educational resources for business educators and/or their students. Such resource people can come from a variety of institutions. Educational institutions can provide teachers and researchers who are willing to share content knowledge, instructional methods, and teaching materials. Private sector consultants and trainers can share their employment and instructional experiences. Professional organizations and businesses can send members or employees who are willing to share their real-world experiences and state-of-the-art knowledge. And government officials can offer a perspective that complements those of representatives of other societal institutions.

Prior to providing education for and about business involving culture, language, communication, and technology, business educators must understand their subject matter and its importance. They must decide upon instructional goals, methodologies, and resources that are appropriate for use in the learning environment.

SUMMARY

In the rapidly evolving global business environment, understanding the intertwined relationships between culture, language, communication, and technology is increasingly important as students look to a future where online global business will be common.

Relationships that deserve special attention include (1) culture and technology acceptance, (2) intercultural communication competencies, (3) factors contributing to successful online international business communication, (4) English and other languages for online business sites, and (5) translation and interpretation services. The power of technology to preserve and destroy cultures and languages and to enable both native and nonnative language users to improve their skills is also important.

As business educators plan for the delivery of instruction about the relationships between culture, language, communication, and technology, they should give serious thought to instructional goals and to approaches that blend the best of teacher-directed, collaborative, and student-directed methodologies using appropriate instructional resources. Guided by the content of this chapter and other sources, business educators can devise and implement critically needed education. This effort will enable students to better understand themselves and others and to better manage themselves and the technologies they use to communicate globally.

REFERENCES

Baxter, J. (1983). English for intercultural competence: An approach to intercultural communication training. In D. Landis & R. W. Brislin (Eds.), *Handbook of intercultural training: Volume II: Issues in training methodology* (pp. 290–324). New York: Pergamon Press.

Bingi, P., Mir, A., & Khamalah, J. (2000, Fall). The challenges facing global e-commerce. *Information Systems Management,* pp. 26–34.

Brock, T. (1998, March 20–26). Your technology is only as good as who uses it. *Denver Business Journal,* p. 28A.

Crystal, D. (1995). *The Cambridge encyclopedia of the English language.* Cambridge, United Kingdom: Cambridge University Press.

Cultural differences can blindside the global villager: Cummings. (1994, January). *Public Relations Journal,* III.

Drucker, P. F. (1998, August 24). The next information revolution. *Forbes ASAP,* pp. 46–58.

Fox, J. (2000). The triumph of English. *Fortune, 142*(6), 209–210, 212.

Hall, E. T. (1959). *The silent language of business.* Garden City, NJ: Doubleday.

Hall, E. T. (1976). *Beyond culture.* New York: Anchor Press.

Hofstede, G. (1980). *Culture's consequences: International differences in work-related values.* Beverly Hills, CA: Sage Publications.

Hofstede, G. (1991). *Cultures and organizations: The software of the mind.* New York: McGraw-Hill.

InterLingua.com—e-commerce service for non-English-speaking Web users started. (1999, December 12). *Business Wire* [Item number CX335B0194]. Retrieved September 19, 2000, from the World Wide Web: http://www.businesswire.com

Keohane, R. O., & Nye, J. S., Jr. (1998). Power and interdependence in the Information Age. *Foreign Affairs, 77*(5), 81–88, 90–94.

Kushner, D. (2000, May 5). Software helps translate languages, alphabets for non-English speakers. *Houston Chronicle* [2 star edition], p. 1.

Mims, B. (2000, May 30). Ute language in danger of withering away: Utes seek to preserve tongue, culture. *The Salt Lake Tribune*, pp. A1, A7.

The new economy: Untangling e-conomics. (2000, September 23). *The Economist: A survey of the new economy: Untangling e-conomics* [Internal supplement], pp. 5–6.

Reed, S. (1999). Want to limit the audience for your business Web site? Keep it English-only. *InfoWorld, 21*(35), 61.

Roakes, S. (1999, June 2). The Internet: A goldmine for foreign language instruction. Center for the Advancement of Language Learning. Retrieved October 31, 2000, from the World Wide Web: http://www.call.gov/resource/essays/internet.htm

Rybczynski, W. (1983). *Taming the tiger: The struggle to control technology.* New York: Viking Press.

Sawhney, M., & Mandal, S. (2000a, May). Go global: Who: Are you ready for globalization? *Business 2.0*, pp. 187–188.

Sawhney, M., & Mandal, S. (2000b, May). Go global: Why: The case for globalization. *Business 2.0*, pp. 179–181, 183.

Scott, J. C. (1985). Human dimensions of information processing. *Business Education Forum, 39*(8), 16–21.

Scott, J. C. (1999). Developing cultural fluency: The goal of international business communication instruction in the 21st century. *Journal of Education for Business, 74*(3), 140–143.

Shannon, P. (2000). Including language in your global strategy for B2B e-commerce. *World Trade, 13*(9), 66–68.

Shneiderman, B. (2000). Universal usability. *Communication of the ACM, 43*(5), 85–91.

Stuller, J. (2000, January). Marketing in a world without borders. *Chief Executive Magazine, 38*, 40.

Swerdlow, J. L. (1999). Global culture. *National Geographic, 196*(2), 2–5.

Ulijn, J., O'Hair, D., Weggeman, M., Ledlow, G., & Hall, H. T. (2000). Innovation, corporate strategy, and cultural context: What is the mission for international business communication? *The Journal of Business Communication, 37*(3), 293–316.

Victor, D. A. (1992). *International business communication.* New York: HarperCollins Publishers, Inc.

Wagstaff, J. (2000, September 14). Technology journal: Machines translate universal talk into online babble. *The Wall Street Journal* [Europe], p. 26.

Writing for the screen. (1998, January). *Editor's Workshop*, p. 1–2.

The Role of Technology in Learning Marketing and Management Concepts

Margaret Crossman O'Connor
Image Consultants
Ringtown, Pennsylvania

Every industry is feeling the impact of technology's rapid growth. Many companies are struggling not only to understand all of the information that is now readily available, but also to determine how to manage the information flow. This is causing many to reevaluate their strategic plans to determine what data management processes are necessary to meet managers' needs (Loshin, 2001). Many are looking at knowledge management as a way of tying managerial objectives to the actual building of information systems within their organizations.

Organizations have never been as challenged by the changing environment—rapidly changing markets, competition, the economy, and world events that have caused consumers to look at things differently—as they are today. Furthermore, channels of communication have changed. As information is more readily available, consumers are becoming less patient in getting their needs met.

Marketing managers are faced with challenges they never anticipated. They have to determine whether or not their traditional marketing expenditures for advertising, promotions, and research are still effective with the advent of the Internet. Additionally, they are uncertain as to how effective the Internet is in capturing an audience for their products and services.

If businesses are struggling with such management and marketing issues, students must also address them. Teachers need a methodology that can focus students on the ambiguities that technology introduces and at the same time integrate approaches actually used in business to resolve these issues.

The purpose of this chapter is to focus on project-based business approaches and demonstrate how they can be integrated into business education. The chapter also shows how instructional projects can be created around technological developments like business Webs, product promotion, current business tools and e-services, and e-mentoring efforts. Some notes on preparing to bring technology into instruction complete the chapter.

PROJECT-BASED INSTRUCTION

Projects can incorporate technology concepts in marketing and business. Project-based instruction allows students to demonstrate problem solving and analysis. Successfully conducting a project requires research and analytic skills, as well as planning, organizing, and communicating with others.

Benefits of Using Projects

At all levels teachers and students are working in a project-based environment assisted by technology. Elementary and secondary teachers have reported that "[w]ell-designed, effective technology-supported projects provided students with a more in-depth learning experience than do traditional approaches" (McGrath, 1998, p. 28). David Dwyer, Apple Computer's director of education technologies, has said that classrooms equipped with technology increase basic skill achievement by 15 percent in 30 percent less time than classrooms that do not use technology (The Futures Channel, 2001). However, "technology must be adapted to fit the curriculum, not the reverse" (Gooden, 1996, p. 8), and in a manner that complements current teaching practices.

Students like the challenge of solving corporate problems. Projects can incorporate the problems companies face today related to technology and change, and students can assume responsibility for fixing the problems. Such projects will develop numerous skills, including managerial, decision-making, problem-solving, and technology-related skills. Furthermore, students will take ownership of their projects and be committed to understanding how to meet corporate objectives effectively. According to Gooden (1996),

> Computers are part of an overall strategy designed to . . . facilitate change and . . . create dynamic learning environments where students help construct knowledge. With computers, students can take greater control over their learning. They are able to take risks in problem solving, engage in computer-generated simulations and experiments, exhibit understanding through creation of multimedia products, visualize abstract concepts, and conduct independent and collaborative research using electronic communications. (p. 156)

Projects can enhance learning of marketing and management concepts. Web-based communication strategies contribute to students' understanding of the impact that the Internet is having on business. According to Bonk and Dennen (1999), utilizing the Web in instructions can

- Extend class discussion across days, weeks, and months
- Increase student involvement and responsibility for their own learning
- Allow for the completion of course requirements whenever and wherever students want
- Create opportunities for students to hear viewpoints beyond [the] classroom and university community
- Allow for fast implementation of instructional ideas and sharing of research findings (pp. 6–7)

The following are a few key points to keep in mind when incorporating technology-driven projects into the classroom:

1. Take an early class assessment as to what technology skills students have. Instructors may be surprised at the wealth of technology knowledge students have, much of which has been self-taught. Designate students who are technology-oriented as technology "experts." They will champion their class role and eagerly learn what they do not know to help the class.
2. Locate campus resources. If technology knowledge is scarce, the instructor may find software and training through other campus programs.
3. Develop contingency plans for technical problems. If multiple groups need help on a particular issue, take a day to regroup, resolve issues, and proceed with the course. Set up appointment times during office hours to cover issues and problem-solve with groups.
4. Provide expectations about timing of assignments on the course syllabus.
5. Supervise students.

Project Scope and Complexity

Teachers must decide on the scope and complexity of each project. Projects can involve teams or individuals and can be broad or limited in scope. The following is an example of the type of project that students will eventually encounter and the steep learning curve that occurs in real-world projects. Other projects may focus on developing knowledge and skills that must be integrated in a capstone project.

A capstone project. Students may need a description of an actual business project as a context for their work. The case study on consulting for a manufacturing subsidiary can be used for this purpose.

Intermediate-level projects. Students benefit from developing competence in other tasks before facing the capstone project. In an advertising management course, for example, students may role-play the interactions required to move a product or service idea from objectives to an advertising campaign resulting in either a commercial or print ad as part of regular instruction. A new project can be created by changing the parameters of this project, such as the medium for the final advertisement. This change builds on prior learning but challenges students to use their creative and analytical abilities.

In an actual classroom, most students chose to develop a Web site for their products, which was a more complex medium than was required and which took more time to develop than a traditional solution would have required. However, class feedback was extremely positive, especially regarding the value of learning new technologies such as FrontPage, Flash, and Photoshop (which students did on their own). Students enjoyed the challenge and requested information about other courses that would enhance their technology skills and complement their majors. This experience encouraged the instructor to build alliances across departments to help meet the needs of students. This is an example of the paradigm shift that Gooden (1996, p. 156) has noted as being a transition "from lone teacher as lecturer to teacher as facilitator and interdisciplinary team member. Students are no longer passive listeners. They actively guide classroom learning and inquiry."

PROJECT CASE STUDY

Consulting for a Manufacturing Subsidiary

A marketing consultant had agreed to complete a project for a manufacturing subsidiary of a large international conglomerate. The subsidiary had moved from the Northeast to the South, but the move had not gone well. Fewer than a dozen employees relocated with the company. Furthermore, the organization's computer systems were outdated, so new hires in the South were overwhelmed by the lack of automation. Much of the day-to-day task knowledge had left the company with its former employees. In an effort to reduce paperwork and automate the sales function, a consultant was brought in to help develop order processing via the Internet, using the current Web site. The project required an extensive collaborative effort between the external consultant and the internal staff.

First, the consultant had to understand the scope of the project and its objectives, construct a budget and timeline, and obtain project approval. The consultant needed to match her specializations to the project for the "best fit" and determine learning needs. The consultant's background was in marketing, necessitating that she learn the sales administration realm task by task. Next, the consultant needed to understand what information was housed on the existing mainframe computer system, what information was necessary for the project, and how to retrieve that information.

Working with the current employee group was essential. In this case, the Computer Information Systems group was overwhelmed with day-to-day problems. There was no LAN (Local Area Network) set up, and training was needed in many areas. Once the consultant evaluated the scope of the project, the project had to be articulated to the Web designers and programmers. As the program went through development, it had to be tested and revised based on actual use.

In an actual situation, a consultant learns through the interaction itself. In this case, the consultant realized that the biggest challenge in the entire project was how to motivate incredibly stressed-out people to meet project objectives and a timetable when there was no extra time in the day for any of them to do so. The consultant could visualize the outcome and knew each employee would improve at the task as each became more knowledgeable. The company needed to change, and so did each employee.

Business Resource and Research Tools

Instructors must enhance students' decision-making skills by incorporating the use of real-world business tools into the course curriculum. Students must research, read, and use the resources that business professionals use, including software and printed or online resources.

Business publications. Nonacademic business publications expose students to current events in business and trigger creative classroom projects, including those that integrate technology. They also help students develop good habits of reading business periodicals. Reading, research, and analysis can support other projects or be primary project tasks.

Teachers can direct students to articles about companies that are being transformed by technology, have them evaluate the positive and negative aspects of these transformations, and develop presentations about the impact of technology on business. Students can select a business problem that interests them as the focus for reading and develop recommendations for a company being studied in the class. The instructor can set the guidelines for the project based on course content. These reading projects can be assigned to teams made of up students from several disciplines.

STUDENT ACTIVITY

Corporate Modeling: Cross-Disciplinary Business Projects

Have teams of students from three or more different business courses work together to solve corporate problems. Current news stories will provide insights on what challenges different businesses and industries are facing today. Students can access contemporary professional online or printed publications as well as business Web sites. Team members should focus on their areas of expertise as they relate to the courses they are taking. The students should become the experts on their selected companies by researching demographics, company history, and other business factors. Then, direct students to develop presentations to share their recommended solutions for the challenges faced by those companies. Have them include charts and graphs. To encourage team spirit and attentiveness, students can also complete peer reviews of their classmates' presentations to be counted as a percentage of their final grades.

Note to teachers: The instructors of the courses need to coordinate objectives for each course that participates. A marketing student might focus on the customers of the company, the effect of the Internet on e-commerce, or competitive advantage. A finance student might focus on shareholder perspectives of growth through technology or investment in infrastructure to ensure competitiveness. A management student might focus on the effects of technology on human resource allocation, operations, and skill development.

The outcome is important—students will have a project they can include on their resumes and discuss during an interview. Studying the impact of technology develops knowledge needed for managerial decision making. The results of exceptional projects can, with student consent, be sent to the actual companies for review. In most cases companies will respond in writing, giving students the confidence of knowing that their ideas may be utilized by the organization they chose to study.

Reviewing the technology sections of periodicals and developing class projects around the content can help students develop critical-thinking skills. The same project can be customized for objectives in different classes. Electronic course delivery systems such as Blackboard (http://www.blackboard.com), InterWise (http://www.interwise.com), and WebCT (http://www.webct.com) allow instructors to conduct interactive group discussions and include business professionals in the discussions. Because the technology and product are new and exciting, student involvement tends to be high. However, teachers may want to limit "chat" groups to six in order to maintain control.

A search for online marketing trade publications will result in an extensive list of resources, only a few of which are presented in Table 1.

Table 1. Electronic Funds Transfer Acronyms and Terms	
Title and Online Location	**Description**
Advertising & Marketing Review http://www.ad-mkt-review.com	Features articles on Internet and digital technology, many information resources, and free downloads from the U.S. Department of Commerce
Advertising Age http://www.adage.com	Covers marketing and media

BtoB
    http://www.btobonline.com
    http://www.netb2b.com
	Covers the online marketing and advertising industry and is a resource for marketers managing business Web sites; includes business case studies, how-to tutorials, a developer directory, and more

Brandweek Online http://www.brandweek.com	Provides current headlines, feature stories, cultural trends, industry events, and other news

Measuring Results

There are several ways to measure the impact technology-infused projects have on a class. Using the following Management by Objectives (MBO) process will enable teachers to evaluate progress strategically and tactically:

1. Determine the key technology objectives to be accomplished by the class (top-down).

2. Define clear goals and how to accomplish them.
3. Develop the course around these objectives and goals and reflect this course direction in the syllabus.
4. Design assignments that reflect the goals developed for the course.
5. Discuss course objectives with students.
6. Request feedback on the agreement of course objectives and course content (bottom-up).
7. Periodically review class performance as it relates to course objectives.
8. Periodically benchmark progress towards objectives and revise the plan as needed.
9. Review the process to determine if the objectives have been met.

When student satisfaction is high, demand for additional courses or even a change of major may reflect the influence the class has had on students' lives. Most importantly, instructors will add value to learning through projects that integrate technology, marketing, and management concepts.

MARKETING AND MANAGEMENT ISSUES

The changing marketplace has caused many marketing and management dilemmas. For instance, does technology make managers better decision makers? Or, does being overloaded with information make people less productive? Furthermore, do companies grasp the true value of technology in the workplace and understand how their infrastructures should change to facilitate the access of information. Many books have been written on the subject, including *Competing on the Edge*, *The Social Life of Information*, and *Managing Interactively*. The bottom line for managers is return on investment (ROI). Cassidy (2000) has addressed many of these issues, looking at gross domestic product (GDP) down to the individual employee.

Current developments in marketing management lend themselves to instructional projects. For example, what infrastructure is necessary to maintain a technology-driven workplace? Should companies begin e-commerce? What type of Web site is best for an organization? What kinds of customer information should be accessed via the Internet? Who will train employees?

Teachers can significantly enhance classroom discussion by addressing these questions. They can also create projects around emerging corporate trends, such as business Webs, e-promotions, e-services, specialized tools, and business mentoring.

The Business Web

A business Web is defined as "a network of suppliers, distributors, commerce service providers, and customers that conduct business over the Internet to produce value for end customers and for each other" ("Business 2.0," 2000). Some business Webs evolve or "self-organize" while others are designed.

Business Web concepts. A business Web has a multidirectional communication flow, but it also reflects the culture established by its participants. Tapscott, Ticoll, and Lowy (2000) have described five models for emerging business Webs. Some business Webs, such as auctions and business procurement sites, bring buyers and sellers together in a manner resembling the open marketplace, or *agora*, where very diverse customer needs can be accommodated. Other Webs are hierarchical, led by a dominant business that sets the rules for interaction by other partners. Retail sites are examples of *aggregate* sites that present many products from many suppliers.

Value chain sites are organized by a broker to bring buyers and sellers of specific types of products together. Sometimes these sites link customers to various resources from which a solution can be created. *Alliances* are, like agoras, online marketplaces with loose structures. Like value chains, however, they are driven by specific customer needs, and suppliers in essence present their products in the hopes of being selected. *Distributive networks* (financial networks and technology groups) provide the behind-the-scenes functionality to promote e-commerce and security. The World Wide Web Consortium (http://www.w3. org) is a value chain Web. The first four types are "content" Webs; the last—the distributive network—is a "process" Web.

The goal of business Webs is to share accurate information quickly among constituencies. Because customers have much more information than they did in the past, companies no longer have the degree of control over interactions that they once had. According to Tapscott et al. (2000), the Internet economy will soon quantify capital through relationships. For instance, customer capital is "[t]he wealth contained in an organization's relationships with its customers and, according to most thinkers, its suppliers" (p. 22). In the Internet economy, customer capital, along with knowledge capital and structural capital, is more important than land or buildings.

Classroom or teaching Webs. Students can simulate business Webs using classroom or other teaching Webs. Through a common Web site, instructors can link students in their classes with students in other disciplines, as well as other instructors and business professionals. Teachers can recruit business professionals through alumni or university internship programs. Teachers can also post assignments and host discussions related to stimulating topics in their fields of study. Teachers and students can post articles and information, making the forum a bulletin board of ideas related to their field of study.

Any design project should include a "before-and-after" comparison to develop critical-thinking skills and facilitate a top-down approach to understanding how a Web-based medium can be used to break corporate objectives into tactical communication programs.

E-Promotion

Branding over the Internet is currently a "hot topic" for marketers. Companies are reevaluating budgeting for advertising, promotion, and market research and wondering if they can improve their ROI through branding over the Internet. Marketing companies

STUDENT ACTIVITY

A Multiple Class Web

Link a marketing class focusing on consumer behavior with an advertising management class to discuss the role of advertising through electronic media. Ask professionals from various advertising agencies—traditional, multimedia, or electronic—to join and discuss the challenges of today's marketplace and the types of clients their agencies serve. Have students review current events in advertising, as well as learn about key trends in the field to prepare for the discussion.

An alternative is to link an instructional technology class with a marketing management or accounting management class. Such combinations can promote discussions of how technology drives business practices and the ramifications of various electronic media used in business practices. (Haynes, Helmi, & Maun [2000] provide additional discussion of Internet teaching methods for multiple disciplines.)

are unsure how to allocate their budgets, not knowing the full value of Internet programs and whether or not the programs are more cost-effective than traditional vehicles such as print advertising (Braunstein & Levine, 2000).

One emerging form of marketing e-promotion is called "viral marketing." "Viral marketing refers to any promotion that is user-propelled via the Internet, typically using e-mail" (Iconocast, 2001). Incentives entice "click-to-click" sharing of information about a brand in order to find new customers for a company's product or service. As a substitute for referrals and direct mail, viral marketing is a cost-effective means to expose potential users to product information. Epinions.com (http://www.epinions.com/) is an example of a Web site that uses viral marketing technology.

Teaching promotional approaches. In teaching this concept, an instructor could generate discussion about how user-propelled promotions vary by company. For example, how would a communication network differ for an educational organization versus an image-driven apparel company? Students can develop Internet-propelled incentives to target the customers of those companies or organizations. Students should research the technology at viral Web sites such as Viralon (http://www.viralon.com/about_viralon.html) and Qbiquity (http://www. qbiquity.com) to further understand this form of promotion. Marketing projects that are Internet driven provide teachers the opportunity to debate current issues regarding privacy, security, and ethics.

Start-up Software and Services

Early-stage start-up companies have a number of software and service options to make doing business easier. Dell (2001) has stated that early-stage start-ups should review industry-specific software and services and incorporate them if they offer value to the new organization. Teaching approaches can incorporate the information and examples from Web sites and the professional software itself. Some educational products simulate professional software.

STUDENT ACTIVITY

Customer Communications

Following a discussion of the concept of customer capital, ask students to analyze various Web sites to isolate customer communication features. Then have students compare and contrast Web sites. Next, have student teams build or simulate Web sites. Have students determine what components to include on their Web sites. Then, have the groups develop methodologies to measure Web site effectiveness.

For example, if a student group has been given the assignment to work as a CPA firm that is trying to attract new business, the group should explore issues such as whether to list current clients on the Web site to draw new business, to develop the Web site in different languages, or to develop a new client contact page.

Note to teachers: You may want to select a particular industry based on the class objectives. You can choose, based on class experience, whether or not to actually build Web sites or develop mock Web sites using PowerPoint or other software. You can develop class discussion around theory and key concepts related to the course objectives, prompting students to discuss how they feel as potential customers or employees about the following questions: What would they want to see on a Web site? How would their parents or other target markets react to the Web site? Class discussion can include privacy, legal, safety, corporate espionage, firewall, and security issues. If students come up with many ideas, you can suggest that they rank them according to importance, given that most projects have a budget and not everything can be accomplished at once.

Professional software and services. An example of a comprehensive customer relationship management approach is illustrated by the products of Salesforce.com (http://www.salesforce.com/us/). This service provides instant information to salespeople. Once cleared through a password system, users are able to go into a database, access customer information, get directions to an office, track orders, and perform other tasks. The Customer Support Management service allows an organization to automate rules for customer contacts so that customer needs are met on a prioritized basis (http://www.salesforce.com/us/services/support.jsp). Sales Force Automation provides analysis of sales transactions to eliminate bottlenecks and identify trends (http://www.salesforce.com/us/services/sales.jsp). Marketing Automation helps assess the impact of advertising and track leads (http://www.salesforce.com/us/services/marketing.jsp).

In addition to services, individual software products can be useful in designing marketing plans. For example, Marketing Plan Pro, a product of PaloAlto.com, "guides [the new business] through the process of writing a marketing plan . . . with an outline, tables, and charts tailored to [individual] needs" (http://www.paloalto.com/ps/mp/be/). Marketing Plan Pro includes sample plans and complements other products such as Web Strategy Pro and Cash Plan Pro (http://www.paloalto.com/ps//mp). A sample marketing plan produced by the software for the business, Interior

Views, is reproduced in PDF format for potential clients and may prove useful as a classroom example (http://www.paloalto.com/sampleplans/protected/mpp4/interiorviews.pdf).

These products supplement the vast resource base of conventional and online publications addressing marketing, distribution, and management areas.

Using software in teaching. Coulter and Stryker (1994) have incorporated professional estate, gift, and fiduciary software packages into a graduate tax course for public accounting majors who are preparing for the CPA exam. The professional or commercial software enhances the learning experience because it reinforces concepts, stimulates interest, and reduces repetitive efforts by students. Coulter and Stryker stated that "[b]y embracing commercial software, instructors can find programs which will ease some of their workload, create a better learning environment, and prepare their students for entry into the real world" (p. 6).

Teachers might include a software product like Marketing Plan Pro (http://www.paloalto.com/ps/mp/) in the curriculum. Marketing Plan Pro provides students with a framework to understand the steps necessary to launch a product or service. The software simplifies the steps in order to focus attention on key areas of discipline. Marketing Plan Pro also provides students with a road map for any future efforts to market a product or service. This is a particularly useful tool for those students who are not marketing majors, but who may take one or two marketing courses for their major.

Marketing plan software varies in complexity. Teachers should be sure to use software geared towards student level. For example, secondary, undergraduate, and graduate levels of instruction warrant different types or versions of software currently available. One adaptable educational program is Marketing Builder Express (Matulich, 1998). A course syllabus designed by Courtnage, a Montana college professor, for undergraduate marketing students illustrates how the software is integrated into the course (http://www.rocky.edu/~courtnal/MARKETSYL.htm).

Students can evaluate software and discuss how software makes business more efficient and how communication strategies are enhanced by software. Students can also evaluate changing skill levels required of salespeople, for example, the need for higher-level research and problem-solving skills. Project-based assignments can be developed using the software and students can critique ease of use and effectiveness.

Mentoring

Mentoring is an important tool for entrepreneurs who realize their need for guidance from experienced professionals in their fields. According to Ball (2001), "Mentoring relationships help foster risk-tolerance in innovative individuals, so entrepreneurial spirit and ability become the primary focus. This unique one-on-one relationship is meaningful, productive and mutually beneficial" (p. 100). The Small

Business Administration sponsors a Business Development mentor-protégé program to help minority-owned firms bid more effectively for federal contracts (http://www.sba.gov/8abd/indexmentor.html).

Current e-mentoring efforts. At one time, mentoring was restricted to the office setting or the telephone. But technology has made mentoring easier through e-mail. In this new generation of business enterprise, mentor-protégé relationships are viable strategic alliances that leverage and establish a dynamic business presence (Ball, 2001).

Catling (2001) has described the environment of the Internet start-up:

> Managers of startups are still completely dependent upon the effectiveness of their team; it's just that the team is smaller and you need people who are effective today. There's little time for development, training or mentoring programs, no 'let's stick him in the sales division for a couple of years, that should round him out.' People get responsibility fast, and they learn fast, or they don't survive. (p. 1)

Whether organizations can afford to do without mentoring, however, remains to be seen, especially when investors' money is at risk. Women in Technology International (WITI) exists to mentor others, stating "WITI has successfully provided women in technology inspiration, education, conferences, on-line services publications and an exceptional worldwide network of resources" (http://www.witi.org/center/aboutwiti/). The list of "Groups Relating to Women in Computer Science/Computing" (http://www.cs.yale.edu/homes/tap/cs-women-groups.html) includes many that have mentoring as a function.

Integrating mentoring in instructional settings. Educators can foster enriching relationships for their students by developing e-mentoring programs. Mahayosnand (2000) has indicated that e-mentoring programs are extremely helpful in building self-esteem and confidence. These programs reduce fears about "unknown" subject matter and build communication skills. Typically, long-term relationships are built and the students' performance is enhanced. Whether residing locally or at a distance, professionals who remember clearly what it was like to begin their careers will want to help others.

Currently, only a few nationally recognized e-mentoring programs exist. More than 100 colleges and universities participate in MentorNet (http://www.mentornet.net/) for female undergraduate and graduate students in engineering and related sciences. Prospective mentors complete a Web-based application. Electronic Emissary at the University of Texas (Austin) was established by the College of Education in 1993 and is the longest running program to date (http://emissary.ots.utexas.edu/emissary/index.html). Funding is provided through grants and endorsements.

Undertaking a national e-mentoring program is time consuming, and currently there is not one for business fields. Teachers can begin by contacting local companies that are interested in helping students learn more about their careers, perhaps companies that already have relationships with the academic community or are related to the academic program or teacher in some other way. Once a mentor group is established, the teacher can connect a student to a mentor via e-mail. Student development can be recorded through journals that document what the student is learning and his or her growth over time.

Using e-mail as a communication device for mentoring is effective. There is some evidence that people have an easier time articulating their needs through e-mail than by telephone or face to face. Perhaps e-mail reduces the emotional impact of resolving conflicts or perhaps people feel less vulnerable to rejection when there is no face-to-face interaction (Gooden, 1996).

BRINGING TECHNOLOGY INTO EDUCATION

Levine (2000) has discussed the emergence of three types of universities: "brick universities," or "traditional residential institutions"; "click universities," or "virtual universities"; and what he perceives to be the most competitive format, "brick and click" universities. How can teachers prepare to integrate technology into traditional classrooms and to take learning online? Many online resources show ways that other teachers have prepared themselves.

Online Courses

Free courses offered over the Internet can enhance instructors' e-learning skills. Meister highlights several free courses offered by nonprofit and commercial groups, including Barnes and Noble University (http://www.barnesandnobleuniversity.com/), which lists free online courses on topics ranging from Shakespearean comedy to business, science, and technology. Motorola University (http://www.motorolacareers. com/ufsd/ university/index.cfm) provides courses in management-skill training such as problem solving in teams and total-quality continuous-improvement tools (Meister, 2001). Online instruction gives instructors the opportunity to be the students, expose themselves to alternative ways of learning and grow in their own knowledge of diverse subject matter.

Web Registries

If instructors are looking for ways to connect their learning through technology, Web registries, or searchable databases of information on different topics, provide a breadth of information. For instance, the Connected Classroom Project Registry (http:/ /www. qesn.meq.gouv.qc.ca/cc/projreg.htm) not only lists project Web sites but also provides links to collaborators.

A community of agile partners in education (CAPE) is an electronic registry consisting of small- and medium-sized K–12 schools and universities that want to use technology to share resources on topics (http://www.acape.org/about/director.html). Developed through the Pennsylvania Department of Education's Link to Learn program, its members can access program ideas, learn about grants, videoconference, and have virtual get-togethers, as well as gather information on a variety of topics. CAPE also provides software development workshops.

EdView is a registry service developed by Apple Computers (http://www.edview. com). The site provides age-appropriate technology information on courses, along with teachers' advice and opinions (The Futures Channel, 2001). For example, a search on business and economics topics provides a link to "20 Reasons to Put Your Business on the WWW" (http://www.net101.com/reasons.html). The Net 101 site provides additional marketing resources and links.

Internet Groups

Instructors can discuss topics related to their fields through Internet groups. A variety of groups discuss current career opportunities, research, curriculum developments, and the latest educational trends. One diverse group called "systers-students" (http://www.systers.org/mecca) "is a mailing list open to all female graduate and undergraduate students studying computer science and related areas." Members include undergraduate through doctoral students in the United States and issues range from dealing with supervisors to the latest research on new technology trends.

Corporate Collaboration

The Hartford Financial Services Group and the University of Connecticut cooperate to offer a Business Mastery Certificate Program to 40 corporate leaders annually. Faculty members instruct participants using a "brick and click" approach, including traditional lectures and online assignments. Bloomsburg University, in Pennsylvania, offers a master of science degree in instructional technology (MSIT). This degree has two career tracks—one for the business sector and one for the education sector ("Instructional Technology," n.d.). The loyalty of the alumni to the program helps to "brand" the university in the field of instructional technology.

Internet Studies

Internet courses are emerging and provide models for developing courses for business curricula. Several universities have already developed and implemented Internet studies as a minor, including Cornell University, Vanderbilt, and the Centenary College of Louisiana. Brandeis University offers a course entitled "The Internet and Society" which covers the basics of security, e-commerce, and Web site understanding and design (Jesdanum, 2001). This course counts toward minors in various disciplines, and this same concept can easily be applied across business disciplines, incorporating key issues related to those fields through technological advancement. Building the course and even including students in the process illustrates the collaboration that is required in today's business environment.

SUMMARY

Project-based business methodologies incorporating the latest trends in technology add value to student learning through interactivity. Developing course content around current business trends involving technology (e.g., business Webs, viral marketing, e-mentoring, business software and periodicals, and other developments) permits instructors to define their instruction as relevant and cutting edge.

Many opportunities exist to examine different approaches to instructional technologies, such as discussion groups, online courses, registries, and others. Teachers can sample from these resources to determine which to incorporate in their classrooms. Instructors' commitment to helping students find and prepare for careers does not change; the techniques used to keep attention and draw students into the learning process do. If educators can use technology-driven tools creatively to attract students, they may be able to hold their attention well into the future.

REFERENCES

Ball, R. (2001, June). Mentor-protégé relationships. *Industrial Distribution, 6.* Retrieved from the World Wide Web: wysiwyg://bodyframe.46/http://ehostvgw2...Num=23& boolcanTerm=mentoring&fuzzyTerm=

Bonk, C. J., & Dennen, V. (1999). Teaching on the web: With a little help from my pedagogical friends. *Journal of Computing in Higher Education, 11*(1), 3–28.

Braunstein, M., & Levine, E. (2000). *Deep branding on the Internet.* Roseville, CA: Prima Publishing

Business 2.0: Relationships rule. (2000, May 1). *Business 2.0.* Retrieved from the World Wide Web: http://www.business2.com/webguide/0,1660,37213|121|0|0|1|a, 00.html

Cassidy, J. (2000, November 27). The productivity mirage: Are computers really that important?. *The New Yorker,* 106–118

Catling, A. (2001, February 2). Crossing the Internet divide: Life running an Internet startup. Retrieved August 25, 2001, from the World Wide Web: http://www.business2.com/articles/web/0,1653,16428,FF.html

Coulter, F. V. & Stryker, J. P. (1994). *Using professional software to enhance teaching excellence* (JC960037). Orlando, FL: Junior Colleges. (ERIC Document Reproduction Service No. ED 390 458)

Dell, A. (2001, January). My best practices. *Fortune Small Business,* 54–58

The Futures Channel. (2001). *A conversation with David Dwyer.* Retrieved August 23, 2001, from the World Wide Web: http://www.thefutureschannel.com/conversations_archive/dwyer_conversation.htm

Gooden, A. R. (1996). *Computers in the classroom.* United States: Apple Press

Haynes, G., Helmi, D. G., & Maun, C. (2000). Internet teaching methods across the disciplines. *The Journal of Applied Business Research, 16*(4), 1–13.

Iconocast. (2001, April 5). Viral marketing. *Iconocast Archives.* Retrieved August 23, 2001, from the World Wide Web: http://www.iconocast.com/issue/20010405.html

Instructional Technology (M.S.). (n.d.). Retrieved August 23, 2001, from the World Wide Web: http://www.bloomu.edu/academic/programs/MSIT.shtml

Jesdanum, A. (2001, April 21). Now you can minor in the Net. Waltham, MA: Associated Press Wire Service. Retrieved from the August 25, 2001, from the World Wide Web: http://www.ap.org

Levine, A. (2000.) The future of colleges: 9 inevitable changes, *The Chronicle Review,* 47(9), B10. Retrieved from the World Wide Web: http://chronicle.com/weekly/v47/i09/09b01001.htm

Mahayosnand, P. P. (2000). Public health e-mentoring: An investment for the next millennium. *American Journal of Public Health, 90*(8), 1317.

Matulich, E. (1998). *Marketing builder express.* Cincinnati, OH: South-Western Publishing/Thomson Learning.

McGrath, B. (1998, April). Partners in learning: Twelve ways technology changes the teacher-student relationship. *T.H.E. Journal, 25*(9). Retrieved August 23, 2001, from the World Wide Web: http://www.thejournal.com/magazine/vault/A1982.cfm

Meister, J. C. (2001.) The brave new world of corporate education. *The Chronicle Review, 47*(22), B10. Retrieved from the World Wide Web: http://chronicle.com/weekly/v47/i22b01001.htm

Tapscott, D., Ticoll, D., & Lowy, A. (2000). *Digital capital: Harnessing the power of business Webs.* Boston: Harvard Business School Press.

Enterprise Resource Planning Concepts and Implementation Issues

Mark W. Lehman
Mississippi State University
Mississippi State, Mississippi

When Belvedere Co.'s order-entry clerks couldn't keep up with constantly changing product lines and couldn't get reliable real-time data on product availability, the company's profits suffered. Customers complained about not getting what they ordered or not getting their orders when they were supposed to. Unhappy customers returned shipments. To solve the fulfillment problems, Mark Waldron, CFO and CIO . . . went shopping for ERP. After the ERP system was installed, Belvedere could process 15% more orders on a typical day—without additional staff. Furthermore, the company was able to reduce inventory by 30%. It began to fill and ship customer orders within 48 hours, down from five days. Customer complaints dropped. (Piturro, 1999, p. 42)

Although the Internet dominates news headlines, another computer revolution has been taking place within corporate America. Driven by users' expectations for immediate information about every facet of organizations, accounting and information specialists are implementing an approach known as enterprise resource planning (ERP).

An ERP system is a collection of related business application software systems that shares data stored in a single database. A typical ERP system supports numerous business applications, including marketing, sales, production, procurement, human resources, financial reporting, and asset management. Employees in virtually every functional area interact with the ERP system.

Billion-dollar companies have been installing ERP systems for decades. Only recently have mid-sized companies begun to install them. Smaller companies have begun to realize that ERP systems enable them to compete more effectively with larger competitors. Thus, students entering today's workplace are likely to be involved with ERP systems either as users or as members of development teams. Business instructors need to ensure that students have, at a minimum, a conceptual foundation of ERP. ERP systems, however, are complex, and the magnitude of information available in journals, books, and on the Internet, makes learning about ERP an intimidating task.

What is a logical method of teaching business education students about ERP? Teachers can start with an overview of ERP, such as the one given in this chapter, which traces ERP's history, components, and benefits. This chapter also includes twelve recommendations for ERP implementation that students should understand. Teachers can use this chapter as the basis for presenting ERP concepts and implementation points in a lesson about ERP or integrate them into current instruction on computerized accounting systems. Student activities are included to help teachers integrate ERP concepts into business classes.

OVERVIEW OF ERP DEVELOPMENT AND CONCEPTS

A brief historical perspective demonstrates how an ERP system differs from traditional computer-based information systems. Describing the components provides an inside view of an ERP system.

Traditional Approach to Information Systems

The accounting (financial reporting) function is the center of a business's information system. A business installing a computer-based information system would typically computerize its accounting function first. Later, with growth in size and technological sophistication, the business would develop other information systems to address marketing, human resources, inventory control, and other applications. The resulting information system would consist of several independent, smaller information systems, each having its own unique hardware and software. Each would have limited ability to interact or share data with other applications.

Figure 1 illustrates how a business enterprise with three distinct information systems processes a customer order, purchases raw materials, and manufactures the product.

Communication between systems requires that data for one system be entered from paper source documents. The first system then generates a new document to communicate the information to the next system. For example, a customer sends the business a purchase order specifying items and quantities. Information on the purchase order is keyed and processed by the order entry system to generate a sales order. A copy of the sales order is sent to the manufacturing and distribution system and keyed into that system. This process continues. Each system uses data entered from a source document generated by another system.

Figure 1. Traditional Information System

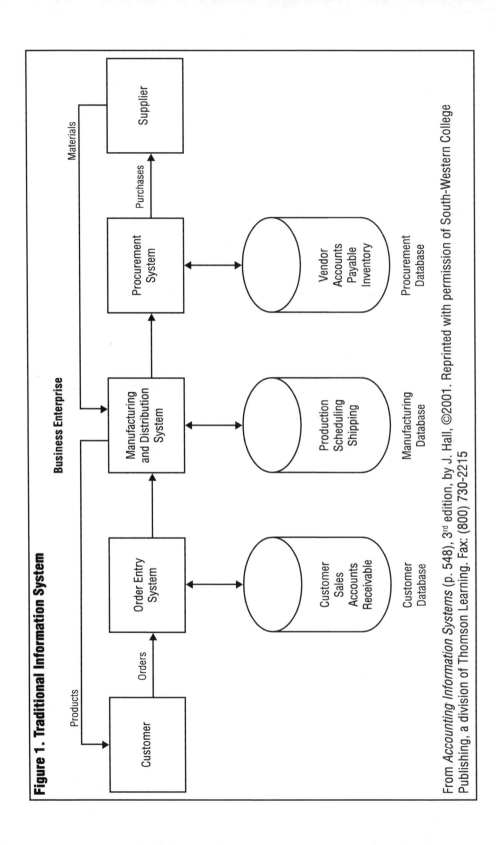

Business Enterprise

From *Accounting Information Systems* (p. 548), 3rd edition, by J. Hall, ©2001. Reprinted with permission of South-Western College Publishing, a division of Thomson Learning. Fax: (800) 730-2215

The inefficiency and human error inherent in this traditional information system are obvious. These problems are compounded when a business has many other smaller information systems, such as human resources, asset management, accounting and financial reporting, and marketing, that must also share data. The obvious solution to the problems of the traditional information system is a single system that uses a single database. This solution is the foundation of the ERP approach.

The ERP Solution

Early ERP systems operated in an environment where all the computing and data storage processes were performed on a mainframe computer. Users accessed information through terminals that possessed no local computing capabilities. ERP systems were initially developed for large businesses that could afford the cost of establishing and maintaining the communication technology required to link terminals to the mainframe computer. SAP, a leading ERP vendor, introduced its first mainframe ERP system in 1974.

In the early 1990s three factors enabled software vendors to develop ERP systems in a client/server environment: (a) advances in communication technology significantly increased the efficiency of transmitting data; (b) the Internet provided businesses, regardless of size, with equal ability to communicate data; and (c) advances in the computing power of personal computers allowed systems to distribute computing and data storage tasks. These factors significantly reduced the complexity and cost of networking. In a client/server environment, a network of computers shares processing and data storage tasks. The ease and relatively low cost of communicating between computers made ERP systems affordable to mid-sized and smaller businesses. SAP introduced its first client/server ERP system in 1992. Today's ERP systems use the Internet to provide access to data from any location.

An ERP system provides a single, uniform solution to the information needs of a business. Unlike traditional information systems, an ERP system is a suite or package of software provided by a single vendor that operates on a single client/server system. Leaders in the ERP software industry include Bean, Oracle, PeopleSoft, SAP, J. D. Edwards, Great Lakes, Lawson, Platinum, QAD, and Ross and Solomon (O'Leary, 2000). Figure 2 illustrates the primary components of an ERP system. Because each business application uses the same software and hardware, data flows easily among applications. Once employees or business partners enter data into the ERP system, those data are available for planning and decision making.

As Figure 2 shows, a customer order prompts the system to decide whether additional inventory should be produced. If additional raw materials are required, the system places an order with the supplier. Knowing when raw material will be received permits scheduling the production of the merchandise and communicating the expected delivery date to the customer. The ERP system should handle these relatively mechanical decisions automatically, enabling employees to perform less structured business planning that improves profitability.

Figure 2. An ERP System

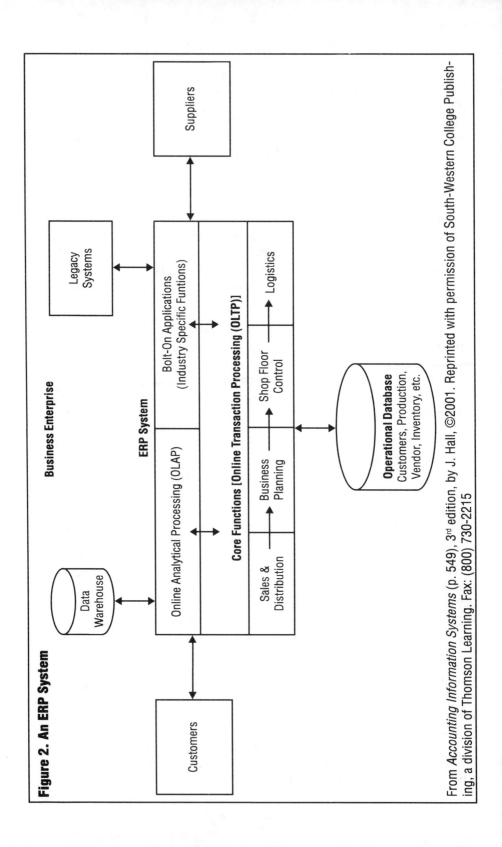

Business Enterprise

Suppliers

Legacy Systems

ERP System

Bolt-On Applications (Industry Specific Funtions)

Core Functions [Online Transaction Processing (OLTP)]

Online Analytical Processing (OLAP)

Sales & Distribution → Business Planning → Shop Floor Control → Logistics

Data Warehouse

Operational Database Customers, Production, Vendor, Inventory, etc.

Customers

From *Accounting Information Systems* (p. 549), 3rd edition, by J. Hall, ©2001. Reprinted with permission of South-Western College Publishing, a division of Thomson Learning. Fax: (800) 730-2215

ERP Components

An ERP system consists of core functions, bolt-on applications, legacy systems, and a data warehouse.

Core functions. Software vendors offer ERP software in a modular format. Each module supports one business function (accounting, financial reporting, accounts payable, or payroll, for example). The modules that are purchased comprise the core functions of the ERP system and handle data input, processing, and output—known as online transaction processing. The ERP data are stored in a single database called an operational database. A business can later add other modules that it needs. A manufacturer can add a production module. If a business wants to sell its product on the Internet, it can add an e-commerce sales module.

Bolt-on applications. ERP software is designed to fit the needs of most businesses but can also be customized to fit the particular needs of a business. Some businesses have unique needs that cannot be met by any ERP system, regardless of its flexibility. Independent software vendors create applications to satisfy these unique information needs. These bolt-on (add-on) applications are written to work with ERP core functions. ERP vendors are eager for independent vendors to create bolt-on applications to their ERP systems (O'Leary, 2000). The Internet sites of ERP vendors typically list available bolt-on applications.

Legacy systems. Businesses with unique information needs often have software that works effectively and is well accepted by employees. Previous information systems can be incorporated into the new ERP system. These legacy systems, thus, continue to operate.

Data warehouse. Just as business teachers can be completely overwhelmed by the demands for attention from colleagues and students at the same time, an ERP system's operational database can also become overwhelmed as hundreds or thousands of users simultaneously perform data input and query activities. Data warehousing solves database overload. The data warehouse is a copy of the operational database available for managers to analyze historical data. Updated on a daily basis, the data warehouse provides sufficiently current information for most managers' online analytical processing needs, such as ad hoc reporting and what-if analysis.

The development of an ERP system using a modular approach with core applications, bolt-on applications, and legacy systems can be compared to the process of upgrading a personal computer system. The student activity on page 170 enables students to make this comparison.

Benefits of ERP

If information is power, then an ERP system is the ultimate power source. An ERP system provides employees with instant access to the information they need to make effective business decisions. ERP systems should enable businesses to achieve the

STUDENT ACTIVITY

Upgrading a Personal Computer Versus Developing an ERP System

Following a presentation on ERP components (core, bolt-on, legacy, and data warehouse components), ask students individually or in groups to evaluate the needs described in the scenario below and relate them to core, bolt-on, or legacy components.

Scenario: *The time had come for Tom to upgrade his computer. His current computer had a great 19-inch monitor, but the computer needed a bigger hard drive, more RAM memory, and a faster modem, as well as a DVD player and CD burner—necessary components for entertainment. Although Tom wanted a speaker system with a subwoofer, he knew he would be unable to play it at the volume he wanted, so that purchase could wait until he went to college. Finally, Tom wanted an ergonomically designed keyboard that, unfortunately, was available only from computer equipment vendors other than the one that could supply the other items he needed.*

Note to teachers: The following notes serve as background for class discussion. Tom's purchase of a new computer system is similar to how a business purchases an ERP system. Tom's computer must have some basic, or core components: a processor, RAM memory, and a hard drive. An ERP system has modules that are basic to an information system—accounting and financial reporting, accounts payable, and accounts receivable.

The DVD player and CD burner are additional components that are offered by the computer vendor and that Tom needs to meet his entertainment needs. The computer system will perform its general functions without the DVD player and CD burner but will not meet Tom's basic needs. Just as a manufacturing business needs to control its production to meet its particular needs and would add the production and procurement modules offered by the ERP vendor, Tom will add additional hardware and software to meet his needs.

Tom already has a great monitor, so he does not need to buy another. Similarly, a business that has an existing information system that works well can integrate that system with its ERP system. Legacy systems are often retained when the ERP vendor cannot offer an equivalent system.

Finally, Tom ordered a keyboard from another computer equipment vendor. The keyboard fulfilled a unique need that his computer vendor could not satisfy. Similarly, ERP vendors have partners (independent vendors) that offer information systems for unique applications. These bolt-on systems are designed specifically for a particular ERP system and are added to the system like the vendor's modules.

following objectives: (a) reduce inventory levels, (b) improve cash management, (c) increase revenue and profits, (d) reduce transportation and logistics costs, (e) reduce information technology (IT) costs, (f) improve customer responsiveness, and (g) improve supply chain management (Janstal, 1999). The ERP system also provides "events-approach" accounting and automated decision making.

Events-approach accounting. An ERP system should enable a business to adopt an events-approach to accounting. In traditional accounting systems, economic events are recorded into journals and ledgers for the purposes of preparing statements following generally accepted accounting principles, or GAAP-based financial statements. In contrast, an events-approach accounting system records all pertinent information related to any event, even if the event does not result in an accounting entry.

The following examples illustrate the events-approach to accounting.

1. Individuals frequently access Internet sites without making purchases. The access of the Internet site is an event. The site should provide an incentive for individuals to register their personal information, especially their e-mail addresses. Capturing the addresses and possibly some demographic information about individuals can allow marketing managers to profile potential customers and gain insights about their buying habits.
2. Many businesses, such as grocery and video rental stores, provide incentives for customers to carry special cards. Scanning the card prior to entering a sales transaction allows the accounting system to identify the customer's name and record of purchases. The business can use this information to analyze customer-buying habits.

Automated decision making. An ERP system should perform routine decisions among business functions without human intervention. The following scenario illustrates the automation of decisions. A sales representative tries to close a deal in a customer's office. Before finalizing the sale, the customer wants a commitment on the delivery date. Connecting to the ERP system through the Internet, the sales representative enters the product and quantity into the order system, which instantly checks the levels of inventory available. Finding an inadequate level of inventory, the inventory system immediately issues an order to produce the item. The production system processes the request, determining a schedule for production based on the availability of labor and raw materials. Any required raw materials are immediately ordered from the suppliers. Within seconds, the production date is determined and communicated to the customer.

A traditional system uses paper documents and independent computer systems, and the order is entered in separate sales, inventory, production, purchasing, accounts receivable, and general ledger functions. In contrast, all the functions of the ERP system happen automatically based on entering the order once.

SUCCESSFUL ERP SYSTEM IMPLEMENTATION

ERP appears to be an ideal solution for developing effective information systems. Without proper planning, however, the ERP system can fail to work properly, spelling disaster for employees who struggle to input transactions, process data, and prepare reports. Twelve recommendations can guide successful ERP implementations. Many of them are not unique to ERP systems. Most reflect standard system development methods. However, the power of ERP systems makes the recommendations more important than ever.

1. Recognize the magnitude of the project. *You've got a tiger by the tail.*

ERP projects can easily cost millions of dollars and require years to implement. Even ERP products designed for mid- to small-level businesses are complex, containing hundreds or even thousands of screens, reports, and data tables. ERP systems often require long implementation periods and higher costs than initially planned. Only 25 percent of companies recently surveyed completed an ERP implementation project ahead of schedule, and only 14 percent of the companies surveyed reported lower than expected costs. One ERP consultant recommends that budgeted costs be increased by 25 to 50 percent (Piturro, 1999).

2. Hire a consulting firm to serve as a partner. *It takes two to tango.*

Implementing an ERP system successfully requires customizing ERP software to the business. IT staffs of most businesses typically work at full capacity. Asking them to absorb the extra work necessary to implement an ERP system could equate to asking airline pilots to load the baggage or serve beverages during the flight. In addition, unless they have experience from previous employment, members of the IT staff will not have firsthand experience in implementing an ERP system. Hiring a consulting firm to assist in every phase of the ERP installation solves these problems. The consultants and the IT staff should form a partnership, with the consultants providing ERP software knowledge and IT personnel providing knowledge of the business.

When selecting a consulting firm, management must ensure that the firm can adequately staff the project with individuals who have experience, preferably in the same industry. Consulting firms are typically independent of ERP vendors and should be able to recommend ERP systems objectively. However, firms may have more experience with one ERP system and may, therefore, be biased in favor of that system.

Hiring a consultant, like any other business venture, is not without its risks. Deloitte Consulting helped Barclays International Funds Group, a European financial services company, customize and implement its Baan ERP system in an amazing six months. Yet the same consulting firm is being sued by W.L. Gore & Associates for its failed implementation of a PeopleSoft system. FoxMeyer Drugs blames Andersen Consulting (now Accenture) for the botched implementation of SAP's R/3 software and the company's having to file for bankruptcy (Osterland, 2000).

3. Model your business processes. *Nothing is ever as easy as you think it is.*

A business process is, quite simply, a procedure for how something gets done. The process must be documented, and a variety of modeling techniques can be used, such as data flow diagrams and systems flowcharts. Some activities seem relatively simple. But interviewing and observing employees performing the activities will reveal special circumstances that impact how the activities are reported in the information system. The following are examples of the types of questions that can be used to learn more about various processes:

- How does an employee report damaged merchandise?
- How are credit sales approved?
- What happens if an item is out of stock?
- How do employees change their tax withholdings?

In addition, business processes evolve over time. For example, the Internet has changed how traveling sales representatives report sales, replacing a written form with an Internet screen. The evolution from one business process to another does not automatically eliminate unnecessary procedures.

A business should not blindly continue to use the same business processes. Installing an ERP system is a perfect time for a business to examine the validity of its processes. A business should not only model what current business practices *are*, but also what business practices *should be*. The ERP system can help direct the modeling process. ERP systems themselves have been developed using a "best practices" approach (O'Leary, 2000), based on the experiences of thousands of businesses. Ultimately, the ERP system should introduce some new business practices that improve the flow of information.

STUDENT ACTIVITY

Modeling Business Practices

Divide the class into groups of three to four students. Instruct each group to identify a common activity in a familiar company or organization, such as a customer's payment of a check at a restaurant. Require the groups to prepare a list of every possible event that could occur in relation to the activity. For example, the customer may (a) pay with cash, check, or credit card; (b) have the credit card rejected; (c) not have adequate cash to pay the bill; (d) leave without paying the bill; (e) complain about charges appearing on the bill; (f) use a coupon; and/or (g) ask the bill to be divided among the diners. All of these events require the business to have operating policies in place and each should result in data being entered into the ERP system.

Note to teachers: Without taking the time to analyze a business process, people generally perceive it to be simpler than it really is. This activity should enlighten students regarding the detail needed to map a company's business processes.

4. Search for available industry solutions. *Don't reinvent the wheel.*

ERP vendors strive to develop comprehensive software that would meet the needs of any business. Even so, some businesses have unique information needs that cannot be met by one-size-fits-all software. For this reason, ERP vendors promote the development of unique applications by independent software vendors.

Bolt-on software is designed to interface with a particular ERP system. Domino's Pizza, for example, uses bolt-on software to give its 4,500 franchises flexibility in ordering supplies:

> A franchise can call and adjust its order even after the truck has rolled away from the distribution center. To help anticipate demand Domino's uses forecasting software from Prescient Systems Inc., which bolts on to their PeopleSoft ERP System . . . [and] a system from Manugistics Inc. to schedule and route the delivery trucks. (Hall, 2001, p. 555)

5. Select the ERP vendor with the best fit. *A good marriage requires give and take.* Once its business practices are modeled, a company can match these processes to the ERP system. ERP vendors should be invited to demonstrate how their systems fit the modeled business processes. Even after selecting the ERP system that is the best fit, differences will exist between how the ERP system and the business conduct some processes. The General Council of the Assemblies of God, an organization of more than 11,000 churches, was ready to roll out its ERP system when it discovered that the system would not handle 16 of the functions needed by its catalog sales operation. Full implementation of the ERP system was delayed while the Council struggled with the estimated $600,000 cost to modify the system (Stedman, 2000).

Changing business processes to meet the requirements of an ERP system may be the least traumatic solution, but may fail to meet user needs. Modifying the ERP system will meet user needs, but the process may be time consuming, costly to implement, and complicate subsequent upgrades of the ERP software. According to Dave Caruso, an analyst at AMR Research Inc., "These [ERP] systems are so complex that what seems

STUDENT ACTIVITY

ERP Best Practices

Divide students into groups of five to six students. Ask students individually to prepare a list of 10 features they would seek when purchasing a new vehicle (e.g., sun roof, side-impact air bags, power steering, antilock brakes, air conditioning, CD player). As a group, have them prepare a list of all the features required by individuals in the group and then pick those that are within the price range you assign. Encourage the group to draw an image of their vehicle. Instruct each student to identify features of the group vehicle that are inconsistent with their individual preferences. Then, instruct the group to resolve the conflicts by creating a vehicle that satisfies each member as much as possible.

Note to teachers: Vehicle features in this exercise emulate business practices in ERP systems. Just as the features of the group's vehicle will not satisfy every individual, an ERP system may have features that are not in synch with a company's practices. Asking students to adapt to a common vehicle should illustrate how companies adapt to fit ERP systems.

like a benign change has a good possibility of upsetting things downstream." (Stedman, 2000, p. 10) Although there is no answer to this dilemma, the final decisions should be made after considering input from users, consultants, and IT staff.

6. Adopt a modular approach. *You have to learn to walk before you can run.*
Problems inevitably arise when transitioning to a new ERP system. The secret to successful ERP implementation is to minimize the number of problems and their impact on the organization. One of the most talked about ERP transition failures involved Hershey Foods. Its $112 million ERP system was designed to support fundamental accounting, track raw ingredients, schedule production, measure marketing efficiency, set prices, and determine how products should be stacked inside trucks (Nelson & Ramstad, 1999).

Hershey implemented its ERP system in July 1999, just before the important back-to-school and Halloween sales seasons. The original 48-month implementation period was shortened to just 30 months. Problems with the new system resulted in shipment delays and deliveries of incomplete orders. Hershey lost sales to its competitors and incurred significant increases in freight and warehousing costs, causing its third quarter profits to decline by 19 percent (Collett, 1999).

What went wrong? The Hershey ERP system involved more than 5,000 personal computers and two bolt-on systems. While most companies install their ERP systems in a staged or phased-in manner, Hershey took the entire system live at once. According to Jim Shepherd of AMR Research Inc., "[A]n all-at-once rollout is tempting because it's faster and potentially cheaper . . . . [However] these systems tie together in very intricate ways, and things that work fine in testing can turn out to be a disaster [when you go live]" (Stedman, 1999a, p. 1).

The moral of this story is clear. The modular construction of ERP software enables the company to phase in its implementation over a period of time. If possible, a single module should be taken live and operated long enough to identify and solve all significant problems before bringing up the next module.

7. Retain effective legacy systems. *Don't throw out the baby with the bath water.*
Business process engineering enables ERP systems to satisfy nearly all the information systems needs of most businesses. Yet a business may have a process that is so unique that reengineering either the ERP software or the existing business process may be too complex and, therefore, unacceptable. In these cases, businesses probably already have effective systems in place. The legacy systems should, if possible, be incorporated into the ERP system.

8. Let the ERP system make routine decisions. *Let the left hand know what the right hand is doing.*
Many of the processes performed in a business organization are routine. For example, if a customer's order reduces the quantity of a particular inventory item

below the reorder point established by management, the ERP system should immediately initiate an order from an approved supplier, following management instructions stored in the system. When the merchandise is received, the system should update the perpetual inventory records and initiate a wire transfer of funds between the business and its supplier.

Automating routine tasks, especially those involving multiple business functions, such as sales, inventory, receiving, and cash disbursements, allows employees to devote their efforts to planning and decision making. Sales representatives who can enter and track orders online can expend more time developing stronger relationships with clients, working to identify additional markets, or pursuing the business of prospective clients.

9. Get connected to the Internet. *Don't get left in the dust.*

ERP vendors offer e-commerce modules that enable customers, suppliers, stockholders, and other business partners to access appropriate data and initiate transactions. For example, Microsoft Great Plains Business Solutions offers a variety of e-commerce modules with its Dynamics ERP software including eOrder, eSell, eView, and eBank (http://www.greatplains.com/dynamics/productinfo.asp).

10. Secure the system from unauthorized access. *Keep employee hands out of the cookie jar.*

Not every employee should be able to access or change every data item stored in an ERP system. A shipping department employee should not be able to change hourly wage rates, nor should the personnel clerk be able to authorize merchandise shipments. ERP systems by default, however, provide all employees with unlimited access to system data.

The system administrator can restrict employees' access to menus and program options based on their job responsibilities. Thus, when sales representatives use their passwords to log on, the ERP system recognizes that they should not have access to the menus necessary to purchase inventory. When entering a sales transaction, the system will enable the sales representatives to view but not change the unit sales prices.

11. Commit to employee training. *An ounce of prevention is worth a pound of cure.*

Employees who are comfortable using one computer screen cannot be expected to embrace the screens of a new system unless they believe the new system is superior. Employees frustrated with a new system may sabotage the system in an effort to force the company to return to the legacy system. Thorough training empowers employees to use a new system effectively.

The city of Oakland, California, learned the importance of training after suffering through a rocky implementation of its $21 million ERP system. Employees complained that they did not feel prepared to use the system and were inefficient at entering data.

As a result, nearly 25 percent of the city's workers received no or incorrect paychecks on the first payroll run. When some applications did not work as promised, employees' frustration levels continued to rise. In response, the city added or redesigned courses to include more real-world examples, significantly improving employees' perceptions of the system and their skill levels (Stedman, 1999b).

12. Make backup and recovery procedures a high priority. *Do or do not, there is no try.*

ERP systems that enable customers and suppliers to access data and initiate transactions must be available "24/7." A system that is unavailable for an extended period is simply not an option. The ERP system must have a backup-and-recovery system in place to ensure virtually uninterrupted access to information.

How often a company backs up its system data depends on the magnitude of recovery expenses. Recovering the system involves loading backup data on the computer system and reentering all transactions since the last backup. For a company using source documents, reentering a day's worth of data would be a nuisance. In contrast, today's electronic businesses cannot rely on source documents to recover recent transaction data. Data storage techniques must store current data in multiple locations so that, in the event of a system failure, the most current data are available for immediate recovery. Too often businesses approach backup-and-recovery systems the way homeowners approach fire alarm systems. They install effective systems but seldom test them. Unpredictable problems can occur when recovering backup data files. Management must insist that its IT personnel test the recovery system regularly.

TEACHING ERP CONCEPTS

Students should be provided with ample opportunities to gain a fundamental understanding of ERP concepts and then develop and apply their knowledge through activities. Several of these activities can be conducted during the presentation of the 12 implementation strategies. The following activities emphasize the whole process. Most involve group work, allowing students to assist in each other's learning.

SUMMARY

Business students are increasingly likely to be involved with ERP systems when they enter the workforce. Whether as users of ERP systems or as members of implementation teams, students will need to understand the fundamental concepts of ERP systems and how they benefit businesses by providing employees and business partners with access to important data.

Of equal importance, students need to appreciate the level of planning and financial resources that are required to ensure that ERP systems are implemented properly so that employees can use them effectively. The twelve recommendations included in this chapter can help guide a successful ERP implementation. Businesses that cannot devote the resources necessary to address implementation issues effectively will probably fail to achieve the benefits of ERP.

STUDENT ACTIVITY

Modeling the ERP System

Divide the class into groups of three to four students and, for the accounting software used in instruction, assign each group one function, such as sales, expenditures, or payroll. Instruct students to create a list of data collected or activities performed by the software that are not required to generate financial statements. For example, entering a customer's account number and selecting the merchandise and quantities ordered to process a sales invoice are not directly required to prepare financial statements. Capturing the customer's zip code is not required to record a sale, but it does enable management to analyze sales by geographic regions.

Note to teachers: Traditional accounting software focuses on capturing the account and amount information of economic events. In other words, the software requires the user to enter the debit, credit, amount, date, and source document reference information. With this information, the software generates GAAP-based financial statements.

The accounting software you currently use for instruction can be classified as an elementary ERP system if it performs functions other than accounting and financial statement preparation. Does your software maintain a perpetual inventory, assist in reconciling the bank statement, or maintain credit limits for customers? If the answer is "yes," the software contains multiple modules and can be considered an ERP system.

Students using a computerized accounting system can quickly relate to many of the problems inherent in implementing a new ERP system. After completing the activity above, ask students to suggest additional features that the software should offer. Then inform them that a new, more sophisticated ERP system will be installed and that they will be tested on the system in a few weeks. What is their reaction? Lead a class discussion on how managers can help their employees transition to a new ERP system.

STUDENT ACTIVITY

Internet Research

Conduct research to identify a company that has recently implemented an ERP system. Prepare a short report that provides the following information:

- The brand of ERP software implemented
- The consultant involved in the implementation
- The legacy systems retained in the new system
- The bolt-on applications merged with the ERP system
- The estimated cost and duration of the implementation
- Problems encountered during implementation
- Lessons learned from the problems encountered

Note to teachers: Not every source will provide the information needed to answer all of these questions. Instruct the students to attach a copy of their sources. Consider asking your students to present these reports orally.

STUDENT ACTIVITY

Data Modeling a Perpetual Inventory

Instruct students to prepare a list of types of data that they believe a local retail business (e.g., Wal-Mart) would need in its inventory. Then ask the students to address each of the following issues for a retail business, instructing them to make any necessary additions or changes to their list. Have students begin each statement with "Your client . . ."

- Sells an item in different units (e.g., each, dozen, pounds) with different sales prices for each
- Purchases an item from more than one vendor
- Stores a product in different locations
- Frequently substitutes other items if an item is out of stock
- Carries an item in many sizes and colors
- Automatically reorders an item when the quantity on hand falls below a reorder point
- Purchases an item at different costs, depending on market conditions
- Does not charge sales tax on certain items (according to state law)

Note to teachers: What data does a business need about its inventory? At a minimum, a business should have a perpetual inventory that contains a part number, description, quantity on hand, and sales price for each item. Yet some businesses have very unique needs that must be handled by the ERP system. This exercise is designed to illustrate how complex a seemingly simple business application can be. Most students' perception of inventory is based on the retail businesses they frequent, where most items are sold in a single quantity for a single price.

It may be helpful for you to identify a local retailer as the client. For example, the local nursery or farmer's supply store has many of the inventory characteristics discussed above. Inviting a manager from that retailer to attend class will provide students with a realistic experience in modeling an ERP system for a client.

REFERENCES

Collett, S. (1999, October 26). Hershey earnings drop as new warehouse, order system falter. *Computerworld Online News.* Retrieved July 29, 2001, from the World Wide Web: http://www.computerworld.com/cwi/story/0,1199,NAV47_STO29274,00.html

Hall, J. (2001). *Accounting information systems* (3rd ed.). Cincinnati, OH: Thomson Learning/South-Western College Publishing.

Janstal, S. (1999). *Enterprise resource planning: Integrating applications and business processes across the enterprise.* Computer Technology Research Corporation.

Microsoft Great Plains business solutions: Dynamics. (2001). Retrieved July 29, 2001, from the World Wide Web: http://www.greatplains.com/dynamics/productinfo.asp

Nelson, E. & Ramstad, E. (October 29, 1999). Kiss your Hershey treats goodbye. *WSJ Interactive Edition.* Retrieved July 29, 2001, from the World Wide Web: http://www.zdnet.com/zdnn/stories/news/0,4586,2384087-1,00.html

O'Leary, D. (2000). *Enterprise resource planning systems: Systems, life cycle, electronic commerce, and risk.* New York: Cambridge University Press.

Osterland, A. (2000). Blaming ERP. *CFO, 16*(1), 89–92.

Piturro, M. (1999). How midsize companies are buying ERP. *Journal of Accountancy, 188,* 41–48.

Stedman, C. (1999a, October 29). Failed ERP gamble haunts Hershey. *Computerworld, 33*(44), 1–2. Retrieved July 29, 2001, from the World Wide Web: http://www.computerworld.com/cwi/story/0,1199,NAV47_STO29314,00.html

Stedman, C. (1999b, December 13). ERP project problems plague city payroll. *Computerworld, 33*(50), 38–40. Retrieved July 29, 2001, from the World Wide Web: http://www.computerworld.com/cwi/story/0,1199,NAV47_STO37818,00.html

Stedman, C. (2000, January 3). ERP problems put brakes on Volkswagen parts. *Computerworld, 34*(1), 8–10. Retrieved July 29, 2001, from the World Wide Web: http://www.computerworld.com/cwi/story/0,1199,NAV47_STO40471,00.html

Managing Knowledge in the New Economy

Pamela Ramey

Kent State University

New Philadelphia, Ohio

The world's latest technological revolution is different from most revolutions of the past, which typically had gradual onsets. The most recent transformation of comparable magnitude is the Industrial Revolution. During the Industrial Revolution education had sufficient time to adjust to the demands of the new industrial society. The current technological revolution, with its impacts on information and knowledge, however, outpaces society's capacity to implement change on many fronts including education.

Today trained human capital is in short supply. The Digital Divide that separates the technologically literate from the technologically illiterate is more than just theory; it is a reality for many individuals in business, government, and education. The academic community has a mandate from many sectors of society to respond to the demands of the era by preparing individuals to meet the challenges of the digital revolution.

One area of business that is starting to receive widespread attention is knowledge management. A majority of today's and tomorrow's students need to add the components of knowledge management to their existing skills to be productive workers in the future. The growing emphasis on knowledge, coupled with the relocation of low-end business functions to other countries, requires business teachers to meet the challenge of helping students who aspire to corporate careers develop intermediate to high-end skills.

Business educators are positioned to provide direction on knowledge management education. Business educators are comfortable with soft as well as hard components of knowledge management. This chapter discusses the technological and knowledge-based environment for which business educators prepare students and the field of knowledge management as it pertains to the educational arena. The chapter also suggests strategies and methods business educators can employ as they prepare an entirely different pool of human capital.

THE NEW BUSINESS ENVIRONMENT

An examination of today's companies would reveal very few that existed in the 1950s had the same names, structures, and products. What allows companies to survive the long haul? The key is for companies to have the vision to reinvent themselves, not just to slightly modify themselves or to maintain business as usual. Vision requires more than data or information; it requires knowledge.

In today's knowledge-based economy, human capital is one of the most significant contributors to corporate success. Muscle power has been replaced with the synergistic strength of a knowledgeable workforce that is enhanced by technology. Corporate executives today realize that both products and production factors are changing. Appreciation for the complex knowledge that the human brain can hold is beginning to surpass the regard for computers, robots, and raw materials.

During an era of dramatic technological change, education and ability are coveted more than they are during other more routine times (Galor & Tsiddon, 1997). The beginning years of this millennium have brought images of individuals able to command phenomenal salaries and move from job to job, each time with a pay increase. These rewards have been the result of the individuals' knowledge and readiness to fit into and contribute to their organizations quickly. Some fast-track companies, particularly those in the Silicon Valley, have promoted a revolving door of knowledgeable and technologically savvy workers to keep fresh ideas coming in. Companies needing to move quickly have sought personnel who were detached from the "we've always done it this way" mentality.

According to PricewaterhouseCoopers, however, 70 percent of the world's 1,000 top-tier companies cite lack of trained employees as their primary barrier to sustaining growth (Urdan & Weggen, 2000). When knowledgeable employees could not be found in the United States, U.S. corporate executives have looked for them elsewhere (Kaiser, 2001). Companies have either imported individuals who have the education to be "knowledge workers," or they have exported job functions to areas where it is more practical to do business.

To meet the shortfall of technologically prepared individuals, the United States has relaxed immigration limits on the H-1B visa for people trained in specialties that require at least a bachelor's degree (Sebelist, 2001). As companies have recognized the minimal return on investment in clerical, data entry, and customer service tasks, they have outsourced these functions to countries with English-speaking workers who will work for lower wages. At the top of the list are India, Ireland, Israel, and the Philippines, whose citizens work for U.S. companies such as General Electric, Microsoft, IBM, Texas Instruments, and Citigroup (Field, 2000; Clifford & Kripalani, 2000).

If companies could clone the ideal worker, it would be someone who would embrace change quickly but who would respect the value of company history as a launching pad for new ideas. Unfortunately, the swift speed at which products are launched leaves little time to negotiate past practice. Company history is often viewed as the "ball and chain" that slows innovation rather than serves as a resource for future initiatives. When technological innovation and implementation follow the path of least resistance, a company's innovations are often framed in the context of existing technological prowess or in existing or potentially accessible locations. "Striking while the iron is hot" allows companies to establish marketplace advantage, but this may be an advantage that is short lived in the knowledge-driven New Economy.

According to Weggen (2000), research analysts for the investment firm W. R. Hambrecht and Company, "The new global economy poses more complex challenges to workers, requiring higher levels of education, computer literacy, critical thinking, information analysis, and synthesizing skills. However, educational deficiencies have brought the United States to the edge of a widening knowledge gap." The analysts went on to note,

> The chasm between the higher demands of a knowledge economy and the educational status of the workforce is deep and must be addressed if the U.S. is to remain competitive internationally. A thorough reexamination of curriculum and teaching methods as they relate to labor market preparation is needed. Academic and corporate environments must be redesigned to adequately prepare people to function in an information society. (p. 2)

Davenport (1999b) suggested this approach: Ask people in companies what they need to know and what would improve performance, sit next to people doing excellent work, and identify skills that could help other workers do things even better. Taking this kind of information back to the classroom will facilitate the flow of information. According to Stucky, associate director of the Institute for Research on Learning, "'communities of practice' . . . are helping [her company's] clients enhance their learning efforts" (Manasco, 2000, p. 1). She has also advocated simulation systems as "particularly effective for representing complex systems that do not necessarily function in a linear fashion" (p. 3).

THE TRANSITION TO KNOWLEDGE

Are educational institutions the ultimate "factories" for information and/or knowledge development? There is evidence to indicate that educational institutions *do* function as information factories. Knowledge factories are a bit more difficult to find, but the knowledge management strategies that elevate existing employees' knowledge quotient in business have applicability to the educational setting in a significant way.

Knowledge management lacks a clear-cut definition and is an area that has not been sufficiently addressed in education. Experts in various areas of knowledge management identify data, information, technology, corporate culture, communication, and people as components of this emerging field (Stratigos, 2001; Boersma & Stegwee, 1996). Because knowledge management has a plethora of interpretations, it is appropriate to revert to a common core of precursors that are present in both educational and business communities.

Educators disseminate *data* to students. In raw form, data consist of nothing more than facts and figures that are the result of observations. There are many countries whose educational systems are based entirely on memorization of data. The potential risk of rote learning is that education will be without meaning or applicability. Unfortunately, assessments of learning are occasionally based on data alone, perhaps disguised as theory. Some would argue that a grasp of data is required for learning to occur. However, facts in isolation have little practical value.

Data become *information* in students' minds when they are taken to the next plateau by adding context or meaning. Boersma and Stegwee (1996) have stated that information consists of data that have a purpose in a particular setting. Data and information are only "carriers" of knowledge; they are not knowledge. *Knowledge* is information that is understood, analyzed, or applied. Students need help to make the transition from data to information to knowledge. According to Stewart (1997), one person's data may be another person's knowledge.

Educators sometimes ignore the accompanying social interactions that aid the transition. For example, three students may be told independently that they have scored in the 60s on a test. When the teacher reveals a high score of 70 for the class, the students have a context for their performance scores. Collectively, they have the knowledge to translate information acquired through sharing into action. They can, for example, ask the teacher to curve the grades.

The highest level of the knowledge management continuum, which often emerges only with time, is *wisdom*. Stewart (1997, p. 115) has described wisdom as "the large generalizations, paradigms, or lessons learned." Is it wise to ask the teacher to curve the grades? Is this a common practice in this classroom? The students must reflect and choose to ask or not to ask.

Dissemination of data and information often marks ineffective educational systems. Knowledge requires engagement of the learner. The image of the teacher as a facilitator is hardly fiction any more. There are many benefits for teachers who engage in the role of facilitator instead of information disseminator and authority figure. Facilitation is every bit as important and as demanding as earlier methods of instruction.

KNOWLEDGE SKILLS IN THE WORKPLACE

Knowledge is the major production factor in knowledge economies. Availability of data and information do not necessarily alter an organization's behavior or competitiveness. But the knowledge needed to interpret the information and to act upon it is critical to organizational success (Boersma & Stegwee, 1996).

Explicit and Tacit Knowledge

To ensure success in the workplace, students need to possess far more than facts and figures. They need knowledge in *both* explicit and tacit form. Explicit knowledge can be stored and passed on to others, while tacit knowledge is personal, carried and transferred by human beings. The ability to convert explicit knowledge into tacit knowledge comes from practice. Corporate executives make it perfectly clear: A premium is placed on tacit knowledge in a knowledge enterprise. Corporate executives value automatic responses that are the result of routines, synchrony, rhythms, and nuances, or the "feeling" that something is proceeding correctly.

Development of Tacit Knowledge

Business educators can use keyboarding knowledge as an analogy. They know that only extensive practice moves students to the routine rhythm that demonstrates keyboard learning. How do business educators articulate to students the sense of recognition that their fingers are not on the home row, that they are going too fast to control for errors, or that certain problematic keystroke combinations can be corrected? This is a very difficult teaching task. Teachers use explicit knowledge to develop tacit knowledge. Brooking (1999) has suggested developing tacit knowledge by multiple means: teaching, analysis, mentoring, repetition, and writing.

Another example of tacit knowledge for business educators is demonstrated in grading business letters. When an excellent letter is submitted, there is a "feel" about it from first reading. No single criterion stands out, but all the components are perfectly in place. An experienced educator can give a novice educator some pointers, some explicit knowledge. The novice will develop tacit knowledge through reading, looking at examples, taking notes, and grading volumes of letters to supplement existing knowledge. In the classroom teachers can help students develop the same tacit knowledge of recognizing high-quality business letters by giving students collections of letters to evaluate on a sliding scale and discussing their reactions.

One more observation of tacit knowledge is worth mentioning. Individuals must separate, isolate, and disregard the unimportant information (what some call noise) that surrounds true tacit knowledge. Educators must help students remove information that is unimportant until they learn how to recognize and remove it on their own.

The more time students have to repeat experiences involving processes and to discuss what they have done, the greater the likelihood that they will develop tacit knowledge. Teachers will need to make time to develop enriched classroom activities. Teachers must learn to trade time. For example, if evaluating class assignments can be used as a valid student learning activity, teachers can free their evaluation time to develop enriched activities. Letting go of the control of grading is a difficult adjustment for some teachers until they recognize the benefits.

Davenport (1999b) has pointed out the holistic approach to knowledge-based decisions and the need to provide opportunities for learners to work in the field,

STUDENT ACTIVITY

Recognizing Well-Written Business Correspondence

Provide groups of students with sets of letters that illustrate a range of writing qualities, such as letter mechanics, conciseness, and orientation to the receiver. Have students evaluate the letters and assign a rating or a grade to each business letter. Then have the students share their results by articulating their reasons for evaluating some letters as excellent.

Note to teachers: This activity does not involve letters written by the students for actual grading. The letters may be from samples collected from businesses or prior classes to ensure that the identity of the writers is not known. In addition, the subject area could be any area for which the objective is to have students learn standards of quality for a product.

confront unfamiliar situations, and even make mistakes. Davenport's words echo a familiar note from apprenticeship perspectives. The apprentice learned the master's skills by working alongside a master, attaching meaning to observations, emulating the master's work, and applying any lessons presented formally or informally. This type of learning by doing builds the intuitive feel for work that comes with experience. This is an example of the tacit knowledge that companies seek. Short of apprenticeships, tackling real business problems in the educational setting with the latitude to experiment and even to fail will yield lasting explicit and tacit knowledge. Nonetheless, educators help students learn to work when they provide examples of productive personal work habits and encourage students to follow suit.

Subcategories of Knowledge

Brooking (1999) has suggested some additional subcategories of explicit and tacit knowledge that are valuable to companies. Explicit knowledge has a subset called *pragmatic knowledge*. Although factual knowledge is the basis for decisions, a competent person demonstrates the ability to use that knowledge pragmatically. A business student's ability to estimate a result in determining the accuracy of a business mathematics calculation involves pragmatic knowledge. Recognizing a reasonable net income figure in accounting requires pragmatic knowledge.

Systematic knowledge can be taught by example in the classroom. This tacit knowledge subset includes problem-solving strategies for getting things done through knowledge of methodologies. Some tacit knowledge is automatic, so engrained and routine that people use it without thinking about it. For example, systematic knowledge is necessary to use the Windows operating system. Applying knowledge automatically and knowing how to get things done can be enhanced in the classroom through repetition and feedback.

KNOWLEDGE MANAGEMENT SKILLS

The results of managing knowledge on the job are innovation and responsiveness. Knowledge management provides new insights into familiar skills and attributes: adaptability, inquiry, communication, decision making, and other skills.

Adaptive Skills

Although explicit knowledge can be disseminated relatively quickly in the form of manuals, charts, blueprints, etc., the time required to acquire tacit knowledge may impede a company's implementation stage. By the time tacit knowledge is assimilated, a company's competitive advantage of early entry into the marketplace may have passed. The composite of explicit and tacit knowledge leads to adaptive skills, one of the most understated assets of individuals, companies, and societies. Individuals who can adapt have the confidence and experience derived from tacit knowledge to embrace more technological changes, thus continuing the cycle of change.

The concept of inertia—that an object at rest tends to remain at rest, and an object in motion tends to continue in motion in a straight line unless acted upon by an outside force—relates to technological development and adaptive skills. Putting countries, societies, or even institutions in motion technologically is difficult when they have been at rest. The same is true for changing the direction of technological motion. Adaptive skills take tacit knowledge to the next level and are the lubricants that keep technological change in continuous motion in a society.

Where there is receptivity to technological change in a society, there will be job opportunities. Companies recognize quick start-up opportunities and locate where there is a trained workforce with embedded tacit knowledge. India is a resource for offshore outsourcing, a $4 billion a year and growing industry (Field, 2000). Compared to its outsourcing competitors, India has a "high-context" culture that requires minimal clarification of instructions.

The good news is that some adaptability can be taught through simulations, the apprenticeship model, or challenging work. In a knowledge-based classroom, the educator first creates situations that have predictable results. Later, the educator establishes a new set of rules that require students to redefine what they already know and place it in a new context. If the educator extends the process one step further to introduce discontinuous change that does not have a logical consequence and then works with the students to obtain a solution, students will experience adaptation at its best.

Once educators identify where student knowledge exists in their classroom, they can move students around to create new contexts in which work will be performed. This movement is what develops students' abilities to adjust to change and to renegotiate social structures that allow them to do their best work. According to Fitz-enz (2000), adaptation can make work fulfilling.

STUDENT ACTIVITY

Developing Adaptability

Ask students to analyze a computer printout with accounting data. Next, have the students analyze the data in an international context by interjecting new variables. Finally, have the students remove some of the traditional constraints from the analysis to see what they could do to optimize the results. Vigorous discussions of lessons learned from the exercise will prove invaluable.

Educators can encourage adaptation by resisting the urge to jump to premature consensus before working through hidden options. If a 45-minute class period is not sufficient time to exhaust a discussion, the discussion should continue during the next class meeting rather than be rushed to closure. This common practice of premature closure does not mirror the business world where discussions go on until the best conclusion is reached even if it means going back to the project the next day. Diverse viewpoints and brainstorming should be encouraged in discussions in knowledge-based classrooms.

Students may need examples that illustrate that different perspectives *do* make a difference, occasionally even perspectives that break the rules. For example, educators can examine and share information about the practices of "free agents" (Davenport, 1999a & 1999b). Free agents keep themselves in demand by keeping their skills sharp and by being willing and able to adapt to new situations at a moment's notice. Both among and within companies, free agents turn the tables of the job search by interviewing the company instead of being interviewed by the company. Companies recognize the value of employees who can adapt and will offer premiums to keep them. The free agent's tacit company knowledge is highly valued. Career development sessions should emphasize adaptability, and classroom visits by people who fit the free agent description should generate meaningful discussions.

Inquiry

Inquiry and research skills take on new meaning in a knowledge-based economy. Students embarking on careers in knowledge management may require a stand-alone research course. Inquiry skills should be taught as a progressive process. The search for information can be expanded by challenging students to make complex discoveries incorporating several disciplines simultaneously.

Students need opportunities to conduct electronic research using tools at their disposal. They must learn to drill down to locate information. The teacher should guide the students to reach conclusions firmly supported by data. Preparing students for knowledge management careers requires students to share results and conclusions as part of their evaluations. For example, students may be asked to research and evaluate company home page designs. In isolation this is a worthwhile assignment, but the benefits reach new heights if students are asked to collaborate with their peers to identify common threads from their findings.

As students engage in serious inquiry, they will quickly realize that there are multiple pathways to bring order to the information uncovered. A 45-minute class session may not be adequate to develop good research skills, and students who enjoy the "hunt" for information will end up frustrated. Other students may want "instant gratification," but they must realize the necessity of ongoing projects in business environments. Students must be taught to prolong their search and not be satisfied with the first "hit" that they encounter. Along the way, exercises that involve scrutinizing information are necessary. With experience, students will become "inquiry savvy"—able to interpret what is important and what is not, what is credible and what is not, and what is appropriate and what is not.

When it is not possible to extend the length of the class session, business educators should consider breaking inquiry activities into self-contained chunks that can be adequately researched during a single class period. Teachers may ask students who are researching international business conduct to focus on greetings one day, business meetings another, and business gifts on yet another day. The topics are small enough that students will have enough time to pursue content-filled pathways as well as appropriate detours.

If textbooks do not provide exercises involving independent research, educators should extend the scope of class work to get students to seek out information to complete tasks. Opportunities for inquiry are prevalent in computer help menus, manuals, online customer support services, directories, indexes, and help desks, to name a few. Students respond surprisingly well to challenges involving inquiry because these challenges resemble puzzles or games in which everyone has a fair chance of winning. Detours satisfy students' curiosity, and curiosity can lead to clarification, validation, or invention.

The patterns of inquiry that students exhibit in educational settings are precursors of knowledge worker behavior. Educators should not assume that research is an innate talent that every student brings to the classroom. Some students do not have a clue about how to begin the inquiry process. Educators should monitor research techniques and suggest pathways for locating information when students experience difficulty.

Communication

Communication and technology play key roles in transforming information into knowledge. Students must be able to receive the information communicated to them as well as disseminate their knowledge to others in understandable and humanistic ways. Social, not technological, networks generate organizational communication. Even if computers are the communicative medium, students need to know how to engage themselves in the social system. The humanistic quality of communication should be emphasized when preparing students for knowledge-intensive careers.

Stucky (Manasco, 2000) has emphasized that knowledge is integrated in the life of communities and the socialization associated with them. These communities of practice are defined as groups of people that "develop a shared way of acting while engaged in real work" (p. 1). Although difficult to accomplish in the classroom, business educators can attempt to create a subculture where students' ideas are built on those of their peers. This will elevate students' desire to learn as they seek entry into and enhance their status within the subculture.

Within the classroom working environment, membership encourages student participation and promotes learning. Partial acceptance as a member of the classroom work team brings limited opportunities to learn, and rejection results in exclusion from learning. Stucky has suggested that classroom simulation systems provide a way to experience interactions that are not linear and that are more like the complex interpersonal systems found in the work environment (Menasco, 2000). The complexity adds realism to learning.

According to Singh (2000), effective knowledge management practices can develop from little more than e-mail and meetings. Students can solve problems via e-mail and can simulate face-to-face meetings.

STUDENT ACTIVITY

Communication Rules and Restrictions
Have students focus on the physical layout of the classroom relative to learning. Ask them to identify the learning purposes that the classroom layout encourages. Ask them to examine barriers to learning. Then ask them to formulate their findings as statements of rules and guidelines for using the classroom. Have them develop alternative rules for classroom use and then propose different layouts that would support the new rules. Ask them to come up with layouts that foster social cohesion and collaboration.

Stucky has focused on collaboration using communities of practice, but has cautioned that true collaboration happens only when there is a degree of social cohesion resulting from a shared experience, shared vision, or shared allegiance (Manasco, 2000). Educators must create healthy, positive classroom climates so simulated communities of practice have a chance to survive. Educators can start with an institutional problem to solve within their school or college. Students can develop an agenda and arrange meetings with stakeholders. Recommendations and plans for implementation will have meaning for students who take ownership of their problem-solving efforts.

Technology brings global communication to the classroom on a personal level. Yesterday's overseas pen pals have evolved into today's global teams of students who collaborate on projects. With face-to-face meetings possible via distance learning and computer meeting software, students can learn to negotiate the subtleties of culture, language, ethics, and rules. Even in the business world, many of the commercial rules that apply globally have not been established, so students will have opportunities to observe firsthand how economic and social policy develops in the Digital Age. Students should also be prepared to interpret complex data and convert it into information and knowledge that can be understood around the world.

STUDENT ACTIVITIES

Interpreting Data

Activity 1. Have students examine a software operator's manual written by a programmer but understood by few others. As an alternative, have students evaluate sections of software help manuals appearing online and recommend improvements.

Activity 2. Have students locate and examine sets of instructions accompanying products made in foreign countries. Have them identify how well the instructions communicate to the customer and suggest improvements. Use this to prompt a classroom analysis of global communication.

International business enterprises will value students who understand how to distinguish previously unidentified and unorganized clusters of individuals as new target markets for products. A starting point is learning how other cultures communicate. For example, according to Microsoft representatives (Microsoft, 1997), the Japanese generally are more visually oriented in their explanations and interpretations and the British are more verbally oriented.

Decision Making

Because of the way that technology affects the configurations of business, decision making occurs at lower levels of the organizational structure than it did in the past. Students will assume these responsibilities earlier in their careers. In the absence of the maturity level traditionally expected for making complex decisions, classroom communities can help students learn to make good decisions.

Students need latitude to make responsible decisions that will affect them and their peers. Teachers should identify a few overriding principles to guide the decisions and then construct exercises that cause students to analyze the sequences or patterns that might lead to different types of decisions. When business simulations and computer simulations first arrived on the education scene, they were linear and very limiting. Some of today's new simulation designs promote creativity and require lateral thinking and complex decision making.

Many commercial products today get to the heart of decision making. For example, Chris Elgood's Management Games and Simulations site (http://www.chris-elgood.co.uk/first.htm) provides descriptions of products available in many areas related to decision making. "Four-Letter Words" by Chris Elgood is a box game designed to encourage student creativity. The activities in *50 Activities on Creativity and Problem Solving* by Cox, Dufault, and Hopkins (1998) are described at http://library.tamu.edu/21stcentury/cbooks.html and provide opportunities for decision making and critical thinking. Both products can be ordered from the Learning Resource Centre at http://www.gowertraining.co.uk/lrcprodfactresources.asp?LC=9G.

Students should work through exercises that develop lateral thinking. Lateral-thinking exercises can be accessed on the Internet at sites such as Grazzmatic's Lateral Thinking Exercises (http://www.geocities.com/SunsetStrip/8295/lateral1.html). These exercises are not only fun but are also excellent classroom tools to get students thinking in different ways.

Labelle (1996) has referred to a tool created by Edward de Bono that will work in the classroom to help students make decisions. It is called the "Six Thinking Hats for Critical Thinking." Each of the six hats represents a different approach to tackling a problem and gives students a chance to view problems from various perspectives.

Data warehousing provides opportunities for individuals to make decisions involving multiple variables. Educators can direct students to isolate variables and later determine interactions. Crossing boundaries to provide interdisciplinary interaction is also a strategy for reaching decisions.

Additional Competencies

Other important competencies and characteristics can also be integrated in business education course work. Students should be taught to maximize team effort and keep egos in check despite their perceived value to the company. Ethics serve as a foundation for all types of technological and knowledge management decisions. Students will need to shift gears quickly, so spontaneity is an asset. Students with the ability to motivate others will thrive. Survival through adversity and uncertainty may turn out to be pluses in today's changing work environment. Although the school of hard knocks is seldom a planned educational strategy, it does have its benefits in the business world.

In the classroom environment students must be given the chance to fail and to regroup. In the past educators too rarely relinquished the controls that prevented failure from occurring. Debriefing, analysis without criticism, and serendipitous discoveries enhance the classroom experience. With classroom safety nets in the background, students will get a chance to acquire knowledge independently. This experience will help them avoid having problems when they move on to technologically rich business experiences.

When a class project is failing, educators should not jump in to offer assistance too soon. Instead, they should help students work through their problems independently as far as possible. This strategy is particularly valuable to students who have a tendency to quit at the onset of frustration. Students should be told that it is acceptable not to know an answer or a solution as long as this is not due to a lack of effort on their part. Students must know how to seek answers. The journey to finding the answers can be as rewarding as the destination.

Anyone who has ever been on a job knows that coworkers learn from each other, and they learn by doing. The apprenticeship model is a method that promotes the development of both explicit and tacit knowledge. To make an apprenticeship experience even more meaningful, students should be encouraged to take it upon themselves to learn as much as they can about their entire work environment, use creativity to solve problems, evaluate what they are doing, and analyze their development of tacit knowledge.

OBSERVATIONS ABOUT KNOWLEDGE MANAGEMENT

Classroom communication is a counterbalance to the isolation that comes from working alone in front of a computer monitor. Business educators are not and cannot be experts in all content areas, possessing the tacit knowledge and wisdom that comes from experience. However, experts do exist in all areas. Efforts to recreate what experts do and know best are a waste of teachers' time. Teachers should provide meaning for information and the transition to knowledge through classroom dynamics.

Educators can work in their classrooms—physical or virtual—facilitating learning, engaging students in social learning activities, and stretching students' capabilities to obtain more knowledge. Teachers can tutor students individually, show students how to deal with stress, and help students learn how getting along with one another can yield big dividends.

Many efforts are under way to bring together educators to collaborate and to serve as instructional resource people. These communities of educators also enhance the classroom through shared knowledge. Two of the more visible efforts are IBM's Reinventing Education Project and Virtual High School.

The IBM Reinventing Education Project (http://www.ibm.com/ibm/ibmgives/grant/education/programs/reinventing/) is a global effort using worldwide resources and innovative technology solutions to improve communities. Data warehouses help school districts pinpoint problems in instruction and administration. Groupware includes tools to create student portfolios and lesson plans online. Communication tools keep parents and teachers connected. Independent evaluations show that technology has dramatically improved schools participating in the project.

The Virtual High School (http://vhs.concord.org/home.htm) is a collaborative effort that allows schools to exchange services for opportunities for students. A school that offers a virtual course is entitled to enroll a given number of students in virtual courses from other participating schools. "Soon, teachers will collaborate across the country with colleagues to develop lesson plans electronically. They, too, will rely less on textbooks as they use intelligent search agents to develop digital projects." Distance learning "will allow students to take virtual field trips, collaborate with experts and students around the world, and do research at the Library of Congress" (Symonds, 2000, p. 119).

Most structures currently in place in education do not foster true knowledge acquisition, communication without boundaries, extended and deep inquiry, adaptation, or decision making with risks. To realize education's potential contribution to the development of human capital requires relinquishing the information dissemination function to computers and liberating educators to create environments that turn information into knowledge.

SUMMARY

Today's economy is knowledge driven, yet organizations find themselves in short supply of trained human capital. While corporations have addressed their needs to some extent by exporting low-knowledge jobs and importing qualified individuals, the need to prepare knowledge workers is pressing. Educators have a mandate from many sectors of society to prepare individuals to contribute to the economy.

While knowledge management is defined in many ways, knowledge itself is characterized as explicit when it can be articulated and disseminated, and as tacit when it reflects an individual's expertise gained through personal engagement with information. Corporations particularly value tacit knowledge for problem solving and pragmatic achievement of complex tasks. The related attributes and characteristics that make individuals valuable are adaptability; inquiry and research abilities; communication and decision-making skills; and complementary attributes such as self-control, ethics, spontaneity, and the ability to motivate others.

Teaching students to acquire knowledge requires more than having them acquire facts and organize them as information. Teachers must let computers be the information managers and prepare students to manage knowledge, that is, to generate and apply knowledge. This requires educational practices that simulate communities within the classroom, require deep research into complex problems, remove safety nets so that problem solving has meaning, promote positive classroom environments, and resist the urge to prematurely conclude discussions. Business teachers are in a particularly good position to prepare knowledge workers because business teachers work effectively with both the soft and hard elements of knowledge management.

REFERENCES

Boersma, S. K., Th., & Stegwee, R. A. (1996). *Exploring the issues in knowledge management.* Presentation at the meeting of the Information Resources Management Association International Conference, Washington, DC.

Brooking, A. (1999). *Corporate memory-strategies for knowledge management.* London: International Thomson Press.

Clifford, M., & M. Kripalani (2000, August 28). Different countries, adjoining cubicles. *Business Week*, pp. 182–84.

Davenport, T. O. (1999a, July). Building the perfect workforce. *Workforce, 78*(7), 56–8.

Davenport, T.O. (1999b). *Human capital: What it is and why people invest it.* San Francisco: Jossey-Bass Publishers.

Field, T. (2000, December 1). Outsourcing: For a few rupees more. *CIO Magazine.* Retrieved from the World Wide Web: http://www.cio.com/archive/ 120100_rupees.html

Fitz-enz, J. (2000). *The ROI of human capital.* New York: AMACON.

Galor, O., & D. Tsiddon (1997, June). Technological progress, mobility, and economic growth. *American Economic Review, 87*(3), 363–82.

Kaiser, R. (2001). *Passport to brainpower.* Retrieved from the World Wide Web: http://www.westbound.com/tribune.htm

Labelle, S. (1996). *Six thinking hats.* Retrieved August 6, 2001, from the World Wide Web: http://www.ozemail.com.au/~caveman/Creative/Techniques/sixhats.htm

Manasco, B. (2000). *Leading lights: An interview with institute for research on learning's Susan Stucky.* Retrieved August 6, 2001, from the World Wide Web: http://webcom.com/quantera/stucky.html

Microsoft. (1997, November 20). *Microsoft Office end user training.* Cleveland, Ohio.

Sebelist, Y. (2001). *Welcoming all skilled immigrants.* Retrieved August 6, 2001, from the World Wide Web: http://www.prairielaw.com/articles/article.asp?channelID=21&articleID=1317

Singh, H. (2000, December). *The convergence of e-learning and knowledge management.* Retrieved August 6, 2001, from the World Wide Web: http://www.elearningmag.com/issues/dec00/converge.htm

Stewart, T. (1997). *Intellectual capital.* New York: Doubleday.

Stratigos, A. (2001, January/February). Knowledge management meets future information users. *Online,* p. 65.

Symonds, W. (2000, September 25). Wired schools. *Business Week,* pp. 116–128.

Urdan, T. A., & Weggen, C. C. (2000, March). *Corporate e-learning: Exploring a new frontier.* Retrieved August 6, 2001, from the World Wide Web: http://www.wrhambrecht.com/research/elearning/ir/ir_explore_a.pdf

Entrepreneurship and Creating the Online Business

Richard Clodfelter
University of South Carolina
Columbia, South Carolina

Not so many years ago, only a scattering of e-commerce sites appeared on the Internet. In fact, the Internet was never built with commerce in mind. In the last several years, the number of commercial Web sites has grown at an exponential rate. Today there are sites on the Internet that sell everything from flowers, candy, and greeting cards to furniture, computers, and automobiles. This is indeed an historic period, a time when individuals with ideas, some guidance, and a lot of hard work can start their own online enterprises. Business educators have a vital role to play in guiding and training potential online entrepreneurs to plan and implement their ideas for new business ventures successfully.

This chapter is, in effect, a teaching guide for business educators for each stage of creating the online business: planning the business, developing the commercial Web site, selecting an Internet business location, promoting the online business, opening for business, delivering the services or products, and providing customer service. Each stage includes Web sites that provide resources that teachers can incorporate into their instruction. The chapter begins by looking at e-commerce from business and educational viewpoints.

INTRODUCTION TO E-COMMERCE

Despite all the hype, e-commerce still represents only a small fraction of all retail sales in the United States, and there are many opportunities and risks that online entrepreneurs face. Education about e-commerce likewise represents new territory with opportunities and challenges for schools.

Trends in Online and Conventional Business

According to Jupiter Communications, online sales amounted to $16.8 billion in 1999, compared with $2.6 trillion in total retail sales (Trout, 2000). The commercial power of the Internet will undoubtedly grow, but prospective online entrepreneurs must not believe that the Web will fulfill all their "get-rich-quick" plans. The early days of the "dot-com" craze can be compared to the gold rush days of the 1800s. Just as too many prospectors rushed to California looking for gold, too many people rushed online to discover their own gold mines.

As the shakeout of e-commerce sites has shown, many online businesses, including a number of high-profile online firms like Petstore.com, Boo.com, and Toysmart.com did not find the gold. Today their URLs lead to "server not found" messages, to sites that are trying to encourage former customers of defunct sites to try new businesses, or possibly to restarted business efforts under bankruptcy options. The Museum of E-Failure features URLs that are part of the short history of the Web (James, 2001).

Many Web sites are producing revenues, however. For example, several companies selling luxury items on the Internet have been quite successful. Blue Nile (http://www.bluenile.com), Ashford.com (http://www.ashford.com), Neiman-Marcus (http://www.neiman-marcus.com), and Tiffany (http://www.tiffany.com) have carved out profitable niches with big-ticket items (diamonds, fine jewelry, fragrances, gifts, accessories, and other luxury items).

Visiting online business sites for purposes other than making purchases can generate many times the value of direct online sales. According to new data from Jupiter Communications, in 2005 U.S. consumers will spend more than $632 billion *offline* as a direct result of research they conduct on the Internet (Wachtel, 2000).

The Internet offers tremendous potential to new entrepreneurs who want to focus on constructing an integrated Web presence that responds to customers' wants and needs. Entrepreneurs must understand that marketing and management basics still apply in the "new" economy. Just because one emerging business model is based on e-commerce does not mean that other, earlier business models are obsolete. Customer service, customer care, good products or services at a fair price, integrity, ethical behavior, and above all proper execution of a business plan are principles that hold true in business, whether the business is online or "bricks and mortar."

Planning for e-commerce is only part of the task that potential entrepreneurs must undertake. Entrepreneurs must also understand the future of conventional businesses. Consumer habits die slowly. At best, e-commerce will selectively replace certain ways of doing things. Currently, "bricks-and-mortar" firms appear to have an advantage because they exploit consumer's tendencies *not* to change. For example, on a good weekend, Wal-Mart still sold more toys than eToys.com did during the entire year (Trout, 2000). This may account for the fact that eToys planned to file for bankruptcy in early 2001 ("Dot-Com Layoffs," 2001) and its Web address now bounces potential customers to another online toy business eager to serve former eToy customers (http://www.kbkids.com/etoys).

All of the traditional "bricks-and-mortar" firms, however, have worked hard to develop an online presence as they plan for the future. For example, after a recent retooling, Wal-Mart's Web site (http://www.walmart.com) now includes over 500,000 items, compared with only 35,000 items on the company's original Web site (Waxer, 2000). In fact, management teams at all the giants of retailing, such as Kmart, Bloomingdale's, and Macy's, have "beefed up" their sites by expanding inventory selections and making improvements to the ordering process (Kanaley, 2000).

Risks in Online Business
At least 130 Internet firms closed during 2000 alone (Swartz, 2000). This trend continued in 2001 with online firms shutting down, selling out, or laying off workers to stay afloat ("Dot-Com Layoffs," 2001). Yet, in the long run this shakeout should make the survivors stronger, and their sales should accelerate.

Why have some online firms failed while many others have remained strong? Certainly, some failures are due to the normal boom and bust of any new industry. Many new online businesses faced the same problems that all new businesses encounter. Too many online enterprises had bad business plans, and too many of the new ventures had no financial safety net. As with many "bricks-and-mortar" businesses, cash flow problems led to failure for many of them. Finally, the explosion of new online businesses spread management talent too thin.

Just as there are not thousands of great ball players, there are not enough great CEOs. This shortage of talent meant that too many dot-coms were managed by poorly trained and sometimes even inept personnel (Maney, 2000). Better-trained managers, however, are becoming more readily available as schools and colleges across the country produce graduates with the skills needed to start and manage online enterprises.

Despite the online business shakeout, however, online shopping is surging, and customer demand grows for convenient shopping alternatives. Potential online entrepreneurs will continue to face the pressures to "get it right," and this translates into executing solid business practices.

Challenges for Business Education
The new economy is also ushering in a new age on school campuses, where increasing numbers of students have already launched Internet-based enterprises. In fact, according to Roper Starch Worldwide Research (Armour, 2000a), more than 60 percent of individuals aged 18 to 29 want to have their own businesses, and many of them aspire to start online ventures.

Students of all ages already have easy access to computer resources, including high-speed Internet connections, streaming video, and other technologies. The availability of these tools allows students to start their own online companies years before they graduate. While there are costs for building good e-commerce sites, those costs are minimal compared with the funds that traditional "bricks-and-mortar" entrepreneurs have needed to translate their ideas into viable businesses. According to one analyst (Bransten, 1999), traditional retailers generate $2 to $3 in sales for every dollar invested in fixed assets such as real estate. Online retailers, however, are able to generate $6 to $8 in sales for every dollar they invest in fixed assets. Today online opportunities abound both for stand-alone businesses and to complement and extend existing firms.

Business educators will provide critical training for future entrepreneurs and have the opportunity to germinate ideas for possible online enterprises among their students. Instruction has taken several approaches and there are many unanswered questions about the best way to include e-commerce in the curriculum. Some educators doubt that dividing e-commerce into a separate course or degree is the best way to train future online entrepreneurs and managers (Flamm, 2000). Many business teachers have developed specific lessons about the Internet and e-commerce and have incorporated them into units of instruction in existing courses.

At secondary schools across the country where entrepreneurship courses are offered, instructors are more likely to integrate Internet technology into their existing curricula than offer stand-alone courses that focus on starting online businesses. The Policies Commission for Business and Economic Education (2000) has encouraged collaboration: "We believe that planning and collaboration across disciplines must be a priority in the delivery of the e-business curriculum and that appropriate resources must be allocated to achieve this initiative" (p. 4).

At Hickory High School in Chesapeake, Virginia, a course in Internet marketing is available to students (http://www.geocities.com/Athens/Pantheon/5307/main.html). The first portion of the course focuses on Internet fundamentals and utilizing the Internet as a job/career tool. The major thrust of the course is examining e-commerce and building Web sites for actual businesses. At the high school level, however, such courses are rare. Oklahoma State University at Okmulgee offers an associate's degree in e-commerce (http://osuecommerce.com), which includes a series of e-commerce courses as well as accounting, marketing, and other business offerings.

A growing number of four-year colleges have developed e-commerce courses, tracks, and degrees. The syllabus for Indiana University's course in e-commerce includes many Web site resources (http://www.slis.indiana.edu/hrosenba/www/L561/syll/commprint.html). The University of South Alabama (http://mcob.usouthal.edu/ec/curriculum.html) has recently launched a bachelor of science degree program in e-commerce with a curriculum that integrates business and technology (Armour, 2000b). Old Dominion University (http://www.odu-cbpa.org/ecomm.htm) and Texas Christian University (http://www.neeley.tcu.edu/programs/undergraduate/major_ebiz.htm) offer degrees in electronic business, and Carnegie Mellon offers a master of science program in e-commerce (MSEC) through its Institute for eCommerce (http://euro.ecom.cmu. edu/program/curriculum.shtml). Program goals reflect business and technology competencies. These are just a few of many programs emerging at the postsecondary level.

In the future, schools at all levels will offer more instruction dealing with e-commerce, but some aspects of the academic picture are still unclear. Few business educators would dispute, however, that e-commerce needs to become a part of the business curriculum in some way. Whatever approach schools take, the curriculum must provide business students with a solid grounding in business.

CREATING THE ONLINE BUSINESS

Those who would like to become online entrepreneurs must combine solid business principles with knowledge of the online environment and technology skills. The stages of creating the online business illustrate this blending of business and technology during business planning, developing the commercial Web site, selecting an Internet business location, promoting the online business, opening for business, delivering the service or products, and providing customer service. Throughout these stages there are risks and errors to be avoided.

Effective Planning

As business teachers begin to develop potential online entrepreneurs, teachers must remember that business fundamentals still apply. Just as in the "bricks-and-mortar" world, the first step that potential online entrepreneurs must take is to find a need. That need must then be met in a unique fashion. Online entrepreneurs need to know what motivates shoppers to buy, and they must incorporate that knowledge in the design and execution of their Web sites.

A Unique Selling Position

The new online business must have a unique selling position. In others words, the company must provide customers with unique advantages over the competition. Customers must be given a distinct reason to buy from the online firm. A compelling image must clearly present what the online business will do for customers that other businesses cannot do. Even before the entrepreneur considers building a Web site, the entrepreneur must create a unique selling position.

Today there are over five million Web sites, and the world is not breathlessly waiting for another one. Without a unique idea that fills an important need, the chances of online survival are minimal. Successful online firms tend to make money almost from the first day. The trick is to be the first business to move into a large market where there are very few significant competitors. Garden.com (http://www.garden.com) is a good example of this strategy. Gardening is a $46-billion industry that is highly fragmented, but Garden.com entered early and was able to stand out. In fact, more than one million members registered at the site during its first year of operation (Trout, 2000).

Specialized Niche Markets

Being first plays a significant role in the success of an online firm, but specialists tend to win the online wars. Specialists focus on one product, one benefit, and one message. Successful specialists have to stay specialized or risk eroding their reputation. Priceline.com is a good example of what happens when a business loses focus. Venturing from hotel and airline reservations into gas and groceries almost destroyed that company (Krantz, 2000).

The Internet is also littered with hundreds of sites marketing "half-baked" ideas and untested products. Chipshot.com is among them ("Dot-Com Layoffs," 2001). The owners of this online venture attempted to make and sell their own brand of golf clubs—an item most customers want to lift and swing before buying—online. The last thing golfers want to do is buy an unknown brand without trying it out.

The Business Plan

Online entrepreneurs do not plan to fail—they fail to plan. A business plan serves as the road map for a company and clearly states what the business is, what it will do, and how it will do it. Besides acting as a plan for the success of a business, a business plan serves another critical function. If the entrepreneur wants to raise money from financial sources, a business plan is essential.

A good business plan helps the online entrepreneur focus on the business concept, provides a framework to develop the business idea, serves as a basis for discussion with investors, and gives both entrepreneurs and investors a way to measure performance over time. The plan also provides a clear understanding of business objectives, strategies, and financial viability. Many online entrepreneurs simply fail to map out solid business plans.

Potential online entrepreneurs may want to download a freeware business plan template called Exl-Plan from Planware.org (http://www.planware.org/exldown.htm). They can choose from different versions of the software based on the size of their proposed business. They can also subscribe to a newsletter such as BizPlanit's free monthly electronic newsletter, which provides insights and useful business planning advice (http://www.bizplanit.com/free/newsletter1.htm).

The business plan should reflect not only who customers are, but also the size of the market and its trends. Entrepreneurs must ask themselves: Where is their market? Is it international, national, regional, or local? Simply because a Web site has global reach does not mean a Web site must sell internationally. Some of the most successful online firms draw customers only from a local area.

An excellent source of statistics about the Internet can be found by clicking on Internetstats.com (http://internetstats.com). It lists Web sites that have business and market information, statistics, and trends new entrepreneurs will need. There is even a search engine to find statistics or market data on a specific industry.

Access to the Internet

Before starting to build their online business sites, entrepreneurs must have access to the Internet. For assistance in finding a service provider, students may want to visit ISP Check at http://www.ispcheck.com or The List at http://www.thelist.com. Both sites provide information about thousands of Internet service providers.

THE COMMERCIAL WEB SITE

One of the first tasks facing new online entrepreneurs is getting potential customers to the Web site. Many factors are involved in this, including the Web address of the business and how a customer-oriented the site is.

The Business Address

An early task is to create a distinctive URL—the address for the Web site. URLs should be short, memorable, and easy to spell. An attempt should also be made to choose an address that relates to the core business being conducted. Selecting a great name, however, is becoming more difficult because many names have already been taken.

To find out whether or not a URL is available, entrepreneurs can access Network Solutions at http://networksolutions.com or Register.com at http://www.register.com. At these sites, students can also find out about current annual registration fees and even register a name themselves if it is not already taken. Web sites like these allow business educators to easily develop and use relevant lesson plans like the one illustrated in the sidebar.

If all the names being considered have been taken, the potential entrepreneur can visit GreatDomains.com at http://www.greatdomains.com. This Web site is a brokerage firm that enables individuals to buy and sell domain names that have already been registered, but are not currently being used. New online entrepreneurs might also consider registering the name they want as a .net or .org domain.

STUDENT ACTIVITY

Student Activity: Selecting a Name for the Online Business

Scenario. *An aspiring entrepreneur wants to open an online business that sells "homemade" cookies and must select and register a name for the new firm on the Internet. After weeks of analyzing hundreds of potential names, this individual believes that cookies.com would be the ideal name for the new venture.* Here are the tasks. Task One: Go to the Network Solutions site at http://www.networksolutions.com and determine if this name has already been registered by someone else. Report the findings. Task Two: Assume *cookies.com* has already been registered by someone else. Identify five other potential names for the online cookie business that have *not* been registered. Task Three: Select one of these five names for the new venture. Explain the benefits/advantages of your new firm using the name you selected.

Customer-Oriented Site

Just as in the "real world," making the first impression count is very relevant in today's virtual environment. Most online entrepreneurs acknowledge that fact and spend a great deal of time, effort, and money on building an attractive, easy-to-navigate, functional Web site that draws in and engages shoppers.

Populating the site with high-quality images of products being sold must not be an afterthought. These images are critical to the credibility and ultimate success of the site. In addition to high-quality images, the site must contain comprehensive product/service information. An online drugstore or pharmacy site, for example, may need to show a particular pain medication in all available forms (e.g., liquid and tablet forms) and every package size. Images must be accompanied by complete, unedited label details so that shoppers can read ingredient or nutritional information, instructions for using the product, and warranty information. An online fashion retailer should show clothing items with available colors, fabric content, laundry instructions, and the like. In addition, the entire product database should be searchable by brand name, product category, and even product attributes. The right content can help ensure that the first impression of a Web site is a positive one.

Errors to Avoid

Potential online entrepreneurs must realize that the fastest way to drive customers away from a site is to confront them with a lot of flashy animation and slick Java applets that require obtaining special plug-ins to view the site. There are millions of potential customers who are still surfing the Web with 28.8K modems. Commercial sites must be designed with them in mind. Security, good prices, great customer service, easy site navigation, detailed product data, and simple ordering procedures are far more important than cool "techno" tricks on a site. The site *must* load quickly. Customers are willing to wait only a few seconds for a site to load before they are off to another site with a click of the mouse (Gladson, 2000).

The homepage for a commercial Web site should be short, fast loading, and to the point. Customers should be given enough information to interest them in learning more about the company or making a purchase. The homepage should let customers know exactly what the company sells. Then, the homepage should direct customers to pages that have more details about products and services being offered or other company information. Graphics should complement sales copy, not replace it. Language should be concise and relevant. Consumers do not read Web pages; they browse them. Short sentences and special bulleted points make the information easy to read and understand. The sales offers should be concise and compelling and should give customers reasons to buy. Making the purchase should be a convenient and secure process.

Potential online entrepreneurs can hire consultants to build their sites, or purchase simple software that walks them easily through the process. Entrepreneurs have alternatives to creating the HTML code needed to build Web pages themselves. Using

Web page editors, business students can have simple Web pages up and running in a few hours. Several public domain editors are available through Tucows.com (http://www.tucows.com).

A Home for the Web Site

After building their sites, online entrepreneurs must consider finding homes for their new online businesses. Each online business needs a host—the computer or server on which the Web site is placed. Thorough consideration must be given to this decision. The entrepreneur should evaluate the host for its performance characteristics and identify risks that accompany online transactions.

Checking the reliability of potential hosts is critical. Customers who find a site unavailable may never return. Each minute a site is offline means lost sales and disgruntled customers. Online entrepreneurs will also want to register their own URL addresses. The addresses given on some free services are not transferable if the entrepreneur leaves that host, which will result in a waste of the entrepreneur's promotional efforts.

The service provider that the entrepreneur selects to access the Internet will probably provide free space on which to build a Web page. Such space can be ideal for small business ventures that will handle customer transactions by e-mail, although security issues may be a concern. There are also Internet sites whose sole purpose is providing inexpensive space for small online businesses. Two of them include Bigstep (http://www.bigstep.com) and FreeMerchant (http://www.freemerchant.com). These sites offer sophisticated, yet easy-to-use, site building through an individual's own browser. Many e-commerce essentials, such as electronic shopping carts, credit card clearing, customer communications, comprehensive reports, and online customer support are also provided at these sites.

Free sites have special appeal for entrepreneurs with limited funds and are great places for students to investigate. However, sites built with these tools start to look similar because the same templates are used. Online entrepreneurs using these sites must also recognize that the host site will attempt to make money from the association. They may leverage the customer base by taking sponsorships from companies who want to market their products and services to the small businesses that have built sites there. Ultimately, value-added services provide the greatest potential source of revenue for these host sites. Site managers expect online entrepreneurs to want more and better technology as they become successful online (Beato, 1999).

Risk Management

Once the host site has been selected, an online entrepreneur must still perform many other critical tasks. For example, he or she must identify and develop the tools for making secure transactions to provide customer protection and minimize risk to the business. Online entrepreneurs must protect themselves from individuals who would attempt to place bogus orders or use credit cards that have been stolen.

In 1999 stolen credit cards were used in 1.2 percent of all Internet sales, forcing online retailers to write off $230 million. During the same period only 0.09 percent of credit card sales at traditional stores were fraudulent (Davidson, 2000). This finding indicates that e-commerce sites are more than ten times more likely to be victims than "bricks-and-mortar" stores are. The good news is that online retailers are increasingly combating the problem by installing software that flags suspicious activity on an account.

A well-thought-out risk management strategy is critical to the survival of an online business. Technology can help identify which orders pose the most risk, but human intervention will probably still be needed. Students should visit VerifyFraud.com at http://www.verifyfraud.com for more information on fraud prevention issues and techniques for online merchants.

Important practices for online entrepreneurs include ensuring that all credit card information from customers is encrypted and/or password protected. Data transmission should be maintained in a secure environment with limited authorized access. All security software must be kept up-to-date and firewalls must be properly configured (Fergerson, 2000).

PROMOTION OF THE COMMERCIAL WEB SITE

Making the site visible to consumers is the next challenge that online entrepreneurs face. Entrepreneurs need to use a variety of means to promote their businesses. Then they must assess the effectiveness of the approaches.

Methods of Promotion

If they have the time, entrepreneurs can put their URL addresses on search engines or Web portals without spending a cent. All search engines and directories have links on their sites that contain procedures for adding addresses; however, potential online entrepreneurs that are strapped for time may consider hiring online services that will perform this activity. For example, SubmitIt (http://www.submit-it.com), a Microsoft bCentral service, and NetPromote (http://www.netpromote.com) will add URLs to various search engines for a small fee. NetPromote, for example, will submit a URL to hundreds of search engines or directories for a one-time fee of less than $50 (Csatari, 2000).

Entrepreneurs should also consider using grassroots marketing efforts that are free or inexpensive. For example, they can exchange links or banners with other sites. Banners can be considered small billboards residing on different Web pages that are visible as potential customers surf the Internet. Such reciprocal linking and banner exchanges may not bring hoards of new customers to a site. Research shows that online users select only about one percent of the banner ads they see (Hanson, 2000). Banners are, however, a cost-effective method of providing a new commercial site with immediate visibility. If online entrepreneurs accept reciprocal links and banners, however, they should not appear on the homepages. Customers should be given the opportunity to see what the company is offering before being shown an exit to other sites.

Other free or inexpensive promotional efforts include placing the site's URL address on every piece of printed material that leaves the company, including all business cards. Online entrepreneurs may even want to consider virtual newsletters or direct e-mail advertising to customers that have made previous purchases. They must, however, be alert to potential dangers. Ads and newsletters must have a *direct benefit* to customers and customers should be given the opportunity to receive or not receive subsequent communications from the company. Customers do not want their e-mail boxes filled with lots of unsolicited advertising.

The Internet can give a small business tremendous marketing power. Through an online firm, entrepreneurs can conduct business with both domestic and international customers at costs far below those of "bricks-and-mortar" firms. Online, the business landscape remains crowded and highly competitive; therefore, dot-coms must distinguish themselves. In other words, they must develop differentiation tactics for merchandising and marketing. Online firms differentiate themselves through product selection, Web content, and service. Sites should offer a breadth and depth of product selection that only the Internet can provide. At the same time, interaction with the site should help customers identify the products that are right for them and maximize their shopping experiences.

At the MVP.com sports shopping site (http://www.sportsline.com/mvp/index.html), for example, customers are given the opportunity—14 hours a day—to talk to product specialists on the phone or via e-mail, and the firm's CEO believes that it is this level of customer service that will enable MVP.com to stand out in a crowded field (Wachtel, 2000). Interaction with customers has also taken other approaches. Some online cosmetic retailers, such as Sephora.com (http://www.sephora.com) and Clinique (http://www.clinique.com), show customers who provide information about complexion and hair color what colors will work best for them.

Promotional Effectiveness

Online, there is also the issue of proving that a firm's advertising is seen and acted upon. Online entrepreneurs must be ready to measure the effectiveness of any promotional campaign. They will want to measure hits, unique visitors, page views, and sales. Monitoring feedback through e-mail comments is another important method that will give online entrepreneurs a clue as to how effective promotion efforts have been.

Today most of the new online firms run their ads using traditional media initially to reach the widest possible audience. During the 2000 Super Bowl, many dot-coms staked $2 million a commercial on their future. Companies like Our Beginning (http://www.ourbeginning.com) and WebEx (http://www.webex.com) ran advertising that gave little information about what they were selling online. In fact, some ads were so vague that it was difficult to fathom what they were for. Being a part of the Super Bowl is great, but not at the cost of losing a business. Pets.com, for example, spent $2.2 million for Super Bowl ads in 2000 and folded 10 months later with a sock puppet mascot as the most valuable asset it had left (Swartz, 2000). Being clever, cute, or hip is not the key to successful advertising for online firms. Promoting online businesses should be more than entertainment; it should be about explaining and selling.

DELIVERY OF GOODS AND SERVICES

Online entrepreneurs must plan and build the "nuts and bolts" of their ventures. Implementing the fulfillment operations that pick, pack, and ship goods or deliver services is a critical piece of the puzzle for online success. Many online retailers have not fully addressed order fulfillment and returns. At too many sites, customers can buy merchandise easily but find it hard to make returns. At some e-commerce sites, there is no mention of how customers can return a purchase. Spending too much time on selling and marketing can result in the neglect of the fulfillment and back-end operations.

Today some online retailers are outsourcing their fulfillment requirements. Acknowledging that the company needed help for its Web operations, TOYSRUS.COM (http://www.toysrus.com) partnered with Amazon.com to operate a cobranded online toy store. TOYSRUS.COM buys and manages the inventory because it has expertise in picking toys as well as the buying power of its offline parent. Amazon.com, a leader in customer service and on-time delivery, operates the Web site, houses the inventory in its warehouses, fills orders, and handles customer service (Grant, 2000).

As online entrepreneurs build their sites, each must include an easy-to-find section that concisely explains the shipping and handling charges and the procedures for returns. In fact, the customer should be given the total shipped price before the credit card number is requested.

CUSTOMER SERVICE BEFORE, DURING, AND AFTER THE SALE

A reason many consumers give for not making a purchase on the Web is a lack of person-to-person contact. Innovative business Web sites use many approaches to providing online customer service. Customer feedback helps to identify problems, and new entrepreneurs benefit from knowing what customers expect.

Online Customer Service

Many Web sites merge the convenience and do-it-yourself control of the online connection with a human connection. Some sites, like Biztravel.com (http://www.biztravel.com), feature their toll-free customer service numbers prominently on their homepages. Others, like Ebags, a luggage retailer (http://www.ebags.com), allow customers to click a button to communicate with a customer service representative via a live, text-based chat. A few sites are experimenting with proactive technology that allows customer service agents to monitor the online shopping patterns of customers and step in to offer live help and even take over the customer's browser to present relevant information on screen. This idea may evoke an image of the salesperson lurking unseen in cyberspace and may raise privacy concerns for many customers, however.

Good online customer service includes e-mail confirmations, multiple means of contact, support outside business hours, guarantees, and return policies. As soon as a customer's order is received, confirmation should be sent via e-mail. The confirmation should include specifics of the transaction. Web sites must always provide multiple ways to contact the company when there are complaints and/or problems. In addition to e-mail addresses, Web sites should provide phone numbers and conventional addresses. An online business is open 24 hours a day, 7 days a week, but customer support typically operates within normal business hours. For customer assistance during times that live customer support is unavailable, a frequently asked question section can address some concerns. Finally, online customers should be guaranteed that they will get their money back if they are not satisfied with the products purchased. According to a recent survey, whether items are purchased online or in stores, there is a least a 30 percent chance they will be returned (Malone, 2000).

Customer Service Effectiveness

How do most e-commerce sites measure up in terms of customer responsiveness? According to Jupiter Communications, nearly 75 percent of e-commerce sites offer toll-free telephone support, but less than half of those call centers operate 24 hours a day, 7 days a week. Response to e-mail inquiries is becoming polarized. About half of the merchants reply to customers within 24 hours, but many others take longer than 5 days or never respond at all (Bly, 2000). Biztravel.com backs its customer service with payments of $10 for slow or unprofessional responses. The site promises the payment if a customer is not connected to an agent for online chat within five minutes or fails to receive an e-mail response within two hours. Online entrepreneurs must understand that it is beneficial to keep all lines of communication open with their customers and to quickly respond to customer concerns.

Credit card security remains the major reason that many consumers give for not making online purchases. Experts agree, however, that online purchasing is relatively safe. In fact, the actual incidence of credit card fraud is low. Today nearly all online merchants use sophisticated encryption and secure servers that scramble credit card numbers, making intrusions into the systems nearly impossible (Suzukamo, 2000).

After credit card security, privacy issues are typically the next major concern for most online shoppers. All commercial Web sites should have a privacy policy that is spelled out and easily accessible from the homepage. Customers must be informed of how any information about them will be used as well as any future plans the company has for the data. Many sites also adhere to the principles of the BBBOnline, a Better Business Bureau program (http://www.bbbonline.com), and display its privacy and reliability seals.

COMMON ONLINE ERRORS

Not delivering on what they promise is the quickest way for commercial Web sites to fail. Customers expect a good product or service, at a fair price, delivered promptly, but responsibility to the customer should not end there. What online entrepreneurs do or do not do after the sale determines whether customers return or make purchases in the future.

Common errors made by too many sites must be avoided. Homepage downloads should be fast, not loaded with graphics. Navigation through the site should be easy and links should be labeled. All customers should have a clear idea of where a link will send them. A site that sells products online or collects customer data should ensure the security of its transactions and communications. In addition, privacy policies should be clearly stated so that customers know how their information will be used now and in the future. Policies related to shipping charges and returns should also be easily accessed. Customers should not be surprised with shipping charges just as they are ready to confirm their order. Too many shopping carts are left at online checkouts when customers learn the full cost of their purchases. Above all, online customers must be respected. A relationship of trust is critical.

A survey completed by Verizon last year found that just 34 percent of firms with fewer than 50 employees had Web sites (Hopkins, 2000). The finding that two thirds of those firms remain offline is significant because small businesses represent as much as 90 percent of the nation's businesses. According to a Forrester Research study, local merchants attracted only 9 percent or $680 million in retail Web sales in 1998 (Beato, 1999). There is great potential for online growth within this business segment.

Established firms have a distinct advantage when going online. Retail giants like Kmart, Wal-Mart, Gap, Best Buy, and Lands' End have extended their expertise to the Internet and capitalized on their existing strengths, name recognition, and customer trust. The Internet, however, levels the playing field and gives a business of any size the image of a large company. Having an Internet presence can build in a potential customer's mind the perception that a business is as credible as any other that is just a mouse click away. Moreover, entrepreneurs of small business sites can employ most of the same online technologies that the corporate giants do. On the Internet a business's size is not as important as whether it builds a strong relationship with customers. In the final analysis, the benefits of going online may have more to do with developing these relationships than with selling products or services.

SUMMARY
Business education students should evaluate the pros and cons—the opportunities and the risks—of developing e-commerce sites. Business teachers should show students how to start and develop commercial ventures on the Internet. Business education courses can provide the entrepreneurship competencies young people need to build and grow fledging firms.

Business educators can teach business, entrepreneurship, and technology concepts and skills by having students learn to plan businesses, develop elements of commercial Web sites, investigate customer service characteristics of effective online businesses, apply risk management strategies, and analyze how and why online businesses succeed or fail. In the 21st century business education is poised to integrate business, entrepreneurship, and technology so that students have a sound educational foundation for seizing opportunities.

REFERENCES

Armour, S. (2000a, April 12). Net firms soar on campus. *USA Today*, p. B1.

Armour, S. (2000b, February 23). New major: E-commerce. *USA Today*, p. A1.

Beato, G. (1999, October). Web-o-matic. *Business 2.0*, 190–197.

Bly, L. (2000, June 20). Personal touch hits turbulence on the Web. *USA Today*, p. 5D.

Bransten, L. (1999, July 12). The bottom line. *The Wall Street Journal*, p. R8.

Csatari, J. (2000, November 26). Do what you love and make money online? *Parade Magazine*, 16–18.

Davidson, P. (2000, July 17). Credit card fraud takes swipe at retailers on Internet. *USA Today*, p. B1.

Dot-com layoffs and shutdowns. (2001, July 25). *The Wall Street Journal at WSJ.col.* Retrieved July 27, 2001, from the World Wide Web: http://www.wsj.com/public/resources/documents/dotcomlayoffs.htm

Fergerson, J. (2000, November). Smart fraud protection. *e-Business Advisor*, 42–45.

Flamm, M. (2000, April 24–30). Electronic commerce joins the college curriculum: A fad or a business fundamental? *Crain's New York Business, 16*(17), 34.

Gladson, T. (2000, July). Make your first impression count. *ERetailing World*, 32.

Grant, L. (2000, February 21). Retailers, dot-coms team up. *USA Today*, p. 5B.

Hanson, W. (2000). *Internet marketing*. Cincinnati, OH: South Western/Thompson Learning.

Hopkins, J. (2000, December 11). Small firms remain offline. *USA Today*, p. 14B.

James, M. S. (2001, July 9). The virtual dead live at the Museum of e-failure. Retrieved July 26, 2001, from the World Wide Web: http://more.abcnews.go.com/s...ailyNews/preservation_efaire010508.html

Kanaley, R. (2000, December 3). Traditional retailers challenge pure plays. *The State*, p. G1.

Krantz, M. (2000, December 4). What detonated dot-bombs? *USA Today*, p. 1B.

Malone, H. (2000, December 3). Check return policy before buying online. *The State*, p. 1G.

Maney, K. (2000, June 22). Dot-com carnage opens door to brighter future. *USA Today*, p. 1B.

Policies Commission for Business and Economic Education. (2000). *Policy statement no. 66: This we believe about electronic business in business education.* Reston, VA: National Business Education Association. Retrieved July 27, 2001, from the World Wide Web: http://www.nbea.org/curfpolicy.html

Suzukamo, L. (2000, December 3). Credit card is safest way to buy online. *The State*, p. 1G.

Swartz, J. (2000, December 13). E-tailers turn net profits. *USA Today*, p. 1B.

Trout, J. (2000, May). Stupid net tricks. *Business 2.0*, 75–78.

Wachtel, N. (2000, July). Differentiation tactics: Standing out in the online crowd. *ERetailing World*, 11–12.

Waxer, C. (2000, April). Wal-Mart takes another crack at the Net. *Business 2.0*, 82–87.

Technology and Career Development

Judith K. Berry

Lansing Community College

Lansing, Michigan

More high school students will go on to postsecondary education than ever before because of the role of technology in the workplace. In 1987 4.1 million, or about 22 percent, of the 20–24-year old age group enrolled in postsecondary education. By 1997 this number had increased to 5.2 million students, nearly 30 percent of that population (Paulin, 2001). This trend will continue. After financial aid grants, students will part with roughly $40,000 to $60,000 for four years of education at a public college or university and even more at private universities ("Great Schools," 2001; Comorow, 2001). With such investments on the line, increasing competition to gain one of these college slots and to succeed will turn up the pressure on students.

At the same time, employer demand for qualified, new talent continues, particularly in business and information technology (IT) fields. The Information Technology Association of America (ITAA) (2001) projected a "12-month demand for IT workers of 1.6 million and a shortfall in filling jobs of approximately 850,000" (p. 1). There is no question that education that addresses the nation's economic needs will justify the investments in education. Yet, there are questions to be addressed in preparing students for these opportunities.

Will our schools be ready for these students? What careers will exist? How will teachers match classrooms to careers and careers to students? How will classrooms keep up technologically with career preparation when many classrooms cannot represent the technology of today, let alone tomorrow? This chapter examines careers and the educational readiness of teachers and their classrooms, suggesting ways for teachers to proceed.

Business educators are continually asked to address careers that are dramatically changing, and administrators expect business educators to implement career programs rapidly. The material in this chapter is designed to help teachers make decisions and anticipate questions about career preparation, standards, technology acquisition, and professional development. This information should facilitate decision making and communication with administrators.

MILLENNIAL TEENS PREPARE FOR CAREERS

The teens of this decade already have technology experiences that set them apart from earlier generations of students. These experiences generate expectations about education and impressions about careers. The careers open to these teens include many that did not exist prior to the last half decade.

Career Categories

The positions for which applicants are being sought today require a combination of technology, business and management, communication, and other education and experience. (For example, see the Monster.com Web site at http://jobsearch.monster. com.) The Bureau of Labor Statistics, the National Workforce Center for Emerging Technologies (NWCET), and ITAA are three major sources of information for categorizing careers and identifying career paths.

The Bureau of Labor Statistics classifies computer programmers, computer systems analysts, computer engineers, database administrators, computer support specialists, and computer scientists as IT occupations (Veneri, 1998). The category for computer scientists includes network administrators and specialists, Web designers and administrators, telecommunication specialists, and virtually all positions not subsumed under the other categories. The *Occupational Outlook Handbook* ("Computer systems," n.d.) includes career information, including information about work environment and earnings statistics according to these categories. The reports incorporate information from the reports of other reputable organizations, such as Robert Half International.

NWCET (2001) (http://www.nwcet.org and http://www.cybercareers.org) identifies eight IT or "cybercareers." The set, shown in Table 1, is very useful for communication purposes. Rather than dealing with the "computer science" category that common usage will treat as synonymous with "programming" or some narrow set of careers, teachers can explain

Table 1. Emerging Cybercareers for the Twenty-First Century
Database Development and Administration
Web Development and Administration
Enterprise Systems Analysis and Integration
Network Design and Administration
Programming/Software Engineering
Technical Support
Technical Writing
Digital Media

the eight careers in a straightforward manner to administrators and parents. In addition, other organizations use these categories for research and reporting purposes.

ITAA (2001) based its study of skills and careers on these cybercareer categories. "The overwhelming majority of companies in this survey (81 percent) have more than one professional advancement level for the eight NWCET categories. Candidates in most career categories can climb a career ladder with three or four non-supervisory steps" (p. 3).

The cybercareers also emphasize the combination of knowledge and skills required in the workplace, a need emphasized for more than a decade in the Secretary's Commission on Achieving Necessary Skills recommendations (SCANS2000 Center, 2001). Engman (2001) pointed out the need for students to weave together a variety of skills that go beyond technical skills to meet workplace needs. Arenofsky (2000) emphasized the need for job applicants to plan their educational goals based on the need for "multiskilled people, such as on-line managers, digital journalists, and intranet designers" (p. 7) and their individual strengths.

STUDENT ACTIVITY

Matching IT Careers to Personal Characteristics

Have students visit and register at the CyberCareers.org site (http://www.cybercareers.org) and complete the IT career interest inventory. The IT interest test is coordinated with a multiple intelligences survey. After students complete the inventory and receive the career analysis, ask them to discuss their results in small groups. Ask them to discuss with others what they learned about the careers, their reactions to the analysis of "best fit" with a career, and their overall attitudes about careers in IT.

Note to teachers: The surveys can be printed and answered by hand, but the interactive version provides students with immediate feedback and graphical analysis of the multiple intelligences results. This activity can be used at the secondary and postsecondary levels in any class that has a career education component. A visit to the Web site may also be appropriate for younger learners.

Net Generation Experiences and Perceptions

Tapscott (1998), who closely watched several hundred Internet-connected teens, tells of a 16-year-old acquaintance. This youth had already created a site on the World Wide Web that received twenty million hits per month. "Imagine being [his] teacher," Tapscott wrote (1998, p. ix). What will business education do for current and future students? The 18-to-21-year old workers who enter the workforce from now on will come face to face with global competition and corporations that have most likely slimmed down. This new generation of teenagers hopes that educational institutions will shift toward more practical education (Tapscott, 1998): life skills, socialization, community training, and civic mindedness. They would also like to see technology, science, and engineering emphasized.

There is little question that postsecondary teachers encounter more students enrolling in classes today who have already pursued learning in a variety of other formats, many of which do not grant academic credit. The *Futurist* ("The Web-connected Generation," 2001) observed that, "America's college class of 2001 is 'virtually 100% connected' to the Internet. . . . More than half of the 2,001 students surveyed (54%) reported visiting career-oriented Web sites such as monster.com, myjobs.com, jobdirect.com, and headhunter.com to help launch their careers" (p. 9). Their younger brothers and sisters in high school are right behind them.

Manfred (2000) observed, however, that "[w]ith all this attention to technology games, gadgets, and instant messaging, you'd think teens would finally view information technology as pretty cool, right? Think again . . . [K]ids . . . see technology professionals as anything but cool" (p. 82). In spite of career opportunities, insufficient numbers of students pursue IT careers to meet the demand for qualified professionals in this field.

An American Association of University Women (AAUW) Educational Foundation study indicated that, "[F]ewer women are considering careers in the New Economy's fastest growing and most lucrative field. It also means that businesses, which are bemoaning a shortage of computer and technical skills are losing out on a substantial source of talent" ("How To Diversify," 2000, p. 32). Federal Express is concerned enough about the inadequate supply of future information technologists to sponsor a technology camp for teens to generate interest for a future five- to ten-year time frame. Cisco is also working to interest teens in IT early through its Cisco Networking Academies (Dash, 2000).

ITAA studied how several hundred third, sixth, ninth, and twelfth graders viewed IT work. Student responses suggested that, as grade level increases, the image of IT as a career field became progressively less attractive. The survey indicated that IT is perceived as "a profession that is populated with 'geeky-nerdy' [males]" (1998). The AAUW report concurred. As reported by *Training* ("How To Diversify," 2000, p. 32), "[G]irls and women often view IT workers as 'alienated and antisocial'—in essence living up to the 'computer geek' stereotype."

Business Education Actions

An overwhelming majority of Americans now work in service and information jobs, with nearly half of all Americans involved in the generation, dissemination, and use of information. New technologies are creating workplaces where creativity, cooperation, and critical thinking are valued at all levels of an organization. If American education cannot equip young people with the skills they will need, they will not be able to play productive roles in society.

As business educators incorporate emerging careers into their work with students, they can help students to understand what it means to be "multiskilled" through an analysis of the knowledge and experience that IT career paths require. Business educators must also address the stereotypes surrounding IT work. "The computer culture must become more inviting for girls," according to Turkle, chair of the AAUW commission ("How To Diversify," 2000, p. 32). WNET (http://www.wnet.org/ wnetschool/tech), New York's public broadcasting station, with support from Toyota, created a multimedia curriculum called, "What's Up in Technology?" to generate interest among high school students in technology fields (Donlevy & Donlevy, 1999).

Business educators are change agents for students and need to address students' attitudes. Teachers must also address the impressions created by administrators, parents, and other teachers who intentionally or inadvertently communicate that technology is the province of men and that the careers do not depend on core business knowledge, but only technical skills. Contemporary career programs that blend business and technology can change attitudes and develop the multiskilled student. Further, business educators can address the broad range of IT positions that take advantage of a wide variety of talents, not just mathematical/logical skills, which have been emphasized in traditional programs of the past.

STUDENT ACTIVITY

Image of IT Careers

Provide students with a simple "position image" rating form. Have students visit a job posting Web site like Monster.com (http://www.monster.com), and search for several of the eight cybercareers listed in Table 1 or other positions that relate technology to business (e.g., project manager, records manager, knowledge manager, document specialist). Assign the career paths so that there are a few students and a mix of male and female students looking at job postings in each career area. Ask each student to read the responsibilities and qualifications for three to five positions and to rate each one for its "image." Then compile the information based on position and gender of respondent. Bring the information back for discussion during another class session. Ask students to discuss what image they want the career they pursue to have.

Note to teachers: A rating form can be as simple as a blank for the position title and company, and four to five brief statements (e.g., "a fun job to have," "an interesting job to study for," "a great job for me," "good earnings"), followed by ratings of one to five for the range from "absolutely don't think so" to "definitely agree."

CAREER PROGRAM FEASIBILITY ASSESSMENT

How can business education address emerging careers? Some schools have already developed curricula and obtained funding. Many business educators may not yet have initiated instructional programs, and this chapter suggests an approach to determining feasibility. The intent is to serve several purposes. Teachers need to know what is involved in delivering instruction, including the availability of resources and their own and their schools' commitments to professional development. Teachers need to be able to decide if the best approach is offering one or more courses, offering a distinct program, or integration within some other instructional setting. Teachers also need to communicate with administrators early in the process to build support and realistic expectations for funding.

Feasibility

After researching a career, teachers should address the following five areas, which are fundamental to determining the feasibility of a program and guiding the actual proposal to establish the program once feasibility is established.

1. **Learner program and/or course description(s).** What does the career path look like when expressed as an educational program and/or course? Does the program title reflect the career path? Do the courses also reflect the career path sufficiently to communicate the scope of the program or learning to administrators and eventually to students and parents? Related to this is the match between the program or course description and business, industry, and educational standards.

2. **Equipment needs for the classroom.** What equipment is required to deliver instruction? What equipment is already available? What needs to be purchased? The issue can be dealt with in several ways, and some solutions have higher price tags than others. Business educators are encouraged to request what they need to deliver a high-quality program. This generally means a one-to-one ratio of workstations to students.

3. **Software and licensing requirements for the classroom.** What software is required? Does the software require server software? What software will be on each workstation? What licensing is required for server and client access?

4. **Course materials and resources for learners and instructors.** Do textbooks and instructional materials exist? Are these materials and resources aligned with the recognized certifications in the career area? What are the estimated costs of these resources?

5. **Professional development requirements for teachers.** The quality, availability, and cost of professional development are among the most important issues to be addressed. Without adequate professional development, teachers may lack the competence and the motivation to undertake program delivery.

REVISED CAREER EDUCATION CLUSTERS

Business educators need to look at the total range of career instruction they might provide. Although the Bureau of Labor Statistics and the NWCET have identified careers, they do not directly address program development. To provide organization to career education, the Office of Vocational and Adult Education (2000) has defined 16 career clusters to represent all jobs in the economy of today and tomorrow and the economy of the local, national, and global marketplace. As shown in Table 2, business education supports some clusters and directly addresses others.

The IT category includes the diverse career set identified by NWCET and the Bureau of Labor Statistics. Business educators must ensure that they are the primary developers

Table 2. Career Clusters and Business Education

Career Clusters That Business Education Supports

Agriculture and Natural Resources

Architecture and Construction

Arts, A/V Technology, and Communication

Education and Training

Government and Public Administration

Health Science

Human Services

Law and Public Safety

Manufacturing

Retail/Wholesale Sales and Service

Scientific Research/Engineering

Transportation, Distribution, and Logistics

Business and Technology Career Clusters

Career Cluster	Sample Occupations
Business and Administration	Human resource administrators, administrative specialists, financial analysts, and international marketing specialists
Hospitality and Tourism	Hotel managers and travel agents
Finance	Stockbrokers and bankers
Information Technology	Web designers and developers, database administrators, multimedia producers, network administrators, technical writers, and software engineers

of programs in the IT cluster because there is an increasing need to merge business foundations with IT instruction.

CAREER STANDARDS

What standards should teachers use as the basis for career instruction when there are several sources for standards that may apply? The National Business Education Association (NBEA) (2001) has issued its standards for business education components, the International Society for Technology in Education (ISTE) (http://www.iste.org) has promulgated a set of standards for IT literacy and applications, and the National Skill Standards Board (NSSB) (2001) has consolidated information about skill standards and recognized certifications for all occupations. Where standards and certifications do not exist, the NSSB has encouraged their development.

STUDENT ACTIVITY*

The Revised CIP Codes

Assign to preservice or graduate business education students the following question for research and discussion: Does the revision of Group 52 (Business Programs) and Group 11 (Computer Programs) in the U.S. Department of Education's Classification of Instructional Programs (2000) affect business educators? In brief, this revision of CIP codes moves certain IT programs traditionally classified in Group 52 to Group 11, and elaborates the emerging IT career programs in Group 11.

Note to teachers: A state consultant for business education and/or the appropriate certification representative may be able to visit and serve as a resource for a class discussion. If distance or time prohibits a class visit, consider hosting a teleconference or electronic discussion.

*For preservice business teachers or graduate business education students

The standards included in the *National Standards for Business Education* (National Business Education Association, 2001) have been identified by business educators and business and industry professionals. Virtually every area of standards affects career development, but Table 3 shows the standards that business educators should focus on in career development.

Table 3. Career Development Standards

Standard Area	Standard
Self-Awareness	Assess personal skills, abilities, and aptitudes and personal strengths and weaknesses as they relate to career exploration and development.
Career Research	Utilize career resources to develop a career information database that includes international career opportunities.
Workplace Expectations	Relate the importance of workplace expectations to career development.
Career Strategy	Apply knowledge gained from individual assessment to a comprehensive set of goals and an individual career plan.
School-to-Career Transition	Develop strategies to make an effective transition from school to careers.
Lifelong Learning	Relate the importance of lifelong learning to career success.

Created by the 1994 National Skill Standards Act and comprised of industry, educational, government, and other voluntary participants, NSSB recognizes standards and certifications developed by various industry groups (2001, Appendices A and B). In the IT career area, there are two types of standards and certifications that are recognized: vendor specific and vendor neutral, both of which are important in career preparation.

Vendor-specific certifications validate the holder's knowledge of a defined product. Whether for Microsoft, Novell, Oracle, or another developer's product, certificates are often recognized by numerous vendors when there is a common base of knowledge involved.

Vendor-neutral standards and certifications generally emerge from professional or industry organizations. The Computer Technology Industry Association (CompTIA) (http://www.comptia.com), for example, "work[s] to develop vendor-neutral standards in e-commerce, customer service, workforce development, and training certification." Often identified as CompTIA certifications, certifications address project management, electronic business, document imaging, Internet technologies, server and networking technologies, and other specializations (2001). Partnerships with technology and business enterprises ensure that these certifications are recognized.

The Institute for Certification of Computing Professionals (http://www.iaap-hq.org) awards the widely recognized Associate Computer Professional and Computer Professional certificates, the first for the emerging professional and the second for the experienced professional. Administrative support skill standards are defined by the International Association of Administrative Professionals (http://www.iaap-hq.org), and the Project Management Institute certifies project managers (http://www.pmi.org).

Academic Credit and Certifications

A final piece of the process is being addressed as certain certifications become recognized for academic credit. Typically, certificates do not convert into academic credit. The Chauncy Group (2000), a subsidiary of the Educational Testing Service, certifies the Associate Technology Specialist who has passed a core examination and two examinations in one of the eight NWCET careers (http://www.e-assessment.org/). The Chauncy Group's Candidate Bulletin (2000) provides a description of its program and sample questions representative of career area testing. The American Council on Education (ACE) College Credit Recommendation Service converts the results of certification to five or six college credits, one credit for the core examination, and the remainder in the career area in which two examinations are completed.

CAREER PREPARATION PROGRAMS

Career programs should be built on a foundation of employability and common technology skills related to communication, mathematics, work habits, problem solving, management and leadership, and economics of work. Career planning should be an integral part of these foundations so that students can identify one or more clusters in which to build their careers. Such foundations should relate IT to the important processes of record keeping, information/media management, and proper use of communication technologies. All careers will require the application of keyboarding, input, spreadsheet, database, multimedia, and technology management skills.

What programs should be offered at the secondary level to prepare students for employment and postsecondary study? Several options corresponding to business career pathways are suggested below. Because IT encompasses so many areas, it is handled as a major section in the chapter.

E-Commerce

E-commerce education leads to recognition and advancement in this emerging industry. E-commerce education can prepare students for technology and design specialist positions. Graduates of e-commerce programs should be able to demonstrate how they can contribute to employers' increased customer satisfaction. At the secondary level an e-commerce program should include the following components:

- Course work in online banking, consumer education, commercial Web site development and maintenance, Internet marketing, product development, advertising, and security.
- Work, cooperative education, internship, or apprenticeship experiences.

E-Biz+ is now a CompTIA certification area. Business Professionals of America has an assessment to validate mastery of Web page design, banking and finance, and marketing. DECA provides assessment instruments that validate mastery of consumer education, marketing, product development, and advertising. Prosoft Training (http://www.ProsoftTraining.com) administers certification examinations for e-commerce designer and Internet positions (National Skill Standards Board, 2001) and has partnered with the NWCET to coordinate selected certifications, such as the Certified Internet Webmaster.

Accounting and Finance

Accounting and finance are recognized business education fields that prepare students not only for employment but also for postsecondary programs in business administration, accounting, and finance. Secondary accounting and finance programs should include the following components:

- Course work in principles of accounting; computerized accounting; money, credit, and banking; securities operations; international finance; financial planning; and economics for finance.
- Work, cooperative education, internship, or apprenticeship experiences.

Business Professionals of America has an accounting and finance assessment instrument. Based on mastery of specific components, the learner can take a variety of assessments at the organization's regional, state, and national leadership conferences in the areas of accounting, finance, international finance, banking, and economics. Certifications in accounting areas are well established. Fields related to accounting, such as audit and security, are also connected to certifications.

Sports and Entertainment Marketing

Students who pursue sports and entertainment marketing can provide employers with a specialty that is customer focused. Graduates of these programs have a competitive advantage in management and marketing fields in an emerging industry. There is not yet an assessment instrument that would lead to certification in this field. Secondary sports and entertainment marketing programs should include the following components:

- Course work in marketing basics, sports marketing, entertainment marketing, recreation marketing, college and amateur sports, professional sports, product and service marketing, technology for entertainment and marketing, public relations, career options in entertainment and marketing, and legal issues.
- Work, cooperative education, internship, or apprenticeship experiences.

Travel and Tourism

Travel and tourism is a recognized industry requiring individuals with increasing levels of skill. Heightened attention to physical and information security and knowledge of various cultures are necessary components of these instructional programs. Students prepared with specific knowledge will enjoy a competitive advantage, especially when they demonstrate sensitivity to customer satisfaction. Secondary travel and tourism programs should include the following components:

- Course work in principles of travel and tourism, people and cultures, travel industry systems applications, travel destinations, and economics for travel and tourism, as well as virtual excursions.
- Work, cooperative education, internship, or apprenticeship experiences.

There are many travel and tourism assessment instruments that lead to certification. Some of the common certificates that can be earned through testing in this industry include National Travel Agent Proficiency Certificate, the Marriott Sales Certificate, the Cruise Line Industry Association Certificate, the Carnival Cruise Line Certificate, the Hertz Certificate, and the Sandals Certificate.

Information Technology

The number of opportunities to provide career preparation for IT careers is growing ever larger. In general, the IT career pathway should proceed from foundation studies in business, communication, management, and IT to the technical studies required to meet standards for performance in particular fields. Following the technical studies, students should complete an internship or cooperative education placement. Because of the continually changing nature of the careers, students should follow an articulated program as they enter postsecondary institutions and develop plans that blend work, certification, and business studies. Lifelong learning must be stressed for these and all careers.

Technical support. Computer support specialists "provide technical assistance, support, and advice to customers and users. . . . These are the troubleshooters responsible for interpreting problems and providing technical support. They answer phone calls, use automated diagnostic programs, and resolve recurrent problems" (Veneri, 1998, p. 46). Two programs and/or courses of study can prepare students for technical support work: help desk and A+ certification programs.

Help desk preparation should focus on help desk concepts, as well as computer user support and customer service skills and experiences in problem solving. There should also be a technical component to provide a basis for delivering help to customers or clients. Help desk professionals often belong to professional organizations, such as Help Desk International (http://www.hdi.org).

A+ certification preparation requires computer installation, configuration, and upgrading instruction. The A+ certificate is a recognized verification of the knowledge and skills required of a computer service technician.

Network administration. Network administration can be approached through a vendor-neutral or vendor-specific program approach. The extensive product options prohibit a thorough presentation of all the possible approaches, but a description of a few should demonstrate the need to decide whether to select a single approach or support multiple products in instruction.

- The Network+ certification program is a vendor-neutral credential acquired though CompTIA. Course work in networking hardware and architecture is required. The examination assesses installing and configuring a client network. On-the-job experience is necessary for hands-on portions of the examination.
- A Cisco Certified Network Administration program (CCNA) should include the following course work: networking fundamentals, networking theory, advanced networking, and network design. Students should design and develop customized business solutions with Cisco routers and switches. The focus should be on both routing and switching, as well as WAN switching solutions across the disciplines of network design and support. Work experience, cooperative education, and internship and apprenticeship options are essential, and on-the-job problem solving should precede the assessment examination.
- The Certified Novell Administrator program requires course work in the administration of an installed Novell network product. Work, cooperative education, internship, or apprenticeship experience is necessary to prepare students for hands-on portions of the assessment.
- The Windows 2000 Microsoft Certified Systems Engineer (MCSE) Network Certification program requires course work in installing, configuring, and administering a family of Windows 2000 products, including Server and Professional products. Implementing and administering a Windows network infrastructure and the directory services infrastructure are essential skills. Experience is essential for the problem-solving and troubleshooting assessment.

Other notes on the IT multiskill set. IT programs can focus on system administration, programming, Internet administration, Web development, and other cybercareers. Business educators must not ignore the fact that some skills are almost universally part of the skill set of IT professionals, yet can also be the focus of specific positions. Project management is such an area, as is record/document management.

Practitioners in almost all cybercareers employ the methodology of project management (Schwalbe, 2001). A search for "project management" on Monster.com yields a variety of cybercareer job titles that include project management as a qualification. Some positions, however, include "project management" in their titles and have project management as their primary focus. A similar result appears when the search term is "records or document management careers." The network basis of electronic systems that disseminate documents and accomplish workflow is the "back office" aspect of document management. The document software products that have content classification, indexing, and retention requirements reflect the changing records management profession. A posting for a New York position in records management advertised a salary between $65,000 and $80,000 and included not only the electronic applications for documents but project management qualifications.

STUDENT ACTIVITY

'Universal"Skill Set

Have students examine the career pages of businesses to obtain descriptions of the positions that are open and profiles of employees who are currently working in various cybercareer areas. Students can use a general search tool, such as the one on http://www.yahoo.com or another portal site, to search for "Web site developer," "e-commerce manager," "project manager," "content manager," "knowledge manager," or other positions and select business Web sites from the results list. Students may also directly select employers they have an interest in.

Have students examine the position descriptions and/or the employee profiles for the main and supporting qualifications. When each student has located at least two positions, have students identify the technical qualifications and the business management and communication qualifications. Have students discuss which skills are more difficult to acquire and how they might set learning goals for school-to-career experiences in both technical and business communication areas. This can be done as a group, individually, or through electronic conference discussion.

Note to teachers: As an example, Keane, Inc., has a career center to attract applicants (http://www.keane.com/careers/). At this site employee profiles introduce visitors to the employees at Keane as well as give prospective applicants some knowledge of what the positions are like. Such profiles can introduce students to positions like technical architect and project manager (http://www.keane.com/careers/qa/ta2_qa.html and /pm_fed_qa.html). Many businesses have such career pages within their Web sites and they make excellent career search resources.

Communication is another skill that is universally sought, but also results in job titles. Documentation specialist positions combine primary skills in both writing and technical areas. Other organizations search for e-business communications managers or communications managers with project management experience. The "weaving" of multiskills is what the business educator does best.

SUMMARY

Business educators excel at developing multiskills, for they have always woven academic, business, and technology skills together in instruction. They must do so even more for the challenging careers that are emerging. In addition, they must work to address attitudes that are impediments to students pursuing careers that are challenging and will provide high earnings potential. Likewise they must address stereotypes that are expressed by the educators and family members who influence students in their choice of careers. Experienced business educators will find that they have been addressing these issues throughout their careers, and business educators who are beginning their careers will find that their commitment to the student will aid them in carrying these important career messages to parents, students, employers, and others in their communities.

In the rich array of career paths that are based on the restructured career clusters, this chapter has demonstrated that there is really no "free lunch" when it comes to delivering sound technology-based curricula. When administrators ask, "Can 'it' be done?" whether "it" is a Cisco academy, a Novell certification program, an Oracle database administration program, or some other technology career program, there is no simple, single answer. Rather there are five basic areas of questioning that can lead to a determination of whether a program is feasible.

Business educators should develop programs to address the shortages of individuals qualified for business and industry. The programs must be standards based and the standards must focus on multiskills. Fortunately, business educators have standards that already address multiple skills, and they have a tradition of meeting employer needs. While the work is demanding, business educators have always been up to the challenge.

REFERENCES

Arenofsky, J. (2000, February/March). Hot careers for the 21st century. *Career World, 28*(5), 6–11.

Chauncy Group International, Ltd. (2000). *Associate technology specialist: Candidate bulletin.* Retrieved September 5, 2001, from the World Wide Web: http://www.e-assessment.com/PDFFiles/ATS%20Candidate%20Bulletin.pdf

Comorow, A. (2001, October 1). The money maze. *U. S. News & World Reports, 131*(13), 58–68.

Computer systems analysts, engineers, and scientists. (n.d.). *Occupational Outlook Handbook.* Retrieved September 28, 2001, from the World Wide Web: http://stats.bls.gov/oco/ocos042.htm

Computer Technology Industry Association. (2001). This is certification. Retrieved from the World Wide Web: http://www.comptia.org/certification/index.htm

Dash, J. (2000, August 7). FedEx grooms teens at technology camp. *Computerworld, 34*(32), 40–41.

Donlevy, J. G., & Donlevy, T. R. (1999). What's up in technology? A multimedia curriculum for exploring high-technology careers. *International Journal of Instructional Media, 26*(3), 249–251.

Engman, J. (2001, April). Trends show that skills must go beyond technical expertise. *Techniques, 76*(4), 36.

Great schools at great prices. (2001, October 1). *U.S. News & World Reports, 131*(13), 69–70.

How to diversify the geek pool. (2000, June). *Training, 37*(6), 32.

Information Technology Association of America. (1998, January). *Task force white paper: Image of information technology (IT) professions.* Arlington, VA: Author. Retrieved August 13, 2001, from the World Wide Web: http://www.itaa.org/workforce/studies/image.htm

Information Technology Association of America. (2001, April). *Executive summary: When can you start? Building better information technology skills and careers.* Arlington, VA: Author. Retrieved July 1, 2001, from the World Wide Web: http://www.itall.org/workforce/studies/01execsumm.htm

Manfred, E. (2000, November 13). Selling teens on IT. *Computerworld, 34*(46), 82–83.

National Business Education Association. (2001). *National standards for business education.* Reston, VA: Author.

National Skill Standards Board. (2001, April 5). *An introduction to the use of skill standards and certifications in WIA programs.* Washington, DC: Author. Retrieved June 2, 2001, from the World Wide Web: http://www.nssb.org/pubs/publications.htm

The National Workforce Center for Emerging Technologies. (2001). Retrieved from the World Wide Web: http://www.nwcet.org

Office of Vocational and Adult Education. (2000, December 26). *Career clusters.* Retrieved September 1, 2001, from the World Wide Web: http://www.ed.gov/offices/OVAE/clusters/

Paulin, G. D. (2001, July). Expenditures of college-age students and nonstudents. *Monthly Labor Review, 124*(7), 46–50.

SCANS2000 Center. (2001). Baltimore: Johns Hopkins University. Retrieved from the World Wide Web: http://www.SCANS.jhu.edu

Schwalbe, K. (2001). *Information technology project management* (2nd ed.). Boston: Course Technology/Thomson Learning.

Tapscott, D. (1998). *Growing up digital: The rise of the net generation.* New York: McGraw-Hill.

U.S. Department of Education. (2000, October). *Classification of instructional programs — 2000: Final draft.* Washington, DC: National Center for Education Statistics. Retrieved September 1, 2001, from the World Wide Web: http://nces.ed.gov/npec/papers/PDF/cip.pdf

225

Veneri, C. (1998, Fall). Here today, jobs of tomorrow: Opportunities in information technology. *Occupational Outlook Quarterly, 42*(3), 44–57.

The Web-connected generation. (2001, October). *The Futurist, 35*(5), 9.

Technology and Effective Communication

Donna R. Everett
Morehead State University
Morehead, Kentucky

Two people shake hands, or perhaps they bow to one another. They exchange information by asking questions. They observe each other's nonverbal cues. This face-to-face conversation employs many senses as well as immediate feedback. The communication is rich. The personal presence of individuals and information from many senses makes the communication "high touch." Each person is, in a sense, his or her own visual aid, creating an image through the skillful practice of verbal and nonverbal communication skills.

As business education graduates communicate more frequently through technology-mediated channels, they will need to use communication media skillfully to compensate for the "high touch" elements that electronic media may not directly convey. They must also deal with information and knowledge management challenges that emerge from these interactions. Communication technology will continue to emerge, affecting how communications are sent and received, how individuals will communicate within emerging systems, and what kinds of skills will be needed to navigate an interconnected workplace.

This chapter is intended to help business educators work with students to use, manage, and apply technology to communicate effectively. This chapter also examines various communication media and the barriers they present to effective communication. Student activities illustrate how concepts can be integrated into instruction. The chapter begins by discussing the implications of technology for the workplace that business education students are preparing for.

THE CONTEMPORARY WORKPLACE

At the current rate of technological change, new opportunities for and means of communicating emerge almost daily. "Just as the personal computer revolutionized the workplace throughout the 1980s and 1990s, . . . information and communication technology [are] on the verge of creating a new revolution [that will] forge the foundation of a new workplace" (Townsend, DeMarie, and Hendrickson, 1998, p. 17). Globalization, instant access to data, high expectations for professional document design and creation, miniaturization, portability, and wireless communications are creating new sets of parameters for how we communicate.

Today's employees deal with a whole range of technology tools, communication media, and information management challenges. They are bombarded with information from coworkers and clients. In addition to messages sent via traditional channels are those coming through e-mail, fax, video- and audioconferencing, mobile telephones, and digital devices that are becoming smaller, wireless, and portable.

Regardless of the sophistication of the hardware and software, "high touch" skills will remain vital. Although there are many benefits to using e-mail, Drake Beam Morin (DBM), a leading outplacement contractor, expects that many employers will be looking closely at how their workforces use e-mail. The loss of the long-standing benefits of traditional communication techniques is a concern of many businesses. "We all suffer from e-communication overload," said Maureen Sullivan, a DBM director. "It's time to get back to basics—to know how your customers prefer to be communicated with, whether it be [via] e-mail, voice mail, telephone, or in person, and to be sensitive to each customer's different communication styles" (Drake Beam Morin, 2001, p. 22).

At the same time, business is also using communication channels and technology skills to build fundamentally new business knowledge. Coupled with the need for basic communication skills is a demand to manage new knowledge and communicate using tools that continually change with the evolution of powerful networks.

Workplace Communication and Knowledge Management

Many of the workplace skills required by employers today relate directly to demonstrating effective communication skills using technology. The SCANS 2000 Center (http://www.scans.jhu.edu), named for the Secretary's Commission on Achieving Necessary Skills, promulgates the workplace competencies and foundation skills that the workforce needs for solid job performance in the 21st century.

Reading, writing, listening, and speaking are basic communication skills. Problem solving and knowing how to learn prepare students for rapid change and uncertainty. Self-esteem, sociability, ability to manage oneself, integrity, and honesty, complemented by flexibility, contribute to the quality of communication. Ability to participate as a member of a team, teach others new skills, serve clients and customers, exercise leadership, and work with diverse populations are other communication skills that are needed in the workplace ("Workplace Know-How," 2000). The SCANS 2000 Center sends a clear message about the context of this skill learning: "Prepare the nation's workforce for continuing globalization, exponentially growing knowledge, and accelerating change" ("Skills for a New Century," 1999).

Knowledge management involves the purposive creation, organization, and effective communication of an organization's collective wisdom and knowledge to further its goals. Many organizations consider it smart business to make knowledge available throughout the organization and to share best practices with colleagues (Guffey, 1999). Knowledge management facilitates communication across organizational lines. By sharing files, databases, manuals, and people's collective knowledge, companies have found they can streamline operations, reduce inconsistencies, and present uniform approaches to sales and product research and development.

Networked technology channels within organizations, such as intranets, support electronic bulletin boards, department pages, and expert contact lists. These applications link employees and customers across organizational and geographical boundaries. Employees need to know which tools to use and how to use them to achieve productive and profitable results (Roebuck, 2001).

Employees must use these skills in a work environment that is increasingly high-tech, problem-oriented, impersonal, evolving and changing, and interrelated in a global economy. Students must be helped to recognize the complexity—problems, demands, rewards, and satisfactions—of the high-performance workplace and taught how to perform appropriately. The expert worker cannot simply "pick up" these competencies; they are acquired in school and refined through on-the-job experience and learning in context. Learning in context entails acquiring, practicing, and applying appropriate methods and technologies available to create, manipulate, and process data into useful information.

Networking and Communication Channels
Successful communication has always depended on networks. Human communication networks are established by selecting the appropriate channel for the exchange of information or ideas and for establishing the feedback loop necessary to complete the communication process. Feedback enhances human communication so that an array of verbal and nonverbal cues can be used effectively.

The enormous benefits of networks in general, and the popularity of the Internet in particular, have prompted companies to use networking to collaborate, communicate, and conduct business with their customers through e-commerce. Many businesses use the same technology internally. Intranets disseminate organizational information and enhance internal employee communication. Networked channels, however, often eliminate or reduce visual and vocal cues and, if the communicator is not skillful, inhibit the feedback loop.

Traditional face-to-face conversation employs the visual, auditory, and tactile senses. A telecommunication channel omits many of these sensory cues. Research suggests that sometimes the medium is the message. Unknowingly, the communication channel that is chosen may create a perceived sense of urgency or convey a lack of personal concern. For example, people may pay more attention to messages received face to face than to messages received through electronic or written methods. An effective communicator matches the technology to the message (Daft, Lengel, & Trevino, 1987).

Working with computer networks calls for taking factors that work in the human environment and making them work in the electronic environment where it is not possible to see the audience, use or exchange nonverbal cues, ask immediate questions, or receive feedback. Speed and timing of responses and personalization are issues that must be addressed in the networked environment. People supply the "high touch" elements that complement technology. Technology enhances response time and productivity and enables organizations to tailor their products and services to fit the needs of clients and customers.

LEARNING COMMUNICATION SKILLS—AN OVERVIEW

Communicators must select the best medium for the culture and the message, choose the appropriate words, and know how to use hardware or software to overcome lack of sensory cues. Teachers must help students develop awareness and skills.

Developing Awareness

Before students can develop the skills and competencies needed to select and utilize communication tools successfully, they must understand the purpose of business communication: to inform, to persuade, and to promote goodwill. Knowledge of a specific business—its services, products, customers, and their cultures—also guides the communicator's choice of medium. The medium itself, however, must be studied, because the potential of different electronic channels to be "rich" or "high touch" varies greatly.

Business educators can help students become sensitive to differences between traditional and technology-mediated communication media and to cultural aspects of technology through activities, such as the following:

STUDENT ACTIVITY

The Virtual Tour

Ask students to take a virtual tour on the Internet (for example, take a virtual business tour at the Knowledge Matters Web site at http://www.knoweldgematters.com). Have them compare what they think they might experience on an actual tour with the virtual tour. A search for virtual tours will reveal additional tour sites, such as those dealing with travel and tourism, real estate, and other areas of business. Museum Web tours can also provide an experience to compare to an actual tour.

STUDENT ACTIVITY

Cultural Differences and Communication

Following a discussion of culture and nonverbal communication, have students research the meaning of nonverbal cues for cultural groups in North or South America, Asia, the Middle East, Africa, or Europe. Students can present their findings in formal presentations, using appropriate software. Students should examine each culture and not assume that what is true for one culture is true for another.

Note to teachers: This can be a group or individual activity. You may need to limit the scope of the project based on available time. The formal presentation may involve multimedia, depending on available classroom technology.

STUDENT ACTIVITY

Media Richness Theory

In college or graduate classes, have students examine Media Richness Theory and suggest applications to communication. Have students use an academic journal search tool to explore the basic theory relative to management communication as well as contemporary research findings on media richness that flow from media richness theory (Daft, Lengel, and Trevino, 1987). Students can examine the relationship of media use to gender, type of position, and capabilities of emerging technology.

Developing Skills

Two topics lead the list of important communication skills for the technological environment: writing for the World Wide Web and online etiquette. Teachers should also consider culminating activities that provide accountability for learned skills.

Writing for the Web. Writing for the Web has become a popular topic to explore and a skill to acquire. Web page development has been made easier with the addition of this function in word processing software. Instruction should address how students can develop a *positive* Web presence. In part, students must practice effective writing. Bovee and Thill (2001) have asked writers to "satisfy [the] online audience's need for brevity." The following are some of their suggestions:

- Be direct so that readers can quickly grasp your topic, main idea, and conclusion.
- Put your most important concept in the first 50 words, in case search engines pick up those words to describe your site.
- Write short sentences and paragraphs to ease the reading process and to fit in narrow columns.
- Use informative, meaningful headings.
- Help readers scan your text for the information they need by using subheads, boldface type, color, bullets, etc.
- Avoid clever, humorous, or jargon-filled phrases that could be misunderstood by readers from other cultures.

Help uninterested readers avoid your site by writing hyperlinks and search engine descriptions that are informative and clear.

Business educators can introduce activities that focus on one or more of these principles. Students can research writing Web sites, such as Ewrite at http://www. ewriteonline.com where Rudick and O'Flahavan (2000) have provided articles on various Web writing topics.

Practicing online etiquette. Communicating on the Internet requires knowledge of the rules of interaction, called *netiquette*. As the Internet and its services have matured, users have become aware of the protocols and procedures for using e-mail, joining discussion groups, and surfing the Web.

Accepted netiquette practices focus on five broad guidelines: (1) avoid sending angry e-mail messages ("flaming"); (2) avoid sending e-mail messages in all caps ("shouting"); (3) lurk (observe quietly) before joining discussion groups; (4) use a short, descriptive subject line for each e-mail message; (5) and remember that the receiver on the other end of the message is a human being and use tact and sensitivity in e-mail communications. Shea (1994) has expanded this set of core rules for netiquette, and excerpts from her works are available at http://www.albion.com/netiquette/corerules.html.

In addition to researching various netiquette sites and articles on the Web, students can analyze cases and create their own guidelines for online interaction.

STUDENT ACTIVITY

Three Ways to Learn Netiquette

- Start a discussion of e-mail etiquette with the following scenario: *Your coworker Hank has such terrible breath that it's become a subject of office gossip. Should you send an anonymous e-mail to warn Hank, tactfully, of the problem?* Discover what Martin (2000) has to say about Hank at http://www.cnn.com/2000/TECH/computing/09/28/email.manners.idg/index.html. A lively class discussion about the appropriate and inappropriate uses of e-mail should ensue from this assignment.
- Have students access a guide to using e-mail, such as Sherwood's *Beginner's Guide* (2001) at http://www.webfoot.com/advice/email.top.html. Ask them to discuss the guidelines and the reason each one is included. Have them create their own guidelines as a brochure (with graphics) to hand out to classmates. Include several World Wide Web addresses in the brochure that justify the guidelines.
- Ask students to collect e-mail messages and to critique them for etiquette and effectiveness. Also have them compare them for ease of reading; language, grammar, and emoticon usage; and tone.

How many of the tips for writing for the Web and online etiquette also apply to traditional written, oral, or nonverbal communication? Have students discuss the fact that principles of effective communication transcend the medium, but using a particular medium requires attention to the capabilities of that medium.

Creating a Web folio. As students work on communication skills, the business educator may assign a culminating activity, such as creating a Web folio that showcases examples of work involving the following competencies.

- **Technology:** selection, use, and manipulation of software to create and format documents; selection of an appropriate site for a Web location; selection, use, and manipulation of software to create and format a Web page, as well as add links, graphics, and headings and upload documents
- **Decision making:** selection of documents to appear on a Web page and attention to formatting, appearance, proofreading, and grammar
- **Communication:** composition of an appropriate written introduction to a Web page with professional information, a title and purpose for the Web folio, writing samples to appear on the Web site that demonstrate attention to readability, ease of navigation throughout the Web site, and appropriate tone (direct, indirect, persuasive)
- **SCANS-related skills:** ability to follow directions, ask appropriate questions to complete the assignment, manage time to meet deadlines, take responsibility for the assignment, read and listen, master new computer competencies, and demonstrate thinking skills, including creativity

DEVELOPING COMMUNICATION-ORIENTED TECHNOLOGY SKILLS

What are the technology-related skills that business educators must teach? First, students must learn to evaluate whether or not software and hardware can enhance communication. Second, students must match particular tools to specific situations. Finally, students must practice basic communication skills as they learn to use various technologies.

Evaluating Software and Hardware

Learning how to evaluate the communication capabilities of hardware and software applications and matching hardware and software with the needs of an organization are crucial skills. Computer savvy, as well as critical-thinking and problem-solving skills and the ability to write, speak, and make decisions are essential.

A good software and hardware evaluation instrument can be found in the "Learning With Technology Course Resources" section (1997–1999) of the North Central Regional Technology Education Consortium site at http://www.ncrtec.org/pd/lwtres/resource.htm#gfes. This learning-oriented evaluation form can be adapted for use in the classroom setting. The following activities should help students develop skills in identifying the communication capabilities of software.

STUDENT ACTIVITY

Communication Technology in the Workplace

- Invite a guest speaker (an employer, a principal or other school administrator, a parent, or other professional) to discuss the kinds of communication technology used in the workplace. Ask them to identify what communication channels are used most frequently, what kinds of documents or presentations are most often created or received, who the audiences are, as well as the challenges of communicating in their organizations.
- Have students attend a career fair and interview various company representatives to find out the kinds of communication media and tools that are used most often in their organizations. Students should ask if communication training is provided. They then can compare the responses of different interviewers or employers.
- Have students complete a service-learning project with a local business. Have students visit and tour the business, conduct interviews with managers and employees to determine needs for hardware and software acquisition or upgrading, and conduct research and make recommendations.

Note to teachers: Each of these activities can culminate in a formal report or a presentation, using presentation software. The reports can be completed individually or in teams.

Matching Technology to Communication Goals

Students must also learn to use the full capabilities of hardware and software. Students must ask the *why*'s of any media selection. *Why* is this hardware needed for this communication? *Why* is this application the best choice to accomplish this communication goal? The following questions can be used to analyze communication and technology situations and make technology selections (Locker, 1998, p. 20):

- What's at stake—for whom and by when?
- Should I send the message electronically or in person?
- What medium should I use?
- Which hardware and software capabilities will I need to know?
- What information should be in the message?
- How should the message be worded?

At both the secondary and postsecondary levels, students should focus on evaluating media using "choose and justify" activities.

These types of activities engage students in discussions of technology use even when the classroom is not equipped with the technology being discussed. Additionally, students can research technologies and share their experiences using various media while developing their critical-thinking skills.

Practicing Basic Skills

A third set of skills needed to promote successful communication involves learning

STUDENT ACTIVITY

Choose and Justify

Have students choose and justify the channel(s) that will provide the most successful communication in a timely manner for each of the following scenarios:

- Feedback to a customer with a complaint: provide some details about the customer and the complaint.
- Performance-related feedback to an employee: ask whether the same medium can be used for feedback on good performance and poor performance.
- Response to rumors of layoffs: select a current event involving layoffs and have students discuss the media used by employers in actual downsizing situations.
- Request for proof of a valid signature on a contract for a meeting in another city in two hours: accompany this assignment with a research project on the current status of acceptability of electronic signatures in your state.
- Response to an e-mail message requesting an appointment: ask students to compare a request for a job interview from a recent high school graduate with a request from a person with several years of relevant experience. If students respond differently, ask them to discuss the basis for the differences.
- Announcement of a change in a company dress code: ask them to compare a change that will be more restrictive than the current dress code with one that will be more relaxed than the current dress code.

and practicing the basic skills of reading, writing, listening, and speaking. New parameters related to miniaturization, portability, and wireless communication are evidenced in the short, crisp, precise "sound bite" messages that are now being utilized. Careful writing to create "sound bites" is complemented by the enhanced listening and reading skills needed to interpret them.

The layout, organization, and content of publications affect readers' attitudes toward an organization, whether the publications are Web pages, brochures, annual reports, presentations, or other documents. Effective communicators know which format— letter, e-mail, Web page, report, press release, or presentation—and which skill— writing, listening, or speaking—are appropriate to reach a given audience. Communicators must also develop appropriate content for their messages.

TECHNOLOGY-MEDIATED COMMUNICATION

Computer networks and communication services include the World Wide Web; e-mail and digital messaging services; telephone, voice mail, and conferencing systems; and many other services and tools. Increasing bandwidth—the capacity of a channel to carry information—and methods of delivering complex information are enabling technology-mediated communications to become richer relative to sensory information. For example, electronic greeting cards and streaming audio and video allow computer networks to add some "high touch" while using high tech methods to deliver messages. Increasingly sophisticated software provides new ways to collaborate, market, train, and create new products and services.

STUDENT ACTIVITY

Look, Listen, Write, Ask, Do (LLWAD)

- Explain and have students practice the LLWAD method to improve listening skills. Have them look at an example, listen to and write down instructions, ask (and listen to others') relevant questions to complete the assignment, and then complete the assignment.

The following is an example of an assignment that could be used: *Visit a computer or technology store and ask for a demonstration of some product you have never used. Tell the class about your visit and what you learned.*

- Build on the LLWAD method by giving only the deadline for a project, not the directions. In the workplace, employees will be given tasks with only the deadline and very limited or no instructions. How the project is accomplished will be up to the employee.

Note to teachers: learning to ask questions, look in files and observe the methods an organization has used in the past, and then use skills and creativity to complete a task are valuable results of these activities.

Streaming audio and video technology can be used to deliver audio or video messages over the Internet or through a company's intranet. Because the audio or video sessions reside on the Internet or on the company's broadband network, no special hardware is needed. Training videos can be delivered directly to the computer desktop; corporate managers can broadcast speeches or announcements to all employees or customers via a company's network; and videoconferences can be connected to a company's intranet for employees to watch (Davis & Gold, 1999).

At this time communication on the Internet is unregulated. Any and all messages may be accessible and made public. Company networks, which are owned by the organization and contain e-mail systems, databases, telephone systems, and intranets, are regulated by organizational policies and procedures.

Misuse of Internet access, e-mail systems, and company information can be grounds for dismissal. When using the Internet and company networks, employees should create and send messages with attention to ethical use of the media, organizational policies, and the proprietary nature of the organization's communication systems. Newspapers and magazines include reports of the fates of many employees who have disregarded one or more of these elements.

Telephone Systems

The telephone continues to perform essential functions in business. As a communication channel, the telephone requires excellent listening and speaking skills. As a technology tool, the telephone provides many communication features. The challenge is to use the telephone to impact the effectiveness and image of an organization. Voice mail may solve the problem of telephone tag. Messages can be sent and received at any hour of the day across any time zone. Voice mail can create a barrier, however, when it

STUDENT ACTIVITY

Misusing Communication Resources

Ask students to analyze how Dow Chemical Company handled instances of employee misuse of e-mail and the Internet. Weiss (2000) has reported on one of a series of incidents that occurred at Dow over several months (http://www.cnn.com/2000/TECH/computing/09/19/dow.firing.idg/index.html). Additional aspects of the story can be found by searching http://www.computerworld.com/ or other news sites.

STUDENT ACTIVITY

Simulating Voice Mail

Have students practice recording voice mail introductions. Students can compare the introductions recorded without notes to those based on notes. Also have students develop a script of menu choices. Students can record the menu selections using any available recording device and then evaluate the recordings in pairs or larger groups. Then have students practice leaving voice mail messages and recording and playing them back. Students can evaluate each message based on the following criteria: Is the message clear? Are names and numbers repeated? Will the message help accomplish the purpose of the original call?

is used to delay returning telephone calls or avoid incoming calls. It is a convenience technology to be used wisely.

The key to using voice mail effectively is to speak clearly when recording an introductory message. Before recording a message, an individual should make notes to follow. The individual then should listen to the recorded introduction for clarity and tone. When leaving information, the caller should speak distinctly, slowly, and in a normal tone. Communicators should spell important words or names, keep messages short, and repeat numbers.

Cellular telephones have become important business tools, allowing calls to be made to and received from anywhere at any time. This technology can become a barrier, however, when used inappropriately. A Siemens Mobile survey (Davie, 1999) reported that leaving the cellular telephone on in meetings and during appointments is unacceptable (85 percent). Respondents also stated that people should not use cellular telephones in elevators or on busses or trains, especially if they talk loudly.

Costs for cellular telephones will continue to drop and usage will continue to increase as multimedia applications, navigation services and guides, and storage and transport of electronic data over cellular technology for e-commerce escalate. As with voice mail, certain techniques will ensure that calls are successfully sent and received: answering promptly, giving a name, listening carefully, taking careful notes, speaking clearly, providing information, and ending the conversation in a professional manner.

Voice technologies will continue to change. To keep the technology discussion on the cutting edge, have students research other channels for voice communication and read about changing voice technologies, the Internet, and alternative telephone services (Dialpad, 2001).

Audioconferencing

Because employees around the world can connect interactively, they can work together regardless of time or location. Employers will seek individuals who have learned to work in teams; are self-starters; can use technology to create, access, and manipulate data; and can communicate in a timely and useful form.

One of the best-known extensions of the telephone is the audioconference that connects two or more people by telephone. Setting up audioconferences today is as easy as placing a regular telephone call. Organizations can use audioconferences to conduct interviews, communicate for other purposes, or replace or supplement face-to-face meetings when time or money must be saved.

Overcoming the lack of visual contact in audioconferences takes special attention. Listening skills become very important, as do clear protocols, or rules, for sequencing and participating in a conference. According to Duarte and Snyder (1999), the leadership skills needed by the facilitator of an audioconference include defining the purpose of the conference, determining the best time for the conference, deciding who should participate, and being prepared. Roebuck (2001, p. 258) has suggested the following format for an audioconference:

1. Ask participants to introduce themselves at the beginning of the audioconference.
2. Establish the ground rules for the conference: how to participate (name first, then comments), how to vote, how to leave the conference, how to use the mute button.
3. Review the agenda for additions or suggested order.
4. Facilitate the discussion by introducing each item, asking for comments from the source of each item, listening for content, asking for clarification and input, resolving differences, and summarizing each discussion before moving on to the next item on the agenda.
5. Conclude by reviewing the actions taken and decisions made.
6. Follow up by writing up the minutes, distributing them by e-mail, and evaluating the effectiveness of the meeting.

In essence, an audioconference takes on aspects of virtual teamwork. Teamwork and communication skills take on particular significance because individuals are working across space and time boundaries. Teachers can work out ways to simulate such conferences or use alternative locations within the school or community to practice these skills.

E-Mail

If memos were once the workhorses of the workplace, they have been supplanted by e-mail. E-mail can be sent via both local area networks and wide area networks. The

STUDENT ACTIVITY

Audioconference

With support from a business partner, advisory committee member, or school service, or through simulation, teachers can have students participate in an audioconference in two phases.

Phase 1. Whether the activity is actual or simulated, students should prepare for the meeting by writing an agenda, agreeing on guidelines for the audioconference, agreeing on how to vote, setting a time limit, and establishing protocols for participation in the discussion.

Phase 2. After participating in the audioconference, students should review the decisions made by the group, prepare and send out minutes, and complete any other follow-up activities.

immediacy of the method contributes to its popularity. But the ease with which e-mail can be sent can also be a disadvantage. Some companies have begun to set parameters on the use of e-mail so that human contact with coworkers is not replaced.

Problems occur when senders assume no one else can read their messages or forget who owns the e-mail. Following a discussion of e-mail, students can be asked to read "What's Your EQ (E-mail Quotient)" at http://www.ewriteonline.com/text.html (Rudick & O'Flahavan, 2000).

Learning how to write an e-mail message is just as important as learning how to write a traditional letter or memo. Time is wasted when messages are sent back from the postmaster due to incorrect addresses. People may delete messages without subject lines. Failing to include a proper signature line can frustrate the receiver if he or she must guess the sender's identity. Other considerations include deciding whether using e-mail or making a five-minute telephone call is the better way to solve the problem, whether a legal signature is required to validate a document, and whether a message may become public knowledge. All of these issues lead into activities that engage students in learning.

STUDENT ACTIVITY

E-Mail

- Ask students to compose and send an introductory e-mail message to you at the beginning of a new class using proper e-mail etiquette. In the e-mail message, ask students to include their experiences with writing and computers. Also, ask them to tell you about their goals for the course.
- Have students research electronic or digital signatures, certification authorities, and current digital signature legislation at the state and federal levels. Ask students to share their findings in a class discussion.

Instant Messaging

While e-mail is a delayed, or "store and forward," technology, instant messaging (IM) services are real time. IM lets employees hold virtual meetings at any time and in any place. IM is more immediate than e-mail and can be more cost-effective than the telephone. IM users can identify who is online at a glance and start chatting in real time across time zones, oceans, and continents.

The software involved in IM is easy to download, install, and use. IM incorporates a variety of collaboration tools that facilitate file transfer, Web browsing, text-to-voice conversion, and "whiteboarding." Teams of workers dispersed throughout various regional offices find that IM helps them build consensus and resolve issues that would otherwise delay projects. However, the use of IM for business has some major drawbacks. For instance, to use IM, groups of employees must be logged on at the same time, and there are risks of security breaches and misuse of company time and resources (Greenemeier, 2000; McCullam, 2000; Miller, 2000).

Other Devices and Software Options

Hardware and software are technology partners, and the variety of devices and features they provide will continue to proliferate. The business educator must be ready to integrate information about these technologies, even if the classroom is not actually equipped with all the technologies. Students can examine the technologies in their community, including in commercial establishments. Sometimes they can bring technologies into the classroom. The following are some of the technologies that require effective communication skills.

Personal digital assistants. These popular handheld devices are equipped with basic personal information management applications such as a calendar, address book, to-do list, memo pad, and support for desktop e-mail. They often include capabilities for wireless Internet access; software applications; and printing, sending, and receiving fax messages. As communication devices, these digital assistants are transforming how information is accessed, manipulated, and transmitted and how business is conducted.

Fax machines. In many offices facsimile, or fax, remains the technology of choice for transmitting printed and signed documents. The merging of faxing with e-mail expands faxing capabilities. Through relay broadcasting, copies of documents can be faxed from one machine to a number of machines in different cities and countries. Network faxing is another viable option for sending and receiving faxes on desktop computers. After a document is received on one's desktop computer, copies can be stored to be accessed at a later time or printed if necessary.

Software Applications

Software applications are becoming increasingly sophisticated, powerful, pervasive, and interactive. Collaborative technology software (also called groupware) holds the promise of advancing group- or teamwork in the areas of brainstorming, list building, information gathering, voting, organizing, prioritizing, and consensus building. Collaborative software is especially helpful in group settings requiring problem-solving, decision-making, and higher-order thinking skills. As with audioconferencing, collaborative work requires facilitation skills to keep electronic discussions flowing, to extend the options to arrive at an acceptable list of solutions or alternatives, and to move discussions toward consensus. A good facilitator knows how to ask questions to elicit the best thinking and responses from a group.

STUDENT ACTIVITY

Collaborative Skills and Software

Have students research the characteristics of a good facilitator and of good questions. Ask them to talk about how to develop the skill of asking good discussion questions. They may want to begin by analyzing good discussion experiences they have had and how questions contributed to the experiences.

Note to teachers: This activity can be done in the context of a particular product or service and how the facilitator would use it. For instance, students can be asked to research groupware, such as the GroupSystems software (Ventana East Corporation, 2001).

The networked workplace allows for collaborative writing projects because ideas and software can be shared across a company's intranet. In addition to writing skills, collaborative writing involves using well-developed verbal and listening skills to produce a final product. Successful collaboration occurs when each group member is open to suggestions, voices opinions, listens to others' ideas, writes clearly, knows how to manipulate software, meets deadlines, and maintains a positive attitude during the process.

Specialized software packages, such as desktop publishing, authorware, and multi-media packages, make the networked workplace truly a one-stop shop. The capabilities of the software, coupled with scanners, digital cameras, and color and laser printers, have enhanced the professional presentation of documents. Attention still must be paid to good document design and layout, spelling, grammar, proofreading, and editing. Communication is enhanced when writers plan, revise, and edit documents with their readers in mind.

These and other software capabilities are creating new jobs while eliminating old jobs. The continuous development of software enhancements will require employees to retrain. No educational institution can guarantee a complete education in a rapidly changing work environment. Learning to learn and making a commitment to continuous learning will open up new career opportunities; training and learning at one's desktop will become the method for the 21st century.

SUMMARY

Consider several new employees—recent business education graduates—as they walk into (or telecommute to) the workplace to start their new business positions. These graduates must deal with a whole range of technology tools, communication media, and information management challenges. Already messages bombard them from traditional and newer media—e-mail, fax machines, pagers, voice mail, etc.

The graduates have learned some essential principles. They have examined how technology-mediated communication differs from face-to-face communication in the richness of sensory information and the immediacy of feedback. They understand that each technology differs in its ability to meet the communication needs of the receiver. Cultural factors will play a role as these graduates select communication media. As they evaluate technology, the ability of that technology to enhance communication will be as important as it price.

The business education graduates also understand that communication with others often creates new knowledge and opportunities for business. Managing the knowledge produced through these communications will be one of the most important challenges they will face. To address each of their communication goals, these graduates will select the best medium from among many media that, on the surface, appear to be equal to the task of communicating effectively. The business education graduates must understand how easily a benefit can be countered by inappropriate use of a medium.

Without effective communication skills, chaos prevails and relationships with coworkers and customers are damaged. The business education graduates are prepared to deal with communication challenges and to know that technology will continue to change, calling for continuous learning. They expect to cope with technologies that affect how communications are sent and received, how individuals will communicate within emerging systems, and how individuals will navigate an interconnected workplace. The business education graduates will also guide others who have not yet learned these essentials. The business education graduates have learned that managing knowledge means applying technology to all forms of communication with the goal of getting the right information to the right people so that everyone can make effective decisions in a timely manner.

REFERENCES

Bovee, C., & Thill, J. (2001, February 6). Email newsletter: Teaching tips, ego surfing, Web writing! In Thill, J. & Bovee, C. (2002). *Excellence in business communication* (5th ed.). Upper Saddle River, NJ: Prentice-Hall.

Daft, R., Lengel, R., & Trevino, L. (1987). Message equivocality, media selection and manager performance: Implications for information systems. *MIS Quarterly, 11*(2), 355–366.

Davie, J. (1999, March 3). Mobile mania—a life necessity of pain in the …? *PhoneChoice*. Retrieved from the World Wide Web: http://www.phonechoice.com.au/

Davis, A. W., & Gold, E. (1999, November 1). The next generation business phone. *BusinessWeek*. 183–192.

Dialpad. (2001). Retrieved July 20, 2001, from the World Wide Web: http://www.dialpad.com.

Drake Beam Morin. (2001, January). Workplace predictions for 2001. *PRNewswire, 22*.

Duarte, D. L., & Snyder, N. (1999). *Mastering virtual teams*. San Francisco: Jossey-Bass Publishers.

Greenemeier, L. (2000, September 25). Teamwork via the Web. *Informationweek, 25*. 211.

Guffey, M. (1999, Fall 1999). The latest in business buzzwords: A primer on knowledge management. *Business Communication News, 18*. Cincinnati, OH: South-Western College Publishing.

Knowledge Matters. (2001). Retrieved July 20, 2001, from the World Wide Web: http://www.knowledgematters.com

Learning with technology course resources: Guide for evaluating software. (1997–1999). North Central Regional Technology in Education Consortium. Retrieved July 20, 2001, from the World Wide Web: www.ncrtec.org/pd/lwtres/resource.htm#gfes

Locker, K. (1998). *Business and administrative communication*. New York: McGraw-Hill Companies, Inc.

Martin, J. A. (2000, September 28). Test your e-mail etiquette. Retrieved July 20, 2001, from the World Wide Web: http://www.cnn.com/2000/TECH/computing/09/28/email.manners.idg/index.html

McCullam, J. (2000, September 11). Instant enterprising. *Forbes, 11*. PO28.

Miller, S. (2000, May 29). Collaboration at warp speed. *Infoworld*, pp. 41–42.

Roebuck, D. (2001). *Improving business communication skills* (3rd ed.). Upper Saddle River, NJ: Prentice-Hall.

Rudick, M., & O'Flahavan, L. (2000). What's your E-Q (e-mail quotient)? Retrieved July 20, 2001, from the World Wide Web: http://www.ewriteonline.com/test.html

SCANS 2000 Center. (2000). The workforce skills Website. Retrieved July 20, 2001, from the World Wide Web: http://www.scans.jhu.edu/

Shea, V. (1994). The core rules. *Netiquette*. San Rafael, CA: Albion Books. Retrieved July 20, 2001, from the World Wide Web: http://www.albion.com/netiquette/corerules.html

Sherwood, K. D. (2001). A beginner's guide to effective email. Retrieved July 20, 2001, from the World Wide Web: http://www.webfoot.com/advice/email.top.html

Skills for a new century. (1999). SCANS 2000 Center. Retrieved July 20, 2001, from the World Wide Web: http://www.scans.jhu.edu/VPGore/SKILLS%20FOR%20A%20NEW%20CENTURY%20A%20BLUEPRINT%20FOR%20LIFELONG%20LEARNING%20-%201.htm

Townsend, A., DeMarie, S. M., & Hendrickson, A. R. (1998, August). Virtual teams: Technology and the workplace of the future. *Academy of Management Executives, 12*(3), 17–29.

Ventana East Corporation. (2001). GroupSystems is. . . . Retrieved July 20, 2001, from the World Wide Web: http://www.ventana-east.com

Weiss, T. R. (2000, September 19). Dow fires more employees over inappropriate e-mails. Retrieved July 20, 2001, from the World Wide Web: http://www.cnn.com/2000/TECH/computing/09/19/dow.firing.idg/index.html

Workplace know-how. (2000). SCANS 2000 Center. Retrieved July 20, 2001, from the World Wide Web: http://www.scans.jhu.edu/General/workplace.html

Keyboarding, Word Processing, and Other Input Skills

Susan Maxam

Maxwood Associates LLC

White Lake, Michigan

Keyboarding and word processing skills are needed by all students for almost every career area, and business educators must continue to provide this instruction. Additionally, the role of business education is expanding to address new technologies, including voice recognition, multimedia, handheld and notebook computers, and assistive technologies that are being used to increase access to technology on the individual level and to increase productivity in business and industry.

Business educators cannot ignore emerging technologies or give up best practices for teaching keyboarding, word processing, and document formatting. This chapter addresses these instructional demands. First, the chapter addresses emerging input technologies that business educators must incorporate in the classroom. Then the chapter addresses keyboarding, word processing, and document formatting skills and identifies learning outcomes and best practices for elementary through adult-level instruction. Activities for students and preservice teachers illustrate how to incorporate this content into instruction.

EMERGING TECHNOLOGIES

New technologies have entered the business and school environment. Assistive technology provides technology access to individuals with disabilities. Voice recognition technology changes the way business data are input into application software. Handheld computers increase the portability of applications. Multimedia content changes the definition of what constitutes a document. Each innovation challenges business educators to reexamine instruction.

Assistive Technology

As students with differing disabilities enter the classroom, business educators must know about assistive technology devices and how they work. These devices vary in function, but all are designed to provide people with disabilities increased access to technology.

Assistive technology software programs allow users to make keystroke shortcuts for frequently keyed phrases and long words, thus reducing input from the keyboard. Visual keyboards can be viewed on-screen. Students can input via the mouse to the visual keyboard rather than through the standard keyboard. Other assistive software allows users to enter information by speaking, as well as receive spoken reminders. For the visually impaired, digitized speech software reads the contents of the user's clipboard. Business educators can work effectively with special educators to open technological doors for students with disabilities. Table 1 lists Internet resources for assistive technology organizations and devices.

STUDENT ACTIVITY

In any computer literacy or computer applications course, have students complete one assignment that investigates one of the Web sites in Table 1. Have students create a memo, post a comment, or discuss in class what they investigated, what they learned, and how they can apply it to their lives or how businesses can use the technology to facilitate employment of people with disabilities.

Voice Recognition Technology

At one time it was questionable that voice recognition technology would ever reach the classrooms, and if it did, whether any changes would be needed in the delivery of instruction. Today voice recognition is in business education classrooms.

In April 2001 Kim Larsh (2001) demonstrated voice-typing to business teachers. Using voice recognition technology, Larsh opened a word processing program, dictated a memo, closed the program, opened a spreadsheet program, dictated a column of numbers, formatted them for currency, summed the values, closed the application, and continued the demonstration in a presentation software program. Larsh did not use the keyboard for any of these tasks. According to Larsh, with training, one can voice-type at the rate of 110 to 160 words a minute.

A number of pioneering business educators were trained in voice recognition technology during the summer of 2000 and taught voice recognition in keyboarding, computer applications, and office procedures courses during the 2000–2001 school year. By the summer of 2001, teachers from 15 states had participated in voice recognition technology training sessions, many through their state business organizations in conjunction with SpeakingSolutions.com (http://www.speakingsolutions.com).

Table 1. Internet Resources for Assistive Technology

Name of Organization or Vender	URL
ABLEDATA	http://www.abledata.com/Site_2/Default.htm
Academic Software Inc.	http://www.acsw.com/
Advanced Peripheral Technologies Input facilitated by positioning the mouse pointer over the desired character on a visual keyboard.	http://www.advancedperipheral.com/propmks.html
Assistive Technology Industry Association	http://www.atia.org/
Fentek Industries, Inc. Assistive technology keyboard products including large print keyboard products	http://www.fentek-ind.com/lrgprt.htm
Gus Communication Free evaluation CD-ROM on assistive technology products	http://www.gusinc.com/
HITEC Assistive Device Center	https://www.hitec.com/hitec.html
Macomb (MI) ISD Assistive Technology, Software and Electronic Resources	http://www.macomb.k12.mi.us/speced/asstres1.htm
Massachusetts Assistive Technology Partnership	http://www.matp.org/
Nextup.com The Power of Spoken AudioDevelopers of Text Aloud and other products; demonstration available for downloading	http://www.nextup.com/
Rehabtool.com High-tech assistive and adaptive technology products, multilingual speech synthesis and voice recognition software	http://www.rehabtool.com/
textHELP! . . . for literacy, language and learning Software designed to help students with their reading and writing processes	http://www.texthelp.com/
University of Buffalo Center for Assistive Technology	http://wings.buffalo.edu/ot/cat
V. I. Guide: Resources for Visual Impairments and V. I. Guide: Assistive Technology	http://www.viguide.com http://www.viguide.com/techtrain.htm
Visual Assistive Technology Center	http://www.at-center.com

Missouri has changed its state business curriculum statements to replace the word "key" with "input," allowing students to choose whether to use the keyboard or voice recognition to input documents. The standards for correct formatting, punctuation, grammar, and spelling are the same; only the method of input is different.

With one in four PC users projected to experience carpal tunnel or repetitive stress injuries, changing to an input technology that will cause less harm to the human body is reasonable. This change in technology is projected to "arrive" this decade. However, the keyboard will still be the major input device in the beginning of this decade, and until it is fully replaced by voice recognition technology, touch keyboarding skills need to be taught.

Palm or Handheld Computers

In many classrooms across the nation, students input their assignments using handheld computers (Soloway, Norris, & Curtis, 2001; see also http://www.palm. com/education/). A University of Michigan initiative on learning is reported at http://www. hi-cd.org, and teachers are developing learning materials to be delivered via palm devices at http://www.palmsheets.org. Top-selling devices include Palm Pilot, with its Palm operating system (http://www.palm.com/products/handhelds/), and a variety of PocketPC devices that use a Microsoft operating system like Microsoft CE (http://www. microsoft.com/mobile/pocketpc/pocketpc2002). Microsoft is reported to be support-ing the Tablet PC on Windows XP, although handwriting is not expected to replace keyboarding and other forms of input on a wide scale (http://www.pencomputing. com/frames/textblock_tablet_pc.html). These and other mobile computing develop-ments are reported in *Pen Computing* (http://www.pencomputing.com).

Handheld computers recognize input from a stylus on a pressure-sensitive screen or through an optional keyboard. Students carry their computers with them, making changes to documents throughout the school day and at home. The technology, when connected wirelessly to the Internet, allows one to "beam" text, images, Web resources, and e-mail from student to student and from student to teacher or teacher to student. When not Internet-enabled, handheld computers can transfer data via uploads and downloads to a PC.

Handheld computers support personal productivity, group collaboration, and learning throughout the business education curriculum. Support for handheld technology systems includes full-speed and portable keyboards, as well as graffiti software that recognizes alphabetic printed input (http://www.palm.com/products/input/) and on-screen keyboards. (Graffiti writing is a simple method of entering letters, numbers, and text into a handheld computer using a stylus.) Software for appointment books, address books, and notepads is often included on these products. Users can create documents to upload to standard word processing, spreadsheet, and database systems. Business teachers need to plan now for the changes these technolo-gies will bring in the way students use technology in the schools.

STUDENT ACTIVITY

Have students in computer literacy and applications courses examine features of handheld computers that are unfamiliar to them, perhaps in the form of a scavenger hunt. Have them brainstorm in small groups to list possible ways that they could use a handheld computer in their daily lives and have each group share the top three "most innovative" ideas with the class.

Multimedia in the Business Education Classroom

Business educators are using multimedia capabilities to add digital video, digital sound, digital imaging, and interactive design to the business education curriculum. While beyond the scope of this chapter, a short discussion of multimedia in the business education curriculum allows readers to visualize the role of multimedia in using computers to solve problems, make decisions, and communicate.

Students learn to input data using the computer keyboard or voice recognition technology in order to communicate information and ideas and publish their work. Multimedia technologies allow students to add graphics, sound, or video to their documents, just as business and industry are doing. A multimedia application that many business educators begin with is presentation software. Students include graphics (both clip art and student-designed), sound, and video in their presentations. However, multimedia technology encompasses much more than basic presentations.

Some middle school and high school business educators are adding animation, Web design, and drawing/paint projects to assignments in their business courses in order to prepare students for real-world applications and capitalize on the excitement that comes with creating more than text-based documents. Advanced computer application courses may include the design and creation of multimedia works that can be published as CD-ROMs or Web sites. Ethical issues surrounding the use of ideas and graphics created by others, the concept of copyright, and what makes a valid and reliable Web site can be part of this instruction. Many Web evaluation resources can be obtained online by doing a search for articles or lesson plans or by visiting university or online libraries.

Compliance with the Americans with Disabilities Act and Section 504 of the Rehabilitation Act and understanding accessibility laws and accommodation for people with disabilities need to be major components of any multimedia assignment. Teachers should ask students to check their sites for accessibility using an accessibility validation tool, such as Bobby (http://www.cast.org/bobby). When teaching students to add graphics to a Web page or other assignment, business educators should explain how to add a rollover to a graphic with a text box for the visually handicapped or a transcript of an audio component for the hearing-impaired. Additional information about accessibility can be found on the Web sites of the HTML Writers Guild (http://www.hwg.org) and the World Wide Web Consortium's Web Accessibility Initiative (http://www.w3.org/wai).

While multimedia development is at the far end of the technology continuum, keyboarding, document formatting, and other input skills are still the foundation of that continuum.

TEACHING KEYBOARDING

Keyboarding is commonly defined as using a typewriter or inputting information into a computer with a typewriter-like keyboard using touch-typing (striking the keys without looking at the fingers to determine correct key location). The principles of psychomotor development, current research on keyboarding, and national standards and objectives form a foundation for discussing instructional approaches.

Psychomotor Skill Development

Keyboarding is a psychomotor skill that develops, as does any motor skill, through cognitive, associative, and autonomous stages (Fitts, 1962). According to Lindsay (1966), the stages of development overlap: (a) familiarization and response orientation (cognition), (b) refinement (association), and (c) fixation and automation (autonomy).

Psychomotor skill theory is evident in traditional keyboarding/input processing instruction. Typically, the first semester is devoted to personal keyboarding skills. The alphabetic keys are introduced in as short a time as possible. The home row presentation is followed by two keys per lesson from then on. Generally, no more than 10 to 12 hours of instruction are devoted to the introduction of keys.

McLean (1995) has provided a complete discussion of psychomotor learning principles. According to stimulus-response theory, a teacher directs students to key a certain letter (stimulus), and students then strike that key (response). During early stages of learning, students may vocalize the letter as they strike the correct key. Students begin to *associate* correct letters with correct key locations in response to certain letter combinations. They will often watch their fingers as they strike the keys. As they develop confidence and learn the location of the keys, they are weaned from watching their fingers.

At speeds below 18 words a minute, students usually display awkward finger stroking and body movements. At about 18 to 24 words a minute, students move into the associative stage of learning. As the students' skills develop, the stimuli may become short words, accompanied by chaining of high-frequency, easily stroked letter sequences and words. As students continue to develop speed, they progress from the cognitive into the associative stage and, in turn, from the associative into the autonomous stage (West, 1983; West & Sabban, 1982).

Current Research on Keyboarding

Keyboarding skill development theory was based on research completed using the typewriter as an input device. Researchers are reporting mixed achievement results when comparing direct teacher instruction of keyboarding using a textbook with skill development using software based on psychomotor skill development theory and other instructional materials such as videos and educational games. Many of these studies are short-term comparisons of different approaches to teaching keyboarding.

When comparing direct instruction keyboarding with a computer tutorial approach, Nichols (1995) found that elementary students were more accurate when taught with the teacher-intensive approach. The computer tutorial students keyed faster but less accurately. Mikkelsen and Gerlach (1988), however, found no significant differences in correct technique among supervised and unsupervised elementary groups using a software package. The supervised group was monitored for proper keystroking techniques; the unsupervised group was not.

In retraining middle school students to use the correct fingers after learning keyboard familiarity, Reagan (2000) found that using a hand cover with drill-and-practice keyboarding software worked better than the drill-and-practice software alone. Russin (1995) compared two groups of sixth-grade students, a group using a teacher-directed approach with a textbook and a group using an interactive computer software program. In this study, students made similarly measurable gains in their progress regardless of instructional approach.

Sormunen (1986) compared keyboarding skill developed through a computer-based educational game with skill developed through a software tutorial based on psychological motor skill development theory. In this study, upper elementary students had higher scores on keyboarding speed achievement using the software tutorial approach than using the educational game. McClurg and Kercher (1989) compared five approaches to elementary keyboarding instruction and found that the textbook group outperformed the software and video groups. However, the best predictor for student performance was a dexterity measure of finger tapping, pencil tapping, and reaction time.

Teaching keyboarding at all levels requires developing touch keystroking and the speed and accuracy necessary to make the skill effective and productive. Initial focus should be given to touch keyboarding techniques, then to speed development, and finally to accuracy (Jackson, 1991; McLean, 1995). Perfect copy practice should not be utilized. Instead, to develop optimal keying speeds, activities that force speed should balance pacing exercises. With the rapid increase in repetitive stress injuries, longitudinal studies should determine whether learning conditions with or without proper keyboarding and positioning techniques account for differences.

National Standards and Objectives for Keyboarding

The National Business Education Association, the International Society for Technology in Education, and the Policies Commission for Business and Economic Education (PCBEE) are three major sources for achievement standards and learning objectives in keyboarding.

The National Business Education Association (2001) issued input technologies standards as part of its Information Technology content area. The achievement standards that describe expected performance at all levels (Level 1 = grades K–6; Level 2 = grades 6–9; Level 3 = grades 9–12; and Level 4 = two-year postsecondary/community college or technical college) are presented in Table 2 (NBEA, 2001, p. 85).

Level	**Table 2. Input Technologies Achievement Standards**
	Achievement Standard: Use input technologies appropriately to enter and manipulate text and data
1	Develop proper input techniques (e.g., keyboarding, scanning, speech recognition, handwriting recognition, and the use of a touch screen or mouse), including safety methods to avoid repetitive strain injury. Enter and manipulate numeric data using the touch method on a 10-key pad. Identify, compare, and explain features of various keyboards. Use a variety of input technologies. Enunciate and read clearly using speech recognition technologies.
2–4	Develop input technology skills for acceptable speed and accuracy levels that adhere to principles of repetitive strain avoidance. Compose original documents using speech recognition and other input technologies. Describe the safe and appropriate use of input tools and techniques.

The International Society for Technology in Education (ISTE) developed the *National Educational Technology Standards* for PreK–12 students. According to ISTE, "prior to completion of grade 2, students will use input devices, (e.g., mouse, keyboard, remote control) and output devices (e.g., monitor, printer) to successfully operate computers, VCRs, audiotapes, and other technologies" (2000, p. 18). In addition, ISTE outlines standards for using technology as a tool throughout the PreK–12th-grade curriculum. The standards emphasize the integration of technology as a learning tool throughout the curriculum.

Representing several business education organizations, the PCBEE (1997) stated,

> After successfully completing 25 to 40 hours of instruction in keyboarding, students should be able to:
> 1. Demonstrate the correct "touch" method for operating alphanumeric keys.
> 2. Demonstrate the correct "touch" method for operating a 10-key numerical pad.
> 3. Demonstrate a straight-copy speed of 25 to 40 words per minute on 1- and 2-minute timed input exercises. Errors should be unacceptable since electronic corrections are part of the 'touch' method on an electronic keyboard. (p. 73)

While a standard keyboarding course can be four weeks, nine weeks, a semester or longer and include speed and formatting skill development, the basic objectives for keyboarding are essentially the same. Besides speed and accuracy development and document formatting, students should be able demonstrate the ability to

- Use correct keystroking and positioning techniques,
- Anchor home row key fingers to assist in key locations,
- Key alphabetic letters by touch without looking at fingers on keyboard, and
- Correctly use all hardware and software (save files, open files, print, and handle disks properly).

Sample Keyboarding Unit Outline

A keyboarding unit outline will vary in the length of time allowed for the course, with speed and accuracy and document formatting becoming part of typical nine-week and semester-long courses. Table 3 shows a basic keyboarding unit outline.

Unit	Content
Table 3. Basic Keyboarding Unit Outline	
I	Care and handling of software and hardware: basic computer terminology (booting up the computer, loading the keyboarding and/or word processing software, and logging off the computer); saving and printing documents
II	Introduction to the keyboard and home row position: familiarization with the keyboard and mouse, anchoring of fingers on home row keys, keystroking and positioning techniques, introduction of capitalization and punctuation
III	Introduction to alphabetic keys, two new keys at a time: reinforcement drills on home row keys and previously learned keys; introduction of new alphabetic keys, two at a time; reinforcement of some formatting such as paragraph indents and spacing after punctuation within and ending sentences
IV	Work habits and workstation care
V	Ergonomic and health concerns

ISSUES IN KEYBOARDING INSTRUCTION

Keyboarding instruction raises questions as the level at which instruction begins changes and the methods mediated by technology are introduced. Two issues are keyboarding at the elementary level and using software to deliver instruction. Student activities for preservice teachers can generate discussion of issues and learning of methodology.

Much of the controversy in teaching keyboarding is focused on the cognitive stage. With computers becoming an instructional tool in every elementary classroom, questions arise about when and how to introduce keyboarding to elementary children. Studies have shown (Sormunen, Adams, Berg, & Prigge, 1990) that children can learn keyboarding at any elementary grade level. Developmentally, students learn best in grades three and above. The PCBEE (1997) has recommended that touch keyboarding be introduced at the point just before students use the keyboard for inputting sentences and fragments of sentences.

"Keyboard familiarization" is the term used to describe the introduction of students to the home row and key locations but not a total touch-keyboarding approach. Keyboard familiarization is recommended for grades PreK–2 (ISTE, 2000). At this level students use the mouse, input "y" for "yes" and "n" for "no," and sometimes using two fingers, key titles and short phrases that go with stories they have written with pictures and graphics.

The need for keyboarding instruction becomes apparent when students use the keyboard to input long phrases and/or key short stories and poems in language arts and other content areas. Cochran-Smith (1991) reported that

> ... regardless of the tasks that teachers assigned during the learning period, children focused their attention on mastering the word processing system and on developing keyboard familiarity, rather than on the content of their writing. They conclude[d] that it is probably not productive for teachers to expect students to use word processing to create the fluid text before they have developed familiarity with the typewriter keyboard and the word processing commands. (p. 145)

Some schools, in an effort to teach keyboarding on a limited budget, use portable word processing keyboards or writing tools (such as AlphaSmart, http://www. alphasmart.com/). Classroom sets that are moved from classroom to classroom can be kept in cabinets. Keyboarding instruction is moving to the elementary grades and multiple instructional strategies are used to teach it, including computer software and tutorials. Keyboarding software is available in many formats, including games and interactive multimedia instructional packages. The keyboarding teacher and/or media specialist must evaluate keyboarding software in terms of sound psychomotor skill development, motivational issues, ease of use, interest level, and instructional and technical characteristics.

Business educators must evaluate their current delivery system for keyboarding instruction and base decisions on sound psychomotor skill development theory. Business educators cannot be complacent about how or when keyboarding is taught. Without adequate keyboarding skills, students are at a disadvantage when they use the technology as a commonplace tool for analyzing data, writing, publishing, and problem solving.

INSTRUCTIONAL METHODS FOR WORD PROCESSING

Instructional methods for word processing vary depending on the level at which the training occurs, the amount of time devoted to instruction, and the level of competence

STUDENT ACTIVITIES*

Activity 1. Using keyboarding technique check sheets (such as Zeliff & Schultz's *Authentic Assessment in Action: Preparing for the Business Workplace*), have preservice student teachers evaluate each other's keyboarding techniques in teams of two. Emphasize proper keyboarding techniques and keystroking. Have one preservice student teacher key the alphabet in order, starting with a, b, c, and so on as the other observes for correct fingering. The preservice student teacher who is keying should key without looking at his or her fingers. The preservice student teachers should then change positions and repeat the process.

Activity 2. Following an introduction to teaching keyboarding, ask preservice student teachers to identify motivational elements that would differ at various grade levels—early and later elementary school, middle school, high school, and postsecondary school. Preservice student teachers may want to refer to NBEA's *Business Education Forum*; NBEA's 1997 *Elementary/Middle School Keyboarding Strategies Guide*, 2nd edition; G. N. McLean's 1995 *Teaching Keyboarding*, which is published by Delta Pi Epsilon; or the Indiana Department of Education's 1993 *Guidelines for K–12 Keyboarding Computer Applications* for age-appropriate keyboarding teaching strategies.

Activity 3. Using sample keyboarding software, have preservice student teachers evaluate keyboarding software based on psychomotor skill development, motivational issues, ease of use, interest levels, and instructional and technical characteristics. Also have preservice student teachers compare their ratings with professional teacher ratings (http://clearinghouse.k12.ca.us/ provides its educators with a review of most educational software). Other links include http://www.superkids.com/aweb/pages/reviews/typing1/sw_sum1.shtml and http://www.itma.vt.edu/Franklin/pollock/portfolio/evaluation.htm.

*For preservice business teachers

desired at the end of the instructional period. For the purposes of this chapter, word processing instructional methods are separated from document-formatting methods, although in many teaching/learning situations, they are integrated. Word processing instruction may range from one session devoted to a specific word processing concept in an elementary class to a comprehensive word processing curriculum at a community college to online proficiency training for software certification for professionals.

Word Processing Teaching Methods

Three word processing teaching methods used frequently are learning by example, learning by following, and learning by doing.

Learning by example. This method provides students with an example of the concept to be learned, such as cutting and pasting. This is followed by verbal or written directions and a problem to complete. In an elementary classroom, this may take the form of a short story presented by the teacher that the students edit by moving sentences around. First the instructor presents the concept of "cut and paste"; next, the teacher presents specific directions for completing this task; and finally, students practice "cut and paste" in an exercise designed to reinforce the word processing concept. From then on, students are expected to revise their writing using these word processing techniques.

Learning by following. This method requires step-by-step directions, which are often provided in word processing and computer applications textbooks as well as online word processing courses. For example, students can be instructed to open a blank document and then proceed through the instructions one step at a time, following the directions for each portion of the document. With this method, there is one correct answer, and students can compare their work against an instructor's key.

Learning by doing. Using this method to introduce a word processing concept, the instructor discusses a concept and demonstrates how to do a procedure. Students apply the concept by solving ill-structured problems. In many cases, no "right" answer is given, and there is no teacher's key for the correct answer. Student answers vary in how the concept has been applied to the given problems. Examples of ill-structured problems abound in the literature and on the Web as teachers at all levels share ideas, lesson plans, creative projects, and simulations. This approach provides learning activities that allow students to adapt to change and transfer their learning to different situations.

Transfer of learning. If word processing software is taught simply by using a specific word processing package, transfer of learning may be minimal. To encourage transfer of learning, students should

- Explain the purposes, functions, and common features of word processing software;
- Explain the meaning of common word processing terminology;
- Compose, organize, and edit information using a keyboard;
- Use touch keyboarding techniques and word processing software to create, modify, store, retrieve, and print documents; and
- Proofread and edit documents for accuracy and content and for correct grammar, spelling, and punctuation (NBEA, 1995, p. 95).

Specific word processing standards are not identified either in the *National Standards for Business Education* (NBEA, 2001) or the *National Educational Technology Standards for Students* (ISTE, 2000). Rather they are implied because these standards emphasize the role of using computer applications to solve problems and communicate effectively.

Typical Elementary Word Processing Objectives

Elementary word processing objectives vary from district to district and from state to state, depending on state and local curriculum standards. Many state standards integrate technology into the language arts, social studies, and other content areas so that students use the technology as a resource and tool to produce their work. According to typical elementary word processing objectives, upon completion of instruction, students might be expected to use word processing to do the following:

1. Open, edit, save, and print documents with minimal assistance.
2. Create, edit, and revise a poem or story to accompany a previously painted or drawn graphic.
3. Use the copy, cut, and paste functions of a word processing program to add graphics and move text and graphics around in a document to create a finished product.
4. Perfect sentence and short story writing skills in conjunction with writing software.
5. Demonstrate an understanding of formatting and appearance of documents by selecting and changing fonts, sizes, and styles; setting tabs; aligning text to the right, left, or center; and adding graphics to text.

This list of objectives reflects only a sample of the many ways elementary teachers integrate word processing into their language arts, social studies, and other content areas as a tool for students to publish their work. Many school districts and states have grade-by-grade objectives for technology that include extensive use of word processing skills. Students may or may not be taught keyboard familiarization or touch keyboarding prior to word processing instruction. If students have not received keyboarding instruction prior to middle school, they may receive combined keyboarding and word processing instruction in a nine-week or semester-long course.

Middle School Keyboarding/Word Processing Curriculum

Middle/junior high school word processing instruction is frequently, but not always, combined with keyboarding in a structured business education class taught by a certified business teacher. Student objectives vary at this level but primarily focus on personal-use applications. According to typical word processing/technology student objectives, upon completion of instruction, students might be expected to demonstrate the ability to

1. Care for and use computer-based technology, including proper disk management;
2. Identify, manage, and use appropriate functions involved in the operating system and software including opening and closing software applications and saving and retrieving data;
3. Use basic word processing functions to produce personal business and academic documents in accordance with stated standards in a timely, efficient manner;
4. Use word processing software techniques and graphics to enhance document presentation;
5. Demonstrate the ability to input material from various sources (keyboarding from handwritten copy and rough drafts, transferring copy from other documents, and using voice recognition software);
6. Critique and edit work for correctness of content and format, professional appearance, and creativity;

7. Work collaboratively to complete complex, multipage documents in a professional manner;

8. Transfer generic software knowledge and skills to other word processing programs; and

9. Exhibit ethical behavior with respect to copyright of software, confidentiality, privacy of documents on-screen, and sharing of disks and information.

STUDENT ACTIVITIES*

Activity 1. Have each preservice student teacher create one Internet scavenger hunt around a particular topic—favorite holiday, period of history, business topic, etc. Before beginning a scavenger hunt lesson plan, preservice student teachers should view sample scavenger hunts at Tonya Skinner's Web site at http://www.angelfire.com/ks/tonyaskinner/scavhunt.html. The class can then share scavenger hunts and expand the number of teaching resources they have.

Activity 2. Have preservice student teachers create two assignments: a conventional word processed business letter and an innovative letter-writing assignment. In the traditional lesson, preservice student teachers must complete the lesson plan, provide the step-by-step directions for students, and provide a teacher's key of the correct answers. For the innovative lesson plan, preservice student teachers should search the Internet for ways to enhance the assignment and then create an unstructured letter-writing activity. There should be no "right" answer for this assignment. An example can be found at http://www.angelfire.com/ks/tonyaskinner/kbletter.html.

*For preservice business teachers

DOCUMENT FORMATTING

At the heart of most business education information processing curricula is the preparation of students for positions in business and industry. Once students have learned basic keyboarding and word processing skills, they begin to learn computer applications that will lead to job opportunities in their chosen career paths. This process requires attention to industry standards, which should be reflected in course objectives and curricula.

Industry Standards

As students use industry standards for document preparation, a considerable portion of class time should be devoted to building speed and accuracy to ensure that students become productive and effective workers. Common business formats for letters, memos, reports, tables, and other documents should be presented in a model that exhibits correct spacing and formatting. Students should then complete problems in which they format documents according to standards. A teacher's key usually includes an example of a document that is prepared according to industry standards. It is important to note that errors should not acceptable since students have the ability to make corrections as they key. Industry preferences are for higher speeds of inputting data, although entry-level positions will allow minimum speeds of 40 words per minute.

Document Formatting Course Objectives

At the completion of this course, students will do the following (without errors):

- Input straight-copy content at a minimum of 40 words per minute. Personal-use speeds should be at least 25 to 30 words per minute.
- Demonstrate knowledge of and ability to use a word processing software program to create, print, store, revise, and edit documents. (See Instructional Methods for Word Processing section for more specific word processing objectives.)
- Create, store, print, and edit personal-use documents.
- Create business documents such as letters, reports, tables, and memos in acceptable business format.
- Use the computer as a communication tool (e.g., for creating documents, sending and receiving e-mail, searching the Internet, and using telecommunication functions).

STUDENT ACTIVITIES*

Activity 1. Have preservice student teachers develop keyboarding lessons that incorporate active learning. They can prepare by reading Moyer's 1991 article entitled "Skills for Active Learning in Keyboarding Classes." Each lesson should focus on a different area of document formatting and present the concept, the learning activities that reinforce the concept, and the process for actively taking notes on the concept. Preservice student teachers should compose steps in their own words and work in pairs to check the steps by having their partners complete the steps.

Activity 2. Have preservice student teachers create informational Web pages that provide links to commercial products. Each preservice student teacher should have a different topic. Before beginning the assignment, preservice student teachers should agree on format and style of all Web pages so that the individual Web pages can be linked together. Topics can include

- The Herzog system of computer keyboarding
- Sunburst's Type Learn software program
- The Diane King Method of rhyming
- KeyWords Elementary software
- Microtype: The Wonderful World of PAWS software program
- Computer Keyboarding: An Elementary Course (South-Western)
- Mastertype computer-based educational game
- Elementary Keyboarding (based on psychomotor skill development)
- Keyboard Training videos and student guides
- Smartype computer tutorial
- *Using a Mnemonic Approach To Teach Fourth Graders To Use a Computer Keyboard* (see B. Chubb's 1994 work, ERIC Reproduction Document No. ED370537)
- ClarisWorks for Kids

*For preservice business teachers

The goal of any document formatting/word processing course should be to prepare students for lifelong learning. Knowledge of basic academic and business standards will empower students in an age of constantly changing technological needs.

Basic Document Formatting Course Outline

Following the introduction to the keyboard and learning touch keyboarding, students should begin simple document formatting exercises, progressing from personal business assignments and academic reports to common business documents. Names of information processing classes at these levels vary from Keyboarding I and II to Information Processing and Computer Applications to Office Assistant I, II, and III. Table 4 presents a sample document formatting course outline.

Table 4. Document Formatting Course Outline	
Unit	**Content Included**
I. Basic Formatting Techniques	Horizontal and vertical centering; setting tabs and inputting short paragraphs; inputting lists, announcements, and menus
II. Improving Language Arts Skills	Learning correct spacing with punctuation, developing language arts skills, proofreading and correcting grammar and punctuation errors, improving input skills, increasing speed in timed-writing materials, developing accuracy
III. Block Letter Formatting	Inputting personal letters in block style with open punctuation and with mixed punctuation, inputting personal business letters in block style with open punctuation and with mixed punctuation
IV. Outline and Academic Reports	Inputting an academic bound report and inputting an academic unbound report, inputting an academic report with references, inputting a report in MLA style, inputting an outline
V. Unbound Manuscript/ Report	Inputting a basic one-page report with or without references, inputting a multipage report with or without references, inputting an unbound report with listed or enumerated items and with text citations
VI. Bound Manuscript/Report	Inputting a bound report with footnotes, inputting a bound report with endnotes, inputting a bound report with long quotations
VII. Basic Table Format	Creating two- and three-column tables, creating tables with secondary headings, creating tables with columnar headings
VIII. Advanced Tables	Creating and filling in a table, inserting and deleting rows in a table, merging cells and changing column widths, creating a table with dot leaders, creating graphs from tables
IX. Employment Documents	Creating a letter of application, creating a resume and online resume
X. Formatting Simulation	Completing documents in an industry simulation, completing standard documents in a social studies curriculum and a math curriculum

The advanced document formatting curriculum includes higher-level formatting skills in each of the basic curriculum areas outlined above. Students should adhere to industry standards and demonstrate timed production work. Even though standard business formats are taught, students should also know that business constantly changes and that they must become aware of those changes through a continual learning process over the course of their careers.

SUMMARY

Business teachers bring methods that are grounded in sound research to all levels of education. By teaching input skills, business educators continue to meet the needs of students to use existing and new technology tools. Keyboarding, word processing, and document formatting skills will continue to be necessary in the workplace. Voice recognition, palm, and multimedia technologies, as well as assistive technologies for people with disabilities, will expand the role of business education in developing input skills.

Innovative and creative business educators who know sound psychomotor skill theory and who are willing to complement keyboarding/computer applications textbooks with lesson plans and other resources found online contribute to the richness of the business education curriculum. The Internet offers students opportunities to pursue a broad range of interests and apply essential career skills. Real-life applications provide internal motivation that solidifies the drive for lifelong learning.

REFERENCES

Cochran-Smith, M. (1991, Spring). Word Processing and writing in elementary classrooms: A critical review of related literature. *Review of Educational Research, 61*(1), 107–155.

Fitts, P. M. (1962). Factors in complex skill training. In R. Glaser (Ed.), *Training research and education* (pp. 177–197). Pittsburgh: University of Pittsburgh Press.

International Society for Technology in Education. (2000). *National educational technology standards for students: Connecting curriculum and technology.* Eugene, OR: International Society for Technology in Education in collaboration with the U.S. Department of Education.

Jackson, T. H. (1991, Winter). Building keyboarding skills at the elementary level. *The Balance Sheet,* pp. 19–22.

Larsh, K. (2001, April 12). *Integrating voice typing in business classes.* Presentation at the convention of the National Business Education Association, Atlanta, GA.

Lindsay, V. J. (1966). Psychological concepts germane to efficient motor skill development in typewriting. (Doctoral dissertation, Indiana University, 1966). *Dissertation Abstracts International, 27*(10), 3346A.

McClurg, P., & Kercher, L. (1989). Keyboarding instruction: A comparison of five approaches. *Journal of Educational Computing Research, 5*(4), 445–458.

McLean, G. N. (1995). *Teaching keyboarding.* Little Rock, Arkansas: Delta Pi Epsilon.

Mikkelsen, V. P., & Gerlach, G. (1988). *Teaching keyboarding skills to elementary school students in supervised and unsupervised environments.* (ERIC Document Reproduction Service No. ED301152)

Moyer, B. (1991, January). Skills for active learning in keyboarding classes. *Business Education Forum, 45*(4), pp. 24–26.

National Business Education Association. (1995). *National standards for business education: What America's students should know and be able to do in business.* Reston, Virginia: National Business Education Association.

National Business Education Association. (2001). *National standards for business education: What America's students should know and be able to do in business.* Reston, VA: National Business Education Association.

Nichols, L. M. (1995). A comparison of two methods for teaching keyboarding in the elementary school. *Computers in the Schools, 11*(4), 15–25.

Policies Commission for Business and Economic Education. (1997). Policy statement 35: This we believe about keyboarding. *Policies statements: Policies Commission for Business and Economic Education.* Cincinnati, OH: South-Western Publishing Company.

Reagan, S. D. (2000). *Increasing touch-keyboarding skills in the middle school student: "KeyWords" vs. "Type to Learn," hand covers vs. no hand covers.* (ERIC Document Reproduction Service No. ED443386)

Russin, I. (1995). *A comparison of the effect of teacher-directed instruction (and textbook use) and interactive computer software instruction on the development of touch-keyboarding skills in two sixth-grade classes.* (ERIC Document Reproduction Service No. ED381132)

Soloway, E., Norris, C., & Curtis, M. (2001, April). Making palm-sized computers the PC of choice for K–12. *Learning and Leading with Technology, 28*(7), 32–34.

Sormunen, C. (1986, Spring). A comparison of two methods for teaching keyboarding on the microcomputer to elementary grade students. *Delta Pi Epsilon Journal, 28*(2), 67–77.

Sormunen, C., Adams, M. E., Berg, D., & Prigge, L. (1990). Teaching keyboarding: Perceptions of elementary school teachers. *NABTE Review, 17*, 7–11.

West, L. J. (1983). *Acquisition of typewriting skills: Methods and research in teaching typewriting and word processing* (2nd ed.). Indianapolis: Bobbs-Merrill Educational Publishing.

West L. J., & Sabban, Y. (1982). Analysis of stroking habits of novice through expert typists. *Delta Pi Epsilon Journal, 24*(1), 1–12.

Zeliff, N., & Schultz, K. (1998). *Authentic assessment in action: Preparing for the business workplace.* Little Rock, AR: Delta Pi Epsilon.

Understanding and Applying the Law to Technology

Richard W. Clark
Stroudsburg Area School District
Stroudsburg, Pennsylvania

The school board in St. Lucie County, Florida, tentatively agreed to a collective bargaining demand that would protect teachers from liability should students access inappropriate material on the Internet. The issue arose after police charged two St. Lucie teachers in separate incidents involving computers and pornography. Both teachers said students, acting without permission, had used the computers to access pornography. Charges ultimately were dropped (Guerard, 2000).

This incident and others provide strong notice to teachers, students, and administrators to be mindful of the legal issues involved in the use of technology in a cyber society. The Internet is one of the top emerging information technologies used to enhance and support instruction by business education teachers in Pennsylvania (Clark, 1999). In other states, as well, business education programs are implementing technology as a resource for enhancing the existing curriculum and as a catalyst for transforming the very nature of teaching and learning. This technological progress forces business educators and others to confront new legal issues, only some of which can be foreseen.

Business educators must understand the law in relation to technology and the implications for the business education curriculum. Students must be aware of the legal implications of the decisions they make in a cyber society. This chapter addresses business teachers' need to understand legal issues involving copyright, trademarks, fair use, privacy and safety on the Internet, free speech, and other pertinent topics. The chapter also suggests ways for students to apply the information.

EDUCATION, INTERNET, AND LEGAL ACTIONS

Within the last decade, the Internet has had a profound effect on education. As the availability of computers and the Internet in schools and classrooms has grown, so has the interest in the purposes of and the extent to which these technologies are being used. A report by the National Center for Education Statistics (Smerdon et al., 2000) stated,

> In 1994, a little over a third of all public schools were connected to the Internet. By 1999, availability had grown to 95 percent, with one computer connected to the Internet for every 9 students. The percent of instructional rooms connected to the Internet grew even more sharply during that time—whereas 3 percent of instructional rooms were connected to the Internet in 1994, 63 percent were connected by 1999. (p. 33)

Many questions arise as school leaders attempt to formulate policies and procedures to avoid lawsuits in an increasingly litigious society. For example, how do business educators protect students from access to potentially harmful material, such as pornography, on the Internet? How are students' rights to privacy and First Amendment rights protected while using the Internet? What is considered "fair use" of copyrighted works? Should filtering software programs be used to safeguard students from accessing unacceptable sites? What is considered acceptable and unacceptable behavior on the Internet?

Several incidents have generated legal actions and provide examples for this chapter. For instance, in the spring of 1998, J. S., an 8th-grade student, created a Web page on his home computer that made crude, derogatory comments about a particular teacher and the principal, and the courts upheld his suspension from school. In another case, however, the district court held that a Pennsylvania school district violated a student's First and Fourteenth Amendment rights by suspending him from school for compiling a list of offensive statements about school administrators.

The case of the "unofficial Kentlake High home page" provides insight into the complexities of the law, information technology, and education. A federal judge in Seattle blocked school administrators from suspending a student because of a Web site he had created on his home computer. The "unofficial" site, a satire of the school, was designed to promote communication among students. The student's Web page included the following disclaimer: "This Web site is meant for entertainment purposes only."

The student's Web site included fake obituaries of other students with their permission, an idea resulting from a creative writing assignment to write mock obituaries. The Web site attracted attention from a local television reporter who suggested that the site had a "hit list" threatening to injure people. The principal suspended the student who had created the site for five days, but the student and his parents contacted the American Civil Liberties Union of Washington and contested the suspension. The chief judge of the U.S. District Court issued a restraining order enjoining the school district from enforcing the suspension. "The judge noted that the school district presented 'no evidence that the mock obituaries and voting were intended to threaten anyone, did actually threaten anyone, or manifest any violent tendencies whatsoever'" (American Civil Liberties Union of Washington, 2000).

Teachers and students need to understand their responsibilities in several areas that concern Internet activities: copyright, freedom of expression, privacy, acceptable use, international business, and e-commerce.

COPYRIGHT AND FAIR USE

Copyright and the doctrine of fair use concern the rights of authors and the rights of the public. Understanding these concepts and the Digital Millennium Copyright Act help teachers and students decide what material is protected and when and how it may be legally used.

Copyright

Copyright essentially offers limited exclusive protection of an author's original work. According to Bielefield and Cheeseman (1997), "…copyright is a bundle of exclusive rights granted to an author. It includes not only the right to reproduce (copy) and publish but also the right to adapt, to perform, and to display a work" (p. 3). "Copyright protects the ability of an author to be financially rewarded for the fruits of her creativity and presentation of ideas" (Howie, 1999, p. 55). Section 102 (a) of the Copyright Law states:

> Copyright protection subsists, in accordance with this title, in original works of authorship fixed in any tangible medium of expression, now known or later developed, from which they can be perceived, reproduced, or otherwise communicated, either directly or with the aid of a machine or device. Works of authorship include the following categories:
>
> (1) literary works;
> (2) musical works, including any accompanying words;
> (3) dramatic works, including any accompanying music;
> (4) pantomimes and choreographic works;
> (5) pictorial, graphic, and sculptural works;
> (6) motion pictures and other audiovisual works;
> (7) sound recordings; and
> (8) architectural works. (p. 7)

The Copyright Act clearly states that an original work of authorship does not extend to any idea, procedure, process, system, method of operation, concept, principle or discovery, unless fixed in a tangible form (17 U.S.C. Sec. 102 b). In addition, copyright law protects the expression of an idea and not the idea itself ("Copyright Law of the United States," 2000).

Copyright is a serious issue in the Digital Age. According to Simpson (1997),

> Every person who writes a document published on the Internet, who creates a graphic or icon, who scans his own photograph or records his own voice into a digital file, who sends an e-mail message, who creates a document for a newsgroup or who designs a Web page owns the copyright to his creative work. (p. 89)

Simpson (1997) has suggested that when students post their work on a Web page, instructors should make sure that the proper rights for the graphics, designs, logos, and photos used are observed and that permissions come from the people authorized to grant such rights.

Students should also distinguish between *copyright* and *trademark* infringement. Perhaps a student writes a short story or research paper on a word processor. The work is protected under copyright as soon as the student saves it. Conversely, a student borrows an image (like the McDonald's golden arches symbol from http:// www.mcdonalds.com) for use in a PowerPoint presentation. According to the law, infringement of a trademark is involved:

> A trademark is defined under the Lanham Act of 1976 as a word, name, symbol, or device or any combination thereof including a sound, used by any person to identify and distinguish goods from those of others. . . . [T]he mark must be used, or promise a "good faith" intent to be used, in commerce. . . .

> Trademarks have been expanded to now include a trade dress that may be a colored design or shape associated with a product. Most franchises are known by their trade dress because the general public associates the color scheme and ambiance of a business with the franchise (e.g., the McDonald's restaurant is red and yellow). (Ferrera, Lichtenstein, Reder, August, & Schiano, 2001, pp. 40–42)

Trademarks are registered with the U.S. Patent and Trademark Office and, once registered, the owner has the right to sue for trademark infringement. According to Ferrera et al. (2001), "A trademark infringement occurs when a party uses a trademark that causes a 'likelihood of confusion' between goods or the relationship between the parties that make the goods" (p. 46). Businesses spend tremendous amounts of money protecting their names as well as building good will. The Registrar Accreditation Overview provides information on registering trademarks (http://www.icann.org/ registrars/accreditation.htm).

Fair Use

The doctrine of fair use imposes an important limitation on authors' exclusive rights. According to Ferrera et al. (2001), "The fair use doctrine . . . is a policy position

STUDENT ACTIVITY

Copyright and Trademarks

Have students work in small groups to create an advertising campaign for an invention they have created. The ad campaign should include a description, a price, and graphics. Ask the students to create a logo for their invention. Have students research the guidelines for a trademark on the Internet and discuss why trademarks are important to businesses. Have students identify what aspects of the campaign are subject to copyright and which are subject to trademark.

taken by Congress that the public interest is best served by placing statutory limitation on the copyright owner's monopoly to its original work" (pp. 80–81). The concept of "fair use" was established in the Copyright Law of 1976 and specifies situations in which copyrighted materials may be used without express permission of the copyright holder, as, for example, the conditions under which teachers can make copies of an author's work for distribution to students.

The Intellectual Property and National Infrastructure Report (U.S. Information Infrastructure Task Force, 1995) has stated,

> The most significant and, perhaps, murky of the limitations on a copyright owner's exclusive rights is the doctrine of fair use. Fair use is an affirmative defense to an action for copyright infringement. It is potentially available with respect to all manners of unauthorized use of all types of works in all media. When it exists, the user is not required to seek permission from the copyright owner or to pay a license fee for the use. (p. 73)

The Copyright Act, U.S.C. 17, Section 107 lists four factors that define "fair use":

1. The purpose and character of the use, including whether such use is of a commercial nature or is for nonprofit educational purposes
2. The nature of the copyrighted work
3. The amount and substantiality of the portion used in relation to the copyrighted work as a whole
4. The effect of the use upon the potential market for or value of the copyrighted work (p. 16)

Lan and Dagley (1999) have provided guidelines for classroom copying of books and periodicals:

> Teachers may make single copies for research purposes or for teaching or preparing to teach from any of the following resources: (a) a chapter from a book; (b) an article from a periodical or newspaper; (c) a short story; (d) short essay or poem, whether or not it is from a collective work; (e) or, a

chart, graph, diagram, drawing, cartoon, or picture from a book, periodi-
cal, or newspaper. The agreement also addresses the making of multiple
copies for classroom use, by permitting up to one copy per pupil in a
course, if the copying meets the tests for brevity, spontaneity, and cumula-
tive effects provided in the agreement, and includes a notice of copyright
on each copy. (p. 27)

Educators who follow these guidelines are presumed to satisfy the fair use doctrine.
School districts should distribute copyright guidelines that incorporate the fair use
provisions to staff members and students. Some school districts include a copyright
provision within their acceptable use policy (AUP).

The Digital Millennium Copyright Act of 1998

On October 27, 1998, the Digital Millennium Copyright Act of 1998 (http://
www.loc.gov/copyright/legislation/dmca.pdf) became the most comprehensive reform
of U.S. copyright law in a generation. The Digital Millennium Copyright Act enables
software publishers, music and film studios, and others to keep their nonprinted,
copyrighted materials from being distributed freely on the Internet, where markets can
be undermined. The Digital Millennium Copyright Act does not specifically make fair
use applicable to works appearing in digital media, but it makes no changes in the fair
use doctrine or other privileges and rights already accorded to users under current
copyright law.

A case that tested the "safe harbor" provision of the Digital Millennium Copyright
Act is *A&M Records, Inc., v. Napster, Inc.* (2000). Napster, a small Internet company,
made its proprietary MusicShare software freely available to Internet users, enabling
users to share MP3 music files with others logged-on to the Napster system. In 2001
the 9th Circuit Court of Appeals in San Francisco ruled in favor of the recording
industry's request that Napster stop enabling users to swap songs for free. This case was
probably the first big battle regarding copyrights in cyberspace, defining how books,
movies, and music are distributed on the Web (*A&M Records, Inc., v. Napster, Inc.*,
2000).

STUDENT ACTIVITY

Defining Terms
Have students research and then define the following terms: plagiarism, patent,
trademark, fair use, and copyright laws. Students should distinguish between fair use
and copyright laws. Ask students to list the guidelines of "fair use" for copying
images, pictures, graphs, charts, and other materials. Then have the class conduct a
debate relative to the "ethical" considerations and the impact on society of copying or
downloading music files as described in the Napster case.

FREEDOM OF EXPRESSION

Students' rights to free speech while at school are not the same as an adult's right to free speech. When a student expresses himself or herself in a manner that disrupts classes or is not in accordance with the school district's policies, the school district has the right to curtail this speech. The First Amendment's provision regarding freedom of expression provides a foundation for this discussion.

First Amendment Rights

The First Amendment to the United States Constitution protects the right to freedom of religion and freedom of expression from government interference. Freedom of expression consists of the rights to freedom of speech, press, and assembly; the right to petition the government for a redress of grievances; and the implied rights of association and belief. The Supreme Court interprets the extent of the protection afforded to these rights. The First Amendment states,

> Congress shall make no law respecting an establishment of religion, or prohibiting the free exercise thereof; or abridging the freedom of speech or of the press; or the right of the people peaceably to assemble, and to petition the government for a redress of grievances.

The nation's commitment to freedom of expression has been tested repeatedly especially during times of national stress, like war or social upheaval. People exercising their First Amendment rights have been censored, fined, and even jailed. Those with unpopular political ideas have borne the brunt of government repression.

First Amendment Rights of Students

The 1969 Court decision in *Tinker et al. v. Des Moines Independent Community School District et al.* recognized the right of public school students to wear black armbands to protest the Vietnam War. The petitioners were 15, 16, and 13 years of age. The school had adopted a policy against the wearing of armbands, but on December 16, 1968, the three students wore black armbands to school to protest the Vietnam War. The students were quiet and passive and did not disrupt or impinge upon the rights of others.

The students were suspended from school until they returned without their armbands. The district court recognized that wearing an armband to express certain views was the type of symbolic act that is within the Free Speech Clause of the First Amendment. The district court found that wearing the armbands did not "substantially" interfere with the work of the school or impinge on the rights of other students (*Tinker et al. v. Des Moines Independent Community School District et al.*, 1969). Problems arise when students in the exercise of their First Amendment rights collide with the rules of school authorities.

In *Hazelwood School District et al. v. Kuhlmeier et al.*, student members of the school's newspaper staff filed suit in Federal District Court in October 1987 against the school district. They alleged that their First Amendment rights were violated by the deletion of two pages that included articles describing students' experiences with pregnancy and the divorce of parents. The newspaper was written and edited by a journalism class as part of the school's curriculum. The principal of the high school was concerned that the story dealing with pregnancy might identify the pregnant girls and that the divorced parents were not given sufficient information to respond or consent to the publication of the newspaper article.

The district court held that no First Amendment violation had occurred. School officials may impose restraints on students' speech in activities that are an "integral part of the school's educational function," including the publication of a school-sponsored newspaper by a journalism class, so long as their decision has "substantial and reasonable basis." The U.S. Supreme Court concurred and ruled that public school officials can censor school-sponsored expression for legitimate educational purposes (*Hazelwood School District et al. v. Kuhlmeier et al.*, 1988).

Landwehr (2000) has described the case of a sophomore who had won a school election but was disqualified by the school. The student's campaign slogan stated, "Adam Henerey, the Safe Choice." Without the approval of school administration, Henerey handed out 11 condoms attached to stickers with his campaign slogan on them. Henerey sued the school district for violating his First Amendment right to free speech.

The court found that Henerey's First Amendment rights had not been violated: " . . . [A] school need not tolerate speech incompatible with the pedagogical mission and . . . may restrict speech that materially and substantially interferes with the requirements of appropriate discipline in the operation of the school or that would substantially interfere with the work of the school" (p. 394). The court applied the *Tinker* ruling that allowed free speech as long as it did not disrupt classes or the learning environment. In the Court's opinion, however, Henerey's speech disrupted the school setting.

First Amendment protection is not limited to "pure speech"—books, newspapers, leaflets, and rallies. These cases indicate that the First Amendment also protects "symbolic speech"—nonverbal expression whose purpose is to communicate ideas.

Disruptions of School or Learning Environments

Rights under the Constitution are not absolute. If a school district wants to curtail speech based on policy, the school district must be consistent in its policies and protect the rights of students. One of the concerns facing school districts is the use of student Web pages. Students are often tempted to use their personal Web space to poke fun at the administration, criticize teachers, or sensationalize school-related problems. For those schools that allow students to create personal Web pages on the school's Web site, there is little problem. The pages can be monitored and edited by school officials or teachers. The parameters of proper Web page content are part of the school's AUP or Web page policy.

Students may, however, create Web sites on their home computers and use free Web space that comes as part of the Web connection fee for their Internet service providers. When such sites substantially disrupt the school environment, taking disciplinary action falls within a "gray area." Suspensions and expulsions are drastic measures that can lead to expensive court costs to defend against First Amendment challenges. The following cases illustrate contrasting legal views relative to student Web pages.

In the spring of 1998, J. S., an 8th-grade student, created a Web page on his home computer entitled "Teacher Sux." The Web page contained crude, derogatory comments about the student's algebra teacher and principal and even requested $20 to help pay for a hit man. A middle school teacher learned of the Web site and reported it to the principal who viewed portions of the site and then called the police and the FBI. After viewing the Web page, the algebra teacher suffered lasting effects including stress; anxiety; loss of appetite, sleep, weight, and general sense of well-being. She was unable to return to school and took a medical sabbatical for the following year.

The trial court, noting that the case involved off-campus activity, applied the *Tinker* standard and found evidence of substantial disruption. The court determined that school officials are allowed to discipline students for conduct occurring off school premises when the conduct materially and substantially interferes with the education process. The court determined that the school district did not violate the student's rights under the First Amendment (*J. S. v. Bethlehem Area School District*, 2000).

In *Killion v. Franklin Regional School District* (2001) the district court held that a Pennsylvania school district violated a student's First and Fourteenth Amendment rights. Paul Zacariah was suspended for distributing offensive remarks about a school administrator via the Internet. Paul, a member of the school's track team, was angered by a denial of a student-parking permit. While at home, he created a "top-ten" list containing derogatory statements about the physical attributes of the athletic director and then e-mailed it to friends. Copies of the top-ten list subsequently appeared in the Franklin Regional High School teachers' lounge and the Franklin Middle School after an undisclosed student reformatted the original e-mail and distributed it on school grounds.

Paul admitted to creating the list and was suspended for 10 days because the offensive remarks were found on school grounds. Paul and his mother sought summary judgment contending that the defendants violated Paul's First Amendment rights because the speech was made off school grounds and in the privacy of his home. The plaintiffs also argued that lack of written notification prior to the suspension violated Paul's due process rights as set forth in the Pennsylvania School Code.

Applying *Tinker*, the court found that Paul's suspension violated the First Amendment. The list was created out of school and there was no evidence that Paul had either been responsible for bringing the list onto school grounds or that there was substantial disruption. The court also ruled that Paul's due process rights were violated because neither Paul nor his mother received advance written communication on the disciplinary proceedings (School Law Information Exchange, 2001).

STUDENT ACTIVITY

First Amendment Rights and Responsibilities

Have students research several Web sites that discuss rights and responsibilities relative to the First Amendment. Have students present this information in a Web page with links to the source material. The class can then conduct a debate focusing on free speech as it pertains to school-sponsored activities.

PRIVACY AND SAFETY ISSUES IN CYBERSPACE

Aidman (2000) has reported, "According to a recent estimate, the number of U.S. children and teenagers online will grow from just under 9 million in 1999 to more than 13 million by 2005" (p. 46). While the Internet is a great place for students to share information with people all over the world, the very communication links that make it possible to converse at a distance have the potential to destroy the privacy of such conversations. Westin (1967) has defined privacy as "the claim of individuals, groups, or institutions to determine for themselves when, how, and to what extent information about them is communicated to others" (p. 22).

There are many methods of gathering information about people who use the Internet, and many reasons for wanting that information. Some of these reasons are legitimate and acceptable. Others are annoying invasions of privacy, but, in a few cases, can be dangerous. Every visit to a Web site leaves a footprint containing personal demographic information. The following are some of the activities that can reveal information about students to others: (1) sending e-mail, (2) posting to newsgroups and mailing lists, (3) participating in online surveys, and (4) surfing Web sites.

Most of the Supreme Court's jurisprudence concerning constitutional rights to privacy has centered on the Fourth Amendment's prohibition of unreasonable searches and seizures. The Fourth Amendment of the United States Constitution states,

> The right of the people to be secure in their persons, houses, papers, and effects, against unreasonable searches and seizures, shall not be violated, and no warrants shall issue but upon probable cause, supported by oath or affirmation, and particularly describing the place to be searched, and the persons or things to be seized. (Lockhart, Kamisar & Choper, 1967, Appendix B, p. 20)

The right to privacy is implied rather than expressed under the Constitution. According to Cate (1997), "Privacy is . . . contextual and subjective. It is neither inherently beneficial nor harmful. Rather, the term connotes a complex aggregation of positive and negative attributes" (p. 31). Although the Fourth Amendment right to privacy is clearly established and routinely applied, it is of limited value outside of the criminal defense context.

E-Mail

Most teachers and students believe that e-mail is private or confidential. Nothing could be further from the truth. While the Electronic Communications Privacy Act makes it a criminal offense to intercept e-mail while it is in transit, any operator of a computer that e-mail passes through may legally read that mail. In addition, electronic communication may be intercepted if at least one party to the communication has given his or her consent to the interception.

E-mail can reveal: (1) the sender's real name, (2) the sender's log-in ID, (3) the computer where the e-mail account resides, and (4) the computers through which the e-mail passed as the message was forwarded. Business educators must instruct students that e-mail transmissions may be stored on several computers during transmission and do not disappear when they are deleted at the sender's or even the receiver's location. In addition, the directory listing may disappear, but the actual message may not. Most computer networks are backed up onto tape or other servers periodically. These tapes can be stored for several months or longer by an institution. Consequently, information about sender's messages can be made available.

Use of Web Page Information

Introduction to Web page design and related courses (e.g., in HTML, Perl, and advanced Web design) have become popular in the business education curriculum. The Policies Commission for Business and Economic Education (2000) has stated, "We believe that business education curricula must include the fundamentals of effective Web site design as it relates to productive operations of e-business" (p. 13). Designing personal Web pages can be fun and an excellent way to share information with people who share similar interests. However, students must be cautious in publishing a page that advertises personal details.

Several federal privacy laws have been enacted since the 1970s that deal primarily with keeping and using personal data about individuals. The most significant of those acts are described below.

The Family Education Rights and Privacy Act of 1974. This act affords students certain rights with respect to their educational records. This federal law applies to all schools that receive funding under most programs administered by the U.S. Department of Education. Students have the right to inspect their educational records, seek to have the records amended, and have some control over the disclosure of information from the records. According to Cate (1997),

> Such institutions must accord parents the "right to inspect and review the education records of children." Students eighteen or older, or in college, are

also entitled to view such records. The educational institution must accord
parents (or students) a hearing to challenge the contents of student records
that they claim are "inaccurate, misleading, or otherwise in violation of the
privacy or other rights of students," and the opportunity to correct or
delete such information or to include in the records a written explanation
of their content. (p. 87)

Educational institutions must inform students and their parents of their rights
under the law. In a recent court action in Exeter, New Hampshire, James M. Knight, a
parent, filed a lawsuit to review the "Internet history log" files from computers maintained by two local school districts. Knight maintained that information stored on the
computers, such as Internet logs, is subject to the state's Right-to-Know law and must
be disclosed on request.

The Rockingham County Superior Court judge found that "students in schools are
not using the computers for personal use but as an integral part of the education
curriculum. Thus the records of such official computer use must be deemed public"
(Kaplan, 2000, p.2). The ruling is subject to appeal.

This case is important because schools must manage and monitor the Internet
content that their students are using relative to the curriculum. The choice of what will
constitute appropriate content will depend in part on local community standards, the
culture of the school or school district, the degree of control that teachers and administrators want to retain, and the extent to which teachers and other school officials are
willing to be involved on an ongoing basis.

Children's Online Privacy Protection Act, H.R. 4328, Section 1303. On October 21,
1998, the Children's Online Privacy Protection Act of 1998 was signed into law.
Effective in April 2000, this first Internet privacy law addressing children's online
privacy states in Section 1303(a):

It is unlawful for an operator of a website or online service directed to
children, or any operator that has actual knowledge that it is collecting
personal information from a child, to collect personal information from a
child in a manner that violates the regulations prescribed under subsection
(b). (p. 2)

To help stop kids from accessing Internet material that is "harmful" to minors, the
Federal Trade Commission has recommended a combination of broader public
education, heightened public awareness of existing technologies, better enforcement of
existing laws, and industry self-regulation. According to the Federal Trade Commission
(1999),

The statute and rule apply to commercial Web sites and online services
directed to, or that knowingly collect information from, children under 13.

To inform parents of their information practices, these sites will be required to provide notice on the site and to parents about their policies with respect to the collection, use and disclosure of children's personal information. With certain statutory exceptions, sites will also have to obtain "verifiable parental consent" before collecting, using or disclosing personal information from children. (p. 1)

Schools need to offer close supervision and well-defined procedures for dealing with online communication. Students must be instructed to contact their teachers or parents if they receive any obscene, suspicious, or threatening messages.

Children's Internet Protection Act. The Children's Internet Protection Act (http://www.techlawjournal.com/cong106/filter/hr896ih.htm) requires schools, libraries, and local educational agencies to

- Enact a policy of Internet safety for students and adults that includes "a technology protection measure" (blocking or filtering software) on computers with Internet access
- Protect against visual depictions that are obscene, child pornography, or harmful to minors
- Enforce the operation of the technology protection measure during the use of [their] computers

Neighborhood Children's Internet Protection Act. The Neighborhood Children's Internet Protection Act (http://www.techlawjournal.com/cong106/filter/s1545is.htm) has three major requirements. First, a policy must be enacted that addresses:

- Access by minors to inappropriate matter on the Internet and World Wide Web
- Safety and security of minors when using e-mail, chat rooms, and other forms of direct electronic communication
- Unauthorized access, including "hacking" and other unlawful activities, by minors online
- Unauthorized disclosure, use, and dissemination of personal identification information regarding minors
- Measures designed to restrict minors' access to material that is harmful to them

Second, the board of school directors must give public notice and hold a public hearing or meeting to address the proposed Internet safety policy. Third, the school board must determine locally what content is inappropriate for minors. The federal government may not establish these criteria, review the board's decision, or consider the criteria employed by the school board in administering the policy. However, if requested, the school district must give the FCC a copy of the policy for its review.

These privacy and protection laws provide a framework for educators to guide students to understand the issues involving Internet content. Educators can also take advantage of other online safety and privacy educational programs. The CyberSmart School Program offers a framework that teachers can use to raise students' awareness of how to make the electronic world safe, valuable, and enjoyable. According to Teicher (1999),

> The CyberSmart program introduces the basics of savvy Internet usage. When carefully implemented, it lays the necessary foundation for community support and contributes to the ultimate success of a school's technology plan. The five components of the program are (S)afety, (M)anners, (A)dvertising and Privacy Protection, (R)esearch and (T)echnology.

Of the five components, "safety" is paramount relative to use of the Internet. According to Teicher (1999),

> The key to online safety is recognizing that communications in the online world have a unique characteristic that can lead to irresponsible behavior: anonymity. When children cannot validate the physical location or identity of an individual on the other end of the message, difficulties can arise. (p. 71)

ACCEPTABLE USE POLICY

Whether or not a school or district ultimately decides to manage students' access to Internet content, the district should still have an AUP in place when it goes online. The AUP provides a framework for student and teacher use of the Internet. According to Crystal, Geide, and Salpeter (2000), "[T]he Acceptable Use Policy is a legal document that pertains to a specific school's or district's technology system and its acceptable use" (p. 26).

AUPs address a wide variety of issues: accessing noninstructional or inappropriate content, online copyright infringement, unacceptable uses of the school district's e-mail system and Web site, limitations on commercial use of the district's Internet resources, misuse of passwords, fraud, considerations related to student privacy, and monitoring students' online activities. The AUP is the combined effort of many stakeholders, ideally "a team comprised of administrators, teachers, 'techies,' parents, students, and teacher's union representatives. . . . [L]egal counsel should be included in these discussions at the beginning, with the final document being approved by the school board" (Crystal, Geide, & Salpeter, 2000, p. 26).

According to the National School Boards Association (NSBA) (Howie, 1999), "Legally, [the AUP] sets forth expectations and puts everyone on notice as to 'acceptable use,' and it helps protect the school against later claims" (p. 2). According to the NSBA, AUPs that are too broad may leave a district open to legal challenge, and districts should consider whether to provide punishment for off-campus behavior, such as creating a "hate site" directed at a teacher or classmate that could cause disturbances on campus. The publication provides a list of 17 elements to be included (Howie, 1999, pp. 18–19).

Most school district AUPs have four major components: statement of purpose, acceptable/unacceptable uses, disciplinary action, and a student/parent release section.

Statement of Purpose

The statement of purpose establishes the reason for using the school or district's telecommunications network system and identifies educational purposes as they relate to the school or district's curriculum, policies, or mission statement. For example, the Charlotte-Mecklenburg district's support for instructional goals and philosophies is clear ("Internet Acceptable Use," 1998):

- To support the implementation of Charlotte-Mecklenburg Schools' Performance Standards and the North Carolina Standard Course of Study
- To enhance learning opportunities by focusing on the application of skills in information retrieval, searching strategies, research skills, and critical thinking
- To promote life-long learning

Acceptable and Unacceptable Uses

This section makes the case for ethical online behavior that parallels "real world" offline behavior. Issues such as confidentiality of user information, "spamming," plagiarism, and copyright violation should also be addressed. The Bellingham School District AUP (http://www.blam.wednet.edu/2313inet.htm) includes the following provision on appropriate student behavior:

Students are responsible for good behavior on school computer networks just as they are in a classroom or a school hallway. Communications on the network are often public in nature. General school rules for behavior and communications apply (see Board Policy 3200). The network is provided for students to conduct research and communicate with others. Access to network services will be provided to students who agree to act in a considerate and responsible manner.

Disciplinary Actions

The section of an AUP that deals with disciplinary actions should contain a clearly defined list of consequences for specific violations. Students must understand that willful or intentional misuse of network resources can lead to disciplinary action or criminal penalties under applicable state and federal laws. The AUP of the Miami-Dade County Public Schools ("M-DCPS Acceptable Use Policy," 1996) states the following warning for improper use of its district network:

Any user violating this rule, or applicable local, state, or federal law or regulations is subject to loss of network access privileges and any other disciplinary actions, reflected in the DCPS Code of Student Conduct (both elementary and secondary) [and/or in the code] of Conduct for Adult Students, the Code of Ethics of the Education Profession in the State of Florida, applicable collective bargaining agreements, and School Board.

Release Agreement

Finally, the AUP is a contract between the student and the school or school district in consideration of the privilege to use network resources. The agreement becomes binding once the student has signed the AUP releasing the school or school district from responsibility should the terms of the contract be violated. The Lexington, Massachusetts Internet AUP ("Internet Acceptable Use Policy, 1994) includes the following statement:

> I release the Lexington Public School System and all other organizations related to the Lexington Internet Connection from any liability or damages that may result from the use of the Internet Connection. In addition, I will accept full responsibility and liability for the results of my actions with regards to the use of [the] Internet. I release the school and related organizations from any liability relating to consequences resulting from my use of the Internet.

From a legal perspective, this is the most important part of the AUP. Here the user signs the AUP and verifies that he or she understands and will abide by it. In the case of users who are minors, a parent's signature is needed to verify that they have read and understand the AUP and that they accept responsibility for the child's use of the technology away from school.

Flowers and Rakes (2000) investigated the presence, origins, contents, and purposes of AUPs being used to address issues related to using the Internet in K–12 schools in the United States. The key issues involved (1) liability, (2) online behavior, (3) system integrity, and (4) quality of content of materials on the Internet.

According to Flowers and Rakes (2000), educators are designing policies to discourage users from accessing inappropriate materials and to protect them from the negative consequences of accessing such material. However, in more than half the schools surveyed, the AUPs did not address issues of limiting access, equal access, censorship, and freedom of information. School districts may want to include these key issues.

An overview of the AUP should be incorporated into the business education curriculum. All students should understand the importance as well as the legal consequences of using the school or school district's telecommunications system (i.e., the Internet and e-mail) properly. The AUP can provide a legal framework for decisions regarding technology usage.

INTERNATIONAL JURISDICTION IN CYBERSPACE

E-commerce has no boundaries and is governed by both national and international law. International laws govern countries' relations and dealings with one another. The basic concepts of law in national legal systems involve status, property, obligation, and tort, as well as substantive law, procedure, process, and remedies.

STUDENT ACTIVITY

Acceptable Use Policy

Have students research the AUPs of three schools in their state by visiting their Web sites. Have students identify any potential pitfalls in each AUP and make recommendations for improvement. Then ask students to work in groups to design their own AUPs. Students should include the basic elements of an AUP.

Concerns over legislating e-commerce emanate from both consumer and business sectors. Consumer concerns include privacy, enforcement of contracts concluded over distance media, ethical standards, and securing communication networks. Businesses favor protections that promote a sense of consumer security when conducting business online (e.g., certificates and privacy policies). Businesses also have strong interests in protecting the security of their intellectual assets and commercial interests through encryption, standards for acceptance of digital signatures, and rules governing the formation of remote contracts.

The future of e-commerce will be dictated by success in meeting these divergent needs while limiting regulation to basic tenets that are globally recognized and supported. Since its inception, e-commerce has been protected and governed by traditional legal principles (e.g., contract, intellectual property, and the Uniform Commercial Code and its international counterparts).

These traditional areas of law will most likely continue to form the basis of legal considerations for the Internet and e-commerce, but they do not specifically address many of the issues that arise when governments, individuals, and businesses interact and transact through this new medium. Governments around the world are addressing issues such as privacy of information collected in the course of e-commerce and protection of intellectual assets in the Internet environment. Several international organizations are playing increasingly important roles in international e-commerce.

Organization for Economic Cooperation and Development

The Organization for Economic Cooperation and Development (OECD) (http://www.oecd.org) is a consultative organization that seeks to help its member countries promote economic growth, employment, and standards of living through the coordination of their laws, regulations, and policies. Since 1997, the OECD has held annual conferences on e-commerce to develop a set of guidelines on consumer protection, as well as ground rules for taxation of electronic sales.

World Trade Organization

The World Trade Organization (WTO) (http://www.wto.org), a specialized intergovernmental organization, administers various multilateral agreements, including the General Agreement on Tariffs and Trade, the General Agreement on Trade in Services, and the Agreement on Trade-Related Aspects of Intellectual Property Rights. In May of

1998 the WTO Ministerial Conference called for the establishment of a comprehensive work program to examine all of the trade-related issues involving global e-commerce.

WORLD INTELLECTUAL PROPERTY ORGANIZATION

The World Intellectual Property Organization (WIPO) (http://www.wipo.int) promotes the protection of intellectual property throughout the world. Recently drafted treaties include the WIPO Copyright Treaty and the WIPO Performances and Phonograms Treaty. The WIPO Copyright Treaty extends copyright protection to computer software, ensures protection of databases, and forbids tampering with electronic coding identifying digitized intellectual property. The WIPO Performances and Phonograms Treaty defines the legal rights of performers, recording companies, and broadcasters and prohibits the circumvention of technological measures, including encryption, that protect those rights.

The information economy, especially the segment that is associated with the Internet, is a global enterprise. The laws and practices of one country cannot be seen as independent of the laws and practices of other countries. Although the United States is not directly subject to active legislative efforts in Europe or elsewhere, Internet activities of businesses within the United States can potentially be subject to the laws of European member countries. It makes good business sense in our global economy, therefore, to adhere to these directives.

STUDENT ACTIVITY

Analyzing a Contract

Have students select a business contract (e.g., automobile agreement) and analyze it: Does the contract include a privacy statement? Does the contract meet the guidelines of the Uniform Commercial Code? Are digital signatures permitted in the agreement? Does the contract include a trademark? Does the contract include verbiage regarding ethics? Ask students to discuss their findings. In addition, have them define the following terms: digitized intellectual property, encryption, multilateral agreement, e-commerce, and tariff.

GUIDELINES FOR INSTRUCTION

Legal issues are complex and can sometimes appear to require contradictory actions. The following are a few guidelines for teaching topics that should be part of business education instruction.

Instruction on E-Mail

Lewis and McGrew (2000) advocate including instruction on using e-mail in basic business communication courses. "Business educators who incorporate e-mail instruction into their courses need to teach their students about the common problems [and perils] inherent in all electronic communications" (p. 27).

Students must understand that e-mail can be stored, reviewed, and forwarded to others by receivers. There is no real privacy. Simpson (1997) has suggested the following:

> For safe parameters, keep e-mail private unless you have express permission of the original writer. Don't forward it to newsgroups or listservs, don't include it in a message to a third party, and don't post it on your web page, unless you receive permission. It's good manners; it's good practice. (p. 93)

Lifto (2001) has concurred and suggested that AUPs include a statement like the following that informs users of the nonprivate nature of e-mail:

> Your school e-mail account is not yours. Messages might travel through multiple networks, and unless they're encrypted, they're not private. Your messages are the property of the school district. They can be retrieved and read, and your use of e-mail can be monitored. (p. 37)

It is important that business educators instruct their students on the proper use of e-mail and its limitations. Incorporating some of these suggestions into a unit of instruction on e-mail may help students avoid embarrassing, or perhaps costly, mistakes.

Web Page Design

Business educators must make sure that students who design Web pages understand that they may not copy a similar site and should strive for unique presentation. Ferrera et al. (2001) have provided the following criteria for copyright protection of a Web page:

1. Originality—The Web site may not copy a similar site and should strive for a unique presentation.
2. Creativity—The Web site need not be novel, as in a patent requirement, but should be an independent creation.
3. Fixed form—The application of the content to the Web site is sufficient to create a fixed form for copyright protection purposes. (p. 68)

Once ideas or expressions become fixed and tangible as school Web pages, students may then file for a copyright at http://www.loc.gov/copyright/reg.html.

According to Simpson (1997), "The more creative the site (i.e., the less factual), the less of the site may be used without prior permission" (p. 94). Simpson (1997) has also warned teachers to instruct students not to "capture" an entire Web site or portion of a site for use offline. Downloading such sites for public display in a classroom may infringe upon copyright works. According to Simpson (1997),

> Remember that under the fair use tests, one of the significant questions is how much of the item will be used. If one captures the entire site, one is

taking 100 percent. Since Web pages are ordinarily highly creative in design and content (the character of the use), the likelihood for a ruling of fair use declines significantly. (p. 94)

The school district may be held liable for any material that is posted on the district Web site in violation of copyright laws. In addition, schools should develop a Web page policy delineating the standards for proper Web design. Business educators should be directly involved with the placement of material on virtually all school Web sites. Using any Web page for classroom instruction involves the display of material. While a display to an individual is expected, display to a public group (such as a class) is not. The Copyright Act of 1976 provides protection for the works of authors; however, business educators should be aware of the fair use doctrine that provides a "safe harbor" for teachers.

STUDENT ACTIVITY

Developing a Web Page Policy
Have students develop a Web page policy as a class project. Students should research other school sites on the Internet to compare and contrast Web page policies. School Web page sites are available at Web66: International School Web Site Directory (http://web66.coled.umn.edu/schools.html). Students will need to consider the following issues: content standards, subject matter, quality, ownership, student safeguards, school board policies, and technical standards.

Other Crimes in Cyberspace
While students need to know about cyber crimes, an open research project can take them to unsavory sites. Table 1 provides definitions and sites for research of these crimes. The student activity suggests that students develop guidelines for searches of sensitive topics.

STUDENT ACTIVITY

Researching the Law on Other Crimes
Have students discuss the role government plays in regulating activities related to the following topics: pornography, harassment, hate crimes, hacking, and spamming. Then have them investigate related community, state, and national laws and policies.
Note to teachers: If students use the Internet for research, they should develop a set of guidelines for accessing sites. Students can write letters to government officials and attend government meetings to get information.

SUMMARY
The business education curriculum will continue to evolve based on changes in information technology. Business education programs will prepare students for the challenges ahead. The business community will demand strong technological skills.

Table 1. Definitions of Cyber Crimes

Pornography. Pornography that involves children is a crime. This could involve the transmission or sale of such images. Law enforcement officials have found that pedophiles are turning to Internet chat rooms to pursue victims. (See http://usdoj.gov/criminal/cybercrime/dagceos.html.)

Harassment. Harassment occurs when someone repeatedly acts in an offensive manner even after being asked to stop by the person(s) subjected to the acts. This includes taunts, profanity, and demands. Most court cases have involved sexual harassment issues in the workplace, schools, government, and the military. (See http://www.vix.com/pub/men/harass/harass.html.)

Cyber Stalking. This form of harassment refers to using the Internet, e-mail, or other electronic communication media to stalk another person. Stalking generally involves repeated harassing or threatening behavior, such as following a person, appearing at a person's home, making harassing phone calls, or leaving written messages or objects. (See http://www.usdoj.gov/criminal/cybercrime/cyberstalking.htm.)

Hate crimes. These crimes typically involve the communication of threatening, hate-filled messages attacking people based on traits such as race, color, sex, religion, ethnicity, or sexual orientation. When hate speech crosses the line into threats and intimidation, there are legal remedies. Threats are not protected under the First Amendment. A threatening private message sent over the Internet to a victim or a public message displayed on a Web site describing intent to commit acts of racially motivated violence can be prosecuted under the law. In a recent case, a college student pleaded guilty to sending derogatory e-mail messages to a number of people with Hispanic last names. (See http://www.usatoday.com/life/cyber/tech/ctb821.htm.)

Hacking. Whether hacking, or unauthorized access to a computer system, is charged as a crime depends on the intent of the perpetrator. Senator Robert Torricelli is proposing legislation to put hackers in prison if they disrupt school computers. (See http://www.wired.com/news/politics/0,1283,45752,00.html.)

Spamming. Spam is unsolicited e-mail or news postings. Spam is a message that the receiver did not request, did not sign up for on a mailing list, or did not provide an e-mail address for on a Web form to get more information. The sender of spam might be liable for a $500 fine per instance. The U.S. Department of Energy's Computer Incident Advisory Center (CIAC) provides e-mail spamming countermeasures at http://ciac.llnl.gov/ciac/bulletins/i-005c.shtml.

"E-learning" will become an important component of the business education curriculum providing students with active, exploratory, and inquiry-based learning online. Teaching ethics will become increasingly important in order to address the safety of students while using information technologies. According to Crystal, Geide, and Salpeter (2000), "Teaching ethical decision-making skills to young people at the start of their exposure to technology is the answer to minimizing the growth of technology crimes and unethical behaviors such as plagiarism and the illegal distribution of copyright information" (p. 31).

Business education teachers must not only keep abreast of emerging information technologies, they must also understand the legal implications of improper use of such technologies. Issues in the United States involving the First Amendment, individual privacy, and intellectual property must not only be reexamined but also kept foremost during instruction. Business educators who teach via the Internet should watch closely the new laws that are on the horizon, while applying institutional ethics and appropriate standards of human behavior and professionalism. By so doing, business educators can provide their students with guidelines for the proper use of emerging technologies and avoid or limit potential lawsuits within their schools and school districts.

REFERENCES

A&M Records, Inc., v. Napster, Inc. (2000, May 12). Retrieved August 19, 2001, from the World Wide Web: http://www.gigalaw.com/library/am-napster-2000-05-12.html

Aidman, A. (2000). Children's online privacy. *Educational Leadership, 58*(2), 46–47.

American Civil Liberties Union of Washington. (2000, March). *Settlement ends attempt to punish student for Web site.* Retrieved August 17, 2001, from the World Wide Web: http://www.aclu-wa.org/issues/students/Emmett-Kentlake.Student.Release3.30.00.html

Bielefield, A., & Cheeseman, L. (1997). *Technology and copyright law: A guide for the library, research and teaching professions.* New York: Neal-Schuman Publishers, Inc.

Cate, F. H. (1997). *Privacy in the Information Age.* Washington, DC: Brookings Institute Press.

Children's Online Privacy Protection Act of 1998. (1998). Federal Trade Commission. Retrieved from the World Wide Web: http://www.ftc.gov/ogc/coppa1.htm

Clark, R. (1999). *A study to identify levels of use and stages of concern in the adoption of new information technologies for classroom instruction by Pennsylvania business education teachers.* Unpublished doctoral dissertation, Temple University, Philadelphia.

Copyright law of the United States of America and related laws contained in Title 17 of the United States Code. (2000, April). Washington, DC: United States Copyright Office, Library of Congress. Retrieved August 17, 2001, from the World Wide Web: http://www.loc.gov/copyright/title17/

Crystal, J., Geide, C. A., & Salpeter, J. (2000). The concerned educator's guide to safety and cyber-ethics. *Technology & Learning, 21*(4), 26.

Federal Trade Commission. (1999, October 20). *New rule will protect privacy of children online.* Washington, DC: Author. Retrieved August 17, 2001, from the World Wide Web: http://www.ftc.gov/opa/1999/9910/childfinal.htm

Ferrera, G. R., Lichtenstein, S. D., Reder, M. E. K., August, R., & Schiano, W. T. (2001). *CyberLaw: Text and cases.* Cincinnati, OH: South-Western College Publishing/Thompson Learning.

Flowers, B. F., & Rakes, G. C. (2000). Analysis of acceptable use policies regarding the Internet in selected K–12 schools. *Journal of Research on Computing in Education, 32*(3), 351–365.

Guerard, E. B. (2000, July 31). *eSchool News online.* Retrieved August 19, 2001, from the World Wide Web: http://www.eschoolnews.org/news/show/Story.cfm?ArticleID=1340

Hazelwood School District et al. v. Kuhlmeier et al., No. 86-836 484 U.S. 260 (Supreme Court of the United States 1988). Retrieved August 17, 2001, from the World Wide Web: http://www.bc.edu/bc_org/avp/cas/comm/free_speech/hazelwood.html

Howie, M. F. (1999). Copyright in the school domain. In *Legal issues & educational technology: A school leader's guide*. Alexandria, VA: National School Boards Association.

Internet acceptable use: Charlotte-Mecklenburg Board of Education policy (6160). (1998). Charlotte, NC: Charlotte-Mecklenburg Schools. Retrieved from the World Wide Web: http://www.cms.k12.nc.us/AUP.html

Internet acceptable use policy, Lexington, Massachusetts. (1994, March). Lexington, MA: Lexington Public Schools. Retrieved from the World Wide Web: http://www.sturtevant.com/lextech/aup.htm

J. S. v. Bethlehem Area School District, 37 SLIE No. 71. (Pennsylvania Commonwealth Court 2000).

Kaplan, C. S. (2000). Ruling says parents have right to see list of sites students visit. *Cyber Law Journal, The New York Times on the Web*. Retrieved August 17, 2001, from the World Wide Web: www.nytimes.com/2000/11/10/technology/10CYBERLAW.html

Lan, J., & Dagley, D. (1999). Teaching via the Internet: A brief review of copyright law and legal issues. *Educational Technology Review, 11,* 27.

Landwehr, A. (2000). A student's right to freedom of speech in light of Henerey v. city of St. Charles school district. *Journal of Law and Education, 29*(3), 393–397.

Lewis, S. D., & McGrew, L. G. (2000, February). Teaching the perils of e-mail. *Business Education Forum, 54*(3), 26–27.

Lifto, D. (2001, January). Working in cyberspace: What school employees need to know about e-mail and the Internet. *Electronic School, 36–37.* Retrieved August 17, 2001, from the World Wide Web: http://www.electronic-school.com/2001/01/0101f6.html

Lockhart, W. B., Kamisar, Y., & Choper, J. H. (1967). *Constitutional law: Cases-comments-questions*. St. Paul, MN: West Publishing Co.

M-DCPS acceptable use policy for the exploration and utilization of the Internet as a tool for learning. (1996, October 23). Miami, FL: Miami-Dade County Public Schools. Retrieved from the World Wide Web: http://www.dadeschools.net/aup/

National Center for Education Statistics. (2000). *Teachers' tools for the 21st century: A report on teachers' use of technology* (NCES 2000–102). Washington, DC: U.S. Department of Education/Office of Educational Research and Improvement Publication. Retrieved August 17, 2001, from the World Wide Web: http://nces.ed.gov/pubs2000/2000102A.pdf

Policies Commission for Business and Economic Education. (2000). Statement no. 66: This we believe about electronic business in business education. *Business Education Forum, 55*(1), 12–14. Retrieved August 7, 2001, from the World Wide Web: http://www.nbea.org/curfpolicy.html

School law information exchange. (2001). *Pennsylvania School Board Solicitors Association, 38*(42). (Killion v. Franklin Regional School District, March 21, 2001).

Simpson, C. (1997). *Copyright for school: A practical guide* (2nd ed.). Worthington, OH: Linworth Publishing, Inc.

Smerdon, B., Cronen, S., Lanahan, L., Anderson, J., Iannotti, N., & Angeles, J. (2000). *Teachers' tools for the 21st century: A report on teachers' use of technology*. (NCES

2000-102). Washington, DC: U.S. Department of Education, National Center for Education Statistics.

Teicher, J. (1999). An action plan for smart Internet use. *Educational Leadership*, pp. 70–74.

Tinker et al. v. Des Moines Independent Community School District et al., No. 21 393 U.S. 503 (Supreme Court of the United States 1969). Retrieved August 17, 2001, from the World Wide Web: http://www.bc.edu/bc_org/avp/cas/comm/free_speech/tinker.html

U.S. Information Infrastructure Task Force. (1995). *Intellectual property and the national information infrastructure: The report of the working group on intellectual property rights.* Washington, DC: Working Group on Intellectual Property Rights.

Westin, A. F. (1967). Privacy and freedom. In F. Cate (Ed.), (1997). *Privacy in the Information Age* (p. 22). Washington, DC: Brookings Institute Press.

Online Investing, Shopping, and Personal Finance

Sheryl Piening
Southeast Community College
Milford, Nebraska

Beth A. Deinert
Southeast Community College
Milford, Nebraska

Research completed during the past several years and current statistics on the nation's saving and debt rates have brought national attention to the need for personal finance instruction. In 1997 and 2000 the Jump$tart Coalition for Personal Financial Literacy surveyed twelfth graders to measure their knowledge of personal finance basics. In 1997 the average score was 57.3 percent; in 2000 the average score was 51.9 percent (Jump$tart Coalition, 2000a). Clearly, the need to improve financial literacy has not been met. At the same time, technology has increased the options for individuals to make personal financial decisions by investing, shopping, and participating in other activities online.

In what ways can business educators integrate technology into the teaching and learning of personal finance? Technology has not changed the key areas of study in personal finance, which include financial planning, banking, consumer purchases, credit, investments, risk management, tax strategies, and estate planning. Technology has, however, affected the terminology, the processes, and the challenges of completing consumer transactions in a competent and safe manner.

Business educators continue to play a key role in delivering personal finance education and facilitating the application of this knowledge. The purpose of this chapter is to help teachers integrate technology into instruction. The chapter begins with financial literacy: What is its current status? What is the status of educational interventions? The major areas of personal finance—financial planning, banking, credit, online shopping, online investing, and taxes—are discussed from a technological perspective. The chapter ends with a discussion of fraud and safety in online consumer activities. Suggested Internet sites, as well as student activities, should help teachers improve financial literacy while integrating technology in instruction.

STATUS OF FINANCIAL LITERACY

Edward M. Gramlich (2000), Federal Reserve Board governor, stated in remarks prepared for the Georgia Consortium for Personal Financial Literacy:

> ... [T]he free market works best if consumers make informed financial decisions about savings, borrowing, investing, and banking. ... Evidence suggests that many families are not well informed about the financial marketplace .... For these present and future families, financial literacy could improve their economic well being by helping them set financial goals, engage in financial planning, and build assets.

The status of the nation's financial literacy clearly shows the need for educational intervention, and there are several areas of the school curriculum where intervention could take place. According to Dara Duguay, executive director of the Jump$tart Coalition, only a few states include personal finance in their curriculum standards. In addition, only 13 states require students to take a course in economics before graduation. Two reasons given for not requiring personal finance courses for graduation are that the curriculum is already full and that parents are responsible for teaching personal finance concepts (Jump$tart, 2000a). However, surveys show that many adults do not fare any better than teenagers on tests of economic literacy knowledge. The National Council on Economic Education (1999) released survey results showing that most U.S. adults and students flunked a basic economics test.

Although improving personal finance literacy is a component of the efforts of the National Council on Economic Education, most economics and personal finance courses differ in their emphasis. Economics courses focus on economic systems and the utilization of resources within those systems. Personal finance courses focus on individual and family choices about using financial resources. Because government and business decisions affect the use of resources by individuals and families, and the choices of individuals and families affect business and government decisions, educating students in both sets of concepts is essential for ensuring the success of individuals and society.

THE ROLE OF BUSINESS EDUCATION

Business educators are committed to improving financial literacy. In 2001 The Policies Commission for Business and Economic Education reiterated this long-standing commitment:

> Financial education issues have been given new emphasis by enhanced use of technology, an ever-changing global economy, and recognition of the need for lifelong learning. ... **We Believe That** business educators should be given responsibility for coordinating the financial education curriculum.

Business programs must provide the foundation for personal and business financial education. (pp. 1–2)

The *National Standards for Business Education* (National Business Education Association, 2001) for personal finance specifically state that students should be able to "function as economically literate citizens in domestic and international venues [and] … select and apply technology tools for making personal and business decisions" (p. viii).

Achieving these standards requires both curricular and instructional approaches. Before designing courses or units on personal finance, business educators should review the complete economics and personal finance section of the national standards. In addition, business educators should review their state and local economics and personal finance standards.

Personal finance may be added to the curriculum by (a) developing a course of study taught by a teacher in one department; (b) drawing on various disciplines through a team approach; (c) incorporating consumer education throughout numerous courses; and/or (d) involving the entire school system, community, and parents through a school-to-career partnership approach (Karjala & Pagel, 1998).

Teaching Personal Finance Concepts

Business educators know that when students apply the knowledge being taught, retention levels increase. The information gathered by the Jump$tart Coalition supports the applied approach to learning. According to Lewis Mandell, researcher for the financial literacy surveys conducted by the Coalition:

> Knowledge of personal finance is not something students can develop by memorizing terms and phrases. It's a skill that students learn when given the opportunity to apply concepts and practices as part of a thoughtfully designed curriculum. (Aversa, 2000, p. D1)

Students with practical experience scored slightly higher on the surveys than those without that experience (Jump$tart Coalition, 2000a & 2000b). Observing parents and having access to the tools, however, is not enough. Students might use a checking account, make purchases, and use a charge card. But without proper training, mismanagement can easily occur.

With the accessibility of the Internet, students in today's classrooms can take on more active roles in the learning process. Teachers can use the Internet to gather information, develop course materials, and locate actual lesson plans. Students can use the Internet to gather information, compare prices and services, perform calculations, and participate in simulations. Although many students are expert Internet surfers, they need structure, direction, and outcome expectations for specific online activities to yield learning benefits.

TECHNOLOGY AND PERSONAL FINANCE CONCEPTS

Although the concepts of personal finance have not, in principle, changed, technology has introduced new terminology and methods of operation for banking, shopping, credit, investing, and other activities. Financial planning, although not inherently a technology-related task, can be facilitated by technology.

Financial Planning

According to Mandell, of the Jump$tart Coalition, "In the financial world, there's so much choice it's bewildering. If people are well informed, they can take advantage of the choices; if not, they become vulnerable" (Aversa, 2000, p. D1). Most personal finance educators recommend that individuals start by constructing a financial plan that realistically looks at available income, necessary and discretionary expenditures, and financial goals. This is an excellent starting place for students, and teachers have many instructional options.

STUDENT ACTIVITY

Financial Planning Spreadsheet

Have students discuss what will be required financially when they move from their parents' homes to apartments, dormitories, or other locations when they graduate from school. Following the discussion, have students create a spreadsheet to list all the expenses they will have. Students should use the Web to find the costs of these items and then fill them in on the spreadsheet. They should then total up the cost of living on their own.

This exercise can be extended to the revenue side by having students identify how they will pay the costs associated with living on their own. This information can be added to the spreadsheet as well.

Note. This activity was created by Shawna Koger, a business educator in the Arlington Public Schools, Arlington, Nebraska.

Besides using the spreadsheet application, teachers can expose students to personal financial planning resources that allow them to develop a budget, write checks, track expenses, and prepare personal financial statements. (See Creating a Budget Student Activity.)

Banking

No banking unit is complete without a discussion of electronic money. Although several forms of electronic banking have existed for about 30 years, consumers have been reluctant to give up their currency and checks. Currency still accounts for 87 percent of the number of payments. Electronic payments account for only 3 percent of the total number of transactions but nearly 90 percent of the dollar value of transactions in the United States (Federal Reserve Bank of Chicago, 1998).

Personal finance software may include access to online banking, but the instructor might find it difficult to provide a hands-on class activity. As an alternative, business

STUDENT ACTIVITY

Creating a Budget

Ask student to select an occupation that they plan to pursue after graduation from high school or college. Students should determine a realistic entry-level salary for that occupation in the area where they plan to live and complete a realistic budget including mandatory deductions for withholding and FICA taxes. For budgeting purposes most students should calculate federal withholding at 15.00 percent, state withholding at the appropriate percentage, and FICA tax at 7.65 percent. Develop 10 typical monthly expenses for the students to address. If budgeting software is available, this is the time to demonstrate it and have students use it for their budgets. Whether or not dedicated budgeting software is available, there are a number of Web resources for budgeting including the following:

- The Chicago Federal Reserve Bank provides both advice and forms for financial planning and budgeting through its Project Money$mart (http://www.chicagofed.org/consumerinformation/projectmoneysmart/budgetingandsaving.cfm) and an online budget worksheet (http://www.chicagofed.org/consumerinformation/projectmoneysmart/budgetworksheetns.cfm#budgeting).
- Creditmania.Com at http://www.creditmania.com/budget.asp includes information about credit cards, online banking, and online investing.
- The National Foundation for Credit Counseling site at http://www.nfcc.org includes information on debt management and related news stories.

educators can invite bankers to demonstrate online banking in the classroom. Teachers should also encourage students to share their experiences. This will help correlate home activities with what students learn about personal finance concepts in class. Students can also explore online banking by participating in the Exploring Online Banking Student Activity.

STUDENT ACTIVITY

Exploring Online Banking

Have students compare traditional banking activities to those performed online. Then ask students to visit Web sites to examine what electronic services different banks offer to customers. Ask students to evaluate the banking sites for features that encourage customers to conduct their banking business online or discourage them from doing so.

It may be effective to combine this activity with a visit from a local banker who can discuss online banking. For the activity, students can ask questions about consumer acceptance, user privacy, operational ease, merchant acceptability (whether merchants are structured for online transactions), and security. Doing so will help structure an otherwise open-ended online banking lesson.

Consumers must be familiar with terms and acronyms used in electronic banking. The Federal Reserve Bank of Chicago (1998) and the Federal Deposit Insurance

Corporation (FDIC) (1998), sources for the material in Table 1, provide many reports for consumers on electronic funds transfer (EFT) and other processes involved in online transactions.

Table 1. Electronic Funds Transfer Acronyms and Terms

Acronym	Explanation
ACH	The Automated Clearinghouse (ACH) is a service provided by Federal Reserve banks and their branches. Instead of clearing paper checks, this service clears direct deposits and electronic bill payments.
ATM	Automatic teller machines (ATMs) provide banking services, such as processing deposits, providing cash, transferring funds between accounts, and paying bills and loans. To activate an ATM, the user inserts an access card (ATM card) into the machine and enters a personal identification number (PIN).
EFT	Electronic funds transfer (EFT) systems move funds in and out of accounts using electronic impulses.
EFT '99	EFT '99 refers to federal legislation requiring that by January 2, 1999, most federal payments, such as Social Security payments, be made electronically.
PIN	The personal identification number (PIN) is a sequence of digits used to verify the identity of an account holder.
POS	The Point of Sale (POS) system is a system of terminals that debits or charges a customer's account and credits or pays a merchant's account to effect payment for purchases at retail establishments.
Terms	**Explanation**
Smart Card	A smart card is a card with an embedded computer chip that can contain a variety of information, including financial, health, educational, and security information. The information can be stored and processed.In 1996 approximately 805 million smart cards had been issued and an estimated 2.8 billion were to be distributed in 2000. A smart card often requires the use of a PIN number. The dollar value of a smart card can be "reloaded." The smart card can also be used for identification purposes. An example is an electronic student ID card. The card can be scanned for identification when the student checks out library books and scanned for a dollar amount when the student eats at the school cafeteria.
Stored-Value Card	A stored-value card is embedded with a magnetic strip or a computer chip that can store a predetermined amount of value. An electronic gift card is a stored-value card.

As part of their personal finance education, students should complete bank reconciliation problems. These can be completed with pen and paper, then completed on financial planning software or using predesigned spreadsheet files. Teachers should encourage students to extend the notion of reconciliation to credit card accounts.

To answer the many questions that arise about banking, students can be engaged in some Internet activities focusing on the history of banking. The How and Why Does Banking Work Student Activities will have an added benefit of reinforcing students' research skills.

STUDENT ACTIVITY

How and Why Does Banking Work
Assign teams of two or three students to research various topics, such as the history of banking, the history of money, the Federal Reserve System, the security of banking online, types of services available online, and new terms. Give students the task of locating information on the Internet and summarizing it for a class report. Have students either submit written reports or give oral and slide presentations.

Excellent Web sites for the study of banking include
• The Federal Reserve System at http://www.federalreserve.gov/
• The FDIC at http://www.fdic.gov/regulations/information/
• FDIC's Federal Deposit Insurance Information site at http://www2.fdic.gov/edie/
• The American Bankers Association at http://www.aba.com (select the "Consumer Connection" link for personal finance information)

Credit
Americans are drowning in debt. By the end of 2000, total household debt had topped 100 percent of disposable annual income. In 2000 the average credit cardholder carried nine cards in his or her wallet and had an outstanding balance of $4,400. Personal savings were at an all-time low. Students start their credit card experience early and charge often. The average undergraduate owed $2,748 on credit cards as well as an average $13,500 in student loans at public institutions (Lim & Benjamin, 2001).

The economy depends on credit, and the consumer must understand his or her rights and responsibilities when using this tool. The student should know how to estimate interest charges and loan payment amounts to determine whether or not a loan fits within his or her budget. The student can use a financial calculator on the Internet, payment functions in a spreadsheet application, or a loan table to calculate interest charges and loan payments. The loan tables and financial calculators found on the Internet do not provide all the figures in one location; however, they can give useful results. Spreadsheet functions make assumptions that students must understand to use the spreadsheet competently, but may not understand at the time of instruction. The benefit of using a table is that it gives the borrower a close estimate of the interest charges, monthly payment, and the total repayment amount. The loan table amount may differ slightly from the actual loan amount because of additional loan cost charges.

Students may want to make a copy of the loan table to use when contemplating future credit expenditures. Students can do research on the Internet for information on various credit topics including credit rights, responsibilities, reports, and protection. Students can then share that information informally with the class and/or prepare short, written reports. Teachers can augment this activity by inviting speakers from consumer credit counseling services.

The following Web sites have information about loans and credit:

- The National Institute for Consumer Education at http://www.nice.emich.edu/ education.cfm has lessons that include learning objectives, background information, discussion questions, an activity, and sources of additional information.
- The Moneymanagement.Com site at http://www.moneymanagement.org/ has a calculator for determining the amount of a loan and interest and for figuring debt ratios.
- The Federal Reserve Board's consumer site at http://www.federalreserve.gov/ consumers.html has banking, credit, home mortgage, and vehicle-leasing information.
- The National Foundation for Credit Counseling at www.nfcc.org/ has information on debt management and related news stories.
- The National Credit Counseling Services at http://www.nccs.org has activities and informational news releases.

Online Shopping

The Census Bureau ("Q1 Sales," 2001) reported that in the first quarter of 2001, total electronic commerce sales had reached $6.994 billion. Although this figure represented only 0.9 percent of total retail sales, total electronic commerce sales were up 33.5 percent from the first quarter of 2000. Young people represented a growing percentage of online shoppers. According to Nickleodeon and Harris Interactive ("Q1 Sales," 2001), 26 percent of young people ages 13 to 18 went online to shop in 2000.

As more young people spend more time online and make online purchases, business educators must include information about using this shopping source. The same principles for making wise consumer purchasing decisions apply to all purchases, whether they are retail, home shopping, catalog, or online purchases. Course information on online consumer purchases should include information about comparison shopping, the pros and cons of shopping online, how to determine the legitimacy of Web sites, and how to order and pay through a secure sight.

STUDENT ACTIVITY

Using Loan Tables

Have student use a loan table to compute interest, monthly payment, and total cost of repayment for purchasing anything from small credit card purchases to a car or a house. The best tools to use in calculating loan amounts are a copy of a loan table (Table 2), a calculator, and a list of directions (Table 3).

Table 2. Monthly Payments for a $1,000 Loan

Months to Maturity	7%	9%	10%	12%	15%	18%	21%	24%
12	86.53	87.45	87.92	88.85	90.26	91.68	93.11	94.56
18	58.68	59.60	60.06	60.98	62.38	63.81	65.24	66.70
24	44.77	45.68	46.14	47.07	48.49	49.92	51.39	52.87
30	36.43	37.35	37.81	38.75	40.18	41.64	43.13	44.65
36	30.88	31.80	32.27	33.21	34.67	36.15	37.68	39.23
48	23.95	24.89	25.36	26.33	27.83	29.37	30.97	32.60
60	19.80	20.76	21.25	22.24	23.79	25.39	27.05	28.77
72	17.05	18.03	18.53	19.55	21.15	22.81	24.57	26.33
Years to Maturity								
15	8.99	10.14	10.75	12.00	14.00	16.10	18.34	20.58
30	6.65	8.05	8.78	10.29	12.64	15.07	17.54	20.02

Table 3. Calculating Monthly Payment, Total Repayment, and Finance Charges

Step 1	To estimate the monthly payment, locate months to maturity and follow that line to the appropriate APR. Note: This chart is for a monthly payment based on a loan of $1,000. To find the monthly payment for a loan of more than $1,000, multiply the monthly payment times the amount of the loan divided by $1,000.
Step 2	To compute the total repayment of the loan plus interest, multiply the monthly payment times the number of months to maturity.
Step 3	To compute the amount of the finance charge, subtract the loan amount from the total repayment amount.

Pros and cons of shopping online. According to Consumer Reports Online (1998), consumers who shop online reported that they do so because online shopping (a) is convenient, (b) may save time, (c) expands the shopping experience, and (d) may give shoppers added perks, such as discounts and announcements of available merchandise and services.

Consumers who do not shop online gave the following reasons for not doing so:

- The online store can show only a picture of the merchandise. The shopper cannot feel, touch, smell, or taste the products they are viewing.
- There may be long, technical delays or the modem may be slow.
- Finding a particular product or store might be difficult if the shopper does not have the exact Web address.
- The shopper may be concerned about the security and legitimacy of the Web site.
- The consumer may fear credit card theft or have concerns about protecting the privacy of personal information.

To address concerns about the safety, security, and legitimacy of Web sites, business educators can discuss a number of issues with students.

Credibility and legitimacy of Web sites. Having a Web site alone does not make a business credible or legitimate, but some questions about appearance coupled with questions about other characteristics of the site can help students make better decisions about shopping online.

Does the Web site have a professional appearance? The more professionally designed the Web site is, the more money the merchant probably spent on preparing the site. The consumer should keep in mind, though, that appearance is not an indicator of the credibility of the site. If the "store" is unfamiliar, students can research it through the Better Business Bureau at http://www.BBBonline.org/.

Does the merchant have a domain name? Merchants have greater credibility if they have their own domain names. A domain is a Web address designated to a specific merchant such as "mystore.com." If the merchant uses free Web space, such as "mystore@hotair.com," consumers would be wise to use extra caution.

There are a number of other items that consumers should consider: Does the site have a digital certificate issued by a trusted certification authority? Does the site provide information about its security? How can the consumer contact the merchant if a problem occurs with the purchase? Does the merchant provide a phone number, fax number, street address, and e-mail address? Does the merchant offer a satisfaction-guaranteed policy? Is there a statement about the return policy? (Fiore, 1998) What about turn-around time? Does the site state how long the purchaser might have to wait before receiving the product? Does the site participate in any programs that permit the consumer to lodge complaints if privacy or good business practices are violated, such as the Better Business Bureau's privacy and practice seal programs (http://www.bbbonline.org)? In addition to these items, students who shop online should examine the payment methods and protocols of sites.

Paying for online purchases. When paying for items or services over the Internet, consumers must confirm that the payment method uses a safe means to transfer funds from a purchaser to the merchant.

Encryption is a technology that allows online merchants to transmit data in a secure manner by taking readable data and "scrambling" or mathematically disguising it during transmission. This process is designed to prevent Internet transmissions from being intercepted by users who should not have access to payment information like credit card numbers.

Users of most current Web browsers already have encryption technology in the browser through a Secure Sockets Layer (SSL) protocol. The Netscape Security Center provides more information about this technology at http://home.netscape.com/security/techbriefs/ssl.html. Customers who regularly access financial accounts can, and probably should, download versions of browser software that have stronger encryption technology than the "default" browser. While SSL is a general security technology, the Secure Electronic Transfer (SET) protocol provides additional security measures specifically for online payments. The Secure Electronic Transaction organization provides more information at http://www.setco.org/how_set_works.html.

Because of risks to consumers, a number of payment products and services have emerged to provide secure payment environments. CyberCash (http://www.cybercash.com) is a software service with an encryption transaction scheme that enables online purchasers to use credit cards and "Internet checks" (money that is electronically transferred from the consumer's account to the merchant's account) in a secure manner. Some payment systems give consumers new ways to carry money for online purchases. The software installs a "software wallet" on your computer. BlueMoney Wallet (BlueMoney, 1999) is the first Internet wallet that operates without software. BlueMoney wallet users must register and have an SSL browser. The wallet is unique because it is on the Internet; therefore, the consumer can make purchases from any computer terminal with Internet access.

Person-to-person (P2P) payment services enable purchasers to pay for products or services without having to write checks or provide credit card information. A purchaser can open a P2P account at a Web site and deposit money into the account using a credit card, debit card, or checking account. The consumer then pays for purchases on the Internet with funds from his or her P2P account. These funds are accessed through e-mail. Consumers may assume some risks if payments for purchases are made through e-mail, a nonsecure transmission. In addition, according to Fiore (2000), while a consumer can deposit money into the account with his or her credit card, the purchase is made with the P2P account money—not the credit card; therefore, the consumer may give up his or her "billing dispute rights."

STUDENT ACTIVITIES

Online Shopping

Activity 1. Have students shop for a particular item on the Internet. Students will not actually order the item; however, they can access information about price, quality, methods of payment, guarantee, return policy, contact information, and payment security.

Activity 2. Have students comparison shop for a particular item at different Web sites.

Activity 3. Have students gather information about various Web payment methods. New methods are constantly being developed.

The following Web sites are good starting points for student research:
- The Chicago Federal Reserve Bank's Payment Systems Resource Center at http://chicagofed.org/paymentsystems/payoverviews.cfm
- Online Shopping with Frank Fiore at http://onlineshopping.about.com

Online Investing

Trading and investing online can save investors time and money, but do not eliminate the necessity of doing research to make informed investment decisions. Investors must still establish specific investment goals that fit within their budgets. In addition, investors must be knowledgeable about various types of investments and understand the risks and benefits of each type. Regardless of the investment medium, whether in person, by mail or telephone, or via the Internet, investors need to ask some questions. The following questions were adapted from a comprehensive list provided to investors by the U. S. Securities and Exchange Commission (2001 a, 2001b, & 2001c):

- Is the investment registered with the SEC and your state securities agency?
- How does the investment match your financial objectives?
- What are the costs to buy, hold, and sell this investment?
- Where is the company incorporated?
- What are the risks associated with this investment?
- How can you get more information about this investment?
- How long has the company been in business?

In addition to asking questions about the investment, investors should evaluate the investment offer in the same way they would any other online purchase. In addition, potential investors should seek the advice of someone knowledgeable about investing, such as a broker, an accountant, or a banker. (See Learning to Invest Student Activity.)

STUDENT ACTIVITIES

Learning to Invest

Activity 1. Have students research an investment opportunity online and answer the above questions.

Activity 2. Have students research the benefits and risks of various types of investments—from CDs to trading on the stock market.

Activity 3. Enroll students in the Stock Market Game at http://www.smg.2000.org/.

Activity 4. Enroll students in a stock simulation at the StocksQuest Web site at http://stocksquest.thinkquest.org/C001759/.

The following Web sites are useful for the suggested activities and for finding investment information:

- Investor's Clearinghouse at http://www.investoreducation.org has calculators and sample investment quizzes.
- Financial Literacy at http://www.fl2010.org provides a downloadable teaching guide, *Basics of Saving and Investing*, and has a calendar for professional development activities.
- The Federal Trade Commission at http://www.ftc.gov includes information about consumer education and a variety of consumer protection laws.
- The University of Omaha site at http://ecedweb.unomaha.edu/teach.htm includes a glossary of investment terms and many useful teaching tools for personal finance education.
- The American Savings Education Council at http://www.asec.org has great resources and activities including the "Ballpark Estimate" for constructing a retirement savings plan.

Note. Activity 4 was created by Chris Gross-Rhode, a business educator at North Bend Central High School in North Bend, Nebraska.

Taxes

Starting with their very first paychecks, students will pay taxes. As full-time students with summer or part-time jobs, students may be exempt from both federal and state withholding. However, they will not be exempt from mandatory FICA payroll deductions. According to research conducted by the Jump$tart Coalition (2000a and 2000b), most students do not understand the impact of taxes on take-home pay.

The material in *Understanding Taxes*, prepared by the U.S. Internal Revenue Service (IRS), provides excellent teaching material and resources for teaching a high school unit on taxes. The material focuses on the history, fairness, and use of taxes, and includes related terms and problems. The material is available to educators free of charge and can be obtained by contacting a regional IRS office. (See Understanding Taxation Student Activity.)

Internet Fraud

The amount of money consumers lose to Internet fraud is increasing. In 2000 consumers lost more than $3.2 million to Internet fraud. The largest percentage of

STUDENT ACTIVITIES

Understanding Taxation

Activity 1. Have students determine take-home pay in different scenarios. Link the tax unit to the budget unit in the financial planning section.

Activity 2. Have students complete a tax form using a simulated problem or using their own figures.

Activity 3. Have students research uses of local, state, and federal tax money.

The IRS provides teachers with many instructional resources. The TaxI, or Tax Interactive, section of its Web site at http://www.irs.gov/taxi has a "Taxes in U. S. History" module that is useful for instruction and student research.

STUDENT ACTIVITIES

Preventing Internet Fraud

Activity 1. Have students gather information and report on Internet scams. They should be able to describe a scam and its intended victims, how the consumer is "recruited," and what is illegal about the scam. Students can search the Internet in general or they can do targeted research through the Better Business Bureau, the state attorney general's office, and any other consumer protection agencies.

Activity 2. Have students share personal or family experience with Internet fraud or scams.

Activity 3. Have students compile a list of steps that victims of Internet fraud should take and where they can file complaints.Useful Web sites for these activities include the following:

- Internet ScamBusters at http://www.scambusters.com
- Better Business Bureau Online at http://www.BBBonline.org
- The Federal Trade Commission at http://www.ftc.gov
- Internet Fraud Complaint Center, a partnership of the Federal Bureau of Investigation and the National White Collar Crime Center, at http://www.ifccfbi.gov/
- Internet Fraud Watch and the National Fraud Information Center at http://www.fraud.org

fraud, 78 percent, was associated with online auctions. Other top sources of Internet fraud included Internet services, general merchandise retailers, and computer equipment/software retailers. According to the Internet Fraud Watch (http://www.fraud.org/internet/lt00totstats.htm) and the National Consumers League (2001), the top five payment types of those reporting losses from Internet purchases were as follows: money order, 43 percent; check, 30 percent; credit card, 11 percent; cashier's check, 6 percent; and cash, 3 percent.

Swindlers are attracted to the Internet because they can reach thousands of consumers inexpensively, quickly, and anonymously. By the time consumers realize they have a problem, the check or money order has been cashed. The perpetrator "virtually"

STUDENT ACTIVITY

Security

Ask students to gather information and compile a list of tips for safe Internet travel. Then ask students to examine the following terms and definitions:

- Hacker: motivated mostly by curiosity and the challenge of trying to hack into other computer systems; the intent of the hacker is not malicious
- Cracker: a hacker with malicious intent
- Cramming: bogus charges on the phone bill as a result of online activity
- Remote Access Trojan or RAT: viruses that access a computer, usually through e-mail, and make it possible for a cracker to manipulate computer files remotely
- Page-jacking: the use of technological tricks to take Internet surfers to different Web sites against their will
- Pump and dump: the act of hyping a stock in an Internet chat room in order for the price to rise high enough that stock can be sold at a profit

Ask students to discuss how each of these individuals or actions might affect payments made on the Internet. After they have finished their discussion, ask students to modify their guides for safe Internet travel.

vanishes, pulling Web site down in seconds. Sharing tips on how to avoid Internet fraud with students and having them expand the list can help prevent them from becoming victims of fraud. The tips listed below were adapted from recommendations by the Nebraska Attorney General's office (Stenberg, 2001), the Nebraska Bankers Association (2000), and the National Consumers League (2001). Some of the tips relate to online purchases and others to online activity in general.

SUMMARY

The information learned in economics, personal finance, and consumer education courses can make a difference in the financial future of young people. Recent research has shown the need for improving financial literacy. Developments in electronic commerce have increased the need to know how procedures, risks, and methods of protection have been affected by technology. Students may experience the most significant learning outcomes when this education is started at a young age and when the information is infused within the entire curriculum.

Students need an understanding of financial planning, banking, credit, purchasing, investing, and taxes. They also need to understand how technology has modified some of these concepts and adopt sound practices for online shopping, online payments, and online investing. They especially need to understand the efforts that could be made to defraud them and how they can avoid being victimized.

Business educators can take a leadership role in implementing a coordinated effort for financial literacy in their school districts. As they plan or modify their curricula, business educators should review the national standards in economics and

Tips For Online Shopping and Other Online Activities

For general safety and privacy:

- If you are under the age of 18, always check with a parent before giving out personal or family information.
- Look for privacy policies when you enter a Web site. Never reveal checking account numbers, credit card numbers, or other personal financial data at any Web site or online service location—unless you are sure you know where this information will be directed.
- Do not give your Internet account password to anyone, even someone claiming to be from your online service. If anyone obtains your password, they can use your account, and you will receive the bill.
- If you are asked for your phone number or home address, use caution.
- Do not download programs to see pictures, hear music, play games, or get other features from Web sites you are not familiar with.
- Invest in virus detection software. If you can afford to do so, invest in firewall software that blocks unwanted intrusions from the Internet.

For shopping safety and credit protection:

- Do business only with companies you know and trust, particularly online. Make sure that any online company has an actual physical location. Test the phone number and mailing address. Check with the phone company to verify that the number is registered with that company and not "John Doe." Look for a digital certificate from a trusted certification authority.
- When transacting business online, make sure your browser's padlock or key icon is active, which is indicated by its being closed, or locked.
- Before making a purchase, understand the offer and ask for clarifying information. Be sure you know what is being sold, the total price, the delivery date, the return and cancellation policy, and the terms of any guarantee. The Federal Telephone and Mail Order Rule, which also covers orders by computer, requires goods and services to be delivered by the promised time or, if none is stated, within thirty days.
- If an offer on the Internet sounds too good to be true, it probably is. Don't accept it.
- Check references. Contact the local Better Business Bureau or state attorney general's office to see if there are any claims on file about an offer or company. Use the Better Business Bureau site at http://www.BBBonline.org when shopping online.
- Pay by credit card through a secured site. When a credit card is used and the consumer has a problem with a purchase, the consumer does not have to pay for the purchase while the dispute is being investigated.
- Print the order information so that you have documentation if you need it.

personal finance for business education, their state standards, and the many resources available for instruction. Teachers can share the statistics and resources from this chapter to convince parents, administrators, and school board members of the vital need for financial literacy. Teachers should also use the information from Policy Statement No. 69 on the role of business education in financial education. That policy states: "A free enterprise economy offers opportunities for financially competent people to be successful, while those without financial skills will struggle with the 'dollars-and-cents' aspect of life" (Policies Commission, 2001).

Many school hours are spent developing the knowledge and skills to have a successful career and earn an income. To be financially independent, though, students must develop consumer knowledge and skills, as well. The school system that devotes disproportionately large amounts of time to preparing students for careers without devoting adequate time to preparing students to manage their financial resources is only completing half the job. To prepare students for the future, schools must teach personal finance.

REFERENCES

Aversa, J. (2000, April 9). High school seniors flunk personal finance. *Lincoln Journal Star*, p. D1.

BlueMoney Software Corporation. (1999). *Network wallet*. Retrieved August 2, 2001 from the World Wide Web: http://www.bluemoney.com/comprod/products/network_wallet.html

Consumer Reports Online. (1998, December). *The pros and cons of shopping online*. Retrieved December 2000 from the World Wide Web: http://www.consumerreports.org/Special/Samples/Reports/9812/shp1.htm

Federal Deposit Insurance Corporation. (1998, June). *Electronic banking: Safety and soundness examination procedures*. Retrieved August 2, 2001, from the World Wide Web: http://www.fdic.gov/regulations/information/electronic/elecbank.pdf

Federal Reserve Bank of Chicago. (1998, July). *Electronic money*. Retrieved August 2, 2001, from the World Wide Web: http://www.chicagofed.org/publications/electronicmoney/electronicmoney.pdf

Fiore, F. (1998, December 28). *Online shopping beginners basics*. Retrieved August 2, 2001, from the World Wide Web: http://onlineshopping.about.com/library/weekly/aa122898.htm

Fiore, F. (2000, October 23). *Person to person payments*. Retrieved August 2, 2001, from the World Wide Web: http//onlineshopping.about.com/library/weekly/aa122898.htm

Gramlich, E. M. (2000, November 21). Remarks by Governor Edward M. Gramlich on financial literacy. Fall Conference of the Georgia Consortium for Personal Financial Literacy, Atlanta, GA. Retrieved August 2, 2001, from the World Wide Web: http://www.federalreserve.gov/boarddocs/speeches/2000/20001121.htm

Jump$tart Coalition for Personal Financial Literacy. (2000a, April 6). *Financial literacy declining among 12th graders: Coalition urges states to include personal finance in curriculum standards*. Retrieved August 2, 2001, from the World Wide Web: http://www.jumpstartcoalition.org/upload/news.cfm?recordid=60

Jump$tart Coalition for Personal Financial Literacy. (2000b, April 6). *2000 Jump$tart questionnaire & results*. Retrieved from the World Wide Web: http://www.jumpstartcoalition.org/upload/news.cfm?recordid=64

Karjala, J., & Pagel, L. G. (1998, April). Personal finance—consumer education at all educational levels. *Business Education Forum, 52*(4), 26–27.

Lim, P. J., & Benjamin, M. (2001, March 19). Drowning in debt. *U.S. News & World Report*, 52–60. Retrieved August 2, 2001, from the World Wide Web: http://www.usnews.com/usnews/issue/010319/debt.htm

National Business Education Association. (2001). *National standards for business education: What America's students should know and be able to do in business* (2nd ed.). Reston, VA: Author.

National Consumers League. (2001). *2000 Internet fraud statistics*. Retrieved May 2001 from the World Wide Web at http://www.fraud.org/news/news.htm

National Council on Economic Education. (1999, April 29). *Major campaign to improve economic literacy among students and adults gets underway*. Retrieved August 2, 2001, from the World Wide Web: http://www.nationalcouncil.org/cel/news.html

Nebraska Bankers Association. (2000, August). *Keep your identity safe* [Brochure]. Lincoln, NE: Author.

Policies Commission for Business and Economic Education. (2001). *Policy statement no. 69: This we believe about the role of business education in financial education.*

Contributions of Research to Teaching Technology

Peter F. Meggison

Massasoit Community College

Brockton, Massachusetts

Probably no other mechanism has contributed more to the advancement of business education than the implementation of sound research findings. Implementing the results of their own research efforts, both formal and informal, and the research efforts of others enables business educators to improve daily classroom performance—whatever form that "classroom" takes. This chapter is designed for the consumer of research—every business educator eager to implement research findings into the emerging content and structure of a changing business education environment.

This chapter examines relevant research findings on methods of teaching technology and the relationship of student attributes to learning technology. Some of this research helps teachers assess the effectiveness of a number of newer teaching approaches when compared to traditional teacher-directed methods. Some studies specifically address the use of technology in delivering instruction. The discussion starts with research on the workplace to provide a context for the other studies.

BUSINESS WORKPLACE NEEDS

Business research provides data about the technology that business education students will find in the work environment and answers questions about the technology skills required to work effectively in that environment.

Technology in the Work Environment

Trend studies provide data on the technologies that will be present in the workplace of the future. Studies of employees portray how contemporary employees have worked with the technology currently at hand. Together the two types of studies reflect what is required to achieve maximum contributions from technology.

The Office of 2005

Officeteam (2000), which declares itself to be "the world's largest leader in specialized administrative staffing," conducted primary and secondary research to ascertain what the office of the future—the office of 2005—might be like. The study included a survey of 1,400 chief information officers throughout the United States and in-depth interviews with a variety of technology and workplace experts. In the office of 2005

- Three technologies will be ubiquitous in the workplace—wireless communication, voice-activated technology, and personal digital assistants.
- Employees will work from virtually any location using wireless, multifunctional technology.
- Computers will cost less, be faster and more powerful, have more functionality, and be lighter and smaller. All types of tools (e.g., cellular phones, electronic organizers, and pagers) will interface with one another as if they were part of a single compact "smart" tool.
- Communication technologies of all types (e.g., voice recognition, real-time video conferencing, cellular telephones, and digital communication devices) will advance as wireless connectivity advances.
- Communication will be transparent, appearing seamless and instantaneous, because wireless computing will focus on connections, not devices like portable PCs, wireless communicators, or smart phones.
- Communications will be recorded in a variety of formats because of advances in storage technology, which will have potentially far-reaching consequences.

This future will bring changes in the way employees will work. How employees fit into the future can be anticipated from studies of employees currently working with technology and employers currently recruiting new employees.

Employee and Employer Studies

Lambrecht, Redmann, and Stitt-Gohdes (2000) conducted a national study using a critical-incident method to identify instances of effective or challenging/problematic work among primary computer users. A primary computer user was defined as an information-processing employee who used a desktop computer for more than 50 percent of his or her job responsibilities. Each of 38 interviewers conducted face-to-face, nondirective interviews with two primary computer users: one employed for at least six months but less than one year and the other employed for at least three years but less than five years.

When asked what they did well in their current jobs, most computer users indicated the ability to demonstrate mastery of computer-based systems or software. Most indicated that they learned informally on the job—by observation and by "picking things up." The chief example of a problem that could not be solved rapidly through one's own expertise was the technical problem, such as a general systems problem or specific software problem. Most employees solved their problems by talking with another person close by or within the firm. The computer users indicated that they felt least competent to learn new software, and the top-ranked experience that would lead these computer users to greater competence was more software or computer training.

The researchers concluded that computer workers needed to work with people and to work independently, the latter being particularly self-evident in the case of software mastery. According to Lambrecht, Redmann, and Stitt-Gohdes (2000),

> The clear message for the business teacher is the need to incorporate such social contexts into their teaching by looking at the social structures of their own classrooms and the opportunities that students have to experience actual business work settings. Using technology means knowing how software works; it also means knowing what a business wants done with the software and whose opinions matter in both judging expectations of work quality and advice for fixing technical breakdowns. (p. 62)

The results of a Center for the Development of Leadership Skills study at Rider University (1999) evidence the continuing dependence of the workplace on technology. In a survey of 428 organizations, computer literacy ranked first in importance among the skills sought in entry-level workers, ahead even of many of the "soft skills" that were also ranked as essential.

End-User Computing Skills

Numerous other studies conducted at the local, regional, and national levels provide data on general and specific end-user computing skills.

Essential computing skills. Entry-level computer skills needed by Fortune 500 and small business employees in Ohio were identified by Olinzock and Lazarony (2001). The researchers cautioned that different entry-level skills may be required depending on the location and size of a business. The following were reported as the most common skills required by the participants in this study: word processing, e-mail, spreadsheet, keyboarding, software, database management, accounting, and scheduling skills.

Arney (1998) examined the computer skills needed by business administration graduates. The 100 largest public businesses in Indiana and the colleges and universities in Indiana offering a baccalaureate degree in business administration were the two populations surveyed. Businesses ranked the following computer applications and skills as most important: spreadsheets, word processing, Windows, keyboarding, and using computers to solve problems. Colleges and universities provided a similar, though not identical, ranking: spreadsheets, word processing, Internet, solving problems with software, and using computers to solve problems.

Henderson (2001) investigated workplace skills and computer literacy skills for entry-level, nonbaccalaureate-degree employees in the computer industry of Silicon Valley, California. Using a Likert-type scale, 116 respondents ranked the importance of computer literacy competencies for entry-level employees. There was unanimous agreement among companies of all sizes in their ranking of the importance of computer skills, as shown in Table 1.

Most organizations offer software-specific training to newly hired employees not familiar with a given software package. In fact, some companies test prospective employees on software applications prior to being hired. However, business graduates are better able to market themselves if they are competent in today's most frequently used software applications.

Spreadsheet competencies. Bush (2001) identified the spreadsheet competencies required by postsecondary business graduates for entry-level managerial positions in business/information systems and accounting. Using a modified Delphi method, a panel of four-year college business educators, accounting managers, and business/ information systems managers responded to a survey in which they identified important spreadsheet competencies. Table 2 includes the 19 competencies—common across the three Delphi panels—that were identified as important.

Table 1. Computer Literacy Competencies

1. Computer literacy (personal computer usage)
2. Ability to use e-mail
3. Understanding of functions and ethical use of computers in society
4. Knowledge of operating system
5. Ability to use the World Wide Web/Internet
6. Ability to use word processing software
7. Ability to use spreadsheet software
8. Ability to use database software

Table 2. Spreadsheet Competencies

1. Copying data with absolute/relative cell references
2. Creating formulas for spreadsheets
3. Printing a worksheet
4. Printing an area of a spreadsheet
5. Changing a cell value
6. Saving to a specific folder/directory
7. Summing a row or column
8. Creating a new spreadsheet
9. Undoing previous actions
10. Creating functions for spreadsheets
11. Entering data into an existing spreadsheet
12. Adding formatting to a cell
13. Creating a chart
14. Cutting/pasting, copying/moving cell contents
15. Changing page orientation
16. Deleting a row or column
17. Formatting cell values
18. Formatting cells
19. Inserting a row or column

Database competencies. Wiedmaier (1997) studied database competencies needed for entry-level employment using a modified Delphi technique. A national panel of 30 individuals from the Association of Records Managers and Administrators and the National Business Education Association responded using a six-point Likert scale. From an original list of 80 competencies, the panel reached consensus on 13 skills necessary for entry-level employment, as listed in Table 3.

Presentation graphics competencies. Alexander (1996) surveyed 306 office

Table 3. Database Competencies

1. Saving a database
2. Entering records into an existing database
3. Selecting drive and directory
4. Printing formatted reports/lists
5. Printing labels
6. Searching for a specific record
7. Copying selected records from one file to another
8. Sorting using multiple relational operators (e.g., AND/OR)
9. Accessing an electronic database
10. Editing/updating queries
11. Using appropriate terminology in context
12. Describing search strategies and using them to solve common information problems
13. Exporting files to use with word processing

professionals sampled from the Professional Secretaries International database and found that the most frequently produced materials were transparencies, handouts, lecture/outline notes, visual slides, audiovisual slides, computer screen displays, and videos. The presentation graphic features most frequently used were clip art graphics, design/style, color, and builds/transitions.

Computer competencies. Groneman (2000) analyzed the demand for computer skills and technologies. A total of 1,006 newspaper want ads from four major newspapers (in Atlanta, Chicago, Los Angeles, and New York) and 22,698 online ads were evaluated. Table 4 presents the top 20 computer skills and technologies ranked by frequency of mention.

Table 4. Top 20 Computer Skills and Technologies

1. UNIX	9. JAVA	17. Web server
2. SQL	10. Cisco	18. Linux
3. Security	11. Intranet	19. Photoshop
4. Windows NT	12. Lotus Notes	20. Visual BASIC
5. C++	13. Microsoft Office	
6. TCP/IP	14. MCSE certification	
7. Internet	15. HTML	
8. A+ certification	16. PERL	

Because the study showed a large number of new Web-related skills and technologies needed by business employees, Groneman suggested that consideration be given to creating new Internet technology or electronic commerce curricula to encompass these emerging skills.

Information systems curriculum content. An international study conducted by Gonzenbach and Davis (1999) examined business employees' opinions about which content areas to include in a collegiate information systems technology curriculum. The 107 respondents were members of the Information Industry Association. Table 5 presents the 13 areas they considered "extremely important."

Table 5. Information Systems Curriculum Content Areas

1. Business communications
2. Telecommunications
3. Programming language(s)
4. Word processing software
5. Database software
6. Groupware and work group computing
7. Project management methodology
8. Information security
9. Disaster prevention/recovery systems
10. Troubleshooting
11. Networks
12. Operating systems
13. Systems analysis and design

Research conducted by businesses and in the business environment provides a profile of workers who, in the near future, will communicate from any location in a seamless, instantaneous manner. Employers will expect employees to use computers to solve problems. Employees will continue to need word processing, spreadsheet,

TEACHING STRATEGY

Using Technology to Solve Problems

Computer instructors often feel that too many components of computer software are taught in isolation. If this is so, students may be unprepared to use multifaceted features to solve problems. Bauer (2001) described a project-based learning activity in which students create their own business (one that interests them and with which they are familiar). Students must connect the business purpose of software to real-world settings. Phases of the project include word processing, spreadsheet use, publishing, database, presentations, and Web design.

With guidelines for the types of documents and related materials to include in each phase of the project, students must build the business. For example, in the publishing phase, students promote their businesses by producing specially designed brochures, cards, and similar materials. The key to the success of this learning activity is that students explore ways of using business software to ensure the success of their "own" businesses. The project lends itself to effective assessment because a rubric can be developed for each phase of the project.

database, and presentation skills. Added to this base are competencies in Internet applications and other Web-related competencies such as network operating system knowledge, programming languages, and a variety of other competencies. The major content areas for collegiate information systems students involve business communications and telecommunications.

METHODS OF TEACHING

What does research reveal about effective instructional methods and materials? The comparative studies selected for review take traditional, teacher-directed instruction as a point of departure for evaluating the effectiveness of alternative approaches. Several studies examine the minimalist philosophy of designing instruction. Other studies present findings relevant to using the Internet in instruction.

Multimedia and Traditional Delivery

Schramm and McEwen (1997) examined the effectiveness of multimedia versus traditional instruction in teaching introductory computer classes. Half of the classes were taught in a traditional fashion with the use of handouts, hands-on activities, the chalkboard, as well as lectures. The rest of the classes were taught using multimedia (PowerPoint slides and computer animation and tutorials). The course was divided into eight units, and the instructor alternated between the two approaches.

Schramm and McEwen reported that students preferred instruction that used multimedia presentation and perceived it to be more effective than traditional instruction in facilitating understanding of computer concepts. The students perceived multimedia instruction as more interesting and effective than traditional instruction in enhancing short-term retention but judged multimedia instruction to be similar to traditional instruction in effecting long-term retention of content. Students perceived both modes of instruction as equally effective in helping them grasp the concepts being presented. Multimedia instruction enhanced academic performance more than the traditional format did. The researchers concluded, "If actual performance on a test is considered more valid than perceptions, then multimedia does present advantages for retention, both short-term and long-term" (Schramm & McEwen, 1997, p. 34).

Parker (2001) studied the effects of different presentation formats on perceptions of football scholarship applicants. This Arizona State University study presented data about a fictitious high school applicant for a football scholarship to three groups of volunteers who rated the football player on a scale of 1 to 7. The first group rated the applicant 4.5 based on statistics presented in typewritten form. The second group rated the applicant 5 based on statistics presented in bar graphs. The third group rated the player 6 based on a PowerPoint presentation using animated bar graphs. The study was replicated using a population of sports fans familiar with sports statistics. The first two groups of sports fans did not differ from the original volunteers in their ratings of the applicant and the PowerPoint presentation, again, received a rating of 6.

Collaborative and Traditional Instruction

Erthal (1998) conducted a quasi-experimental study to determine whether mode of instruction (i.e., lecture, application, or demonstration) and student's preferred learning style were related to success in a computer class. One class used a cooperative learning method, and participants were encouraged to continue this method outside of class. These students were given instructions verbally.

Students in the other class were taught in a traditional manner. They watched the instructor complete an assignment and worked through the assignment as the instructor presented it. They were then responsible for learning and completing assignments on their own. The same instructor was responsible for both groups while all the students completed the same assignments and tests. Common applications such as word processing, spreadsheets, presentation graphics, and Internet use were covered.

Erthal reported that teaching method was unrelated to previous computer class experience, grade point average, or computer ownership. However, teaching method was related to final course grade; in this case, students in the class who were responsible for learning and completing assignments by themselves received higher grades. As a result, computer instructors should incorporate a variety of instructional delivery modes into class presentations, thereby facilitating students' learning and the transfer of the concepts to other tasks. In computer application classes, students should work both in groups and alone to prepare for today's work environment.

Guided Practice and Traditional Instruction

McDonald (1997) studied two methods of teaching spreadsheets. In the guided-practice method group, each student sat at a computer and received hands-on instruction. The second group practiced learning activities independently following instruction in a traditional classroom using the lecture/demonstration method. The instructor used one computer for demonstration purposes in this arrangement.

McDonald found that both methods produced similar results in student performance relative to content knowledge of spreadsheets. The students using the guided-practice method, however, achieved significantly higher skill scores. The researcher concluded that, when teaching brand-specific software, having each student practice at a computer using step-by-step instruction results in higher student skill achievement than independent skill practice. Willoughby (1997) also compared two approaches to teaching spreadsheet software: one utilizing a teacher demonstration method and the other using a hands-on approach. She concluded that students learn similarly regardless of which method is employed.

Systematic and Minimalist Instruction

Lambrecht (1999) examined computer teaching practices in schools judged to be exemplary. Six educational institutions (five community/technical colleges and one technical high school) participated in the study, based on their innovation and responsiveness to diverse students' needs. The researcher used a critical-incident technique to identify significant program aspects and interviewed 40 teachers, students, and employers of program graduates.

In the beginning phases of instruction, the dominant mode of instruction focused on software. At this stage, teachers viewed themselves primarily as software instructors. A systematic, step-by-step process ensured the comprehensive coverage of the software's multifaceted features. Lambrecht contrasts this with the minimalist approach that incorporates a discovery approach to learning software. This approach, if present at all, was evident only in advanced office technology classes.

With the minimalist approach, the learner views the software as necessary to solve a business computer problem. Thus, students learn through their mistakes. Carroll (1990, 1998) found that when transfer of learning to different software and situations is the goal of instruction, the minimalist approach to software instruction is superior to the traditional "push-button" approach, which employs detailed verbiage describing how to execute various computer commands or functions.

Lambrecht recommended closer examination of learning situations in which the minimalist approach is used, as well as investigation of the methods that would ensure that students are engaged in realistic uses of software to solve business problems, produce projects, and evaluate cases.

Minimalist and Traditional Materials

In a quasi-experimental study, Millslagle (1996) compared instructional materials based on minimalist concepts with the traditional, structured materials used in computer applications courses. The minimalist materials attempted to reduce textbook verbiage. Cues to prior knowledge and similarities of computer functions facilitated concept formation. The traditional classes used well-structured textbooks containing step-by-step directions. The study attempted to examine the variation in skill acquisition and transfer of learning. Students using the minimalist materials were encouraged to work in teams at the computer in order to observe and learn from one another.

Millslagle found no significant differences in skill acquisition or transfer of learning between the students using the two sets of materials. The minimalist materials were as effective as the structured materials, and students using the minimalist materials attained the same skill level as traditional students. However, the researcher cautioned that the traditional approach may be more appropriate for teaching software to students with little prior computer software experience. Neither set of materials was superior at enhancing the transfer of skill from one application package to another. However, students learning diverse software over an extended period of time may form a more complete model of software usage that would facilitate transfer as a result of the self-discovery learning inherent in the minimalist approach.

Internet and Traditional Instruction

Wilkinson and Echternacht (1998) conducted one of the first studies of the use of the Internet as a teaching tool in business education classes. The researchers assessed the learning of students in risk management classes, the time they spent on homework, and their attitudes toward subject matter under two homework conditions; one involved Internet activities and the other involved traditional activities.

The researchers sought to determine if there was a significant difference in scores on subject-matter achievement, time spent on homework, and student perception of risk management between students assigned Internet homework activities and students assigned traditional homework activities.

Wilkinson and Echternacht concluded that instructors may use both Internet and traditional types of homework assignments in risk management classes with equal effectiveness. They also concluded that student perception of risk management subject matter is not affected by the homework method used. However, students completing Internet homework activities took twice as long to complete them as the students completing traditional-type assignments. Wilkinson and Echternacht pointed out several advantages to using Internet activities including the currency and real-world relevance of the information and activities, the introduction to people and places, and the ability of students to complete Internet activities outside the classroom.

Bartel (1998) examined students in microcomputer applications courses taught on-campus and those taught via distance education. She concluded that the performance levels of beginning computer applications students taught using either method were equal. Likewise, the use of distance education did not affect the perceptions of students. The researcher concluded that distance education should be perceived as a positive, academically enhancing environment because as performance increases so do the positive perceptions that students have of the course. As would be expected, for students in both environments, as grade point average and expected course grade increased, student performance in the course also increased.

Similar conclusions regarding distance learning and on-campus instruction were reached in a study completed by McDonald and Bartlett (2000) involving the teaching of a resume unit in a business communications class. Specifically, the researchers attempted to determine if there was a difference in the knowledge gained and the skill level achieved by self-directed students learning via the World Wide Web and students who experience the lecture method. In addition, the researchers sought to determine the general perceptions of the students participating in the quasi-experimental design study.

The study revealed no significant statistical differences between the two delivery methods employed. The researchers suggested that because there were no differences in terms of content and skill-level achievement, teachers without the resources at hand to employ self-directed learning via the Web may use the traditional lecture format. On the other hand, the researchers suggested that Web instruction in this area of business communication may provide new and enriching opportunities for students and instructors alike.

Research provides a number of ways to evaluate the effectiveness of alternative instructional methods. While alternative methods do not appear to exceed traditional methods in effectiveness, they appear to produce equivalent levels of learning and may increase student interest and involvement in learning. Significantly, the same conclusion applies to using the Internet to deliver instruction. Learning that employs the Internet is at least equivalent to traditional learning and provides added benefits. Minimalist approaches appear promising because students must depend more on themselves to solve the types of software problems they will encounter on the job. These approaches offer opportunities for further research.

TEACHING STRATEGY

Using Technology to Support Decisions

There are, at present, no computer application textbooks that use the minimalist approach per se. Some authors do include problem-solving activities, generally for advanced phases of instruction. To facilitate transfer of learning, students need computer-based projects that require using software for decision support. Ray (2001) has suggested using the following "inputs" to teaching problem solving in a computer applications class:

1. Exercises requiring total student construction of files—not simple manipulation of publisher-provided files.
2. Preparation for problem-solving assignments through class discussion and practice problems.
3. Exercises preceded by general descriptions of desired outcomes but not step-by-step instructions about how to produce those outcomes.
4. Totally unstructured problems to be solved using the software—either through learner-developed files or large, realistic instructor-supplied files. (p. 78)

Ray (2001) has recommended using "industrial-grade" problems rather than simple examples that have limited value beyond teaching introductory concepts. He describes how this methodology may be applied to developing spreadsheet mastery:

> The Human Resources Manager at ABC Company wants a spreadsheet that can be used to project the future value of company-matched employee contributions to a 401k-retirement plan. Preferably, the spreadsheet will be designed so that basic input data can be keyed into a few cells and the spreadsheet will calculate the value of the investment at specified future times; for example, 5-, 10-, and 15-year intervals. The preparation should include a brief discussion of 401k plans, employer contributions, employee contributions, reasonable rates of return, and the future value spreadsheet function. Students might be asked to investigate spreadsheet protection if that topic has not been covered. (p. 79)

INDIVIDUAL FACTORS IN LEARNING TECHNOLOGY

What does research reveal about the role of perceptual or learning style differences and confidence in using technology? Research may tell teachers when they must develop multiple approaches to teaching subject matter or working with students.

Perceptual and Learning Style Differences

Lyons-Lawrence (1994) investigated the role of field dependence/independence in acquisition of office systems concepts through computer-based instruction. Learners who were field-dependent (not visually oriented) and field independent (visually oriented) were compared. Field-independent students scored higher on a posttest (a pencil-and-paper exam designed to measure knowledge and understanding of office systems concepts) than the field-dependent students. The researcher cautioned, though, that while computer-based instruction is an effective technique for individualizing instruction for some students, it may hinder learning for others.

Truell (1999) studied differences in student attitudes toward and evaluation of Internet instruction based on learning style (field-dependent, neutral, field-independent), gender, and student status (undergraduate or graduate). Eighty-two students enrolled in a university telecommunications course taught via the Internet participated in the study. Student attitudes toward Internet instruction were positive, but no significant differences were related to learning style, gender, or student status. Because students as a whole had positive attitudes toward Internet instruction, teachers can feel confident that this mode of instruction will be well received by the majority of students.

Simon (2000) reported a correlation between learning style, training technique, user satisfaction, and computer use. Using structural equation modeling, Simon examined three training methods—instruction, exploration, and behavior modeling. Simon's study of 450 members of the U.S. Navy indicated that trainees whose learning style matched the training methodology were more successful in training outcomes, had higher computing satisfaction, and had higher levels of computer use. Behavior modeling trainees were not affected by learning style and reported the highest levels of satisfaction and computer use. Typically, behavior modeling utilizes a combination of exploration and pedagogy that focus on observation and performance while imitating a "role model."

Fournier (1993) studied learning style and attitudes involving voice-input technology. The study's 50 participants completed a learning style instrument and a background sheet. They then participated in a one-hour session of voice-input training, practice, and dictation. Learning style did not relate to performance in dictating a paragraph or reported attitudes toward voice input. No relationships were apparent between (a) performance scores and learning styles or (b) performance scores and attitudes toward voice-input technology. The study did not indicate the need for special teaching methods based on varying learning styles.

Computer Self-Efficacy

Smith-Weber (2000) examined computer self-efficacy (one's ability to use a computer) and its relationship to sources of self-efficacy: mastery experiences, vicarious experiences (observing, role modeling, imitating), social (verbal) persuasion, and physiological state. To determine how these perceptions changed before and after computer technology education, Smith-Weber administered the Torkzadeh and Koufteros Computer Self-Efficacy Scale to university students during precourse and postcourse sessions. Pre- and postcourse computer self-efficacy were significantly and positively correlated. Pre- and postcourse scores were also significantly related to mastery experiences and physiological state. Students' overall perception of computer self-efficacy increased after course completion, and no gender effects occurred.

NEEDED RESEARCH

Delta Pi Epsilon (Rader & Wilhelm, 2001), the national graduate business education honor society, recommends areas of research needed in business education. These recommendations guide prospective researchers as they formulate significant research questions. Using a modified Delphi technique, selected business educators developed and then ranked a list of research topics in order of importance. Table 6 presents the research topics related to technology.

Table 6. Technology-Related Business Education Research Topics

1. The characteristics of effective computer teachers
2. Traditional skills needed by prospective computer teachers
3. The impact of e-mail upon workforce productivity
4. The effects of online vs. traditional computer instruction
5. The integration of basic business competencies into computer applications instruction
6. Technology instruction with group support systems compared to traditional instruction
7. Internet/Web skills present in the high school curriculum
8. Computer literacy components desired by industry
9. The effect of accounting software programs such as Quickbooks and Peachtree on traditional accounting instruction
10. The impact of distance learning on the business curriculum
11. The most effective way to develop word processing production skills
12. Effective assessments for evaluating competencies in spreadsheets, presentation graphics, and databases
13. The advantages and disadvantages of distance learning
14. Employers' perceptions of the importance of technological skills vs. soft skills
15. The impact of technology on cheating

SUMMARY

The implementation of sound research findings enables business educators to devise creative and valid ways to impact learning. Research on the work environment identifies the technology skill base that students need to develop. Dealing with technical problems leads employees to desire more instruction or training, but also indicates that students will need to network with other employees to develop problem-solving abilities.

Research on teaching methods generally demonstrates that student-directed, multi-media, and collaborative approaches produce achievement comparable to traditional approaches and often offer additional benefits for learners. Research suggests that achievement in advanced instruction under minimalist conditions is also at least comparable to learning under traditional conditions.

Estimates indicate that 1.6 million students are enrolled in distance education courses (Boettcher 2000). Business education research has examined both distance and Internet-delivery of instruction, showing similar results. Learning with these delivery methods is at least comparable to learning with traditional delivery options, and students display positive attitudes toward technology and may experience added benefits from using it.

Individual factors, such as learning style and self-efficacy, are more complex to interpret. In some studies matching learning style to instructional approach appears to have some positive effects. Learning styles do not appear to affect students' attitudes toward distance education or to be an indicator of performance for users of voice-input technology. Gender appears unrelated to self-efficacy; both females and males attain a higher level of computer self-efficacy as a result of computer instruction. What appears across several studies is that as students' experience with technology increases, there are corresponding positive results in other areas.

This review should encourage further research. As all types of alternatives to traditional, teacher-directed instruction are developed, teachers, students, and other stakeholders will want to know whether these new approaches will yield benefits. At a minimum, they will want assurance that no educational harm will be done to the learner. Gradually, patterns will emerge from new research and replication studies. Business educators at all levels should engage in finding answers to the important questions affecting their instructional practices. As the Delta Pi Epsilon list of needed research demonstrates, research on technology as content, delivery method, and instructional tools is essential. As Pullis (1981) has asserted, "The primary concern of all business educators should be the scientific identification of teaching methodologies which are most beneficial to our students."

REFERENCES

Alexander, M. W. (1996). Use of presentation graphics software by administrative support personnel: Implications for business educators. *The Delta Pi Epsilon Journal, XXXVIII*, 139–154.

Arney, J. B. (1998). A comparison of computer skills needed by business administration graduates as perceived by colleges and universities and human resource managers in Indiana. *NABTE Review, 25,* 44–48.

Bartel, K. B. (1998). *A comparison of students taught utilizing distance education and traditional education environments in beginning microcomputer applications classes at Utah State University.* Unpublished doctoral dissertation, Utah State University.

Bauer, J. S. (2001). Project based learning. In D. Briggs (Ed.), *Best practices in business instruction* (pp. 68–71). Little Rock, AR: Delta Pi Epsilon.

Boettcher, J. V. (2000). The state of distance education in the U.S.: Surprising realities. *Syllabus, 13*(7), 40.

Bush, M. L. (2001). *Spreadsheet competencies needed for entry-level managerial positions in accounting and business/information systems.* Unpublished doctoral dissertation, Utah State University.

Carroll, J. M. (1990). *The Nurnberg funnel: Designing minimalist instruction for practical computer skill.* Cambridge, MA: The MIT Press.

Carroll, J. M. (Ed.). (1998). *Minimalism beyond the Nurnberg funnel.* Cambridge, MA: The MIT Press.

Erthal, M. J. (1998). Analysis of performance in a microcomputer applications class. *The Delta Pi Epsilon Journal, 40,* 36–49.

Fournier, R. S. (1993). *Voice input technology: Learning style and attitude toward its use.* Unpublished doctoral dissertation, Virginia Polytechnic Institute and State University, Blacksburg.

Gonzenbach, N. M., & Davis, D. C. (1999). Business employees' perceptions of content areas to be included in an information systems technologies curriculum. *NABTE REVIEW, 26,* 58–62.

Groneman, N. (2000). Business demands for Web-related skills as compared to other computer skills. *Book of Readings: 2000 Delta Pi Epsilon National Conference,* 3–5.

Henderson, D. K. (2001). *Basic workplace and computer literacy skills for entry-level, nonbaccalaureate-degree employees of the Silicon Valley computer industry.* Unpublished doctoral dissertation, Utah State University.

Lambrecht, J. J. (1999, November). *Developing employment-related technology skills.* Final Report. MDS 1199. Berkeley, CA: National Center for Research in Vocational Education.

Lambrecht, J. J., Redmann, D. H., & Stitt-Gohdes, W. L. (2000). *Organizational socialization and adaptation: Learning the ropes in the workplace by primary computer users.* Little Rock: Delta Pi Epsilon Research Foundation.

Lyons-Lawrence, C. L. (1994). Effect of learning style on performance in using computer-based instruction in office systems. *The Delta Pi Epsilon Journal, 36,* 166–175.

McDonald, M. (1997). *Teaching microcomputer software applications (electronic spreadsheets): Guided practice vs. independent practice.* Unpublished doctoral dissertation, University of Missouri-Columbia.

McDonald, M., & Bartlett, J. E., III. (2000). Comparison of Web-based and traditional delivery methods in a business communications unit. *The Delta Pi Epsilon Journal, 42,* 90–100.

Millslagle, J. (1996). *A comparison of the structured approach and the minimalist approach to the design of materials for teaching microcomputer software.* Unpublished doctoral dissertation, University of Minnesota, Minneapolis.

Officeteam. (2000). *Office of the future: 2005.* Retrieved March 2001 from the World Wide Web: http://www.officeteam.com

Olinzock, A. A., & Lazarony, P. J. (2001). 21st century entry-level computer skills needed by Fortune 500 and small business employees in central Ohio. *NABTE REVIEW, 28,* 46–50.

Parker, I. (2001, May 28). Absolute PowerPoint: Can a software package edit our thoughts? *The New Yorker,* pp. 76–87.

Pullis, J. M. (1981). Variables afffecting achievement in shorthand. *NABTE Review, 8,* 34.

Rader, M., & Wilhelm, W. (Eds.). (2001). *Needed research in business education* (6th ed.). Little Rock, AR: Delta Pi Epsilon.

Ray, C. M. (2001). Teaching problem-solving in computer applications courses. In D. Briggs (Ed.), *Best practices in business instruction* (pp. 78–79). Little Rock, AR: Delta Pi Epsilon.

Rider University. (1999). *Who is most likely to succeed?* Lawrenceville, NJ: The Center for the Development of Leadership Skills.

Schramm, R. B., & McEwen, B. C. (1997). Effectiveness of multimedia versus traditional instruction. *NABTE REVIEW, 24,* 30–34.

Simon, S. J. (2000). The relationship of learning style and training method to end-user computer satisfaction and computer use: A structural equation model. *Information Technology, Learning, and Performance Journal, 18,* 41–59.

Smith-Weber, S. M. (2000). Computer self-efficacy: An examination of the sources and the impact of computer technology education. *NABTE Review, 27,* 53–58.

Truell, A. D. (1999). Student attitudes toward and evaluation of Internet instruction. *Book of Readings: 1999 Delta Pi Epsilon National Conference,* 127–132.

Wiedmaier, C. (1997). *Database competencies perceived as necessary for entry-level employment and employment advancement.* Unpublished doctoral dissertation, University of Missouri-Columbia.

Wilkinson, K., & Echternacht, L. (1998). Internet homework activities and traditional homework activities: The effects on achievement, completion time, and perception. *The Delta Pi Epsilon Journal, 40,* 214–230.

Willoughby, L. J. (1997). *A comparative analysis of teaching methodologies used with application software tools: Hands-on vs. teacher demonstration.* Unpublished doctoral dissertation, Utah State University.